Paul Celan: Poet, Survivor, Jew

Leningrad

Stockholm

Moscow•
Vitebsk •   Tarusa •

Hamburg
Amsterdam   Bremen
Moisville   Frankfurt   •Berlin
• Paris   Oświęcim   •Kiev
Stuttgart   Prague   •Kraków   Lemberg (Lvóv)
Todtnauberg•   •Tübingen   Sadagora   BUKOVINA
Zurich•   Bodensee Vienna•   •Czernowitz TRANS-
                                              NISTRIA
Sils-Maria   Budapest•   •Paşcani
                              Piatra-Neamţ•
                              Tăbăreşti•
La Ciotat•   •Assisi   Bucharest•

Elbe River
Bug River

Heidi Perov

Paul Celan: Poet, Survivor, Jew

WITHDRAWN

John Felstiner

Yale University Press   New Haven and London

Published with assistance
from the Mary Cady Tew
Memorial Fund.

Designed by Sonia L. Scanlon.

Set in Berkeley type by DEKR Corporation,
Woburn, Massachusetts.

Printed in the United States of America by Vail-Ballou
Press, Binghamton, New York.

Library of Congress Cataloging-in-Publication Data

Felstiner, John.
Paul Celan : poet, survivor, Jew / John Felstiner.
p.   cm.
Includes bibliographical references and index.
ISBN 0-300-06068-8 (cloth: alk. paper)
0-300-06387-3 (pbk.: alk. paper)
1. Celan, Paul.   2. Poets, German—20th century—
Biography.
I. Title.
PT2605.E4Z599   1995
831'.914—dc20   94-33942
[B]   CIP

Paul Celan's writings used by permission: from *Mohn
und Gedächtnis* (1952), *Von Schwelle zu Schwelle*
(1955), © Deutsche Verlags-Anstalt GmbH, Stuttgart;
from *Sprachgitter* (1959), *Die Niemandsrose* (1963),
© S. Fischer Verlag, Frankfurt am Main; from
Atemwende (1967), *Fadensonnen* (1968), *Lichtzwang*
(1970), *Schneepart* (1971), *Gesammelte Werke* (1983),
© Suhrkamp Verlag, Frankfurt am Main; from *Poems*
(1988), © Persea Books and Anvil Press Poetry Ltd.

A catalogue record for this book is available from
the British Library.

The paper in this book meets the guidelines for permanence
and durability of the Committee on Production
Guidelines for Book Longevity of the
Council on Library Resources.

10 9 8 7 6 5 4 3

For Alek and Sarah

and

for the victims of "that which happened," 1933–1945

Contents

Acknowledgments

On first encountering Paul Celan's poetry in 1977, I knew I would have to find my way into it before doing anything else. This process proved consuming, and to reckon debts now means reviewing a whole dimension of my life.

Gisèle Celan-Lestrange, the poet's loyal widow, whom I met in 1984, was right away open and helpful. I immersed myself in her husband's Paris and Normandy libraries, and our talks illumined Celan's poetry for me. Gisèle remained a spirited, scrupulous friend until her death in 1991. I am also grateful to their son Eric for his friendly support and for permission to reproduce two of Gisèle's etchings, each titled by Paul Celan.

Ilana Shmueli of Tel Aviv has for twelve years helped me see what it meant to be uprooted from Czernowitz and to survive as a German-speaking Jew. Her knowledge of Celan's youth and his 1969 visit to Israel, along with her acute sense of his poetry, have enriched this book and my life as well.

Pearl Fichman of New York, another friend I could not have foreseen, conveyed to me her experience (parallel to that of her contemporary, Paul Celan) of Czernowitz, the war, and its aftermath. Her fine memoir, *Before Memories Fade,* deserves a wide audience.

Petre Solomon of Bucharest, whom I regret not having met, was a wise correspondent from 1983 until his death in 1991. His friendship with Celan typifies the Bucharest period and its bearing on the later years.

Jerry Glenn, at the University of Cincinnati, has so bolstered my study of Celan that his name goes in invisible ink on my title page. Besides his pathbreaking survey (1973) and superb bibliography (1989), he aided me in countless ways, as Germanist and friend. He bears out the ethic that is sought by Celan's poetry.

Jamie Lyon, at the University of California at San Diego, has also shown uncommon scholarly fellowship, sharing his research, ideas, and contacts, alerting me to other work in the field, and engaging with what I wrote.

Esther Cameron, in Jerusalem, was a spur to insight into Celan's poetic purpose. I learned from her writings and from her demands on Celan interpretation.

George Steiner, Celan's strongest advocate, has been a stimulus over the years—through his penetration of Celan's writing and his thinking on translation.

Cyrus Hamlin of Yale University, during the 1950s when we were students together, reconnected me to German, the language my father knew as a child. In our comradeship since then, his engagement with Hölderlin—in search of the religious underpinnings of poetry and its call to dialogue—has set a high standard for my own study.

So many friends have helped or encouraged me that to list them all might seem perfunctory. But they each know (or knew), I hope, why I thank them: Chimen Abramsky, Robert Alter, Yehuda and Chana Amichai, Larry Berman, T. Carmi, Ari Cartun, Craig Comstock, Sidra Ezrahi, Michael Fishbane, Joseph Frank, Gregory Freidin, John Friedmann, Myron Gubitz, Geoffrey Hartman, Erich Heller, Kathryn Hellerstein, William Heyen, Al Hoelzel, Patti Joplin, Shirley Kaufman, Dori Laub, Melissa Monroe, Cynthia Ozick, Dan Pagis, Johnny Payne, Tony Rudolf, Claudio Spies, Danny Weissbort, Elie Wiesel, Shira Wolosky, Luitgard Wundheiler, Marilyn Yalom, and James Young.

Other friends and acquaintances aided me with their support and their own literary work, for which I am grateful: Jean Bollack, Bernhard Böschenstein, Martine Broda, Israel Chalfen, Amy Colin, Peter Demetz, Joel Golb, Michael Hamburger, Michael Jakob, Erez Kalir, Larry Langer, Joachim Neugroschel, Leonard Olschner, Benzion Orgad, Kevin Perryman, Otto Pöggeler, Edouard Roditi, Shimon Sandbank, Steven Schwarzschild, and Manfred Winkler.

Friends of Celan and others kindly gave me interviews, letters, and information: Erhard Bahr, Ilse Blumenthal-Weiss, Rolf Bücher, Isac Chiva, Klaus Demus, Robert Freedman, Bengt Holmqvist, Walter Jens, Alice Kahler, Alvin Rosenfeld, Gershom Schocken, David Seidmann, Moshe Shalvi, Jared Shlaes, Elmar Tophoven, Sigfried Trichter, René Wintzen, Rudolf Wittkopf, and Zvi Yavetz.

I am indebted to Peter Frank, Sonia Moss, and Henry Lowood of Stanford University Library, to Helen Solanum of the Hoover Institution, and to the Yivo Institute for Jewish Research for their help. My editor, Jonathan Brent, astutely recognized the improvements the manuscript required, and Jean van Altena copyedited it intelligently and scrupulously.

Several organizations generously supported my research, travel, and writing: the Rockefeller Foundation, Memorial Foundation for Jewish Culture, Pew Foundation, Guggenheim Foundation, Stanford Humanities Center, National Endowment for the Arts, National Endowment for the Humanities, and the Djerassi Resident Artists Program.

A number of journals have housed the essays through which my book evolved: *ACTS, American Poetry Review, Ariel, Commentary, Comparative Literature, Encyclopaedia Judaica, Holocaust and Genocide Studies, Modern Poetry in Translation, New Literary History, New Republic, Northwest Review, Orim, Parnassus, Prooftexts, Religion and Literature, Representations, Sequoia, Stanford Humanities Review, Stanford Slavic Studies, Studies in Twentieth Century Literature, Sulfur, Tel Aviv Review, Threepenny Review, TriQuarterly.*

First and last I feel blessed in thanking my wife, Mary Lowenthal Felstiner—*du meine Wahre.* Throughout the years in which she was writing her own book, on the artist Charlotte Salomon in the Nazi era, she pitched in at every stage of my work, from suggesting the right word in translation to rigorously, wisely, and repeatedly critiquing essays, chapters, the whole manuscript, while cheering me on and sharing the disheartenments she also knew well enough.

Introduction

Because Paul Celan lived—or rather, survived—through the poetry he wrote, this book tries to give a sense of his life's work. Either a biographical or a textual study alone would miss Celan's reason for being. Every day he felt his era's and his own history pressing on the poems he wrote, which "had to pass" (as he said of the German language itself) "through the thousand darknesses of deathbringing speech."[1]

Born in what soon became the wrong place and time, Celan absorbed his misfortune but never grew immune to it. His family were German-speaking Jews from the eastern reach of the Austrian Empire. They lived in Czernowitz, capital of the Bukovina region, which passed to Romania just before Celan's birth in 1920. After Soviet, then German occupation in 1940 and 1941, after forced labor, his parents' deportation, and the Russians' return in 1944, Celan left home for Bucharest and then Vienna, and in 1948 he settled in Paris. There he studied, taught, translated, married, and kept faith with his mother tongue, creating a poetry that "thought with and out of this time," as he said, "thought it through to its end."[2]

What it meant to be Paul Celan evolved in the 800 poems he wrote from 1938 to 1970. So far, a Collected Works has been published in German, and three of his eight volumes have come out in the long-awaited historical-critical edition, with dates and draft versions but no sources or notes. A thoroughgoing sense of Europe's most significant postwar poet, who plumbed his native language and others as well, and who ranged among literary traditions and theological, philosophical, scientific, historical, and personal data—a sense of this full-memoried poet is hard to come by, asking much of the reader.

Celan's work demands an "encounter" like that in his writing of poems, where "I went with my very being toward language." For such an encounter, he said, "there would have to be readers again."[3] After "that which happened" to both humankind and language between 1933 and 1945, poetry more than ever meant a reaching out. "A handshake," he called it, or, more hazardously, "a message in a bottle" (3:186, 177).

Celan's lyrics seek "an addressable thou": the poet himself, his mother, wife, or sons, a loved one or friend, the Jewish dead, their God, Osip Mandelshtam, Nelly Sachs, Rembrandt, Rosa Luxemburg, Spinoza, Saint Francis, Queen Esther, Prague's Rabbi Loew, King Lear, a plant or stone, a word, the Word, the Hebrew letter Bet, Babel, or often something indeterminable, present only because the speaker calls it *du*. That word is voiced some 1,300 times in over three decades of verse. "Hear deep in / with your mouth," a late lyric ends, and Celan's last poem takes the refrain "You read."

For an English-speaking audience it is here, at the point of response, that translation enters. The translator becomes answerable for what a poet's lines have to say, and I take encouragement from Celan's own lifelong commitment to translation—his versions of Mandelshtam, Shakespeare, Dickinson, and others. My book assumes no knowledge of German on the reader's part. Instead, it brings to light the overlooked process of voicing a poem anew.

To begin with, every critical resource—from history, biography, literary tradition, theory, philology, and prosody—can work toward guiding a foreign poem into our own language. Then, the intimate options need articulating, the to-and-fro of finding and losing equivalent rhythms, sounds, overtones, and ambiguities. "Poetry no longer imposes, it exposes itself," Celan said near the end of his life (3:181), and the same may be said of translation. To expose the process that one verse translator goes through, the decisions and revisions, will vivify the poetry in question, with the bonus of a new poem in English.

Celan's lyrics, being in German, pose a particular challenge. For the "Thousand-Year Reich" organized its genocide of European Jewry by means of language: slogans, slurs, pseudo-scientific dogma, propaganda, euphemism, and the jargon that brought about every devastating "action," from the earliest racial "laws" through "special treatment" in the camps to the last "resettlement" of Jewish orphans.

Celan has become an exemplary postwar poet because he insistently registered in German the catastrophe made in Germany. With his world obliterated, he held fast to the mother tongue that was both his and the murderers'—literally all he had left. Insofar as it was language that had been damaged, his verse might repair that damage.

To uproot and rewrite Celan in translation runs the risk of alienating an already alien voice. Yet this voice needs translating because of its very obscurity. Often his lines seem only half emerged from shadow, as if recovered from some lost tongue and needing further translation even for native speakers. New or odd or archaic words, ruptured syntax, ellipses, buried allusion, and contradiction fill the poet's "true-stammered mouth" (2:42).

That mouth, after the wartime "darknesses," resisted simple speech. When a European Jewish poet's turn came for the Nobel Prize in 1966, the more accessible Nelly Sachs got it, not Paul Celan. Along with a gradual recognition of his difficult genius, doubt has been voiced: Why the "insistent minimalism" of his poems and his "unwillingness to commit himself to accessibility"? Why their "discontinuous, alogical, and arbitrary" behavior?[4]

Celan's writing may baffle the reader unready to give it that "attentiveness" he considered "the natural prayer of the soul" (3:198). To grow attentive, especially in translating, is to activate these poems. Their truth, after all, may consist in obscurity or ambiguity, as also in occasional radiance.

For years Celan has been a distinctive figure, at times a contested commodity. Many claims for his identity are in the air, some more valid than others, but all pointing up a complex, migrant fate. His childhood found him embedded in the German-Jewish cultural matrix of Bukovina. Two years in Bucharest (1945–47) solidified a Romanian dimension. A 1948 sojourn in Vienna and his family's Hapsburg Empire origins have led some to call him an Austrian writer. His perfect French, his mature decades in Paris, and his marriage to the artist Gisèle de Lestrange gave him a connection with France, though that country never embraced him. His frequent trips to Germany and regular publication there make it easy to label him a German poet. His long-deferred visit to Jerusalem and Tel Aviv in 1969, where he was welcomed fervently by the German-speaking community, and some lyrics he wrote immediately thereafter tightened a link with Israel. His youthful leanings toward socialism, his solidarity with Republican Spain, his mystical tendencies, and his closeness to certain literary and philosophical doctrines have each gained him adherents.

No one element alone accounts for Paul Celan. He was above all a poet—perforce and by choice a Jewish poet: that is, a poet and a Jew of his time, the two identities interpenetrating to such an extent that any other definition seems partial.

In Celan the "strain" of Jewishness means both the trace and the tension of it. Years ago, after I had spoken at a colloquium in France, an eminent academic warned against *surjudaïsant* Celan, "over-Judaizing" him. I keep that in mind and welcome the risk, especially in view of a tendency (with some exceptions) to neglect that strain in him. While examining Celan's Hebrew Bible in 1984, for instance, I found that someone from a German research team, unable to identify the volume, had placed in it a slip saying *Wichtig?* ("Important?").

Though Celan never spelled out his Jewishness, he aligned himself more stringently with the Jews than with the non-Jews in his pantheon: with Kafka and Mandelshtam, for instance, though he also prized Hölderlin and Rilke; with Heinrich Heine, but also with Georg Büchner; with Gustav Landauer, and Peter Kropotkin; with Martin Buber, and Martin Heidegger; with Gershom Scholem, and Meister Eckhart; with Nelly Sachs, and Ingeborg Bachmann. Celan's allegiances can be traced through his lyrics, prose fiction, translations, speeches, letters, conversation, and the books he bought and marked, so often concerned with the question of coexistence between Jewishness and Germanness.

No less critical in shaping his allegiance was the hurt Celan felt, from the late 1950s on, at German and other hands. Recrudescent anti-Semitism along with neo-Nazism, plus a malicious plagiarism charge, aroused his defiance and provoked verse that took new risks. It was a distress which made for rich poetic interest.

Scripture, above all, pervades Celan's poetry—Biblical names, places, images, liturgical figures, overt and covert allusions, Hebraic citations and wordplay—though always ironically, against the grain. Often the Psalms speak for his need, fluctuating as they do between lament and praise. At times, Hebrew terms or phrases occur abruptly in Celan's verse. Beyond their immediate sense, they test whether Scripture holds good anymore. They bring out Celan's design on language and on German, on his audience and on himself, on literary and on sacred tradition.

That the word *Shulamith,* from the Song of Songs, closes his first published poem and *Sabbath* his last is symptomatic of the strain of Jewishness in Celan. Yet, with so multifarious a writer and linguistic genius, no single way of hearing him will do, and every way begins and ends in the "speech-grille" of his poems. "With a changing key," Celan advised himself, "you unlock the house where / the snow of what's silenced drifts" (1:112). My eighteen chapters use a "changing key" to present this poetry, which moves from symbolist through surrealist lyrics to a modernist stance and beyond. While my own approach to the strain of Jewishness in Celan, plus the empathy evoked in translating him, stems from a kindred strain in myself (as a Diaspora Jew decisively less at risk), in fact Celan wrote for every possible reader, and this book aims the same way.

To engage with the life's work of Paul Celan is a difficult venture. Out of darkness and wounding he made striking poems, which challenge the way of our world. In encountering these poems and becoming conversant with them, I have felt a grim energy verging on elation. Does this belie the burden of Celan's voice, or is elation akin to something the poet knew?

Part One
Stricken

Then came my tears. I wove the shawl.

1
Loss and the Mother Tongue
(1920–43)

"First of all forgive me, please, for not writing. I've got no reason for it, either."[1] This earliest extant writing by Paul Antschel (he renamed himself Paul Celan only after the war), a letter to his aunt, opens with a familiar plea. It is January 1934, two months after his bar mitzvah, and Aunt Minna, who lived with the Antschel family during Paul's childhood, has just emigrated to Palestine. "So pardonnez-moi, please!" he goes on, exhibiting a penchant for languages other than his native German. Then he mentions that "by rights" he should be ranked first in his class, not second. To explain this mischance, he cites (with mock-legalistic phrasing and emphasis) his "belonging to the *Jewish* branch of the *Semitic* race. . . . Yes, as for anti-Semitism in our school, I could write a 300-page opus about it." He tells his aunt that even now he would not be writing to her, but "today I couldn't go to school, because yesterday I fell on the ice and cleverly bruised my behind." He closes by asking her how it's going with the languages: "Und wie geht's mit den Sprachen? Speake-you English? Und Hebräisch?"

The child's word *Popo,* for that bruised "behind," sits oddly with his acute ear for racial jargon—"the *Jewish* branch of the *Semitic* race." That same ear, after Hitler's twelve-year Reich, kept the poet from ever using *Rasse* ("race") in his writing.[2] Within Paul's 1934 letter, the onset of persecution at home coincides with his aunt's departure for Palestine. This slight tension is eased by his jocular manner—"a 300-page opus"—but will stay with one who remained in Europe during and after the catastrophe.

The thirteen-year-old's pleasure in "pardonnez-moi" would later become an exile's choice to settle in Paris. And his attempt at a language he hadn't yet studied, "Speake-you English?," led eventually to bold translations of Shakespeare and Emily Dickinson. The question closing his letter, "Und Hebräisch?," wonders how a Jew of the Austrian Empire can possibly migrate from German to Hebrew, from the mother tongue to the holy tongue.

Paul Antschel's mother tongue came bonded with his mother. Through her, German passed to him in everyday speech, classic authors, fairy tales, and songs such as one he later recalled, "the Maybeetle song that stayed motherly, summerly, bright- / blooded at the edge / of all cragged / cold winterhard / syllables" (1:290). A photo he kept of his mother shows her at about twenty-one, with full, soft features and a warm gaze, a large floppy hat, and her hand in a suede glove resting on a book.[3] Most likely a standard photographer's prop, one of several a client might choose from, the book fits what we are told about Fritzi Schrager: "She especially liked to read the German classics, and in later years she vied with her son in quoting their favorite authors."[4]

On the back of the photo Celan has written: "Mama, during the first World War, in Bohemia–." The handwriting, as well as the hindsight of "first" World War, dates from after the next war, from which refuge proved impossible. Around 1915 Fritzi Schrager, as yet unmarried, had fled west with her family to Bohemia—"the three-year-land of your mother, it wanders everywhere, like language" (1:285). Celan's paternal grandparents had also fled from the Russians, while their son, Leo Antschel, served and was wounded in the Austrian army. Both sides of the family, then, stemming from Galicia and Bukovina, five hundred miles east of Vienna, belonged to the Hapsburg Empire—its "easternmost" part, Celan emphasized.[5]

He knew his ancestors to be religious Jews: his mother's grandfather, a

Celan's mother, ca. 1915 (Eric Celan)

pious Hasid who made the pilgrimage to Safed in Palestine, and his own grandfather, a Biblical scribe.[6] Celan's mother was born in Sadagora, a Hasidic center near the Bukovinan capital Czernowitz, and once he mentioned approvingly that his great-grandmother came from the Karaites, "adherents of Scripture."[7] He called himself a "posthumously born *Kakanier*," someone native to the Kingly Kaiser's Hapsburg Empire though born two years after its demise in 1918, when Bukovina passed to Romania. Franz Josef's regime had been liberal toward its Jews, and within Paul's own household, claims of Jewish alongside Austro-German culture blended in an undefined yet viable form, as for countless other such petit bourgeois families.

Celan's childhood during the 1920s and 1930s took shape in a polyglot milieu. Bukovina held speakers of Ukrainian, Romanian, German, Swabian, and Yiddish, as well as other languages and dialects. In Czernowitz, where Paul was born on 23 November 1920, nearly half the 100,000 inhabitants were Jews—"Little Vienna," they called their city. At home he grew up speaking German, and at school became fluent in Romanian. He also understood Yiddish and before the war probably shared the High German-speaker's disdain for it. But a schoolmate recalls that when a teacher belonging to the Fascist Iron Guard called Yiddish a ludicrous language, Paul objected that even Shakespeare had been translated into Yiddish![8] Sometimes he would recite the fables of a Yiddish author from Czernowitz.

Years later Celan recalled his "first encounter with poetry," and his memory of it is phrased revealingly: "I was six years old and could recite 'The Song of the Bell,'" by Schiller. "Who knows whether the impression it made on my listeners didn't release everything that came later?"[9] It comes as no surprise that a child in the orbit of orthodox Judaism should have taken pride in mastering a classic German author. But that Celan thinks the impact of his recital inspired him points to his deepest impulse as a writer—the need to be heard, to reach another person.

Without question it was the German mother tongue, the *Muttersprache,* in which he flourished. While Paul's father stressed the son's Judaic education, his mother considered "the German language more important, and all her life she took care that a correct literary German should be spoken," as distinct from the impure German current in Czernowitz.[10] "At home we always spoke High German only," Celan once said; "dialect for me remained—unfortunately—quite distant."[11] A school friend recalls, "We had no natural language. To speak good German was something you had to achieve. You could do it, but it didn't come of itself."[12] The memories of his mother that are woven through Celan's poetry bind her to the *Muttersprache*: "the motherword led me," he would say (1:110). By contrast, his father's almost complete absence from Celan's poetry seems to reflect their distant, difficult relationship.

Leo Antschel had an Orthodox upbringing and strong Zionist convictions, and Paul, an only child, felt the burden of these. At six, he was taken out of a liberal, German-language elementary school and sent to a Hebrew school, the Safah Ivriah. This school had earlier encouraged Jewish assimilation to Austro-German culture, then later felt the Yiddishist influence of the Jewish-Socialist Bund. During Paul's three years there, from 1927 to 1930, Zionism and Hebrew instruction were in force. In fact Chaim Weizmann, as president of the World Zionist Organization, came to Czernowitz in December 1927, gave a rousing speech, and visited the Safah Ivriah, where he "was visibly very impressed by all he saw and heard."[13] Paul Antschel was less happily impressed. After entering a state school in 1930, he still had to continue Hebrew with a tutor at home—even over the Christmas holidays, he wrote to an aunt in Vienna.[14] As it turned out, then, before learning Romanian as a schoolboy, he had become (resentfully) proficient in Hebrew.

It would falsify the dynamics of this middle-class, Central European Jewish household to say that Paul associated the secular German language only with his mother and the Hebrew tongue with his father. Family Sabbaths would have been celebrated by both parents together, in both German and Hebrew. Still, he grew up averse to his disciplinarian father and close to his mother.

Celan appears kindred here to certain other European Jewish writers: Proust; Freud, whose father evoked Oedipal instincts; Martin Buber, who from the age of three keenly felt his mother's absence; Osip Mandelshtam, who remembered his merchant father's "Judaic chaos" as against his mother's sonorous Russian speech; and, above all, Franz Kafka. Indeed, Celan once told a friend that Kafka's bitter *Letter to His Father* had to be written over and over again in Jewish homes.[15]

Celan most likely could not have brought himself to compose a memoir on his middle-class Jewish upbringing, along the lines of Kafka's *Letter* (1919) or Mandelshtam's *The Noise of Time* (1925). These writers were tutelary spirits for Celan, yet his own recovery of childhood could not have had their ambivalence tinged with disgust at the loose ends of Central European Jewish assimilation; for that world was violated by Nazism.

After his bar mitzvah in 1933, Paul dropped Hebrew (whence his curiosity about how Aunt Minna was coping with it in Palestine). Not long afterward he began taking up political ideas that troubled his father. Like other left-leaning students, he dropped out of the Zionist group Davidia. At a time when Czernowitzers were listening to Hitler's harangues on the radio[16] and Communist activity was punished by torture and imprisonment, Paul joined a suspect anti-Fascist youth group composed mostly of Jews. They produced a mimeographed magazine called "Red Student," writing their own articles and translating Marxist texts from German into Romanian.[17] Then in 1936

Celan in school, 1936 (Edith Silbermann)

he helped collect money for the Spanish Republicans. Their rallying cry, "No pasarán" (They shall not pass), later turned up twice in his poems. He even invented an older sister and recounted her doings in the Spanish civil war, only to be asked later what had become of her.[18]

Soon he gave up his Communist allegiance, but he never lost an affinity with anarchism and socialism. Celan called himself "one who grew up with the writings of Peter Kropotkin and Gustav Landauer" and recalled learning a Viennese "Solidarity" song as a boy in Czernowitz (3:190).[19]

In literature, Paul's schoolboy leanings were less radical. He read Goethe and Schiller as well as more congenially stirring writers such as Heine, Trakl,

Celan in Czernowitz, 1937 (Pearl Fichman)

Hölderlin, Nietzsche, Verlaine, Rimbaud, and later Hofmannsthal and Kafka. Friends remember his uncanny sensibility for lyric poetry. He and a classmate, Immanuel Weissglas (who was then translating Rilke into Romanian), each composed poems on common themes, and the two boys tried making German versions of Apollinaire, Éluard, Shakespeare, Yeats, Housman, Sergei Esenin, and the Romanian Tudor Arghezi.[20] Above all, he cherished Rilke. One of his early schoolmates recalls a summer walk they took together into the countryside.[21] They lay down in the shade of a tree, and suddenly Paul began reciting Rilke's poem "The Olive Garden" about Jesus in Gethsemane: "He went up then under the graying leaves / all gray and wasting in the olive groves." They didn't walk very far, the friend adds, because that would have been risky for two young Jews in Romania of the 1930s.

Paul Antschel was a handsome young man, as can be seen in photos from that time. One of these, taken in Czernowitz in February 1937, provides the earliest candid picture of him.[22] A sidewalk photographer chanced to be taking a shot of two of his friends as Paul passed the couple and looked back—just when the photo was snapped. The result, cropped and enlarged, shows a slender figure in a dapper cap and long overcoat with astrakhan collar and a clear, sensitive countenance. Paul's friend Pearl Fichman, who kept the photo, showed it to me years later, describing him then as "slim, with dark hair and dark eyes, a handsome, poetic-looking man with a quiet, rare laughter. . . . Paul was rather reserved, with an almond-shaped face. . . . His voice melodious and soft . . . a soft lilting voice. His humor was sharp, biting, and often condescending."[23]

It was around this time, at age fifteen or sixteen, that he began composing poems. They run much in the melancholic vein of romantic and symbolist verse, with rhymed and cadenced stanzas, bearing titles such as "Lament," "Wish," "Summer Night," "Twilight," "Les Adieux," and "Clair de Lune," and colored with blue, gold, and purple, weaving "shadow," "slumber," "dream," and "death" with "sand," "wind," "rain," and "tears."[24]

Antschel's earliest known poem is dated by him "Mother's Day 1938," in May. At seventeen, he was just graduating from Czernowitz's liberal Ukrainian Gymnasium, to which he had transferred because of anti-Semitism in the Romanian state school. This sonnet to his mother, with its share of over-wrought language, presents a delicate task for the translator: to expose without parodying the sentiments of a teenager. He speaks of "scattered homesickness at night" and "clasping prayers anxious for your face," then says that her "soft solicitude braided with light" keeps him from turbulent dreams. The sonnet ends:

> You've naught to do with those who flee from rest,
> where motley crowds are swarming, thick and cheap—
> For you are stillness, Mother, shimmer from the deep. [F 9]

The final line extends the sonnet's meter by two syllables, as if the word *Mutter* had surged up into the midst of things—*Denn du bist Ruhe, Mutter, Schimmer aus dem Grund*. The speaker gains a point of balance, while echoing Schubert's "Du bist die Ruh'," a serene and cherished song.

Paul's mother and father envisioned their son as a doctor, but Romanian medical schools had quotas against Jews, and by the time he left high school in spring of 1938, German troops had marched into Vienna. His father wished to reserve the family's moderate funds for emigration. But Paul leaned toward further study and was backed by his mother. On 9 November 1938 he left for France to take premedical courses in Tours. His train went through Berlin just at the time of "Kristallnacht," the first Nazi-fomented pogrom. Celan later glanced back at that moment—

> you caught sight of some smoke
> that was already from tomorrow   [1:283]

—that beginning of the end of European Jewish life.

Not long after arriving in France, Paul looked up his uncle Bruno Schrager, his mother's brother, who had settled in Paris to become an actor. Only fifteen years older than Paul, Bruno took him to see Montmartre and Montparnasse. During these months abroad, Paul also visited an aunt who had fled from Nazi-occupied Vienna to England, and there for the first time he heard Shakespeare performed in English. While in France, he encountered refugees from Spain and probably studied the avant-garde more avidly than medicine. The Romanian-Jewish surrealists Eugene Ionesco, Tristan Tzara, Benjamin Fondane, and Ilarie Voronca had come to Paris years before, and in 1938 Breton, Éluard, and Duchamp organized a notorious international exhibition, in effect the culmination of the surrealist movement.

Paul's own verse was not yet open to the surrealist spirit. For Mother's Day in May 1939 he wrote another sonnet. This time he was away from his mother, and war was likely. After a tender opening stanza, foreboding intrudes:

> The mother, softly healing, keeping near,
> whose gentle evening fingers brush our skin,
> clears precious space for us, as for the deer
> who draws in welcome breaths of morning wind.
>
> We pick our steps into the stream of things
> and she must be there, cleansing like a death
> that holds off night for us, and quickly brings
> our journeys home, when thunder makes its threat.   [F 14]

My imperfect rhyme in each quatrain—"skin" with "wind," "death" with "threat"—can suggest the poet's own straining after rhyme. Really troubling, though, and (à la Rilke) difficult to grasp, his image of the mother "cleansing like a death" hints at bereavement in excess of the case, or perhaps in anticipation.

While Germany was threatening Poland in summer of 1939, Paul Antschel returned home, and after war broke out, he began studying romance philology in Czernowitz. Scenes of menace tinge his verse, couched in legendary or epic terms. "Ballad of the Extinct World" speaks of sand and "countless tents": "(But what, / but who is in the tent?) / They all went under?" (F 18). Or from his feverish "Ballad of the Flight of the Three":

> Then they came,
> they came and pled: fire gorges all our homes!

Then we laughed,
we laughed and quelled their fires.   [F 19]

A harsher force moves "The Dead Man":

The stars whipped at his gaze:
their thorn entered his ways

so that he claws at grass,
his heart grasps winds that pass,

where briars pull and rend
and night makes him its friend.

The crickets stand at bay—
Now no more crickets play . . .

Poppies scrape blood from him:
kneel now and drink it in!   [F 28]

This allegory fits the anxiety over a war now imminent.

After the Hitler–Stalin nonaggression pact and the outbreak of war in September 1939, Romania was forced to cede northern Bukovina to the USSR, and in June 1940 Russian troops occupied Czernowitz. The new Soviet leveling meant that petty university reforms hobbled Paul's studies, and a Stalinist presence, with arbitrary deportations to Siberia, rid him of any lingering illusions. "Now I am a Trotskyite," he said.[25] Yet Soviet occupation did accelerate his command of Russian and also of Ukrainian, which he was obliged to study. A university classmate remembers hearing a sympathetic Ukrainian teacher reciting poems by Esenin and the "non-person" Osip Mandelshtam.[26]

At that time Paul came to know a young actress in the Yiddish State Theater, Ruth Lackner, and, through her, several Yiddish literary figures. Still he was writing copiously in his mother tongue, the language of Rilke and Hölderlin. That allegiance may in part have disposed him to remain with his parents in Czernowitz when a German invasion threatened in June 1941.

Expectations of any sort vanished when Hitler broke the Russo–German pact and invaded Soviet territory on 22 June. Some of Paul's friends fled with the Russians, and others were commandeered into the Soviet army. Throughout Bukovina, Bessarabia, and Moldavia, Romanian soldiers took over, surprising even the German army with their savage assaults on Jews—reputedly the worst instance in Axis Europe. The SS Einsatzkommando 10B, part of Einsatzgruppe D under Otto Ohlendorf, reached Czernowitz on 5 and 6 July 1941. Since Romania had meanwhile joined the Axis, its army and police aided the Germans in obliterating a six-hundred-year Jewish presence: burning the Great Synagogue; imposing the yellow badge; plundering, torturing, and slaughtering community leaders and three thousand others during the first twenty-four hours; driving Jews into a ghetto; and later deporting tens of thousands. Conditions in the ghetto were *sehr eng* ("very cramped"), one woman recalls;[27] forty-five people to a small apartment, says another.[28] Friends of Paul's remember the short-lived ghetto experience of six to seven weeks as not wholly wretched, owing to the intense communal feeling there. They sang Yiddish songs, and Paul even worked on translating some Shakespeare sonnets.[29]

In his own lyrics, private emotion bears the brunt of political upheaval. Thus "Darkness" (1941):

The urns of stillness are empty.

In branches
the swelter of speechless songs
chokes black.

Blunt hourposts
grope toward a strange time.

A wingbeat whirls.

For the owls in the heart
death dawns.
Treason falls into your eyes—

My shadow strives with your scream—

The east smokes after this night . . .
Only dying
sparkles.   [F 37]

The sequence of surreal images attests to emotional disarray if not altogether to "speechless songs."

As one among many victims of the general trauma, Paul Antschel fared better than some and worse than other Bukovinan Jews. He was put to work hauling debris from the Prut River bridge and clearing rubbish from the ruined post office. Later he had the task of collecting and destroying Russian books. During this first year of occupation, after July 1941, he went on writing—poems pervaded by grief and intimations of death but attuned to the German Romantic tradition. "Notturno" plays its melancholy musical rubric against a dire landscape:

Sleep not. Be on your guard.
The poplars sing and stride
with war troops by their side.
The ditch runs with your blood.   [F 54]

Then, after an expressionist stanza in which "green skeletons dance" and "your dream bleeds from the lance," this nocturne closes:

The world's a laboring beast
creeps naked under night sky.
God is its howling. I
feel fear and I freeze.

An echo of Yeats's "rough beast" and that lopped final line strain the poet's craft. Aware that a well-tuned lyric manner could not serve him anymore, he was searching for a voice.

After leaving the ghetto in the fall of 1941, Paul's family escaped the next wave of deportations, thanks to authorization permits issued by Czernowitz's well-disposed mayor, Traian Popovici. Paul risked walking in the public garden, hiding his yellow star. But those permits became useless when, during June 1942, Bukovina's Romanian governor again began deporting "undesirable Jewish elements."[30] On Saturday nights, arc lights in the city were left on bright, and before dawn, Gestapo or local gendarmes routed people out of bed, into trucks, and then to cattle cars at the railway station: families, children and old people, orphans, the sick, and the mentally ill. After two such overnight "actions," 6 and 13 June, Jews were forewarned. Over the weekend they could stay elsewhere or send their children away. But which families would be hit, and when? It may never be clear just what occurred on the night that so altered Celan's life and art.

He could never readily give an account of this event of 27 June 1942. According to his friend Ruth Lackner, she found him a hiding place in a cosmetics factory. Paul urged his parents to seek refuge with him, but his mother was resigned: "We can't escape our fate. After all, there are already lots of Jews living in Transnistria."[31] (She had no way of knowing that by this time, two-thirds of the Jews deported to Transnistria had died.) Paul is said to have had an argument with his father and stormed out. Another friend remembers that Paul's parents wanted him safely out of the house, and that on the night in question, a Saturday, he and Paul went to a gathering at the home of two friends and, because of the curfew, stayed overnight. The next day, when Paul returned home—this much seems definite, wherever he had been or whatever his dealings with his parents—the house was empty, the front door sealed, and his mother and father gone.[32]

After an earlier roundup, an acquaintance of Paul's had gone to the station and managed to get her parents off the train, thereby saving their lives.[33] And two poet-friends of Paul's, deported in June 1942 with their parents, stayed with them for almost two years and returned to Czernowitz with them.[34] Celan remained conscious of not having done as much.

Another report on that night seems revealing, if unlikely. In 1960, explaining to some friends his anguish from the war years, "Paul said his heaviest guilt was a betrayal. He broke into tears. He told how one day the Nazis came and arrested him and his parents. That was in 1942. They were put into a concentration camp. A barbwire fence separated them. Then Paul stretched his hand through the barbed wire and grasped his father's hand. A guard saw it and bit Paul's hand very hard: 'And I let Papi's hand go—just think, I let *go* of his hand and ran away!' "[35] This does not tally with other reports, but the story embodies an essential trauma.

What befell Paul's parents next is reflected in accounts of the few Jews who survived deportation east to Transnistria, across the Dniestr River into German-occupied Ukraine: a five-day journey in summer heat, packed in cattle cars; housing in stables just across the southern Bug River; arduous work on the roads or in a gravel pit; and brutal treatment by SS and Ukrainian guards. His parents' transport also held a younger cousin of Paul's, Selma Meerbaum-Eisinger (1924–42), a gifted, fervent poet who wrote about a blooming rose that "it dies, dies and has never lived its life."[36] The diary of a Bukovinan artist, Arnold Daghani, notes Selma's death from typhus and also this on 17 September 1942: "Thirty craftsmen are to be removed to Gaissin. Amongst them . . . the builder Anschel," Paul's father. On 20 September: "Hammerling and Anschel have arrived from Gaissin, to fetch their wives and things. They are rather reticent as to life there."[37] Nothing more is known firsthand.

As for his own hardships, twenty years later Celan drily mentioned "the war years, which off and on I 'spent' in so-called labor camps in Romania."[38] Less than a month after his parents' deportation in June 1942, Paul had to join a labor battalion which Romanian authorities forced the Jewish Council to organize. He was sent 400 kilometers south of Czernowitz to Tăbăreşti, in Wallachia, to a camp run by the Romanian army along with the Todt Organization of German military engineers. In a letter to Ruth Lackner, he said: "You write that I should not despair. No, Ruth, I don't despair. But my mother gives me such pain, she was so sick in the last days, she must always be wondering how I am, and now without ever saying goodbye I'm gone, probably for ever."[39] And again on 2 August 1942: "In my own hands I have seen life changed into utmost bitterness, but finally into a humanness that once laid out a path which I tried to follow and still will follow, upright and assured."[40]

To uphold that humanness, that *Menschlichkeit*, Paul Antschel composed verses whenever the prisoners' regime permitted. Along with this letter to Ruth, written on a Sunday when the men were given time off, he sent a poem called "Mainland." Beginning "Sister in darkness, reach your healing balm / toward a blanched white life and muted mouth" (F 57), these resolutely rhymed and measured verses stand against a background of shoveling rocks and road building, rough conditions and minimal rations. The composing and the composure of poems gave him a reason to go on living. Much of this writing he sent to Ruth, in the remote hope that it might become a book.

"Shoveling!" is what he would say when asked, on brief returns to Czernowitz, what work he did.[41] A companion in Tăbăreşti recalls him as "very taciturn, never speaking about the fate of his parents."[42] Others remember his "gallows humor."[43] As a Jew in these years, Celan later recalled, he learned that "language doesn't only build bridges into the world, but also into loneliness."[44]

Published accounts of Celan's life say he was in one labor camp only. But he himself spoke of "camps," and other reports mention places besides Tăbăreşti: Piatra-Neamţ and Paşcani, closer to Czernowitz, and Pleşeşti, in Romania's western mountains.[45] At these camps he met intellectuals, along with Jews from less familiar walks of life. As he later told a friend, he learned much Yiddish in the camps.[46] During his nineteen months at forced labor, he wrote poems regularly while also translating Shakespeare sonnets, Verlaine, Yeats, Housman, Éluard, Esenin, and others.[47] At least seventy-five poems survive from this period, almost all rhymed, many in traditional quatrains.[48] Imbued with melancholy, homesickness, and longing for his beloved and laden with expressionist nature imagery, they also deal in literary and mythological references. "Out of the Depths," "Morning Song," and "It is raining, sister," all written within a few days, recall the Psalms, medieval lyric, and Verlaine. He was casting about among traditions.

One poem from the fall of 1942 adopts a popular title, "The Witching Hour," and the rounded couplets common to Romanian folk songs. Observing their form while releasing a raw impulse, the poem was "depicting something inward and unspeakably immense," as he put it then.[49]

> The stillness gasps. South winds bring so much gloom?
> Come, gillyflower, crown me. Come, life, bloom.
>
> Who's mirrored? What is changing? End this dream.
> Who hears how soft, who sees how white you seem?
>
> The darkness wanders. Can night cry in pain?
> The darkness toils! It tears free from its chain!
>
> Four daggers feel a star chase in their wake.
> It whirls on further. Wonders rage awake.
>
> It grows now. Splits our bright house through with holes.
> And singing as it goes fans out our souls.   [F 63]

The tossing from one symbolic event to another sounds forced yet displays real force.

Paul's father died from typhus in the fall of 1942. A few months later he heard "in bits and pieces," he later said, about his mother's fate.[50] Sometime in late 1942 or early 1943, during an exceedingly cold winter, he learned from a relative who escaped Transnistria that his mother had been shot as unfit for work.[51]

Under this impact he wrote some quatrains called "Winter," straining to grasp a ghastly, unknowable Ukrainian scene.[52] "It's falling, Mother, snow in the Ukraine": this first line opens in the middle to address her, like the end of the 1938 sonnet: "For you are stillness, Mother, shimmer from the deep." But now the verse names a real place and drives imagination there—not nostalgia this time but its antithesis:

> It's falling, Mother, snow in the Ukraine:
> The Savior's crown a thousand grains of grief.
> Here all my tears reach out to you in vain.
> One proud mute glance is all of my relief . . .
>
> We're dying now: why won't you sleep, you huts?
> Even this wind slinks round in frightened rags.
> *Are* these the ones, freezing in slag-choked ruts—
> whose arms are candlesticks, whose hearts are flags?
>
> I stayed the same in darknesses forlorn:
> Will days heal softly, will they cut too sharp?
> Among my stars are drifting now the torn
> strings of a strident and discordant harp . . .
>
> On it at times a rose-filled hour is tuned.
> Expiring: once. Just once, again . . .
> What would come, Mother: wakening or wound—
> if I too sank in snows of the Ukraine?   [F 68]

For the first time a place name enters Celan's poetry, a locale that rebuffs any mythic reach toward some exotic "there"—Keats's "warm South," let us say, or Yeats's Innisfree. "Ukraine" rhymes twice—a feature worth retaining in translation. Its name closes the first and last lines and our own lines of sight.

The "Savior's crown" has less pathos than irony—that a Christian icon might succor a Jewish victim. And where the victims' "arms are candlesticks," the word *Leuchter* also keeps its sense of "menorah," the candelabrum ordained in Exodus. Given the universal currency of Jesus' passion, it is easy to miss a bitterness here and in other early lyrics that set Jewish suffering against Christianity.

A deep-seated Judaic tradition is threatened when the only run-on line breaks as "torn / strings of a strident and discordant harp." Harps show up often in the early poems, standing for exile. "By the rivers of Babylon, there we sat down," Psalm 137 begins; "yea, we wept, when we remembered Zion. We hanged our harps upon the willows." Around this time, Antschel wrote "Chanson juive," then retitled it "By the Waters of Babylon." Its first word tells: "Again by darkening pools / you murmur, willow, grieving" (F 70). In "Winter," torn harp strings adopt from the Psalms not praise or anger so much as despair.

This poem's last question opens toward the poet's mother and toward his audience-to-be:

Was wär es, Mutter: Wachstum oder Wunde—
versänk ich mit im Schneewehn der Ukraine?

Word for word: "What would it be, Mother: growth or wound— / if I too sank down in the snowdrift of the Ukraine?" Again Mutter centers the line, and instead of "growth" for Wachstum, "wakening" balances the question of suffering—

What would come, Mother: wakening or wound—
if I too sank in snows of the Ukraine?

—the question whether death in Ukrainian snow can awaken a poet's growth.

The paradox animating Paul Antschel's "Winter" turns up again in a 1943 poem originally entitled "Mutter," then "Schwarze Flocken." "Black Flakes" recalls (or, more likely, recreates or imagines) the moment of receiving a letter from his mother telling him of his father's death. No poem before this had shown such reach, revising loss through memory. The son speaks the first stanza, the mother the next, then the son returns at the close.

Snow has fallen, with no light. A month
has gone by now or two, since autumn in its monkish cowl
brought tidings my way, a leaf from Ukrainian slopes:

"Remember, it's wintry here too, for the thousandth time now
in the land where the broadest torrent flows:
Ya'akov's heavenly blood, blessed by axes . . .
Oh ice of unearthly red—their Hetman wades with all
his troop into darkening suns . . . Oh for a cloth, child,
to wrap myself when it's flashing with helmets,
when the rosy floe bursts, when snowdrift sifts your father's
bones, hooves crushing
the Song of the Cedar . . .
A shawl, just a thin little shawl, so I have
by my side, now you're learning to weep,
this hard world that will never turn green, my child, for your child!"

Autumn bled all away, Mother, snow burned me through:
I sought out my heart so it might weep, I found—oh the summer's
    breath,
it was like you.
Then came my tears. I wove the shawl.   [3:25]

Ranging from the present to the past to the ancient past, "Black Flakes" frames memory around experience. Only this once does a poem by Celan mention his father, and even then, it is only through his mother's voice. It is her letter embedded in the text that calls up Jewish lore—Jacob, the Song of the Cedar.

Subtly this poem sets its face against facile expectation, against the old theme of love counteracting winter from the sixteenth-century German folk song "The snow has fallen," in which a lover begs his beloved to wrap him in her arms and banish winter.[53] No such homeliness, Paul Antschel insists by echoing this song, will dispel the winter of 1943. Nor is Christian consolation to be had. Where his German says "autumn in its monkish cowl / brought news," the word for "news," *Botschaft,* also has the Gospel sense of "tidings." Here and in autumn's "monkish cowl," an edge to the voice gets at pious folk who stood by or aided the persecution near idyllic "Ukrainian slopes."

The mother's tidings are not of great joy. Saying, "Remember, it's wintry here too," she has millennial suffering in mind—"the thousandth time now." In his mother the poet finds a muse of memory. Because she's absent and probably dead, he makes her present by folding her letter into his poem.

Of course, this letter only *seems* to speak for his mother. It is himself whom he is reminding of "Ya'akov's heavenly blood, blessed by axes." Instead of the standard *Jakob,* he uses a Hebraicized German spelling with two *a*'s: *Jaakob.* This form seldom occurs in Jewish literary or religious texts: not, for instance, in a 1921 Viennese edition of the Hebrew poet Bialik, nor in a 1935 German Jewish encyclopedia that Celan owned.[54] But Martin Buber's and Franz Rosenzweig's translation of the Bible, begun in 1925 and meant literally to breathe the spirit of Hebrew Scripture, spells it *Jaakob.* In this three-syllable form, transliterating Jacob's Hebrew name, the father of the twelve tribes has been axed to death. Jacob's blood is "blessed" by axes in a Christian word, *benedeiet,* used in Lutheran and Catholic Bibles following the Annunciation: "Blessed art thou among women, and blessed is the fruit of thy womb" (Luke 1:46). In Antschel's poem, the Virgin Birth for a moment grates across the voice of a Jewish mother.

Instead of calling her persecutor a name that Jews have used for centuries—Amalek or Pharaoh or Haman—she is specific: *Hetman* ("headman"), the Ukrainian Cossack Khmelnitsky, whose massacres in 1648 decimated East European Jewry. From Jacob through the seventeenth century into the Second World War: the poet gets this grasp of persecution and endurance through his mother's voice.

But at our own remove, how can we enter the mind of someone who routes the news of his father's murder through his absent mother's words? Translation, the art of loss, can take risks now and then. "Oh for a cloth, child, / to wrap myself," she says, *wenn schneeig stäubt das Gebein / deines Vaters*—"when snowdrift sifts your father's / bones." A German friend devoted to Celan says that "sifts" is wrong, for *stäuben* connotes dust flying up. Yes— and there's no "drift" here in Antschel's German. But the poem's saddest pitch can take this music.

Translating has drawn me to look further into certain words. When the mother's letter speaks of "hooves crushing / the Song of the Cedar," this song points to the Biblical cedars of Lebanon and the anthem of the First Zionist Congress (1897): "There where the slender cedar kisses the skies / . . . there on the blue sea's shore my homeland lies." Paul had resisted his father's Zionist persuasion, and it would be decades before he ventured to that "homeland." But when he wrote "Black Flakes," it looked as if the Song of the Cedar was being crushed irreparably.

Readers have taken the poem's middle section, the part in quotation marks, as verbatim transcription of an actual letter received by the son. But that seems doubtful, given the dislocations of the period and the allusions to "Ya'akov," "Hetman," and "the Song of the Cedar"—allusions an exhausted widow would hardly have managed. What matters is that they're voiced through the mother, revising an elegiac tradition that events may outstrip.

When the mother's voice says "Oh for a cloth, child," and later begs for "A shawl, just a thin little shawl" (*Ein Tuch, ein Tüchlein nur schmal*), this reversal, this pathos of a parent seeking her child's help, must have cost the poet dearly. (A childhood friend remembers that Paul's mother knitted colored sweaters for him.[55]) Her word for hard times, *Enge* ("narrowness," "straits"), later found its way into Celan's 1960 Meridian speech: "With art go into your very selfmost straits" (3:200). A true poem must go the hardest way.

"Black Flakes" goes into the poet's selfmost straits—the presence most lost to him—and emerges tentatively. We overhear his mother saying *du* ("you") to him, and again he names her at the fulcrum of a verse:

Autumn bled all away, Mother, snow burned me through:
I sought out my heart so it might weep, I found—oh the summer's
        breath,
it was like you.
Then came my tears. I wove the shawl.

He finds the same word she used, "weep," and it takes him through the straits of winter to "the summer's breath"—*es war wie du* ("it was like you"). Here the shortest, simplest line converts this poem into dialogue, his *du* returning hers.

To close, this elegy again poises growth against wounding: *Kam mir die Träne. Webt ich das Tüchlein.* At first I tried to match those five-syllable cadences: "Tears came to me then. I knitted the shawl." But *Webt ich* means "I wove." The advent of tears balances the weaving of a shawl, the unmaking force of grief meets the poem's own making: "Then came my tears. I wove the shawl." Answering loss with language, this poem weaves a text against winter.

"Schwarze Flocken" (Black Flakes) holds in a single moment the European Jewish catastrophe, Paul Antschel's private loss, and a poet's calling. We hear his mother ask for a shawl: he writes a poem, restoring to her something, at least, in the mother tongue.

2
A Fugue after Auschwitz
(1944–45)

"What the life of a Jew was during the war years, I need not mention," Paul Celan said in a 1949 biographical note.[1] With a discretion that seems to spare his German readers, Celan offset the trauma. Like many people who lived through those years, he gave almost no factual testimony about them—which gives his poetry a testimonial charge. Yet the war years bore down absolutely.

Exactly when and where his period of forced labor—from July 1942 until about February 1944—came to an end and how he returned to Czernowitz remain obscure. An East German émigré poet published a dramatic but dubious account, supposedly given him by Celan, of a camp "selection." With one group of prisoners headed for "the gas chamber," another for immediate release, Antschel slipped from the first to the second, and the SS waved some other man to his death. All Celan's writing was thus "a futile attempt to silence the voice of his guilt."[2] This story contains implausible elements, though it does suggest how chance and choice worked upon victims under Nazi control. Perhaps in the division of a camp, Paul was one of those who stayed while others went to a severer camp. But Jews in Romanian labor battalions were not sent to Auschwitz. What is certain is that as the Red Army pushed west in 1944, Antschel either escaped or was released, returning home (possibly by way of Kiev) before the Soviets reoccupied Czernowitz in March of that year.[3]

One of the first lyrics he wrote then evoked that fatal season, autumn closing upon winter, which had occupied "Black Flakes" a year earlier. This is "The Lonely One":

More than the dove, more than the mulberry
it's me that autumn loves. Gives me a veil.
"Take this for dreaming," says its stitchery.
And: "God's as nearby as the vulture's nail."

But I have held another cloth instead,
coarser than this, no stitchery or seam.
Touch it and snow falls in the bramble bed.
Wave it and you will hear the eagle scream.   [3:24]

Twice these lines yoke dissonant ideas with a firm rhyme: "veil" is answered by a "vulture's nail," then "seam" ties needlework to a "scream," exposing lyric decorum to savagery.

By 1944 there was no doubt, despite his early study of medicine, that Paul Antschel was a poet. "Black Flakes" made his first clear claim to a lyric call: "I wove the shawl." Now "The Lonely One," written when he knew himself to be orphaned, again takes up a *Tüchlein,* a cloth that this time works a dismal magic: snow and an eagle's scream.

Though pastoral elegy no longer held good, Antschel still linked his lost mother to a solace in nature. Some couplets written "after the return from Kiev" (as he noted it years later[4]) question the maternal source of his mother tongue, challenging poetry itself. First they call to mind Goethe's famous lyric, "Kennst du das Land wo die Zitronen blüh'n?" (Knowest thou the land where the lemon trees bloom?). But this verse by an orphan in Czernowitz, entitled "Nearness of Graves," orients him toward no such paradise: *Kennt noch das Wasser des südlichen Bug,*

Still do the southerly Bug waters know,
Mother, the wave whose blows wounded you so?

Still does the field with those windmills remember
how gently your heart to its angels surrendered?

Can none of the aspens and none of the willows
allow you their solace, remove all your sorrows?

And does not the god with his blossoming wand
go up in the hills climbing hither and yon?

And can you bear, Mother, as once on a time,
the gentle, the German, the pain-laden rhyme?   [3:20]

The rhymes and rolling meter native to folk song give grief a way to move. Yet again, as in "Black Flakes" and "Winter," Antschel's verse centers on "Mother," though I have had to drop something vital—*ach, daheim*—from the final couplet:

Und duldest du, Mutter, wie einst, ach, daheim,
den leisen, den deutschen, den schmerzlichen Reim?

Literally:

And can you bear, Mother, as *oh, at home,* once on a time,
the gentle, the German, the pain-laden rhyme?

That schmaltzy "oh, at home" would overflow my four-beat line. Yet it seems a shame to edit the poet's nostalgia for the place where he first heard songs in the *Muttersprache,* songs whose cadences these lines echo. When the mother tongue came to serve his mother's murderers, a pall fell across it. Antschel could never answer or stop asking this poem's ultimate question, which he sealed with a rhyme in and against German.

German and Jewish motifs mingle strangely in one lyric, "Russian Spring," written toward the end of the war. By that time Antschel had absorbed various influences, among them the epic *Nibelungenlied*.[5] Attracted to Middle High German as a distinctive and historically pristine state of his mother tongue, he also knew how Nazism after Wagner had used heroic Nordic legend. By evoking medieval Germany, his poetry was seeking its own standpoint within a compromised tradition.

"The blood-brimmed helmet is fallen: what blossom can bloom?" (*F* 143). This archaic lament, recalling a gruesome scene from the *Nibelungenlied* and even imitating its epic verse, came after the Soviets had reoccupied Czernowitz during their 1944 offensive. The title "Russian Spring" and the dire opening mark a season of renewed oppression, which Celan later called "anti-Semitism Soviet-style."[6] Even Jews who had somehow survived were accused by their

Russian liberators of having collaborated with the Germans, and they risked resettlement in Siberia, forced labor, or conscription. But why would a Jewish student orphaned by the SS summon up tragic German warriors?

His current of feeling is hard to trace. Turning to Siegfried's bride, the poem asks: does she know that "there lingers, 'mid Ukrainian green, the faithful, Flemish death?" Knightliness verges upon Transnistrian killing fields, and "Flemish death" quotes an old song that Paul liked to sing, though it was a German nationalist favorite.[7] In this poem he is trying his cultural legacy against the death assigned by Nazism.

Leaving the *Nibelungenlied,* "Russian Spring" gravitates to Jewish motifs, addressing the poet's beloved:

Stay not my love now Katyusha has started its singing!
Kneel, amid old organ voices it's time now to kneel.
Loud rumblings now, and must I still wrestle with Ya'akov's angel?
Alone among Jewish graves, beloved, I know you are weeping.

In naming Katyusha, a rocket launcher that Russian soldiers also called the "Stalin organ," Antschel notes the mixed blessing of Soviet troops retaking Eastern Europe. Rhyming *singen* ("sing") with *ringen* ("wrestle"), he asks: *und ich muss mit Jaakobs Engel noch ringen?* Here his Hebraic spelling of "Jacob"[8] fills out a cadence: "and must I still wrestle with Ya'akov's angel?"

Yet "Russian Spring" comes back to the *Nibelungenlied:*

Dreamily he holds my hand and in streaming azure sings
for all those lying here—Herr Volker von Alzey.

The commemorative care of the dead, including those in "Jewish graves," falls to this valiant Teutonic minstrel and swordsman, a strange proxy for the poet.[9] Antschel's lament is struggling for a genuine voice in German.

No image has caught the dynamic of Jewish existence so graphically as that of Jacob wrestling the angel. Anxious about what is to become of him, Jacob spends a night alone, wrestles until dawn with a strange man, barely prevails, then takes the angel's blessing in a new name, Israel. In this agonized encounter, Jacob's wrestling speaks to the poet's struggle—with sacred authority and with an adverse time.

Soon after returning from forced labor in early 1944, Antschel put together a typescript of ninety-three poems. Later he made another collection for his friend Ruth, handwritten in a small black notebook, with the poems grouped in titled cycles.[10] Under Russian occupation, he avoided military service by working as an aide in a psychiatric clinic.[11] To earn money, he also did translations from Romanian to Ukrainian for a local paper. Then in the fall, he began studying English at the Soviet-sponsored university. All the while, he was aiming to publish a book of poems and, now that his homeland was being absorbed into the Soviet Union, to leave Bukovina for a freer milieu.

Meanwhile another cold winter set in, with shortages of food and kindling. "Life continued to be brutally hard," Pearl Fichman remembers, "sullen and joyless."[12] The Nazi camps were beginning to disgorge. Some few Jews returned, most did not. Paul must sooner or later have learned the fate of his uncle, Bruno Schrager, who had remained in Paris after the outbreak of war. His name, with the birth date "2.4.03," appears on the roster for transport #57 of 18 July 1943, the first convoy dispatched by Eichmann's SS deputy Alois Brunner from Drancy to Auschwitz.[13] Thirty of the transport's five hundred men survived.

Some of the Bukovinans deported to Transnistria came back to Czernowitz in 1944. At the home of Rose Ausländer, an older poet, Paul met his former classmate Immanuel Weissglas and also Alfred Kittner, poets who, together with their families, survived the same resettlements to the River Bug that Paul's own parents did not. Kittner thinks that Paul "suffered a severe psychic shock he never overcame, and felt a heavy burden of conscience—the thought that maybe he could have prevented his parents' murder in the camp, if he had gone with them."[14] This would help to explain Celan's later reticence and the variant reports on why he was not picked up along with his parents in June 1942. Whatever his portion of trauma and guilt, Paul was alone in late 1944, when personal and newspaper accounts of the horror were emerging.

Out of those months that saw the war ending and its Jewish catastrophe revealed, Paul Antschel wrote one lyric that drives far beyond private anguish, forming the benchmark for poetry "after Auschwitz": "Todesfuge." Its title in English might be "Fugue of Death," "Death's Fugue," "Death Fugue," or "Deathfugue."

This astonishing piece of writing has drawn more passionate attention than any other poem from the war. What looms largest is its public career since 1952, when it came out in Germany. The *Guernica* of postwar European literature, "Todesfuge" has become a historical agent, accumulating its own biography. Lyric poetry rarely has an effect like that of judicial precedent or scientific experiment, upsetting assumptions or forcing new choices. Here, Neruda's "United Fruit Co." and Yevtushenko's "Babi Yar" come to mind, as do Owen's "Dulce et decorum est" and Yeats's "Easter 1916." But no lyric has exposed the exigencies of its time so radically as this one, whose speakers—Jewish prisoners tyrannized by a camp commandant—start off with the words *Schwarze Milch der Frühe wir trinken sie abends,* "Black milk of daybreak we drink it at dusk."

The prolonged impact that "Todesfuge" has had stems partly from its array of historical and cultural signals—some overt and direct, some recondite or glancing. Practically every line embeds verbal material from the disrupted world to which this poem bears witness. From music, literature, and religion and from the camps themselves we find discomforting traces of Genesis, Bach, Wagner, Heinrich Heine, the tango, and especially *Faust's* heroine Margareta, alongside the maiden Shulamith from the Song of Songs. To realize these traces in translating Celan's verse can identify the poem, with its indictment of so-called Judeo-Christian culture.

"Todesfuge" has startled its listeners, shocking some and convincing others by its metaphors: milk that is black, graves dug in air, hair of ash, dances fiddled for gravediggers. These embellish the raw matter of Auschwitz, reviewers complained. But they aren't metaphors at all, they're plain fact, survivors claim. A translator need only convey *aschenes Haar* as "ashen hair" and *ein Grab in der Luft* as "a grave in the air." Yet we must have grasped the ironies of those images for their shape and rhythm to work in English.

Our closest access to "Todesfuge" comes by way of its rhythm, driven by repetitive risings and fallings:

> *wir* trinken *und* trinken
> we *drink* [it] and *drink* [it]

When Germans and others listen to Celan's recorded voice, they are drawn into its intensifying cadences.[15] Some are beguiled, others abruptly enlisted, as the inexorable beat forms this lyric's prevalent metaphor. Rhythm and repetition take in every other element of "Todesfuge."

What touched off this fugue of death, when and where it was composed, Celan never stated publicly. Its true origin, the only one we really need to know, we know already: "l'univers concentrationnaire," Nazism's "concentrationary universe." Still, it may help to review what is certain and what is probable about the genesis of this unprecedented work.

Friends from Czernowitz assign the poem to 1944. Alfred Kittner recalls coming back from Transnistria in the late spring of 1944: "It can't have been long afterwards, one morning outside the iron railing of Czernowitz's archdiocesan cathedral in Siebenbürger Street, that he read me the '*Todesfuge*,' written shortly before."[16] If this report is accurate, it makes Celan's most famous piece of writing all the more arresting. Instead of a lyric from soon after the war showing surprising composure, we have a consummate piece from the very uncertainty of wartime.

For a 1962 anthology, Celan dated "Todesfuge" 1945, and later he annotated it "Bucharest 45."[17] Perhaps a first version came in Czernowitz and a final one only after he emigrated in April 1945. That was the impression of Petre Solomon, Paul's close friend in Bucharest, whose 1947 Romanian translation was the poem's first publication. Solomon said the poem was "brought from Czernowitz, but doubtless finished in Bucharest, after numerous revisions."[18]

My early dating would root the poem close to its first cause. While autumn 1944 was still early for survivors from Hitler's Polish death camps to have directly prompted the poem's voice, not only Auschwitz or Maidanek or Treblinka or Sobibor or Chelmno but any Nazi camp finds its quintessence here. What Paul Antschel underwent in his own person gave him the wherewithal for these lines, though they probably bear the imprint of survivors he listened to as well. Moreover, accessible reports existed in 1944. Celan once remarked that "Todesfuge" arose from something he read about Jews playing dance tunes in a Nazi camp.[19]

He might have seen a pamphlet dated 29 August 1944, on "The Lublin Extermination Camp" (Maidanek).[20] In July 1944 the Red Army took Maidanek, and what they discovered was publicized worldwide, as propaganda. This pamphlet, issued by Moscow's Foreign Languages Publishing House, appeared in various cities and languages. Written by Konstantin Simonov, it reports that tangos and fox-trots were played during camp functions, and it contains other details suggestive of "Todesfuge."

The earliest notice of Celan's poem may connect it to the Simonov pamphlet. "Todesfuge" first appeared not in German but in Romanian (it was Celan's first published poem and his first under the name "Celan"). In May 1947, the Bucharest magazine *Contemporanul* printed Petre Solomon's translation, prefacing it with this note: "The poem whose translation we are publishing is built upon the evocation of a real fact. In Lublin, as in many other 'Nazi death camps,' one group of the condemned were forced to sing nostalgic songs while others dug graves."[21]

Because the abomination staggers belief—mass murder orchestrated, music gracing death—Celan's Bucharest editor, so soon after the war, needed to assure his readers that "a real fact" authenticated this outlandish lyric. Maybe, too, the magazine's readership needed orientation, because in 1947 Romania was going Soviet and any surrealist extravagance would be suspect. The same issue of *Contemporanul* included a long and no doubt heartening poem entitled "The Tractor."

Something surprising marks this appearance in Bucharest—namely, Celan's title: not the now famous "Todesfuge," but the Romanian "Tangoul Morții" (Tango of Death), as if romantic rhythms might sveltely shape the business of grave digging.[22] For Celan to call the poem "Death Tango" was to annul the dance that fascinated Europe during his childhood—the essence of life as urbane, graceful, nonchalant.

Not far from Czernowitz, at the Janowska camp in Lemberg (now Lvov), an SS lieutenant ordered Jewish fiddlers to play a tango with new lyrics, called "Death Tango," for use during marches, tortures, grave digging, and

TANGOUL *Morții*

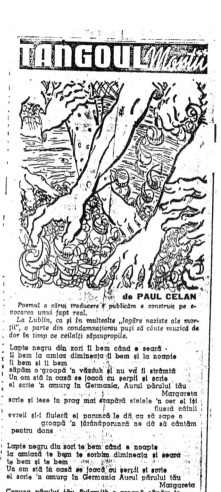

de PAUL CELAN

*Poemul a cărui traducere o publicăm e construit pe e-
vocarea unui fapt real.*

*La Lublin, ca și în multealte „lagăre naziste ale mor-
ții", o parte din condamnațierau puși să cânte muzică de
dor în timp ce ceilalți săpaugropile.*

Lapte negru din zori îl bem când e seară ·
îl bem la amiaz dimineața îl bem și la noapte
îl bem și îl bem
săpăm o groapă 'n văzduh și nu va fi strâmtă
Un om stă în casă se joacă cu șerpii și scrie
el scrie 'n amurg în Germania, Aurul părului tău
                                            Margareta
scrie și iese în prag mai scapără stelele 'n cer el își
                                            fluerâ câinii
evreii și-i fluieră el poruncă le dă ca să sape o
            groapă 'n țărânăporuncă ne dă să cântăm
pentru dans

Lapte negru din zori te bem când e noapte
la amiază te bem te sorbim dimineața și seară
te bem și te bem
Un om stă în casă se joacă cu șerpii și scrie
el scrie 'n amurg în Germania Aurul părului tău
                                            Margareta
Cenușa părului tău Sulamith o groapă săpăm în
                    văzduh și nu va fi strâmtă
El strigă săpați mai adânc iar ceilalți cântați
arma o 'nșfacă, o flutură, albaștrii i-s ochii
săpați mai adânc iar ceilalți cântați pentru dans mai
                                            departe

Lapte negru din zori te bem când e noapte
te bem la amiază dimineața și seara te bem
te bem și te bem
un om stă în casă, aurul părului tău Margareta
cenușa părului tău Sulamith el se joacă cu șerpii

El strigă cântați mai blajin despre moarte căci
                    moartea-i un meșter german
el strigă plimbați un arc mai cețos pe viori veți
                    crește ca fumul atunci
veți zace 'ntr'o groapă în nori și nu va fi strâmtă
Lapte negru din zori te bem când e noapte
te bem la amiază e moarte un meșter german
te bem dimineața și seara te bem și te bem
e moartea un meșter german albaștrii i-s ochii
cu plumb te împroască din plin și adânc te lovește
un om stă în casă aurul părului tău Margareta
câinii spre noi și-i asmute ne dăruie-o groapă 'n
                                            văzduh
se joacă cu șerpii visând emoartea un meșter german

aurul părului tău Margareta
cenușa părului tău Sulamith

Traducere din limba germană
de PETRE SOLOMON

"Tangoul Morții," *Contemporanul,* May 1947 (Petre Solomon)

Orchestra playing "Death Tango" in Janowska Road Camp, Lvov,
ca. 1942 (Yad Vashem Archive, Jerusalem)

executions.[23] Then, before liquidating the camp, the SS shot the whole
orchestra. This "Todestango," of which a recording exists, was based on the
Argentine Eduardo Bianco's greatest prewar hit.[24] In fact, Bianco's band played
in Paris while Paul Antschel was there in early 1939 and later that year
entertained Hitler and Goebbels, who preferred the tango to the "decadence"
of Negro jazz.

At Auschwitz too the orchestra played tangos, and prisoners elsewhere
used the term "Death Tango" for whatever music was being played when the
Germans took a group out to be shot.[25] So Celan's early title, "Todestango,"
gave his poem the ring of reliable evidence: that this person knew whereof
he spoke, that he was surely there and must have written the poem there.

At least once, Celan's firsthandedness has given rise to a revealing confusion between the poem's actuality and the poet's. A catalogue of Anselm
Kiefer's paintings, which embody phrases from "Todesfuge," tells us that
Celan's poem "was written in a concentration camp," and a *New York Times*
article repeats this information.[26] But it was not so. If "Todesfuge" seems to
speak straight from a Nazi camp, that is due to its first-person, on-the-spot
present tense: *wir trinken und trinken*.

The immediacy of "Todesfuge" is compelling because compelled to voice
something hitherto unheard-of.

Deathfugue

Black milk of daybreak we drink it at evening
we drink it at midday and morning we drink it at night
we drink and we drink
we shovel a grave in the air there you won't lie too cramped
A man lives in the house he plays with his vipers he writes
he writes when it grows dark to Deutschland your golden hair
    Margareta
he writes it and steps out of doors and the stars are all sparkling
    he whistles his hounds to come close
he whistles his Jews into rows has them shovel a grave in the ground
he commands us play up for the dance

Black milk of daybreak we drink you at night
we drink you at morning and midday we drink you at evening
we drink and we drink
A man lives in the house he plays with his vipers he writes
he writes when it grows dark to Deutschland your golden hair
    Margareta
Your ashen hair Shulamith we shovel a grave in the air there you won't
    lie too cramped

He shouts jab this earth deeper you lot there you others sing up and
    play
he grabs for the rod in his belt he swings it his eyes are so blue
jab your spades deeper you lot there you others play on for the dancing

Black milk of daybreak we drink you at night
we drink you at midday and morning we drink you at evening
we drink and we drink
a man lives in the house your goldenes Haar Margareta
your aschenes Haar Shulamith he plays with his vipers

He shouts play death more sweetly this Death is a master from
    Deutschland
he shouts scrape your strings darker you'll rise then as smoke to the sky
you'll have a grave then in the clouds there you won't lie too cramped

Black milk of daybreak we drink you at night
we drink you at midday Death is a master aus Deutschland
we drink you at evening and morning we drink and we drink
this Death is ein Meister aus Deutschland his eye it is blue
he shoots you with shot made of lead shoots you level and true
a man lives in the house your goldenes Haar Margarete
he looses his hounds on us grants us a grave in the air

he plays with his vipers and daydreams der Tod ist ein Meister
  aus Deutschland

dein goldenes Haar Margarete
dein aschenes Haar Sulamith   [1:41]

Against disruption, Paul Antschel in 1944 Czernowitz came up with this pattern of repetition and refrains, feeding the victims' words through his own fresh memories so as to find a voice for what happened.

Celan's own recorded voice—he read with "a cold heat," one friend said[27]—gives us quickenings, emphases, retards, pauses, caustic articulation, and even a phrase misspoken. Over the years, alone or with family or friends or students or in public, I have listened a hundred times to Celan reciting "Todesfuge" and have watched people who don't understand German register a dumbstruck recognition that deepens my respect both for the poem and for the nearly possible task of translating it.

Nearly possible—which means ultimately impossible. We get a revealing sense of "Todesfuge" by exposing the transit from one tongue, Celan's own, to another, not his own. Yet we can also hear the poem back toward its own state in German, hear its resistance to translation, its rude integrity.

Translation is already bred into this poem, since a Romanian version saw the light before the German original. Such anticipation in a foreign language seldom occurs, and when it does—as with Wilde's *De Profundis*, Broch's *Death of Vergil*, Neruda's *Heights of Macchu Picchu*, Pasternak's *Dr. Zhivago*—usually war or censorship or exile has intervened. If only because Paul Antschel emigrated (with this poem?) from Czernowitz's German-speaking milieu to the Romanian capital and "in strict collaboration" helped Petre Solomon turn the unpublished "Todestango" into "Tangoul Morţii," his premier piece of writing can be said to reach us under the sign of translation.[28]

There are at least fifteen published English translations of "Todesfuge," from Michael Bullock, Clement Greenberg, and Jerome Rothenberg in the 1950s to Christopher Middleton, Joachim Neugroschel, Michael Hamburger, and others later on.[29] Still, I see some point in rendering once more this poem that goes on speaking in a continuous present. Practically every word, phrase, and cadence broaches questions for the translator. Poetry is "news that stays news," Ezra Pound once said, and this speaks also for new versions of poems.[30]

When Celan, after his poem's Romanian debut, crossed out *tango* in a typescript and substituted *fuge* (though he left "play up for the dance"), this small change made an immense difference. It was to bring on decades of debate, the term *Todesfuge* offending against acceptable modes of meaning. What is this absurd genitive, this irreconcilable compound? "Fugue of Death," a correct translation, loses the accentual (and atrocious) symmetry of *Tó-des fú-ge,* while also loosening the German possessive's compactness—the compact between death and music, nullity and order, which are the word's two sides. Yet "Death Fugue" does not convey the sense of belonging, a train of events belonging to death. "Death's Fugue" sounds disjointed, and "Deathsfugue" coins too strange an equivalent.

That small revision by Celan, from *tango's* two syllables to *fuge's,* deepened the reach of this lyric, since "Art of the Fugue" was the summa of Johann Sebastian Bach, our paragon *Meister aus Deutschland.* Now Celan's term *Todesfuge* throws into doubt the acme of music, which is itself the quintessential art. That doubt was already blatant when Bach fugues were heard from the commandant's residence at Auschwitz.[31] Unlike (the Naziphile) Ernst Bertram's popular lyric "Die Fuge" (1930), Celan's verse undermines any high idea of music ordering our lives.[32]

Or our deaths. For "Todesfuge" enters a profound tradition in German and Austrian culture: the bond of music with death, as in Schubert's "Der Tod und das Mädchen," Wagner's "Liebestod," Brahms's *Ein deutsches Requiem,* and Mahler's *Kindertotenlieder.* Celan's poem blights this tradition. Even if death camp music sometimes "humanized" the German staff or kept up prisoners' spirits or (temporarily) exempted the musicians, that world's negation of values still rendered music and the idea of music grotesque.

Music itself is of the essence as "Deathfugue" confronts art with history. There is verse music in Celan's varying rhythms, his refrains and recurrent motifs, his alliteration and rare rhyme. His speakers also talk of music: the whistling, the playing and dancing and singing, the fiddles and the fugue. No wonder this word *Todesfuge* has thrived over the years.

The surreal conjunction in Celan's title feeds into his most famous paradox: *Schwarze Milch* ("Black milk"). This opening, which becomes the refrain of "Todesfuge," is the only line starting with a stressed syllable. And the line works a small but momentous grammatic turn. In the beginning, so to speak, *Schwarze Milch* seems to occur in the nominative, announcing the poem's initial motif: "Black milk of daybreak." Then this subject, while keeping syntactic and rhythmic primacy, turns out to be the object: "we drink it at evening." All four stanzas start with "Black milk," then dole it out over and over.

Black milk—a flagrant metaphor (like "Black Flakes"). It takes metaphor, our figure of speech that asserts something contrary to fact, to convey a fact. This metaphor is extreme, bittersweet, nullifying the nourishment vital to humankind.

But maybe we have no metaphor here. Maybe camp inmates were given a liquid they called "black milk" simply by way of description.[33] If so, *Schwarze Milch* insists that in Nazi-ridden Europe, reality overtook the surreal. In Paris a Gestapo officer asked Picasso, "Did you do this?," gesturing at *Guernica,* and the painter replied, "No. You did."

"What shall I take to witness for thee? what shall I liken to thee, O daughter of Jerusalem? What shall I equal to thee, that I may comfort thee?" This outcry from Lamentations (2:13) questions the potency of figurative language to even represent extreme distress, much less heal it. Yet the solitary city "as a widow" who "weepeth sore in the night" sits at the source of Judaic lamentation, and "Todesfuge" inherits this tradition, taking "black milk" to witness to Jewish affliction.

Just where Celan came up with *Schwarze Milch,* there's no knowing. The image occurs in a 1939 volume by Rose Ausländer, an older Jewish poet from Czernowitz, and could have some remoter origin.[34] It could have been distilled from Lamentations—"Her princes were . . . whiter than milk . . . Their visage is darker than black" (4:7–8)—or could have arisen independently. *Schwarze Milch* discloses a paradox so arresting that young Germans to whom I have mentioned Celan recall those words before anything else about him. Later Celan regretted any metaphorical ingenuity in "Todesfuge," since ingenuity could distract from the poem's burden. Traumatized by the loss of his mother, he would have winced at Bruno Bettelheim's reading of "black milk" as "the image of a mother destroying her infant."[35]

The antagonism to life embedded in Celan's opening comes through with extra force in Hebrew translations.[36] For "Black milk of daybreak" they have *Chalav shachor shel shachar,* using the root shared by *shachor* ("black") and *shachar* ("dawn")—words spelled the same, שחר, with only a vowel sign distinguishing them. In the twinkling of an eye (the Hebrew version implies), dawn can go dark.

For the first line of "Todesfuge" I would like to say "Black milk of daybreak we drink it at dusk," so as to let alliteration imprint the day-in, day-out fatality of camp existence. But "evening" rather than "dusk" for *abends* keeps Celan's rhythm and leads familiarly to "morning" in the next line. Simonov's 1944 report on Maidanek recounts a mass death march: "Scores of loudspeakers began to emit the deafening strains of the fox-trot and the tango. And they blared all the morning, all day, all the evening, and all night." Imagine the twenty-four-year-old poet reading this and then beginning a poem "Black milk of daybreak we drink it at evening / we drink it at midday and morning we drink it at night." The leap from fact to verse arrives at psychic actuality.

Fact also touches the nerve of sacred memory. Along with the scenes and rhythm that I believe found their way from Simonov's account into Celan's lines, another source deepens the reach of "Todesfuge." In the beginning I hear—or persuade myself I hear—the creation sequence from Genesis: "And God called the light Day, and the darkness he called Night. And there was evening and there was morning: one day." If the Bible reverberates through Celan's opening lines, "day . . . night . . . evening . . . morning," then the word "dusk" cannot parody Scripture as does "evening . . . and morning"— though a more radical parody occurs by turning this poem into Hebrew, which has words to refute Holy Writ in the holy tongue itself.

For forty years now, what Celan wrote has imprinted itself on readers and audiences through a relentless cadence that cannot be gainsaid. As his only poem not stopped by punctuation, "Todesfuge" finds a beat by the first line—

> *wir* trinken *sie* abends
> we *drink* it at *evening*

—and prolongs that rising and falling right through to the end. Celan recited these lines without relaxing tempo or tension. Here we have the poem's elemental gesture, a timing of degradation, a senseless inescapable cycle such as Nietzsche called the "most dreadful" aspect of eternal recurrence. *Wir trinken und trinken*: "we drink it and drink it," or "we're drinking and drinking," a rollicking beat that calls up much-loved German songs—from the Munich beer-hall, let us say, where Nazism arose. *Wir trinken und trinken*: you can see the torsos swaying and hear the tankards clanking . . . until you remember who it is in Celan's poem that is saying *wir* ("we").

This first-person plural enlists and defies us to credit the time and place it recounts. Like Dante, the poet is a listener or a mouthpiece for those speaking. To assume the voice of Jews at their most hellish moment took a stroke of verbal nerve. For Celan, as for most survivors, the difficulty of bearing witness engenders the need. And hidden within the voice he adopted—"we shovel a grave in the air"—runs his own suffering. Recall his answer when friends asked what work he did in the labor camp: "Shoveling!"[37]

Another reverberation occurs three times over: *da liegt man nicht eng* ("there one doesn't lie narrowly"). The word *eng* counted for a lot in Celan's semantic universe. In "Black Flakes" the poet's mother begged for a shawl to withstand the "straits" of the world, and years later he spoke of "your very selfmost straits" (3:200): *eng* came to signify those extremities which make art authentic.

For years I have tried one way after another to bring *da liegt man nicht eng* into rhythmic, idiomatic English: "there you won't lie too tight"—but this makes an unwanted rhyme with "we drink it at night," in a poem where rhyme would prettify. Celan's laconic phrase gives a proverbial ring to the notion that these prisoners will not be jammed into rough narrow bunks anymore, once they have gone up in smoke. Or else: "there you won't lie crammed in," but I would rather end on a hard consonant as Celan does on *eng*—which he actually pronounced *engk*. Hence "there you won't lie too cramped," with its harsh cutoff.

Verse translators are always weighing whether to try for musical effects at the spots where such effects occur in the original. "A man lives in the house," we hear, then the treble alliteration in *der spielt mit den Schlangen der schreibt*, which connects playing, snakes, and writing. To say "he plays with his snakes he writes" creates some resonance, but "he plays with his vipers he writes" moves the rhythm along and ties "vipers" to "writes," uncovering something deadly in the act of writing.

Celan's sounds sometimes defy any English equivalent: *der schreibt wenn es dunkelt nach Deutschland*. Rather than "he writes when it grows dark to Germany," we can keep the jolt of *dunkelt* and *Deutschland* by extraditing the name into English: "he writes when it grows dark to Deutschland."[38] Those two syllables grip the rhythm better than "Germany," and, after all, why translate *Deutschland*, drilled into everyone by Nazism's "Deutschland, Deutschland, über Alles." The word occurs this once in Celan's poetry, then never again.

What Celan has the commandant write home to his loved one, "your golden hair Margareta," cuts doubly into the German romantic ideal. For one thing, she is a namesake of Goethe's tragic heroine—Goethe, whose famous oak near Weimar the SS carefully preserved in Buchenwald.[39] Just what it feels like to hear *Faust*'s Margareta, the eternal feminine, maudlinly invoked on SS lips is probably best attested by native Germans (including German Jews) who grew up revering Goethe as the quintessence of the Enlightenment. (In a French version "Marguerite," gathering gorgeous overtones from Gounod's and Berlioz's *Faust* operas, boosts the irony of music counterpointing deathliness.)

A second presence in "Todesfuge" is Heinrich Heine, like Celan a German-speaking Jewish poet exiled in Paris with ambivalent feelings toward the fatherland. When the commandant cherishes his beloved's *goldenes Haar*, he is aping the premier Romantic lyric, Heine's Lorelei, whose siren "combs her golden hair" when the evening "grows dark" and sings a seductive melody while her jewels "sparkle." Heine's poem had been declared an anonymous folk song by Nazi cultural commissars, and Celan, aware of this purging, came to identify himself with Heine.[40] For the fatal music in "Deathfugue" to subvert a fair-haired nordic ideal, Heine furnishes a verbal jewel, *goldenes Haar*, which can't help but seduce German listeners, even those who sense the anger in this poem.

Once, in "Todesfuge," the cadence alone summons a protest ballad by Heine. "The Silesian Weavers" (1844) denounced the repressive *Vaterland* with a well-known refrain:

We're busy weaving day and night—
Old Germany, we weave your shroud,
We weave the threefold curse in it,
　　We weave and we weave it!

Wir weben, wir weben! One century later, in "Todesfuge," we hear *wir trinken und trinken*—a brave echo. The trouble is, Celan's speakers must drink their own doom, not weave the doom of their oppressors. And even those Silesian workers were put down, not far from Oświęcim, which in German is Auschwitz.

As the historical burden of "Todesfuge" underscores the musical, its verse sounds both brutal and fluent. With this poem's longest line, English syllables can equal the German: *er schreibt es und tritt vor das Haus und es blitzen die Sterne er pfeift seine Rüden herbei*: "he writes it and steps out of doors and the stars are all sparkling he whistles his hounds to come close." To catch in *blitzen* a glimpse of Hitler's *Blitzkrieg*, his lightning war, the stars could be "flashing." But "sparkling," a hackneyed poeticism, fits this nocturne better.[41] And *es blitzen die Sterne* half-quotes a song popular during (and after) the Third Reich, *Heimat, deine Sterne*: "Homeland, thy stars / shine on me even in distant climes." This nostalgic tune, which SS officers demanded from the Auschwitz orchestra,[42] brings a bitter taste to Celan's poem, especially if a Star of David can also be seen hovering over his line.

A sharp counterpoint follows on the sparkling stars: *er pfeift seine Rüden herbei / er pfeift seine Juden hervor.* Literally, "he whistles his hounds to come near / he whistles his Jews to appear." This matches the German, but its smooth rhyme on "near" and "appear" distracts from Celan's abrasive off-rhyme of *Rüden* ("hounds") and *Juden* ("Jews"), one word with an umlaut, the other not. Making a slight change—"he whistles his hounds to come close / he whistles his Jews into rows"—the voiced *s* in "rows" grinds against the unvoiced *s* in "close." Nazi guards used to call their Jews "dogs" and their German shepherds "men."

Because the victims' words pervade this poem, we are struck when they report another voice: "he commands us play up for the dance" (*er befiehlt uns spielt auf nun zum Tanz*). That imperative, "play up," sounds harsher coming via "us," his Jews. The dance jibes with Celan's early title, "Todestango," and with such things as *Tanz mal Jude!* ("Start dancing, Jew!"), which survivors remember the SS shouting. At the same time, the implacable rhythm gathering in this poem gives to *Tanz* the force of a *Totentanz*, a dance of death, or *danse macabre*—though this medieval emblem pales next to the speakers' present agony. When Celan reads the command "spielt auf nun zum Tanz," his voice—almost despite himself—becomes clipped, as if in mouthing SS speech some memory possessed him.

If "Todesfuge" managed no more than a compulsive repetition, it would only be going back helplessly over the trauma. So the fuguelike pattern breaks. Again *Schwarze Milch* starts a stanza, but instead of saying "we drink it," the voice now addresses "black milk" directly: *wir trinken dich*—"we drink you" or "we drink thee," letting the intimate German *dich* prompt a usage that English has lost except in the Psalmist's idiom. For these speakers to face up to black milk—is it crematorium smoke?—seems a start at resistance.

Although Celan's second stanza virtually repeats the first, a new speech breaks in on the "master" and his romantic manner. After "your golden hair Margareta," it cannot still be the commandant who says "Your ashen hair Shulamith." Though these two phrases occur in parallel, a line break keeps them apart, and Celan's own tone turns gentler after the break.

Shulamith is no ash blond but the "black and comely" maiden in the Song of Songs, a princess "the hair of whose head is like purple" and whose dancing feet are beautiful in sandals. Akin to *shalom* ("peace") or *Yerushalayim* (Jerusalem), her name guards its identity, occurring only once in the Bible. Celan had already summoned such a figure from the Song of Songs in "Legend" (1939): "It is my sister, my love" (*F* 20). Shulamith is the beloved par excellence and is seen as the Jewish people itself: "Return, return, O Shulamite; return, return, that we may look upon thee" (Song 7:1). Since the Song is read at Passover, she figures as a promise of return to Zion, and mystical tradition interprets her as the Shechinah, who wanders with the community of Israel.[43] When "Deathfugue" twins Shulamith with *Faust's* devout, ruined Margareta, nothing can reconcile them. Celan's word *aschenes* tells why.

So much depends upon differing voices—the Jews are vehement then pensive, the German is commanding then sentimental—that it jolts to hear victims quote their persecutor in staccato tones:

> He shouts jab this earth deeper you lot there you others sing up and
> play
> he grabs for the rod in his belt he swings it his eyes are so blue
> jab your spades deeper you lot there you others play on for the dancing

When Celan comes to this passage in the only recording he made of "Todesfuge," he bites off the words, almost barking some of them.[44] And he momentarily misreads one phrase—a highly unusual incident for so exact a speaker. After *ihr andern* ("you others") in the first verse, instead of saying *singet und spielt* ("sing up and play") he anticipates the phrase that two verses later will follow a second *ihr andern* and says *spielt weiter zum Tanz auf* ("play on for the dancing"). He sounds driven by the poem's SS voice into his own unnerved repetition.

That brusque "sing up and play" exposes the outrage of exile as did the Psalmist's "For they that carried us away captive required of us a song. . . . How shall we sing the Lord's song in a strange land?" (Ps. 137:3–4). Now the modern lyric foists music on killing:

> He shouts play death more sweetly this Death is a master from
>   Deutschland
> he shouts scrape your strings darker you'll rise then as smoke to the sky
> you'll have a grave then in the clouds there you won't lie too cramped

Celan's *spielt süsser den Tod* ("play death more sweetly") brings into earshot Bach's aria *"Komm süsser Tod"* (Come sweet death). Then "strings" rubs in that irony, what with Europe's countless good and not-so-good fiddlers who perished along with their fellows. Besides the crassness of playing death sweetly, Celan articulates a twist of thought that English cannot manage:

spielt	*süsser*	*den Tod*	*der Tod ist ein Meister*
play	more sweetly	death	death is a master

At the line's midpoint, *den Tod der Tod,* "death" as the object of sweet playing pivots directly on "death" as the subject of mastery. *Tod* wedges up against itself, making death both outcome and origin.

Now the poem confirms its title: *der Tod ist ein Meister aus Deutschland.* This has become a tag line, gracing articles, monographs, anthologies, documentaries, and works of art. It translates readily, yet *Meister* can designate God, Christ, rabbi, teacher, champion, captain, owner, guildsman, master of arts or theology, labor-camp overseer, musical maestro, "master" race, not to mention Goethe's *Wilhelm Meister* and Wagner's *Meistersinger von Nürnberg,* which carries overtones of the 1935 Nuremberg racial laws and the postwar trials. Any other choice but "master" would lose the loaded sense of *Meister.*

As this motif takes over, the verse itself falls into step and turns up the poem's only rhyme:

> *der Tod ist ein Meister aus Deutschland sein Auge ist blau*
> *er trifft dich mit bleierner Kugel er trifft dich genau*
>
> this death is ein Meister aus Deutschland his eye it is blue
> he shoots you with shot made of lead shoots you level and true

The celebrated purity of that icy nordic eye calls for a folk idiom, a singsong wordiness to bring out the childlike tone, and a hackneyed rhyme.[45] Goethe too rhymes on *genau* ("exact") in his ballad on death, the "Erlking," ardently set by Schubert.

By the time this "master from Deutschland" is named three and then four times, "Todesfuge" has evolved its own span of real time. Rhythm and repetition have become systemic, there is no escaping them, and that is precisely their metaphoric burden. Morning and midday and evening and night: the poem's own reiterations bear out the fatality of "l'univers concentrationnaire."

Then suddenly this mind-emptying repetitiveness makes the poem easier to translate: *wir trinken dich mittags*—I've solved this already, and this: *der Tod ist ein Meister aus Deutschland*. The next time they come round I've got my version, then the next and the next. There's no use in thinking anymore, and that points to a rare option, given the poem's *fugue* of death: that is, to drive home its motifs as Celan himself does. The catch phrase *der Tod ist ein Meister aus Deutschland* appears four times. Let this sentence gradually revert to German. First, so that the reader comprehends, say "Death is a master from Deutschland." The second time, "Death is a master aus Deutschland." Then "Death is ein Meister aus Deutschland." And finally, "der Tod ist ein Meister aus Deutschland"—a German contagion of English.

What makes it possible to do this is the logic of "Todesfuge"—its musicality, for better or worse. By veering more and more to the original, my version gets a ring of truth, an identity with verse written by Paul Celan. In this gradual reversion, unavailable to German readers, we re-enter the darkness of deathbringing speech.

Near the end of his recording, Celan's enunciation grows slow and precise: "er spielt mit den Schlangen und träumet der Tod ist ein Meister aus Deutschland." The verb *träumet* is eerily drawn out, which leads me to extend it from "dreams" to "daydreams": "he plays with his vipers and daydreams der Tod ist ein Meister aus Deutschland." While "daydreams" fills out the meter and intensifies the vowels, it also lends a deceptive innocence. Celan's syllable-by-syllable precision, speaking his key phrase now, sounds tender and surgical: "der - Tod - ist - ein - Mei - ster - aus - Deutsch - land." Maybe he articulates so carefully because it's his last chance.

Finally, I leave the litany of appeals to Margareta and Shulamith wholly in German. The translator's voice moves into unison with the poet's, recouping a little of what has been lost in translation. The twin motifs that have shadowed each other throughout this poem join at the end—

dein goldenes Haar Margarete
dein aschenes Haar Sulamith

—in a chord that makes discord, a coda with no closure. When any poem ends, it has come to its limit of representation. This poem comes to that limit with a vengeance. Instead of a promising Biblical parallelism, the figures of Margareta and Shulamith undercut each other—*dein goldenes Haar . . . / dein aschenes Haar*. The German and Jewish ideals will not coexist.

German-Jewish: the hyphen alone signals a lost world, as do "Todesfuge'"s closing lines. Because couplets pull things together, it's plausible to hear reconciliation and even forgiveness. But these are precluded by Celan's speaking voice (if by nothing else) when its tension catches slightly on the *a* of *aschenes,* Shulamith's "ashen" hair, in almost a glottal stop: *dein—aschenes Haar Sulamith.*

Paul Celan's fugue runs out on a name that resonates as strangely in German as in English and preempts them both, being Hebrew. Darkened by ash, "Shulamith" ends the poem holding onto what Nazism tried to erase: a rooted identity. Archaic, inalienable, she has the last word, not to mention the silence after.

3
Song in the Wilderness
(1945–48)

"How would it be, for example," Paul Antschel remarked early in 1945 about leaving Soviet-controlled Czernowitz—"How would it be to arrive in Jerusalem, go to Martin Buber, and say: 'Uncle Buber, here I am, now you've got me!'"[1] Buber, who had left Germany in 1938, mattered enough to him, as did Palestine to his family and friends, for this remark to be only half jocular, masking a sense that he really should be emigrating now or should have done so with his parents before the war. That option became for Celan the road not taken, which would have made all the difference to a poet, if indeed he remained a poet at all.

Antschel's native city, spelled "Chernovtsy" by then, along with the rest of northern Bukovina, lay in Russian hands. He was acquainted with the dangers and constrictions of the Soviet regime and its hatred of Jews. For someone whose family stemmed from the Austrian Empire, Vienna was the place to be reached, but Vienna after Nazi domination and Soviet occupation held little promise at the time. So that left what lay closest, to the south, where the border with Romania remained fairly open.

As he rode a crowded Russian army truck from Czernowitz toward Bucharest in late April 1945, Antschel was crossing a personal as well as a political border.[2] Behind him he left not only his physical homeland, now lost to him, but the mother and father and childhood and youth set in that matrix. Carrying a few prized books, money he had earned since returning from forced labor, and his poems in manuscript, he and some companions ventured to the Romanian capital, which was no longer in league with the Axis.

On arrival, Antschel took the poetry he had already written in Czernowitz (probably including "Todesfuge") to the doyen of Bukovina's Jewish poets, Alfred Margul-Sperber, who welcomed it. He found work with a new publisher, Cartea Rusa ("The Russian Book"), reading manuscripts and translating Russian literature into Romanian: Chekhov sketches, Lermontov's novel *A Hero of Our Time,* and a play called *The Russian Question* by Simonov, who had written the 1944 pamphlet about Maidanek. These books were well received, and though Paul Antschel signed them in various ways—Paul Aurel, Paul Ancel, A. Pavel—they were his first publications and gave him particular pride. "If only my mother had lived to see it!" he said to a friend. "I think she sometimes had her doubts about me."[3]

Paul came to translation with some handiness already. He had tried German versions of French, English, and Russian poems since his mid-teens, had rendered Marx into Romanian for a student magazine, and, more recently, had worked as translator for a Ukrainian newspaper in Czernowitz. What is more, translating was akin to crossing borders, his own plight. Translate, transmigrate—seeking likeness within strangeness, sustaining identity.

His first poem after resettlement dates from 1945. "Ein Lied in der Wüste," he called it (1:11), "A Song in the Desert"—or to echo the King James Bible, "A Song in the Wilderness," since *in der Wüste* translates the Hebrew *BaMidbar,* the title of the Book of Numbers: "And the Lord spoke unto Moses in the wilderness of Sinai." Besides exilic wandering, Antschel's title evokes a song sung by Moses, Miriam, and the Israelites after their exodus from Egypt. Against that divine deliverance, the modern song begins (in the meter of "Todesfuge"):

A garland was wound out of blackening leaves in the region of Acra:
I reined my dark stallion around and stabbed out at death with my
    dagger.
From deep wooden vessels I drank the ashes of wells there at Acra,
and dropping my visor I charged straight ahead 'gainst the ruins of
    heaven.

When this violence headed up Celan's first major book (1952), one reviewer
called it "a pure play of language for its own sake" and identified Acra as a
Saudi Arabian city.[4] Liking the poem's knightly impulse, German scholars
have noted that Acre, or Akko, was once the site of Crusader activity in
northern Palestine. (The Crusades, they might have added, accounted for
many thousands of European Jewish martyrs on the way to rid the Holy
Land of other infidels.) But Celan's Acra may be the citadel built by the tyrant
Antiochus, overlooking Jerusalem's Temple mount.[5] It figured strategically
for the Jews rebelling against both Greek and Roman rule.

The black-leaved laureate tilting at heaven's ruins brings to mind perennial
persecution:

The angels are dead and the Lord has gone blind in the region of Acra,
there's none in the night who will guard for me those who have gone to
    their rest here.

Lamenting his wounds, he thinks of those who "pray in Acra":

So I have become now their smiling brother, the ironclad cherub of
    Acra.
And still do I utter the name and still on my cheek feel the blazing.

Though golden cherubim guarded the ark in the wilderness and in Solomon's
Temple (Exod. 37:7, 1 Kings 6:23), the poet after so much death is an
"ironclad cherub" profaning—by uttering—the name of God. What then is
this blazing on his cheeks? Moses at the burning bush? The hot coal touched
to Isaiah's lips? Ezekiel beholding the fire between two cherubim? A holocaust?

The years in Bucharest, from April 1945 until December 1947, were not
wholly wilderness years. Paul saw them as a transition, a time to earn money
toward resettling in Vienna. This time saw as well a first flush of liberation
before Romanian Communism set in. "From the age of 21 to 25," says his
contemporary Pearl Fichman, who also left Czernowitz in 1945, "I had not
heard a concert, seen a performance or read any new book."[6] These were
relatively happy years, to judge from his friend Petre Solomon's 1989 memoir.
In a revealing photo, the two men are glancing up, Celan with a magazine
held half-open in his fingers. A life could be lived then. After wartime
deprivation, some release could come.

Celan and Petre Solomon, Bucharest, 1947 (Yvonne Hasan)

Beneath it, though, ran anxiety. The editor who published Celan's "Tangoul Morţii" remembers him at a New Year's Eve party singing an old Germanic ballad he had favored before the war, one also sung by the Hitler Youth: "Flanders in distress, in Flanders rides death."[7] Celan was sitting on the floor and after each stanza would rhythmically thump his fist, articulating the word *ge-stor-ben* ("perished").

Something else in this Romanian interlude reflects a lifted spirit and also an escapist impulse: the penchant in Paul's circle for pun making and language games. Petre Solomon recorded some of Paul's witticisms, among them: "A poet doesn't wait for the dial tone to make a call."[8] The wordplay of this period was in Romanian with French asides. Celan later called it "cette belle saison des calembours" (this high time of puns).[9] But ardent punning shows more than a delight in words. John Keats, mortally ill in Rome in 1820, said he "summoned up more puns, in a sort of desperation, in one week than in any year of my life."[10] A pun, as a takeoff on literal sense, also takes off from the intractable fact of things.

Although *jeux de mots* enjoy a brief life span, those from Bucharest have a dark-tinged *joie de vivre,* as in this example, written down by Celan, of the surrealist "question–answer" game:

What is the poet's solitude?—A circus number not announced in the program.

What is forgetting?—An unripe apple with a spear stuck into it.
What is return?—Almost nothing, but it could be a snow flake.

Paul liked to transform his friends' names: Margareta Dorian became "Gar-gareta," and by an anagram, his own name in Romanian, Ancel, became Celan. This change of name, occurring early in 1947, had a professional as well as a psychological motivation: for a modern writer, "Antschel" smacked of the Old World. He also came up with a self-definition: "Paul Celan: persona gratata"—the poet as *persona non grata,* isolated by a grate and grated.

While in Czernowitz, Paul had discovered Kafka's writings, and later he introduced his Bucharest friend Petre Solomon to them. In May 1946, the French Communist weekly *Action* published an article entitled "Faut-il brûler Kafka?" (Must we burn Kafka?), deploring the influence of "black literature" on societal health.[11] For two months, *Action* ran responses, mostly liberal-minded though neglecting Kafka, from René Char, François Mauriac, and others. Celan's own reaction was to translate—into Romanian—four of Kaf-ka's short parables: "Before the Law," "Excursion into the Mountains," "An Imperial Message," and "The Passersby."[12]

Through translating from Russian and German and absorbing everyday speech, Celan became more at home in Romanian. Yet it never displaced German. Asked how he could still write in German after the war, he replied: "Only in the mother tongue can one speak one's own truth. In a foreign tongue the poet lies."[13] But at the urging of friends, it seems, he wrote some Romanian pieces: eight short lyrics, which were published posthumously, and eight prose poems.[14] "Tristeţe" (Sadness) begins:

> The dreams, the storm wind of evening's dawning,
> the sea asleep in sunken water lilies,
> you come to freeze them with your silence, black
> sister of him who set the jag-toothed
> snowy sky as a wreath upon your brow.   [F 157]

What starts as a neo-Romantic landscape turns toward harsh expressionism. And "Poem for Marianne's Shadow," the strongest of the Romanian lyrics, begins:

> The love-mint has grown like an angel's finger.
> Believe it: an arm sprained by silence still rises from the earth,
> a shoulder scorched by the heat of extinguished lights,
> a face, the eyes' gaze black blindfolded,
> one huge wing of lead and the other of leaves,
> a body, spent, at rest, rinsed clean.   [F 160]

After "Todesfuge," a fresh hand is dealing in bizarre rather than atrocious phenomena.

This freedom derives from the new medium, Romanian, and from Celan's habitual wordplay in Bucharest. Clearly surrealist innovation affected these lines from "Regăsire" (Rediscovery):

On green chalk dunes it will rain tonight.
Wine kept till now in a dead man's mouth,
poured in a bell, will wake the landscape with bridges.
A human tongue in a helmet will peal derring-do. [F 178]

Chalk dunes might have appeared in Celan's earlier poetry, and wine and a bell, but not green chalk dunes or wine in a dead man's mouth or bells with a human tongue. Dreamlike, disjoined images loosen up his Romanian writing, which can also turn ominous: "we'll go back upstairs to drown ourselves at home."

Celan's prose poems from 1946–47, which, like the lyrics, remained unpublished during his lifetime, have an even freer whimsy. As a student, he had been enthused with Paul Éluard and others. Then, after the war, he frequented Bucharest's avant-garde, which was as zealous as any in Europe. The short prose he wrote makes use and makes fun of surrealist audacity. "Partisan of an Erotic Absolutism," for instance, speaks about "brainless members of the Universal Poetic Conspiracy" (F 195). Even at their most absurd, the prose poems shape their spontaneity. Celan was still finding his way.

One of these pieces presents a slate pencil skipping over the tablet of the earth. This parable (the only one in German) could pass for something by Kafka. It is worth quoting a sample, not least for the pleasure of translating with Kafka near one's fingertips.

"Noiselessly a slate pencil skips across the blackish earth, tumbles over, spins on across the endless tablet, pauses, looks around, spots nobody, goes on wandering, writes" (F 191). A little later, where "the way is far, the surface unwritten-on,"

A man pops up, on foot, he follows the shimmering and often broken trail. Snow, he thinks, but he knows it's not snow, although we're far into December. And yet he goes on thinking it is snow, and smiles because he knows that it's something else and he has no name for it.

No doubt about it, yesterday was a day of mirrors. When he went to the window to check whether he'd left it open overnight—for nobody had been there during this last night of waiting—he found it closed, bolted from outside, a hand must have fooled with it, a deft noiseless hand (he was a light sleeper, he'd even waited up and still heard nothing), so the hand he dreaded for years, just today it had come and barred entrance to him. In the glass, however, he glanced at himself and saw he was wearing a coat, though he hadn't intended to go wandering—oh, that's why no one had come, because he'd lain there clothed, ready for the road!—and on looking closer, he ascertained that he'd thrown the coat over his naked body and buttoned it up, the coat had countless buttons and strangely enough: every button was a small glass cube with a light burning in it, and if one peered carefully—O God, that was actually himself, even these cubes were mirrors! And more terrible yet: it was not him, that is, not his whole shape, but only his head, a bit averted and with closed eyes.

Finally the man stands looking at his "outstretched toes doing some sort of wandering."

The pace and humor in this sketch have a semi-antic, semi-manic tone, as in the piece by Kafka that Celan translated around this time, "Excursion into the Mountains": "'I don't know,' I cried out soundlessly, 'I just don't know. If nobody comes, well then nobody comes.'" À la Kafka, troubling signs appear in Celan's sketch. The slate pencil travels over "blackish earth," and the man steps through snow that is not snow but "something else and he has no name for it." Not long before, "Black Flakes" had found death in the snow, and "Todesfuge" had dealt with blackness and earth. In Celan's Bucharest sketch, the window bolted from outside at night may have to do with the door Paul found barred after his parents' arrest in 1942. And the man sleeping with a coat on, ready for the road, could be set to flee Bucharest at any moment. The verb "wander," used several times, ties Jewish wandering to what the pencil does—"goes on wandering, writes"—as if writing were tantamount to wandering.

Ominous fantasies run through Celan's Romanian prose, along with erotic innuendo. One piece ends tortuously: "Night has set in, you push backward, the mirrors on your house keep bending down to seize your shadow, stars fall and rip your mask off, your eyes drop into your heart, where the sycamore's leaves are kindled, the stars come down there too, all but the last, a small bird, death, circling around you, and your dreaming mouth utters your name" (F 189). Surrealist stirrings plus the unencumbered Romanian language were freeing Celan to try out an exile's identity.

"On the second day after the deportations began," another piece starts, "Raphael came at night, he had on an immense despair of black silk, with a hood" (F 199). After "a similar despair" is placed on the narrator's shoulders, he says: "I bowed to my mother, kissed her, incestuously, and left the house." At the railway line, Raphael shows him a giant candelabrum (or menorah) that will save the people before daybreak if they climb on it to the sky. The narrator climbs up, but ends his account crying "Where is the sky? Where?" Elsewhere, Celan never wrote about the deportations from Czernowitz. Maybe in 1946 this was possible only in Romanian, not in the familial mother tongue.

Yet Celan did not go for over two years in Bucharest without composing poems in his native language.[15] Like "A Song in the Wilderness," his other German verse of this period hints at apocalypse. "Over the steppe an ice wind hangs the gallows-light of your eyelashes," "Harmonica" begins, and there's word of "frozen roses," fruit "hoisted on jagged towers," "peaks of ash," and "God's wolfish bosom" (3:34, 41). Surreal energy has skewed the universe: "A grinding of iron-nailed boots in the cherry tree. / Your summer foams out of helmets" (1:24). Every one of these poems, Celan wrote to an editor in 1946, is "accompanied by the feeling that I've now written my last poem."[16]

The poet's universe retained a single flaw. To address his mother, he adapted from Romanian folk song the elegiac *doină*, whose couplets typically make some plant or tree witness to personal despair. Thus, for example, in a traditional *doină*:

> Green leaf of the ribwort,
> Heavy pain stalks my heart.
> Pale leaf of the blue lilac,
> My mother does not come back.[17]

And in another:

> What leaf trembles
> when no wind blows?
> The aspen leaf,
> my love, with grief.[18]

Celan's "Aspen Tree" (1945) does without rhyme, answering the question from a year before: "And can you bear, Mother, as once on a time, / the gentle, the German, the pain-laden rhyme?" If "Espenbaum" goes rhymeless, though, its firm beat measures human against natural events:

> Aspen tree, your leaves glance white into the dark.
> My mother's hair never turned white.
>
> Dandelion, so green is the Ukraine.
> My fair-haired mother did not come home.
>
> Rain cloud, do you linger over the well?
> My soft-voiced mother wept for everyone.
>
> Rounded star, you coil the golden loop.
> My mother's heart was cut by lead.
>
> Oaken door, who hove you off your hinge?
> My gentle mother cannot return. [1:19]

Celan published "Espenbaum" three times in 1948, which shows its impor-
tance to him.[19] When it came out again later, he made one almost impercep-
tible change in the sixth line, of *weint'* to *weint*: "wept" became "weeps,"
keeping the rhythm but shifting grief into a perennial present.

It is art itself that feels corrupted in "The Sand from the Urns" (1946),
which depicts a surreal minstrel at work:

> Mould-green is the house of oblivion.
> At each of its blowing gates your beheaded minstrel goes blue.
> He beats a drum for you of moss and bitter pubic hair.
> With an ulcerous toe he traces your brow in the sand.
> Longer than it was he draws it, and the red of your lip.
> You fill up the urns here and nourish your heart.   [1:22]

Poetry would live in the house of memory rather than that of oblivion, were
it not for sand. "Sand art," "sand people," "sand glass": in Celan's work these
signify a people's desert wandering, their multiplied seed, their life running
out—sand like ashes in the urns. The last line names the poet's task: "You
fill up the urns here and nourish your heart."

Celan saw little future in Romania as a German-language poet under the
aegis of socialist realism. Just before the king abdicated under Communist
pressure in December 1947 and a People's Republic was declared, Celan fled
Bucharest with no papers, only a rucksack of poems. This was the last possible
moment. Hungary had started sending Romanian fugitives back, and Romania
was arresting and shooting them. All told, forty thousand Romanian Jews
reached Vienna in 1947.[20] Celan made a dangerous border crossing (paying
a smuggler exorbitantly) and a "dreadfully hard journey" across Hungary in
winter, he said, sleeping in unused railway stations, heading toward Vienna,
the lodestar of his childhood.[21] Hungarian farmers helped him, and he
stopped in Budapest for a week, but no poem ever touches on this journey.

Except, perhaps, for a passage from his only prose fiction, "Conversation
in the Mountains" (1959). There, a narrator named Jew Klein remembers
something "back then": "On the stone is where I lay, back then, you know,
on the stone slabs; and next to me, they were lying there, the others, who
were like me, the others, who were different from me and just the same"
(3:171). Are these "others" the emigrants of 1947—Jewish, like Celan, but
different, because he had not so identified himself? Perhaps a common
condition was brought home to him—or so he later realized—by his search
for a place to settle.

Vienna. For years I had the impression that my father was born there. In
fact he came from Lemberg, Galicia, north of Czernowitz. People living in
those outposts of the Austro-Hungarian Empire saw Vienna as their spiritual

home. "What was reachable, distant enough," in his prewar life as Celan remembered it, "what had to be reached was named Vienna" (3:185). So that city became his postwar destination, a German-speaking place not Germany. With him when he fled Romania, Celan carried a letter of introduction from his mentor, Alfred Margul-Sperber, to Otto Basil, an Austrian man of letters, announcing "*the* poet of our west-easterly landscape . . . the most original and unmistakable of the recent German generation."[22] Sperber called Celan's poetry "the only lyric counterpart to Kafka's work."

On reaching Vienna, Celan straightaway presented his letter. "One day" in December 1947, Basil remembers, "there appeared in the office of *Plan* a young man of slender countenance and dark sad eyes. He spoke in a soft voice, seemed modest, withdrawn, almost frightened. It was Paul Celan. He looked hungry and shabby, having had to make his way across Hungary to Vienna, sometimes for long stretches on foot. . . . Along with a manuscript of poems he brought me a letter from Margul-Sperber."[23]

But the high auspices of this letter could not fully certify a young Czernowitzer in the metropolis. "He came literally out of nowhere," a Viennese friend of his recalled in 1970 (to the distress of Celan's Bukovinan and Romanian compatriots).[24] And a Swiss editor publishing his poems in February 1948 introduced them this way: "Paul Celan is a young Romanian who, growing up in a Romanian-speaking village, has learned German through remarkable application and been drawn into our poetry. In his own surprisingly beautiful way, he has raised his voice in its choir, born again as poet in an element that was foreign at first."[25] So much for the young man whose mother had shared Goethe and Schiller with him in the mother tongue, and who had long cherished the poets from Hölderlin to Rilke.

A few days after that note appeared, Celan wrote to Sperber about reading his work to a gathering in Vienna and receiving "much praise."[26] His gratification seems an index of how needy he was at the time: "Believe me, God knows I was happy when they told me I was the greatest poet in Austria and—so far as they knew—in Germany as well." Yet Celan was wary of his new acquaintances, for what they may have done during the war. When a certain author extolled him, Celan thought that this man, who had held a position in Viennese radio under the Nazis, had "probably had other things to say to a Jewish poet back then." In a letter to Bucharest he signed himself "sad poet of the Teutonic tongue."[27]

In a city with more pressing concerns, Celan's poetry did meet with some success. Basil published a generous selection in his avant-garde magazine, while others helped him to get a book published and to read on Austrian radio. He was befriended by a well-known surrealist painter, Edgar Jené, "who is," Celan assured Sperber, "definitely free of prejudice."[28]

Under Jené's influence, he translated a French poem by the West Indian surrealist Aimé Césaire and also a short text on Jené by André Breton.[29] Together with Jené he wrote a piece of skeptical humor. "A Lance" begins like this: "Again the huge hammer swings and whom should it crush, when it whistles down? A creature no longer like unto man, a misbirth out of Sodom, Methuselah's last offspring, begot in his death hour: Surrealism."[30] He also helped organize a surrealist exhibition in March 1948 and there gave his first public reading to an enthusiastic audience.

At this time Celan wrote a revealing essay, the foreword to a brochure of Edgar Jené's work (3:155–61).[31] He even entitled one of Jené's figures "The Son of the Northern Lights" and identified with this decaying bust whose empty eyes loom over a landscape of icy fragmented trees. "Man is bound numb in the snow woods of his despair," Celan writes. As for "his eyes: they have seen what all have seen, and more."

"Edgar Jené and the Dream of the Dream," as Celan called this essay, does more than interpret Jené's pictures. It opens with the "wandering" of an "unappeasable discoverer," a blend of William Blake, Alice in Wonderland, and Wittgenstein: "I am to say a few words that I heard in the deep sea, where so much is silenced and so much is happening." Celan denies any "rational" means of "giving words their own (primitive) meaning again." "What has happened," he urges—and a decade later he would call the European Jewish catastrophe simply "that which happened"—is not just an addition to history but a "metamorphosis" (*Verwandlung*, echoing Kafka). Human beings cannot speak, because their words "groan under a thousand-year burden" of false sincerity (recalling Hitler's "Thousand-Year Reich"). Our age-old struggle for expression has now felt "the ash of burnt-out meaning and not only that!"

Asked to introduce pictures, Celan writes a philosophical fable. "How should what is New," he asks, writing as a German-speaking survivor and a sometime surrealist—"How should what is New now come up Pure as well?" The task this essay proposes is to "never leave the depths and keep holding dialogue with the dark wellsprings [*finstern Quellen*]." Several poems from the Vienna period also take on this task. "We watch each other in the deep sea's mirrors," says one (1:32). These love lyrics reach down for contradiction, to make "what is New now come up Pure as well." Nothing quite like them had evolved in Czernowitz or Bucharest.

"Praise of Distance," for example, takes *Quell* ("source," "wellspring") as its keynote and paradox as its technique:

In the springs of your eyes
live the nets of the fishers of Wildsea. . . .

Blacker in black, I am more naked.
Only faithless am I true.

I am you, when I am I. . . .

A net trapped a net:
embracing we sever.

In the springs of your eyes
a hanged man strangles the rope.   [1:33]

In Celan's invented *Irrsee* ("Wildsea"?), *irr-* can mean wandering, error, insanity—a fit setting for what follows. "Praise of Distance" reverses good sense: "a hanged man strangles the rope," and "Only faithless am I true" (which could also be translated "Only apostate am I faithful," as a bereft survivor might say).

Signs of life gone topsy-turvy occur in "Memory of France," dedicated to Jené, which ends simply: "We were dead and could breathe" (1:28). Another poem from Vienna, called "Late and Deep," refutes the Resurrection by involving it with Jewish persecution.[32] "We swear by Christ the New to wed dust to dust," say the poem's plural speakers (1:35). "You blaspheme!" cries an Inquisitional voice, whereupon the speakers as much as accuse Christian dogmatism of crushing the Chosen People in Auschwitz: "You grind in the mills of death the white meal of the Promise." Again, "You blaspheme!"—to which they reply ironically, using words that Matthew put into Jewish mouths at Jesus' trial (27:25): "Let the guilt be upon us." The poem ends: "Let a man come forth from the grave." Not just Jesus. However "late and deep" it may be, let just one *Mensch* come back to life.

Christian–Jewish dynamics also move Celan's last major lyric written in Vienna, "Corona," which invokes—while revoking—Rilke's marvelous "Autumn Day."[33] First, here is Rilke's 1902 lyric, beginning *Herr: es ist Zeit. Der Sommer war sehr gross*:

Lord: it is time. The summer was immense.
Stretch out your shadow on the sundial's face,
and on the meadows let the winds go loose.

Command the last fruits to be full in time;
grant them even two more southerly days,
press them toward fulfillment soon and chase
the last sweetness into the heavy wine.

Whoever has no house now, will build none.
Who is alone now, will stay long alone,
will lie awake, read, get long letters written,
and through the streets that follow up and down
will wander restless, when the leaves are driven.

Now Celan's "Corona," moving from autumn to Rilke's "It is time":

Autumn nibbles its leaf right from my hand: we're friends.
We shell time from the nuts and teach it to walk:
time turns back into its shell.

In the mirror is Sunday,
in dream goes sleeping,
the mouth speaks true.

My eye goes down to my lover's loins:
we gaze at each other,
we say dark things,
we love one another like poppy and memory,
we slumber like wine in the seashells,
like the sea in the moon's blood-beam.

We stand at the window embracing, they watch us from the street:
it's time people knew!
It's time the stone consented to bloom,
a heart beat for unrest.
It's time it came time.

It is time.   [1:37]

The appeal that opened Rilke's poem, "Lord: it is time," waits until the close of Celan's. And after two world wars what's missing is the word *Herr* ("Lord"). Just before composing "Autumn Day," Rilke wrote the elegiac "Autumn": "The leaves are falling, falling distantly . . . And yet there still is One who holds this falling / unendingly and gentle in his hands." No such presence undergirds Celan's lines. They can only implore, like the Psalmist: "It is time for the Lord to work" (119:126).

To arrive at *Es ist Zeit*, at once complaint and demand, "Corona" settles into Celan's rising-falling rhythm:

wir lieben einander wie Mohn und Gedächtnis,

we love one another like poppy and memory.

They both must forget and remember their pasts, maybe because one of them is Christian and the other not. Also divided, the word "corona" suggests Christ's crown of thorns and a new time come round. The lovers' union has a civic dimension—"it's time people knew!"—and a prophetic one as well: "It's time the stone consented to bloom." For Celan, who shoveled stones at forced labor and could not give his parents a gravestone, "stone" already stood for mute grief. If a stone is to bloom, then there must come—to borrow from "Late and Deep," written shortly before—a "wind blast of conversion."

Vienna, rid of its Jews by Eichmann's agent Alois Brunner,[34] was not congenial for Paul Celan or for the other refugees streaming in. "Happy the man who forgets what can't be changed" runs a refrain from *Die Fledermaus,* Vienna's darling operetta. By late 1947, when Celan arrived, Austria's mild denazification process was already coming to an end, and in 1948 the government gave blanket absolution to all minor offenders.[35] Celan was on his guard. In this light, his friendship with Ingeborg Bachmann (1926–73) mattered vitally. She was writing a dissertation on Heidegger and was sensitive to the limits of poetic language, especially after fascism.

Celan's Vienna poems mostly address Bachmann, as we see in her 1971 novel *Malina,* with its fable of a princess and a "stranger" from the east with dark warm eyes, a compelling voice, and a long black cloak. Into this fable Bachmann weaves phrases from Paul Celan's love poems, above all from "Corona," creating an effect of preternatural kinship. "Must you go back to your people?" the princess asks, and the stranger says: "My people is older than all peoples of the world and is scattered to the winds."[36]

A photo of Celan, taken in Vienna, shows something of this stranger— still youthful, with an inward gaze.[37] There were certainly friends—Edgar and Erica Jené, the writers Milo Dor, Klaus Demus, and a poet also born in Czernowitz in 1920, Alfred Gong, whose work Celan helped revise.[38] But, given hard living conditions, a divided city, and the unlikelihood of furthering his education or finding proper employment, Celan decided to leave the Austrian capital for Paris, even though his first collection of poems—*The Sand from the Urns,* featuring "Todesfuge"—was to come out soon. "I didn't stay long," Celan said; "I didn't find what I'd hoped to find."[39]

On 5 July 1948, journeying west, he stopped near Innsbruck, laid flowers and a willow twig on Georg Trakl's grave, and visited the eminent old editor Ludwig von Ficker. Celan nervously read aloud some poems and wrote to Sperber the next day:

> You can imagine my joy on being told I was destined to be the heir of Else Lasker-Schüler. At first I didn't know just what to make of these words, because—I'm ashamed to admit it—I'm much less attracted to Else Lasker-Schüler's poems than to Trakl and Éluard, and also because I didn't know what Ludwig von Ficker thought of her poems. But then Ludwig von Ficker took from his desk Lasker-Schüler's latest volume, *The Blue Clavier,* it was a copy of the book published in Jerusalem, and began speaking of this poet in such a way that I saw she meant every bit as much to him as Trakl. He also thought Trakl himself was often very indebted to her. And he talked to me as if even I were one of them. What especially delighted me was that he really entered into the Jewishness of my poems—as you well know, that counts a great deal to me.[40]

If Vienna, "that which had to be reached," proved impossible to settle in, Paris offered more incentive. Celan spoke French fluently and had tasted the city during his prewar student year in France. Baudelaire, Verlaine, Rimbaud, the surrealists—he had grown up on them and had started translating their work as soon as his own poetic calling emerged. Heinrich Heine lived out his voluntary exile in Paris. Rilke's Malte Laurids Brigge came there in the fall of 1902, like Rilke himself.[41] Tzara and Ionesco were in Paris, and Celan would also have been aware of other Romanian-Jewish writers in France who had not survived: Benjamin Fondane, rounded up in 1944 and gassed at Auschwitz, and Ilarie Voronca, an immediate postwar suicide. What is more, his mother's younger brother, Bruno Schrager, who had welcomed Paul to Paris in 1938, had been deported from there and had died in Auschwitz. A brief lyric of Celan's, "While Traveling," marks his arrival in July 1948: "It is an hour that makes the dust your escort" (1:45).

Despite the promise of Paris (once studied reverently by Czernowitz schoolchildren), translating himself out of a German-speaking ambience was not a carefree process. Already in Vienna Celan had brought one poem to a close with the line "I sing before strangers" (1:31). This anxiety—echoing the Psalm of exile, "How shall we sing the Lord's song in a strange land?"—only intensified in France. Why did he go farther west, when May 1948 saw celebrations in Vienna and elsewhere of the founding of the state of Israel? A couple of weeks after reaching Paris, Celan wrote to relatives in the new, threatened state, trying to justify "my destiny to you, who stand at the very center of Jewish destiny." What might have pushed him toward Israel was also what kept him in Europe: the trauma of loss, the precarious hold on his native tongue, and the struggle to see his work in print. "There's nothing in the world," he says, "for which a poet will give up writing, not even when he is a Jew and the language of his poems is German."[42]

4
"German" Author in Exile
(1948–53)

"Perhaps I am one of the last who must live out to the end the destiny of the Jewish spirit in Europe," Celan wrote to his Israeli relatives in August 1948.[1] But why "must"? Because a poet cannot stop writing, "even when he is a Jew and the language of his poems is German." All this "may be saying a lot," Celan added. Just how much it was saying would take him years to realize.

On first reaching Paris in 1938, he had visited Bruno Schrager, who lived near the Sorbonne on the Rue des Écoles. Ten years later, with his uncle killed and himself an orphan and exile, Celan decided to settle in the same street.

France would have to serve now, since Bukovina was Soviet, Romania Communist, Austria hopeless, and Germany out of the question. A sense of this moment in 1948 issues from the first poem Celan composed in Paris. Like his earliest poem in Bucharest, "A Song in the Wilderness," this one takes its title from the Bible. "In Ägypten" translates the Hebrew *B'mitsrayim* ("In Egypt"), which stands for slavery and exile—"I have surely seen the affliction of my people which are in Egypt" (Exod. 3:7). Housed only within his mother tongue, Celan in Paris let a terse phrase tap an old story.

"In Egypt," which he published three times before it came out in any book,[2] responds to the strain of exile with a set of commandments, but positive not negative ones:

> Thou shalt say to the eye of the woman stranger: Be the water.
> Thou shalt seek in the stranger's eye those thou knowest are in the water.
> Thou shalt summon them from the water: Ruth! Naomi! Miriam!
> Thou shalt adorn them when thou liest with the stranger.
> Thou shalt adorn them with the stranger's cloud-hair.
> Thou shalt say to Ruth and Miriam and Naomi:
> Behold, I sleep with her!
> Thou shalt most beautifully adorn the woman stranger near thee.
> Thou shalt adorn her with sorrow for Ruth, for Miriam and Naomi.
> Thou shalt say to the stranger:
> Behold, I slept with them! [1:46]

Defiant? Honorable? These verses adapt the Lutheresque model of the Ten Commandments—*Du sollst . . . Du sollst . . .*—to expose the liaison with a stranger, a Gentile. (And with a Biblical warrant, translating Celan's *du* as "thou" conveys its intimacy.) He does not deal harshly with himself for a sexual option that would have astounded his parents. Instead, he frames that option in sacral, tribal terms.

Ruth and Naomi and Miriam "are in the water," rising from collective memory, all linked with exile. They were also the names of Celan's women friends in Romania, as against the *Fremde* ("stranger").[3] So the commandments he voices, the encounter between 1948 France and 1945 Romania, root his predicament in mythic ground. The poem seems balanced but leaves us oriented less toward the *Fremde* than toward Ruth and Naomi and Miriam. It is with sorrow for them that the stranger is adorned. "In Egypt" ends: "Thou shalt say to the stranger: / Behold, I slept with them!"[4] "In Ägypten" admits the claims of a Jewish past, though why Celan speaks only nine commandments, not ten, is anybody's guess. Maybe he simply had to be at odds with religious dogma.

During his first months in France, Celan was still caught in "the struggle over publishing my book," his collection of poems from 1943 to 1948.[5] Already in early February 1948, in Vienna, he had said: "my book will be ready in five or six weeks."[6] But five months later he left for Paris with proofs not yet made and his book in the charge of Edgar Jené, who was contributing two lithographs. When *Der Sand aus den Urnen* finally appeared, in August 1948, the poet was dismayed by the cheap binding and paper, as was common then, and a few misprints, some of them altering his meaning.[7] Celan blamed Jené and renounced the whole edition. "Maybe I should try to write poems without thinking of publishing them," he said that fall.[8] After three years, fewer than twenty copies had been sold. By 1952 he had earned 350 Austrian shillings on the book, the equivalent of $14. Celan had his Viennese friend Klaus Demus withdraw and pulp it.

Meanwhile the French metropolis provided what it could. A German writer remembers visiting Celan: "There could have been no better guide through the city. We walked, walked, and now and then, pausing, he broke into our talk, our silence: 'Up there in this house Verlaine died.' 'Rilke wrote *Malte* in this hotel.' 'Here's where Baudelaire lived.'"[9]

Celan's own vocation felt tenuous in those early postwar years. When a German magazine founded right after the war and named *Die Wandlung* ("The Transformation") asked for some poems in 1949, he gave them "Corona," "While Traveling," and "In Egypt," along with a biographical note whose tone and tacitness tell more than anything else. "I will allow myself—since I'm aware that it can't be wholly indifferent to you to know how an unknown author's life has passed until now—to mention what little my outward life comprises." Then he says: "What the life of a Jew was during the war years, I need not mention."[10]

During this lonely period in Paris Celan composed few poems, partly because everyday life was difficult, partly for deeper reasons. "For months I haven't written," he told the Swiss editor Max Rychner in October 1948, because "something unnamable is laming me." And he added, as if living out Kafka's parable "In Front of the Law": "When a door opens . . . I hesitate so long that this door closes again." Then in March 1949: "The more convulsively I cling to my poems, the less I can do for them. My ambition seems so great, it shackles my hands."[11] When a German publisher refused his new collection of poems that September, Celan was downcast and felt himself "struggling with heaven and its abysses."[12] In December he called 1949 "a dark and shadow year,"[13] and later he sent the Jenés his "few Paris poems," saying he couldn't write anymore, owing to aftereffects of the upheaval in his youth.[14]

Celan's malaise fills a February 1951 letter to Ludwig von Ficker, who back in Austria had greeted his work. He starts by talking about "silence, which was a not-able-to-speak and thus believed itself an ought-not-to-speak."[15] After seven tortuous paragraphs, he offers to send his accumulated work in manuscript: "Sometimes it's as if I were the prisoner of these poems . . . and sometimes their jailer." All this sounds much like Hugo von Hofmannsthal's Lord Chandos letter (1902), a confession of poetic inadequacy that had struck Celan years earlier.[16]

Again in August 1951 he says he has "not written anymore." Yet we have a poem from that same month, in a futile vein:

On the shore
a thought wanders muffled and listens:
for nothing
steps forth in its own form.   [1:71]

Celan wrote seven or eight publishable poems a year from 1948 to 1952—a meager number, due to his angst and to his circumstances. He was "struggling along as a factory worker, interpreter, and translator," a note on him said.[17] He also gave German and French lessons and was pursuing studies in philology and German literature at the École Normale Supérieure. Meanwhile many poems lay buried in his abandoned Vienna collection. All this, plus the awareness that "nothing / steps forth in its own form," was enough to inhibit a poet in postwar Europe.

Celan's desire to make his way led to an episode that later had disastrous consequences. His mentor Margul-Sperber had suggested he look up Yvan Goll (1891–1950), an Alsatian Jew living in Paris. Goll, allied with surrealism, had translated Joyce's *Ulysses* into German and dealt in themes of loneliness and Jewish wandering. In November 1949 Celan gave Goll and his wife a copy of *Der Sand aus den Urnen,* and—according to Claire Goll—complained of feeling misunderstood as a poet.[18] Yvan Goll, dying in a Paris hospital, took to Celan and his poetry. Shortly before his death in February 1950, Goll began writing again in German and asked Celan to translate his French poetry into German. Celan promised and did three collections, which went unpublished because, Claire Goll later claimed, they bore too clearly the "signature" of Paul Celan. The upshot, as of 1950–51, was a sour twist on Celan's encounter with an older Jewish poet and on his first major undertaking as a translator of poetry.

Around this time, Celan published translations of Romanian and French surrealists.[19] But he was breaking with the movement. Witness a lyric of his own in the same surrealist magazine as those translations. Its title, "Kristall," speaks for pattern and solidness in poetry and spurs a memory of Nazi "Kristallnacht," the rupture within this poem:

Seek not your mouth on my lips,
nor a stranger at the gate,
nor a tear in the eye.

Seven nights higher, red wanders to red,
seven nights deeper a hand raps at the gate,
seven roses later the well gushes up. [1:52]

From one moment to the next, expectation is forced higher, deeper, later, and sevenfold—a messianic number in Jewish tradition. Roses for Celan blended vulnerability with beauty, whether they were lyric (a "rose-hour" hung on a broken harp in 1941 [F 68]) or Judaic (an ark sheltering the "rose-race" against winter in 1946 [3:42]). And "the well gushes up" like tears or like an oracle from the wells of Celan's Bukovina homeland.

These wells dot the landscape of Celan's *oeuvre*, starting with the wartime poems of longing and loss. "A Song in the Wilderness" speaks of drinking "the ashes of wells there at Acra" (1:11), and "Aspen Tree" recalls his mother: "Rain cloud, do you linger over the well?" (1:19). In Paris in 1950, Celan shaped a lyric around his mother "in a land of wells." These untitled quatrains, whose brief lines stress strict rhymes, work strange effects by that means:

So bist du denn geworden
wie ich dich nie gekannt:
dein Herz schlägt allerorten
in einem Brunnenland,

wo kein Mund trinkt und keine
Gestalt die Schatten säumt,
wo Wasser quillt zum Scheine
und Schein wie Wasser schäumt.

Du steigst in alle Brunnen,
du schwebst durch jeden Schein.
Du hast ein Spiel ersonnen
das will vergessen sein. [1:59]

To render Celan à la Emily Dickinson:

So you are turned—a Someone
As I had never known—
Your heart a drum that summons
Through Land where Wells once flowed

Where no Mouth drink—and nothing
Will cleave where Shadows form—
Where Water wells to Seeming
And Seeming falls—to Foam

You rise in every Wellspring—
Through every Seeming—run
You've conjured up a Playing
That begs—Oblivion

This pastiche risks giving Celan unlikely wittiness.[20] But wit (like Dickinson's) can carry a burden. Celan said this "poem for the dead" addressed his mother—an unwonted admission.[21] "So bist du" locates her in a spectral landscape, a transient Bukovina. She rises in the wells, she hovers everywhere, but it's "a Playing / that begs—Oblivion."

Behind my quirks of phrasing and rhyming, Celan's verse itself has unusual regularity, sharing a little in Dickinson's hymnlike quatrains. In fact, his cross-rhymes and alternating 7-6-7-6 syllable count recall the Baroque hymns on which German Christians were raised. Take the famous Passion stanza by Paul Gerhardt:[22]

O Haupt voll Blut und Wunden,	O head all blood and wounded,
voll Schmerz und voller Hohn;	all pain and full of scorn;
O Haupt zum Spott gebunden	O head with mocking bounded
mit einer Dornenkron.	by this one crown of thorn.

Celan's *So bist du denn geworden* mimics the old Baroque cadence with its comfort in Jesus' suffering. He titled his next poem "Die feste Burg" (1:60) after Luther's hymn "A mighty fortress is our God"—a gaping irony for a Jew from lands where Luther's call to burn synagogues had just been taken literally.

It was too soon, in 1950, to think of Germany "coming to terms with the past." For Paul Celan it would always be too soon. Instead, he wrote to keep that past active, as in "The Travel Companion" (1951):

Your mother's soul hovers ahead.
Your mother's soul helps sail around night, reef upon reef.
Your mother's soul lashes the sharks on before you.

This word is your mother's ward.
Your mother's ward shares your bed, stone upon stone.
Your mother's ward stoops for the crumb of light.   [1:66]

In Hans Christian Andersen's fairy tale "The Travel Companion," an orphan is "lashed."[23] By contrast, this poem stresses a mother's protectiveness. Celan's German leads *Mutter* to *Mündel,* "mother" to "ward": *Dieses Wort ist deiner Mutter Mündel.* Even in death the mother remains a guardian of the speech she fostered. Luckily, English turns up a consonance for *Wort* and *Mündel:* "word" and "ward." They clinch the mother's role as muse—"This word is your mother's ward"—even as that ward shares a "bed," or *Lager,* the word echoing *Konzentrationslager,* a Nazi coinage. Precisely because of such coinage, "This word" and any word the poet might utter must now stoop for crumbs of light.

The Paris poems of 1950–51 often evoke a "sister"—maybe his mother cut off too young or the sibling Paul never had or the "sister bride" from the Song of Songs who embodies Israel's peoplehood. This figure of absence and desire also connects with language: "Sistermouth, / you speak a word that fades outside the windows" (1:55).[24] Or here: "She knows the words, and yet she only smiles" (1:72). In one lyric "the sister's eye spun snow into thoughts" (1:73). Mother, sister, well, rose, night, snow, stone, eye, mouth, word: words go on speaking in face of the "silence" Celan named in 1951, "which was a not-able-to-speak and thus believed itself an ought-not-to-speak."

Summing up this span of writing, in April 1952, Celan composed a poem that would close his next collection. Because the poem has no title and opens with three crisp imperatives, an English version should retain their cadence exactly.

ZÄHLE die Mandeln,
zähle, was bitter war und dich wachhielt,
zähl mich dazu . . .

COUNT UP the almonds,
count what was bitter and kept you waking,
count me in too:

I sought your eye when you glanced up and no one would see you,
I spun that secret thread
where the dew you mused on
slid down to pitchers
tended by a word that reached no one's heart.

There you first fully entered the name that is yours,
you stepped to yourself on steady feet,
the hammers swung free in the belfry of your silence,
things overheard thrust through to you,
what's dead put its arm around you too,
and the three of you walked through the evening.

Render me bitter.
Number me among the almonds.   [1:78]

The poet is speaking to his mother. Later he called her an "almond-eyed shadow" and recollected "the almond eye of the dead" (1:110, 121). The *Mandeln* he wants to be numbered among call to mind the almonds she baked in breads and cakes, as well as the Yiddish lullaby about Zion's widowed daughter, "Raisins and Almonds," from Goldfaden's operetta *Shulamis*. Blooming earliest in Israel, yielding sweet nuts and bitter, oval like the Levantine eye, almonds now betoken Jewishness for Celan. The Israelites' menorah in the wilderness has almond blossom designs (Exod. 25:33), and Aaron's rod bears ripe almonds (Num. 17:23). When the prophet Jeremiah is summoned, a play on "almond" (*shaked*) proves that the Lord will "keep watch [*shoked*] over My word to perform it" (Jer. 1:11).[25] This pun surfaces in 1952—"Count up the almonds, / count what was bitter and kept you waking"—after the lapse of the divine promise.

Celan's triple imperative on *zählen* ("count") also rings of the *Zählappell*, a head count in Nazi camps. And it's possible, though only just, to think here of the smell of almonds given off by Zyklon B, the gas the SS used. Against such atrocity, we hear now of attempts—the poet's, his mother's—at connecting, at naming, and "you" sounds twelve times in as many lines: "There you first fully entered the name that is yours." The word *Namen* ("name") resounds throughout Celan's writing, restoring identity to those despoiled of it. Finally, when this poem ends on two more imperatives, *Mache* and *Zähle*, I want more ceremonial verbs than "make" and "count"—

Render me bitter.
Number me among the almonds.

—to seal his kinship.

Shortly after writing "Zähle die Mandeln," Celan traveled to Germany for the first time since 1938. Sponsored by Ingeborg Bachmann and his Austrian friends, he went to a meeting of Group 47, founded after the war to promote new voices in German literature.[26] Two anecdotes from this May 1952 visit give a glimpse of Celan's sensitivity vis-à-vis postwar Germany. Walking along a street in Hamburg, he came upon a dog struck by a car and some women lamenting the accident. "Bei einem *Hund* jammern sie!" (For a *dog* they're yammering!) Celan exclaimed.[27] Another acquaintance, remembering him "laconic and reserved," quotes him as saying: "I was really curious about my first encounter with young German authors. I asked myself, what are they likely to talk about? And what did they talk about? Volkswagens."[28]

Group 47 held several tenets that were bound to affect their reception of Celan. They liked responding with instant, frank criticism to the work presented; they were exercised over the merits of "engaged" versus "pure" poetry; and they wanted verse read as monotonously as possible.[29] None of this boded well for an East European poet who had recently impressed someone in Paris with the "soft timbre" of his reading, the "urgent whisper" of his "psalmodic voice."[30]

Celan recited "A Song in the Wilderness," "In Egypt," "Count up the almonds," and also "Todesfuge," still virtually unknown. Witnesses differ as

Celan, *right*, at Group 47, Niendorf, 1952, with Reinhard Federmann, Milo Dor, Ingeborg Bachmann (R. Piper & Co. Verlag, Munich 1983)

to how the reading went, but no one called it a wild success. Celan spoke rapidly, with pathos, and had "an almost hypnotic effect," one person thought. But afterward some writers went around "sarcastically scanning: *Schwarze Milch der Frühe . . .* ," and the Group's organizer said that Celan recited "in a singsong straight out of a synagogue."[31] One review found "the Austrian Paul Celan's *poésie pure* astonishing with its unobtrusive mastery of language and precision of imagery." Others called him "not *engagé*," "ununderstand-able." "Oh yes, these soccer players," Celan later remarked about Group 47, one of whom told him, "You even recited in the tone of Goebbels."[32] His pathos and "visionary articulation" went over poorly, yet German radio wanted to broadcast him, and a publisher signed him up.[33]

Celan's next poem, from autumn 1952, was *engagé* to the point of stub-bornly recalling a destroyed homeland:

I saw my poplar descend to the water,
I saw how its arm grasped down in the depth,
I saw its roots pray heavenward for night. . . .
And saw my poplar no more.   [1:85]

As in an earlier lyric that began "You lofty poplars—humans of this earth!" (1:74), the sound shared by *Pappel* and the Latin *populus* linked the tree to a people.

A yet stricter engagement with the dead emerged in September 1952.

That summer Celan had visited his Austrian friends Klaus and Nani Demus in the Tyrol.[34] The bus journey home over an alpine road gave rise to this:

Nocturnally pursed
the lips of flowers,
crossed and folded
the shafts of spruce,
moss greyed, stone jolted,
jackdaws roused to unending
flight over the glacier:

this is the region where
those we've caught up with are resting:

they will not name the hour,
nor count the flakes,
nor follow a stream to the weir.

They stand sundered in the world,
each one near his night,
each one near his death.

In their own landscape, those arrested by untimely death press on language itself:

They pay off the guilt that sparked their origin,
they pay it off upon a word
that persists unjustly, like summer.

A word—you know:
a corpse.

Come let us wash it,
come let us comb it,
come let us turn
its eye heavenward.   [1:125]

With a ritual pulse of ministering to the dead, we are told not to shut the corpse's eye but to make it look upward.

Celan cast another poem as a burial ritual in autumn of 1952, this time with a twist. On 18 November Paul Éluard died, a mainstay of world communism, and three days later Celan wrote an elegy. To sense its depth exactly, we need some political data.[35] When a Czech Stalinist tribunal in 1950 condemned Zavis Kalandra, a surrealist poet and survivor of Hitler's camps, André Breton urged Éluard to intercede for the comrade they had both known. Éluard solemnly refused, and Kalandra was hanged. Against this background, Celan's liturgic lines for a writer he valued, "In Memoriam Paul Éluard," bind poetry to solidarity and death:

Place in his grave for the dead man the words
he spoke so as to live . . .

Place on the lids of the dead man that word
he denied to the one
who said thou to him . . .   [1:130]

From his first draft (penciled into a copy of Gerard Manley Hopkins's poems), Celan removed the words "gallows" and "guilt," making this memorial an even subtler critique of the poet, Éluard, who himself had written nobly about liberty and love and "the power of words" but had not, Celan thought, acted accordingly.

Just before Christmas of 1952, Paul Celan married Gisèle de Lestrange (1927–91), a lively, earnest woman he had met in 1950 when she was just back from a liberating trip to Spain. She was a graphic artist, apt to work for hours on a detailed abstract image with Baroque music playing in the background. Her parents, French nobility who during the war had no sympathy with De Gaulle or the Resistance, could hardly accept a poor, East European, Jewish survivor-poet with no family and a scant livelihood. The couple did little more than make ends meet, but they had in common a fierce seriousness about genuine art.

They lived in Paris, where Celan took translation jobs, some for money, others more out of an affinity (though the fees helped too). In translating Marianne Moore's reflective lyrics "The Mind Is an Enchanting Thing," "Poetry," "What Are Years?," and "A Grave" for a 1952 German edition of *Perspectives USA*, he responded to her verbal acumen with his own, and without mind-bending exertion (5:360 ff.). The first two poems went into German cleanly, though without her intricate rhyming and syllabifying. And "What Are Years?" had a clear call on him:

> All are
> naked, none is safe. . . .
> He
> sees deep and is glad, who
> accedes to mortality
> and in his imprisonment rises
> upon himself as
> the sea in a chasm, struggling to be
> free and unable to be,
> in its surrendering
> finds its continuing.

Moore's sinuous truths fit Celan's own ever-aggravating struggle.

Her title "A Grave" pointed him back toward "Todesfuge"'s "We shovel a grave in the air." Although in Moore the grave is the sea, not East European soil, there are striking coincidences. Of the drowned she says, "their bones have not lasted," as in Celan's "Black Flakes" where "snowdrift sifts your father's bones." Moore's fishermen lower nets "desecrating a grave," and the "blades" of their oars translate as *Schaufeln,* which in German also means "shovels."

Moore's oar blades move "as if there were no such thing as death." At this point Celan, spurred by bones, a grave, shoveling, and death, breaks into his own idiom. Her blades make wrinkles "beautiful under networks of foam," but his German fractures this fluent syntax: *unter Schaum, Netzwerk—schön* ("under foam, network—beautiful"). And when the wrinkles "fade breathlessly while the sea rustles," Celan cuts this up too, turning "fade breathlessly" into two verbs on a line of their own: "breathe their last, fade away." Reinforcing the action of loss was his way of signing the translation.[36]

Celan had a longer and closer attachment to Guillaume Apollinaire. In school he had vied with a friend at translating the French poet, and later he studied him in Soviet-occupied Czernowitz.[37] Apollinaire, who died in 1918 of a war wound, was fascinated by the Wandering Jew, and his symbolist melancholy stirred Celan. Allusions to Apollinaire show up throughout Celan's verse, along with the poets' shared motif of remembered loss. During the 1950s Celan published six translations from *Alcools* (4:780). Where Apollinaire mourns his love under the sign of autumn, Celan sharpens that season of loss—it being ten years "since autumn in its monkish cowl / brought tidings my way." Celan's preoccupations show through as his German phrasings bend and break the original, sometimes repeating what occurs only once in French, stopping where the verse flows evenly, or adding stress through shifting syntax. Making it new, the translator makes it his own.

Take a stanza from Apollinaire's "Signe" (Sign) and Celan's translation, "Zeichen." With a literal English version of each, we can observe Celan setting these verses to his own voice and concerns:[38]

Mon Automne éternelle ô ma saison mentale
Les mains des amantes d'antan jonchent ton sol
Une épouse me suit c'est mon ombre fatale
Les colombes ce soir prennent leur dernier vol

[My eternal Autumn oh my mental season
The hands of yesteryear's lovers strew your soil
A wife follows me she is my fatal shadow
The doves this evening take their final flight]

Du ewige, du Herbstzeit, du der Gedanken Jahr:

die Hände, die mich liebten, du häufst sie ohne Zahl.
Ein Schatten folgt: die Frau ist's, die mein Verhängnis war.
Am Abend fliegt die Taube, sie fliegt zum letztenmal.

(You eternal, you Autumn-time, you year of thoughts:
the hands, which loved me, you heap them without number.
A shadow follows: it's the woman who was my fate.
At evening the dove flies, she flies for the last time.)

Many wayward or willful things have happened here, yet all within the original frame of rhymed hexameters. To begin with, Celan breaks up Apollinaire's fluent opening, confronting the "mental season" directly as *du*. He then replaces *mentale* with *Gedanken* ("thoughts"), veering toward *gedenken* ("bear in mind"), just as his *Herbstzeit* ("Autumn-time") and *Jahr* ("year") together suggest the Yiddish *Yortseit,* the yearly commemoration of a parent's death. Turning the female lovers (*amantes*) into "hands that loved me"—they can now include his mother's—Celan makes autumn active: "you heap" those hands. He stresses "A shadow," he whose own lyric at the time called his dead mother an "almond-eyed shadow." Finally, the dove in German "flies, she flies"—a repetition that gets the firsthand truth of loss from the second-hand work of translation.

Even in so candid a lament as Apollinaire's "L'Adieu" (The Farewell), Celan makes his own mark:

L'automne est morte souviens-t'en
Nous ne nous verrons plus sur terre

[Autumn is dead remember this
We'll no more see each other on earth]

Der Herbst ist tot—sei eingedenk.
Auf Erden scheiden wir nun beide.

(Autumn is dead—bear this in mind.
On earth we part now both of us.)

Apollinaire's nostalgic future tense, "We'll no more see each other," falls to Celan's hard present fact of separation.

More than "L'Adieu," Apollinaire's "Schinderhannes" brought out a new voice. This satirical ditty on an eighteenth-century German folk hero, a brigand murderously cruel to Jews, would have been worth translating in any case. The poem ends on a light tone masking anger, and Celan's version reads in translation like this:

Today when dusk falls on the Rhine,
That rich Jew will be mine to slay.

When resin torches brightly shine,
florins are ours like flowers in May!

The gang sits down to eat awhile,
farts, laughs, digs in with fork and knife,
then softens up, in German style,
and goes and snuffs out one more life.

This soft "German style," segueing into the murder of a Jew, recalls Celan's sentimental commandant in "Todesfuge." His translation, in print, said the gang "f---s." Maybe German readers in the mid-fifties were not ready to be shown obscenity linked with murder, at least not by a Jewish publisher and a Jewish translator.[39]

A long-awaited upturn in Celan's fortunes, in December 1952, gave him the foothold he craved as a poet, though not a release from translation and teaching jobs. A Stuttgart publisher[40] brought out *Mohn und Gedächtnis* ("Poppy and Remembrance"), poems from 1944 to 1952, including part of the ill-fated Vienna collection, with "Todesfuge" in a section of its own and closing with "Zähle die Mandeln." The book's title, drawn from Celan's 1948 poem "Corona," would remain heraldic for him: poppies of oblivion, but also those seeds on Jewish festival pastry and the Sabbath challah loaf, back in his Bukovina childhood.

No less telling are some changes Celan made in readying poems for *Mohn und Gedächtnis*. A line from 1950 originally said "Sistermouth, / you speak a word that fades outside the window" (1:55). Celan changed "fades" so that her word now "lives on" amid the poem's "ashflowers." A small change, but in the economy of one who had sent his poem to friends saying that he could not write anymore after the upheaval of his childhood, a hopeful one.

In "Todesfuge," after five years, Celan only added an optional *e* to *Aug* in the last stanza: *sein Auge ist blau* ("his eye it is blue"). This syllable perfects the rhymed singsong with *er trifft dich genau* ("shoots you level and true"), fine-tuning his poem on the verge of its becoming a national obsession in Deutschland.

"Todesfuge," placed at the center of *Mohn und Gedächtnis,* interested some, but by no means all, of Celan's readers. Its reception in Germany could be a morality play of Art against History.

For the poet in Paris waiting to hear how his words fell on German ears, the first reviews of *Mohn und Gedächtnis* touched a nerve, though they were not all unwelcoming or undiscerning. In March 1953 Karl Krolow, initiating three decades of attention to Celan, noted his "surrealism . . . with a special gift for imagery" and "verse of a tender beauty and depth."[41] In a review entitled "Schwarze Milch der Frühe," in the *Frankfurter Allgemeine Zeitung,* Celan read that "he grew up in Vienna," lost his parents dreadfully, and "expresses the unspeakable."[42] Paul Schallück ended this notice by quoting "Todesfuge," predicting that people would come to study Celan's sources and the influences on his work; "But we will remember that we never read such verse before." In Hamburg's *Die Zeit,* a German friend of Celan's was sympathetic yet made no mention of "Todesfuge" or the realities conditioning the poetry—loss, death, Jewishness.[43] A Viennese Catholic journal acknowledged Celan's origins and wartime trauma, compared him to Chagall and Lasker-Schüler along with Trakl and Mallarmé, and pointed to the interweaving of reality and visionary depth in his poems—again without mentioning "Todesfuge."[44]

"His lyrics are *poésie pure,* magical montage, comparable to Marc Chagall's paintings," began another 1953 review, which must have given him pause.[45] "They have French sheen and Balkan glitter, the suggestiveness of the *chanson* and the modulations of melancholy. They exist wholly on metaphor. . . . Reality is transposed into the secret script of poesy!" All this from the Christian poet Heinz Piontek, who also alluded to "glittering *arrangements,*" as if this were not a Chagall but an effete Whistler, and urged Celan to publish only when "he has something to say that is really pressing him—but not his *études* and finger exercises." Piontek's Gallicisms seem to credit Celan, ensconced in Paris, with little more than frippery. You would never guess that the volume under review contained "Todesfuge"—"something to say that is really pressing him," indeed!

We may wonder how audible the poem was in 1953. One reviewer liked "Todesfuge" for its "removal of everything concrete" (hounds? iron rod? graves?) and its "absorbing rhythm, romanticizing metaphor, lyrical alchemy," and he got a "Zen-Buddhist satori experience" out of Celan's opposing "*atrocitas* and *suavitas.*"[46] That very opposition—never mind the glossy Latin—would have been worth mentioning if it noticed "Todesfuge"'s actuality. Instead we hear this: "A Celan poem is wholly without intention. It wants to be nothing but breath, sound, image—effortless and almost singable."

Imagine Paul Celan at a newsstand in Paris, seeing "the words he spoke so as to live" (Celan on Éluard applied to himself) labelled "finger exercises." At least, he would never write another poem like "Todesfuge." At best, his credo spoke straight to himself:

Whichever stone you lift—
you lay bare
those who need the protection of stones . . .

Whichever word you speak—
you owe
to destruction.   [1:129]

This let his readers in on a fearful symmetry.

Struck by the attention given to *Mohn und Gedächtnis*, Claire Goll addressed an "Open Letter" in August 1953 to various German publishers, authors, and critics.[47] In it she "disclosed" Celan's "borrowings" and his "cleverly assimilated utilization of phrases and images" from a 1951 volume of Yvan Goll's German verse, citing several "parallel passages." The widow's claims proved groundless—in fact, Celan's passages in some cases predated Goll's. Years later he bitterly recalled this incident, but there is no record of his reaction at the time.

Celan had other concerns. His personal library shows him delving into Heidegger's work from at least 1951. In March 1952 and again a year later, he studied *Sein und Zeit*. Then in summer of 1953, he took up essays from Heidegger's *Holzwege*, marking passages on Hölderlin and Rilke.[48] He underscored the philosopher's remarks on Hölderlin's elegy "Bread and Wine," especially that poem's question, "what use are poets in a destitute time?" (*wozu Dichter in dürftiger Zeit?*). Celan also greeted Rilke's ideas about "the Open" as that unbounded realm where the human self can set itself free and Rilke's sense of death as the richly present other side of life.

Gisèle was pregnant in 1953, but that fall they lost their first child within days of his birth. "Epitaph for François," addressing a newborn whose death has opened the passages into and out of life, is the only poem Celan ever printed with its date:

> Both doors of the world
> stand open:
> opened by you
> in the twinight.
> We hear them beating and beating
> and bear it uncertainly,
> and bear the green into your Ever.
>
> *October 1953*   [1:105]

Celan had come across gates of day and night in Parmenides,[49] and Martin Buber quotes a Hasidic saying about man passing through two doors between this world and the next.[50] Rilke's fervent ideas about death and "the Open" are also at work here; one poem of his discovers a "green really green" in death.[51] Yet Celan's wordplay is simpler than all this: instead of Eden's "evergreen" we see green taken "into your Ever," life borne into death.

This death—"it was hard, hard, hard," Celan told a friend[52]—caused him to shape the central section of his second book around it. Entitled "With a Changing Key," this sequence, arranged out of order of composition, forms a commemorative unit. It opens with "Epitaph for François" and includes lyrics on death. One of these, "Ich weiss" (I know) (1:119), echoes "I know that I must die soon" by Else Lasker-Schüler, whose books Celan had bought.[53] Another poem here arose from his visit to Assisi in November 1953.[54] Echoing Catholic piety, "Assisi" poses the humility of Saint Francis— "Umbrian night with the stone you hauled here"—next to an impossible consolation. The poem ends:

> Radiance that will not comfort, radiance.
> The dead—they still go begging, Franz. [1:108]

The Celans' son François may have died on Saint Francis's name day, 4 October, or been named after the poet's country of exile. This poem's last lines also call up the Czech Jew who found no comfort in the "radiance" of the Law.

The title poem of Celan's sequence keys the writer's "word" to duress:

> With a changing key
> you unlock the house where
> the snow of what's silenced drifts.
> Just like the blood that bursts from
> your eye or mouth or ear,
> so your key changes.
>
> Changing your key changes the word
> that may drift with the flakes.
> Just like the wind that rebuffs you,
> the snow packs around the word. [1:112]

Snow, which marked his parents' death, now visits his son's. Celan's lyric almost eliminates metaphor,[55] so interpenetrable are the literal and the figurative: "the snow packs around the word."

The most demanding poem from this sequence, and the longest Celan had yet written, confronts Christian salvation with Jewish custom and does so in the person of the poet's mother. "In Front of a Candle" takes its stance where she herself should be standing. It begins:

> Out of beaten gold, just
> as you bade me, mother,
> I formed the candlestick—from it
> she darkens up to me among
> splintering hours:
> your
> being-dead's daughter. [1:110]

The memory of a mother blessing candles cedes to a memorial candle: her absence now demands a shaping act, something like weaving the shawl in "Black Flakes." Since "beaten gold" is what God told Moses to use for a candlestick (Exod. 25:31), a murdered mother rounds out that nearly extinguished covenant. Celan calls her "your being-dead's daughter," arrested in time, uncannily becoming as young as her son (and giving him the sister he never had). An "almond-eyed shadow," she then rises to the *Scheitel des Jetzt*, the "peak" or "crown of the Now"—except that in Yiddish, *Scheitel* also denotes the wig worn by Orthodox wives. Such wordplay eludes translation.

"I speak the blessing," Celan goes on, but instead of the Sabbath blessing, it is "In the name of the Three." After touching on Christ's passion, the poet faces his mother again:

I speak you free
of the Amen that deafens us,
of the icy light that edges it.

Recalling Saint Paul on Christ—"For all the promises of God are . . . in him Amen" (2 Cor. 1:20)—the poet's speech frees his mother from Jewish guilt for Jesus' death and even from the accepting "So be it," the Amen of faith.[56]

Speaking to the stalled-young spirit of his mother, Celan's "In Front of a Candle" closes: *Du bleibst, du bleibst, du bleibst,* "You remain" or

You are still, are still, are still
a dead woman's child,
consecrated to the No of my longing,
wed to a crevice in time
the motherword led me to,
so that just once
the hand should throb
that on and on grasps for my heart!

In a ritual vein she is "consecrated," but to his baffled longing; "wed," but to the rupture between time before and time after. Seeing his mother as a "child" points to his own child's death.

To close the cycle that began with "Epitaph for François," Celan wrote an anniversary poem in October 1954, "Andenken" (Remembrance). He and his wife were vacationing at La Ciotat in Provence, on the Mediterranean shore. In September he had bought Heidegger's *Introduction to Metaphysics*, recently issued without any comment on the philosopher's 1935 lectures, which hailed "the inner truth and greatness" of National Socialism, "namely the encounter between global technology and modern man."[57] Next to this statement Celan in La Ciotat put two exclamation marks.

Against Heidegger's neglect, Celan's title was "Remembrance":

Nourished by figs be the heart
wherein an hour thinks back
on the almond eye of the dead.
Nourished by figs.

Steep, in the seawind's breath,
the shipwrecked
forehead,
the cliff-sister.

And full-blown round your white hair
the fleece
of the summering cloud.   [1:121]

Figs, which Celan mentions nowhere else until a late poem on Jerusalem, turn up throughout the Bible, a sweet full fruit indigenous even to Paradise. When the Law goes forth from Zion, "nation shall not lift up sword against nation . . . but they shall sit every man under his vine and under his fig tree" (Mic. 4:3). By the Mediterranean in autumn, Celan found himself "Nourished by figs," remembering a father who never reached the land on its eastern shore. One could translate *das Mandelauge des Toten* as "the dead man's eye," for *Toten* is masculine. But "almond eye of the dead" makes room for the poet's father and son alike.

That it is Celan's father ("the shipwrecked forehead"?) who emerges in this elegy becomes clear when a fleecy cloud surrounds "your white hair." (Leo Antschel's hair went gray under the duress of occupation and deportation.[58]) A grazing, "summering cloud" and Jason's quest for the Golden Fleece almost conceal that someone has vanished into this sky.

Rather than "Remembrance," I am inclined to retain the title in German, the homage to Celan's precursor Hölderlin. The typescript of his poem shows its title penciled in on top, "Andenken" (1:293). An afterthought? Not really, because almost every phrase in Celan's poem recalls Hölderlin's, which harks back to the poet's sojourn near the French coast and, like its modern namesake, has to do with memory. Celan marked only one line in the 1803 poem: "But memory / Is taken and given by the sea."[59] Traces in his writing manifest a lifelong spiritual affinity with Hölderlin, from his youth and university days in Czernowitz until the time (and even the hour) of his death.

"Nourished by figs," coming twice in Celan's opening, points to the nurturing presence of Hölderlin's poem. There we hear: "I am glad to bethink myself" of the gardens at Bordeaux, "But in the courtyard a fig tree grows." There also, remembering the "windy point of land" and the "steep bank" of the Garonne where "Cradling breezes move," Hölderlin thinks of friends who are gone. "But memory," he assures us (in lines translated years ago by Cyrus Hamlin),

> But memory
> Is taken and given by the sea,
> And love as well takes hold of our eyes,
> But what abides is founded by poets.

Celan had little practice or faith in what abides, even if his life left him nothing but that to seek.

5
Saying No To Say Yes
(1953–54)

"What a game!" (*Welch ein Spiel!*), Celan said in a 1954 letter, "So short-lived, so kingly too." He had in mind the writing of poems and his own evolving struggle. "The circumstances of my life, living in the domain of a foreign tongue, have meant that I deal much more consciously with my language than before—and yet: the How and Why of that qualitative change the word experiences, to become a word in a poem, I'm unable to define more closely even today. Poetry, Paul Valéry says somewhere, is language *in statu nascendi,* language becoming free." A poet can hope only "to overhear the word becoming free, to catch it in the act . . . yet the word lays claim to uniqueness, lives and sometimes even feeds off this claim, this arrogance, still believing it can represent the whole of language, can give check to the whole of reality."[1]

Language *in statu nascendi* ("in a state of being born") and "language becoming free" (*freiwerdende Sprache*): poetic process can deliver language from previous nonbeing. "Whichever word you speak—," Celan wrote only months before, "you owe / to destruction" (1:129). He called the making of poems a game. Yet being "so short-lived" and "so kingly too," this game had a tense, divided feel to it.

Precisely here, between possibilities—"poppy and remembrance," for instance—Celan's finest poems hold forth. Sometimes the tension occurs in a single word: the imperative *zähle,* saying "number me" among the Jewish people but also recalling the vicious head count in Nazi camps, or the word *Mandel* ("almond"), both bitter and sweet, as also in the ruined, brilliant Mandelshtam. Unless we can tolerate flat-out contradiction, we are not seeing Celan's verse face "the whole of reality."

Sometimes this tension generates an entire poem, such as "Sprich auch du" (Speak you too). "Speaks true who speaks shadow" (*Wahr spricht wer Schatten spricht*), runs a line from that 1954 poem, as if the poet had been misheard and must tell himself to hold fast to the difficult way. "Speak you too" is probably Celan's response to an April 1954 review of his *Mohn und Gedächtnis* (1952) in the respected monthly *Merkur.* The latter was published by Deutsche Verlags-Anstalt, who had brought out *Mohn und Gedächtnis* and were doing a second edition, so Celan took a heightened interest in it. Billing itself "A German journal for European thinking," it ran essays by Buber, Adorno, Toynbee, Jaspers, Eliot, and Habermas, fiction by Beckett, and later in 1954, some poems by Celan. The April issue featured Gottfried Benn, Germany's senior poet, whose ideas on poetry as artifice—not to mention his early Nazism—did not sit well with Celan. This issue also contained the review "Five Young Poets."[2]

Hans Egon Holthusen, an influential poet and critic, devoted six pages to *Mohn und Gedächtnis,* welcoming a talent that "translates certain principles of modern French lyric into the German language. . . . Here one sees language taking fire not from an object confronting it, but from itself." Readers of this review came upon one word more than any other, *Phantasie*—"imagination," "fantasy," "fancy." In Celan's writing Holthusen saw "fantastic associations" and "unqualified arbitrary lyric imagination" working on "the reader's fancy."

Holthusen did mete out praise, citing Celan's paradoxes—"Blacker in black, I am more naked . . . a hanged man strangles the rope"—which "mock the complacency of logical thinking, mobilizing dream truth against reality." Yet this review could still be describing something by the author of "Jabberwocky" or "A Child's Garden of Verses." Though Celan's volume ends by saying "Render me bitter. / Number me among the almonds" (from a poem that Holthusen had anthologized), the critic dwelt on "playful freedom," "self-inspired, purely lexical configurations," "not meaning but form," "absolutely musical effects," "Mallarmé . . . Mallarmé . . . Mallarmé." Again, as with Group 47, Celan became a whipping boy in the dispute between "engaged" and "pure" poetry. Admittedly *Mohn und Gedächtnis* harbored plenty of fantastic imagery and verbal music, but this critique disengaged them from their basis in exile, loss, and mass death.

To Holthusen's credit, he closed his review by celebrating "Todesfuge," in which "instinct and suffering coincide with the kairos [opportune time] of a great motif." Yet, designating the Jewish catastrophe with "kairos," a term steeped in Christian theology—"when the fullness of time was come, God sent forth his son" (Gal. 4:4)—betrays a careless ear.

Celan has "mastered" a technique of repetition, says Holthusen, disregarding the use of "master" in "Todesfuge." He is congratulated for "singing" a ghastly event, even as the commandant tells his Jews to "sing up and play." The poet has "overcome" a staggering theme—here Holthusen's verb is *bewältigen,* as if Celan were part of Germany's *Vergangenheitsbewältigung* ("overcoming the past"). This gruesome theme "can escape history's bloody chamber of horrors to rise into the ether of pure poetry." But it was the Jews in Celan's poem who rose into ether, never the poem; not "Todesfuge" but its German readers who wanted to "escape history's bloody chamber of horrors." Thus they apotheosized Celan's poem: "one of the grandest poems for our time," says Holthusen.

Celan felt used within Germany's cultural recovery after the Third Reich. With a nascent vocation in the early 1950s, but sensitive to the costs of recognition, he forged his poetry partly in response to an audience that threatened to skew what he wrote. "Speak you too," he insists after the *Merkur* review,

> *Sprich auch du,*
> *sprich als letzter,*
> *sag deinen Spruch.*

> Speak you too,
> speak as the last,
> say out your say.

> Speak—
> But don't split off No from Yes.
> Give your say this meaning too:
> give it the shadow.

Give it shadow enough,
give it as much
as you know is spread round you from
midnight to midday and midnight.

Look around:
see how things all come alive—
By death! Alive!
Speaks true who speaks shadow.   [1:135]

"Speak you too," the poet tells himself, and then "speak as the last." Not long before, Celan had called himself "one of the last who must live out to the end the destiny of the Jewish spirit in Europe."[3] Speak as the last, and you speak as the one on whom that destiny hangs.

For the command to say your *Spruch,* I like the stubborn idiom "say your say," but *Spruch* can also mean a Biblical parable, a motto, oracle, scriptural text, proverb of Solomon, verdict, or sentence. Celan's early version had "proclaim your verdict" (*künde den Wahrspruch*) instead of "say your say." Maybe the Biblical "proclaim" felt too grand, and "verdict" too juristic. And/or maybe Celan wanted a more compact cadence.

In Scripture, speech itself brings about God's will. Breaking in on Celan's "Speak—" comes the poem's only negative command: "But don't split off No from Yes." Anything affirmed about God or history or humankind or art, anything positive, must admit denial, for split vision (or even blindness) verifies perception. "But don't split off No from Yes" also rebuts the *Merkur* review, which "joyfully says Yes" to certain images in Celan's volume but rejects others, calling the "mills of death" trivial and "white meal of the Promise" a dead metaphor.[4] It galled Celan to see the burden of his writing stripped away. "Give it shadow enough," his poem says, "as much / as you know is spread round you from / midnight to midday and midnight." In draft that last line was simply "midday and midnight." Celan's ear told him the line needed lengthening, and his change redefined the Jewish day: not from evening to evening but from midnight to midnight.

An Ezekiel-like vision clinches the next section—*Beim Tode! Lebendig!* ("By death! Alive!")—where *bei* can mean "near," "in," or "with," as in "With God all things are possible." Then the imperatives—"Speak you too . . . But don't split off No from Yes . . . Give it shadow enough"—are answered by Celan's proverbial *Wahr spricht, wer Schatten spricht*: "Speaks true who speaks shadow." Since by words came death (to adapt Saint Paul), the German language must go dark to speak the truth.

"But now," this lyric closes tentatively,

But now the place shrinks, where you stand:
Where now, shadow-stripped, where?

Climb. Grope upwards.
Thinner you grow, less knowable, finer!
Finer: a thread
the star wants to descend on:
so as to swim down below, down here
where it sees itself shimmer: in the swell
of wandering words.

Speak true by speaking shadow, and you find your standpoint shrinking. *Schattenentblösster* could be "stripped by shade," but maybe the poet also feels stripped *of* shade.[5] Celan had recently used the verb *entblössen*: "Whichever stone you lift— / you *lay bare* / those who need the protection of stones" (1:129).

The hazard of "wandering words" occupies several lyrics from 1953–54— "the word star-overflown, / sea-overflowed." *Jedem das Wort,* Celan writes (echoing the maxim "To each his own" inscribed over the gate to Buchenwald), "To each the word that sang to him, / when the pack snapped at his heels" (1:138).

Celan chose the title "Shibboleth," a password, to declare himself a prophet without honor even in a *foreign* country:

Together with my stones
wept large
behind the bars,

they dragged me
to the midst of the market,
to where
the flag unfurls that I
swore no kind of oath to.   [1:131]

This vignette of oppression then recalls "the dark / twin redness / in Vienna and Madrid"—that is, the destruction (with Nazi help) of two popular movements: Austrian socialism in 1934 and Spanish republicanism. In solidarity the poet tells himself:

Heart:
make yourself known even here,
here in the midst of the market.
Cry out the shibboleth
into the alien homeland:
February. No pasaran.

"Cry out"—the prophetic summons. Celan's title alerts us to an Israelite tribal password that the Gileadites used at the river Jordan against Ephraimites fleeing back west, who on pain of death mispronounced it "sibboleth" (Judg. 12:4). It is bracing to hear a "Hebraic title" (as Celan called it[6]) above an embattled secular lyric, "here in the midst of the market." The alien Hebrew "shibboleth" serves as password for the poet himself: can he pass into the realm of Goethe and Schiller by proving his identity with a Biblical password?

"February. No pasaran." His shibboleth includes a rallying cry from the Spanish civil war: *No pasarán*, "They shall not pass." From February 1934, when a Viennese workers' uprising was suppressed, to February 1936, when Spain's Popular Front was elected (and supported by students in Czernowitz), to February 1939 at the battle for Madrid, where banners proclaimed "No pasarán," the progressive cause rose and fell. These calamities posted the way to world war. Less well known, the French said "Ils ne passeront pas" when slaughter began at Verdun in February 1916.[7] Writing in Paris, a victim of the second Great War, Celan could not help facing back, like Walter Benjamin's "angel of history," who sees "one single catastrophe that keeps piling wreckage upon wreckage and hurls them in front of its feet."[8]

Still, this act of recollecting adversity has a strong basis. An ancient Jewish bent of mind marks the coincidence of various historical events in a single date. Thus the ninth of the month of Av, it is said, saw the destruction of both the First and the Second Temples, the defeat of Bar Kochba's revolt against Rome, the expulsion of the Jews from Spain, and even the onset of the European Shoah in 1939. For Celan to bundle up February events close to his heart, clinching them with "No pasaran," says that the poet will not abandon his hard dark ambiguities.[9] "No pasaran": I'm curious as to why Celan did not put these words in italics with the proper accent. In any case, to translate this phrase, the first that he drew from a foreign tongue, would void his oath of fidelity to a hard-bought history.

When Celan gathered his poems of 1952–54, he called the 1955 collection *Von Schwelle zu Schwelle* ("From Threshold to Threshold"). His previous book could have been datelined "Czernowitz–Bucharest–Vienna–Paris, 1944–1952" (though not with the allure of Joyce's "Trieste–Zurich–Paris, 1914–1921" at the end of *Ulysses*). *From Threshold to Threshold*, dedicated to Gisèle, was the first book to arise wholly from Paris. Its title sounds forward-looking, unless this wanderer, like Franz Kafka or Walter Benjamin, is reaching thresholds but cannot cross them.

The book traces memories and encounters. "Epitaph for François," "Assisi," "In Front of a Candle," "With a Changing Key," "Remembrance," "Whichever Stone You Lift," "In Memoriam Paul Éluard," "Shibboleth," "Speak You Too": these respond to the poet's firstborn, Saint Francis, Parmenides, his mother and father, a Communist surrealist, political subjugation, his earliest German critics. To close this collection, Celan (unchronologically) used "Islandward," a ballad to his spectral cohort:

the foreign and free ones are rowing,
the masters of ice and stone:
are tolled at by foundering buoys,
are barked at by shark-blue seas.
They're rowing, and rowing, and rowing—:
You dead ones, you swimmers, lead on!   [1:141]

Only the poet's rhythmic vehemence drives these path-breakers.
An elegy to that same cohort comes just before the end of *From Threshold to Threshold* and asks even more attentiveness than usual. "Die Winzer" (The Vintagers) stems from September 1953 and ingrains autumn into itself: an elegy and at the same time a meditation on poetic process, impelled by rhythmic repetition.

Any lyric verse is pervaded by repetition of all sorts. For Celan, starting from "Todesfuge," repetition takes on a significance of its own. In "The Vintagers" its possibilities range from the momentary to the immense. We notice first the visible or audible instances of repetition: alliteration and assonance, punning and rhyme, parallelism and recapitulation, and doubling of all sorts—morphemic and lexical, grammatic and syntactic, metric and stanzaic. We also find one sense doubling another: paradox, contradiction, metaphor, citation, self-correction. And repetition works as memory, ritual, belatedness, even redemption. The range of repetition extends, we might say, from Moses' stammer to Yahveh's "I am that I am."

Since any translator is making a repetition, the very process of translation bears an affinity to this poem which not only works by repetition but also works toward it. They who "harvest the wine of their eyes" do it "so that a mouth might thirst for this, later— / a latemouth, like to their own." This "latemouth" (*Spätmund*), the poet's, belongs in turn to the poet's translator, who in voicing the repetitions of "Die Winzer" becomes an even later *Spätmund,* a touch closer to the end of days hinted at in Celan's closing line by *endlich* ("at last").

In translating "Die Winzer"'s two twelve-line stanzas, I listen (having listened repeatedly to Celan's three recordings[10]) for the small and the far-reaching arguments of meter—the timing, because time is of the essence here.

Die Winzer

Für Nani und Klaus Demus

Sie herbsten den Wein ihrer Augen,
sie keltern alles Geweinte, auch dieses:
so will es die Nacht,

die Nacht, an die sie gelehnt sind, die Mauer,
so forderts der Stein,
der Stein, über den ihr Krückstock dahinspricht
ins Schweigen der Antwort—
ihr Krückstock, der einmal,
einmal im Herbst,
wenn das Jahr zum Tod schwillt, als Traube,
der einmal durchs Stumme hindurchspricht, hinab
in den Schacht des Erdachten.

Sie herbsten, sie keltern den Wein,
sie pressen die Zeit wie ihr Auge,
sie kellern das Sickernde ein, das Geweinte,
im Sonnengrab, das sie rüsten
mit nachtstarker Hand:
auf dass ein Mund danach dürste, später—
ein Spätmund, ähnlich dem ihren:
Blindem entgegengekrümmt und gelähmt—
ein Mund, zu dem der Trunk aus der Tiefe emporschäumt, indes
der Himmel hinabsteigt ins wächserne Meer,
um fernher als Lichtstumpf zu leuchten,
wenn endlich die Lippe sich feuchtet.

The Vintagers

For Nani and Klaus Demus

They harvest the wine of their eyes,
they crush out all of the weeping, this also:
thus willed by the night,
the night, which they're leaning against, the wall,
thus forced by the stone,
the stone, over which their crook-stick speaks into
the silence of answers—
their crook-stick, which just once,
just once in fall,
when the year swells to death, swollen grapes,
which just once will speak right through muteness, down
into the mineshaft of musings.

They harvest, they crush out the wine,
they press down on time like their eye,
they cellar the seepings, the weepings,
in a sun grave they make ready
with night-toughened hands:

so that a mouth might thirst for this, later—
a latemouth, like to their own:
bent toward blindness and lamed—
a mouth to which the draught from the depth foams upward, meantime
heaven descends into waxen seas, and
far off, as a candle-end, glistens,
at last when the lip comes to moisten.   [1:140]

Even the title words *Die Winzer* start a cadence that will move throughout both stanzas and at the end make up a near-perfect couplet. Those three syllables *Die Winzer,* like the phrase beginning each stanza, *Sie* herbsten (or *wir* trinken und trinken in "Todesfuge"), make a metrical foot (an amphibrach, ⌣ / ⌣) scarcely used in English but worth repeating in translation: *Sie herbsten den Wein ihrer Augen,* "They harvest the wine of their eyes." The end of my line already lacks one light syllable, but compensations occur too. Along with the cognates "wine"/*Wein* and "eyes"/*Augen,* another crops up: "harvest" and *herbsten,* the poem's first verb, its motive idea.

Sie herbsten den Wein ihrer Augen,
sie keltern alles Geweinte, auch dieses,

They harvest the wine of their eyes,
they crush out all of the weeping, this also.

English cannot pick up Celan's suggestive if well-worn pun on *Wein* ("wine") and *Geweinte* ("what's been wept"), because the harvesting of grief brings weeping, not whining.

As we unscroll this autumn elegy, even the simplest words touch off questions. To begin with, who are "They," who will appear twelve more times? Vintagers, yes, but "they" persist as a third-person plural—a people, evoked again and again throughout Celan's work. A 1952 poem located "those we've caught up with," the older dead: "They stand sundered in the world" (1:125). Other poems name them outright: "The dead swim by twos, / by twos, swirled in wine . . . / they dwell near each other" (1:101). Or "they're rowing—: / You dead ones, you swimmers, lead on!" (1:141). In a later poem, "They dug and dug . . ." (1:211).

Despite this ever present "they" in Celan, critics who are sure that "Die Winzer" concerns the poetic process itself identify those who "harvest the wine of their eyes" as poets taking on our pain and transforming it.[11] Perhaps, but this disregards the people who first found voice in "Todesfuge," whose wartime suffering sifted through European earth. It's they, a buried people, who are leaning against night in "Die Winzer," against the shooting wall, and who speak "into / the silence of answers." To say that "they" are poets is off by a generation.

What's more, this poem in draft was called "Die Menschen" (The Humans), a seemingly banal title. In Nazi-Deutsch, however, the term *Mensch* excluded Jews, while Yiddish called someone decent a *mensch*. Likewise for Celan, the words *Menschen* and *Juden* seem interchangeable—a 1962 poem speaks of "the wander-East . . . the humans-and-Jews" (1:278). *Die Menschen*: they are mortal, both vulnerable and redeemable—the more Jewish, the more human.

The change from "The Humans" to "The Vintagers" added a pastoral irony, since in German Romantic poetry the *Winzer* figures as a rejoicing worker. In Hölderlin, "The vintager's brave joyous cry / Rings pure on sun-warmed vineyard slopes."[12] Closer to Celan is Isaiah's prophecy: "upon thy harvest the battle shout is fallen. . . . And in the vineyards there shall be no singing . . . no treader shall tread out wine in the presses" (16:9–10). Desolation threatens the harvest and the song alike.

They *herbsten* ("harvest") the wine, from *Herbst,* meaning "autumn." The season signals loss and death, even when Celan in 1953 is translating Apollinaire: "Autumn is dead remember this / We'll no more see each other here" (4:790). Moreover, on 16 September 1953, when "Die Winzer" was composed, Celan's wife was soon to give birth to their first child, and the baseless plagiarism charge against Celan had just been initiated in Germany.[13] There is no telling how much these things may have touched upon a poem beginning with growth and grief.

Images of wine turn up in Celan's early poems, not like the Psalmist's "wine that maketh glad the heart of man" (Ps. 104:15), but mixed with autumn and tears.[14] And shortly before writing "The Vintagers," Celan had read Heidegger on Hölderlin's 1801 elegy "Bread and Wine,"[15] in which Dionysus goes between humankind (*die Menschen*) and "they," the gods. Celan marked Heidegger's phrase, "poet in a destitute time: singing on the trace of the departed gods."

"The Vintagers" corresponds in a score of words to "Bread and Wine" and still refutes it. The later poet does not invoke gods or the mystery of water being turned into wine or wine into the blood of redemption. When, in Celan, "they cellar the seepings, the weepings, / in a sun grave they make ready / with night-toughened hands," we are to think not of Dionysus's priests or Jesus' disciples but of people forced to dig their own graves.

"They harvest the wine of their eyes": throughout Celan's writing, eyes gaze from or at the Jewish dead, and *Aug* is used twice as often as any other noun.[16] "I sought your eye," says a 1952 poem to his mother, "when you glanced up and no one would see you." And the "almond eye of the dead" appears in Celan's "Remembrance." Contrast Hölderlin's "Remembrance," in which "love seizes hold of the eyes," or his "Bread and Wine," whose wise men's "eyes moisten" at the descending light of Christ.

Primed by the opening of "Die Winzer," I have tried to mimic its cumulative syntax and cadence, where each recurrence straddles a line break: "the night, / the night," "the stone, / the stone," "their crook-stick . . . / their crook-stick," "which just once, / just once." Repetition like this makes for the purest ambiguity. Is it deathly night or fruitful? stone that stifles or braces? the crook-stick blind and mute or visionary? just once because gone now or consummate?

Repetition can impede speech yet propel it, as both stammer and eloquence. Celan also links contraries by alliterative ricochet: *spricht—Schweigen* (speaking—silence), *Tod—Traube* (death—grape clusters), *Stumme—spricht* (muteness—speaking). Heeding Celan's alliteration, I moved to his verb—"swells to death, as sweet grapes"—but sweetness seemed too facile for this poem. Eventually I tried my own repetition: "when the year swells to death, swollen grapes," keeping the syllabic measure of Celan's German, which matters for a poem yielding its speech in time, in season. The issue, as always, is what comes of suffering and death. Now the only answer is "the silence of answers."

Celan's only revisions to his first stanza augmented the rhythm while introducing no new words at all. After "their crook-stick speaks into / the silence of answers," he made elementary changes—a second "crook-stick," a third "just once"—yet they build a cadence that any missed beat would skew:

> *their crook-stick,* which just once,
> just once in fall,
> when the year swells to death, swollen grapes,
> *which just once* will speak right through muteness, down
> into the mineshaft of musings.

In this stanza that shapes a single sentence, each clause gropes and probes, correcting the previous one. Rather than "once" or "one time" for *einmal,* "just once" may catch what is precious and precarious about this autumn moment. Three times the word *einmal* resounds (thanks to Celan's revision), like a spell or litany, speaking something into being.[17] These rephrasings do not so much hark back as reach forward, as in Kierkegaard's sense of repetition.[18] Much is at stake here, and in a later poem:

> JUST ONCE,
> then I heard him,
> he was washing the world,
> unseen, nightlong. . . .
> Light was. Salvation.   [2:107]

In "Die Winzer," "just once" helps Celan's stanza end with six identical feet in two lines: "which just once will speak right through muteness, down / into the mineshaft of musings."

Adhering to Celan's meter creates other spin-offs too. For the German *spricht* ("speaks"), "will speak" lifts to a prophetic present. And speaking "right through" instead of "through" muteness stresses Celan's doubled preposition *durch: der einmal durchs Stumme hindurchspricht.* When he told a German audience what their language had passed through, he used that same form, *durch . . . hindurch:* "through frightful muting, through the thousand dark-nesses of deathbringing speech" (3:186). Given Celan's severe economy, the echo of his 1953 verse in that 1958 speech binds a survivor's poem to a poet's testimony.[19]

The language that passed through muting and death, Celan said in 1958, could "come to light again, 'enriched' by all that"—"enriched" being a mining term, like the "shaft of what's been thought up" in "Die Winzer," the *Schacht des Erdachten.* And his word *erdachten* recurs in 1959: "They dug and dug" and "thought up" no language (1:211). So in "Die Winzer" we touch the generation of poetic speech, like the deep source of Hölderlin's imagery in "Patmos": "Indeed the pit bears iron." Celan's resonance in *Schacht des Erdachten* needs a strong equivalent. I tried "cave of conceivings," but that makes Gothic romance out of the downward, lightless shaft where speech is mined—hence "mineshaft of musings," even though it may be a bit over-done.

Now we can dwell within the stanza break—and not only because this silence constitutes the translator's only unalloyed success. Time passes be-tween stanzas, enough for "the mineshaft of musings" to renew a cycle, like yearly festivals.

A second stanza, a twelve-line (or month?) sentence,[20] compacts the poem's opening lines. These said "They harvest the wine of their eyes, / they crush out all of the weeping." Now we have: "They harvest, they crush out the wine, / they press down on time like their eye." Remaking grief sounds like what Freud called "repetition compulsion," a fruitless acting-out of past trauma.[21] But "The Vintagers" keeps accruing all that has been wept, as the next line lengthens within Celan's basic meter:

sie kellern das Sickernde ein, das Geweinte,
they cellar the seepings, the weepings.

This beat in English turns out singsong, "the seepings, the weepings," but at least it echoes Celan's repeated pun on *Wein* and *Geweinte* by rhyming wine with tears.[22] Another word for "seepings" could be found in Keats's "To

Autumn": "Thou watchest the last oozings hours by hours." But Keats, even apprehending death, would bring Romantic promise to "Die Winzer" and its "sun grave," a metaphor for the seasoning of cellared wine and still the poem's bleakest image. There is no call here for organic forms from European poetry: tree, bird, urn, torso, fountain, stream. Instead, we have wall, stone, stick, shaft, grave, stub. What happens in Celan's autumn poem happens "late," we are told, and "later"—later than Keats or Hölderlin.

From here on the sentence moves to its end through a ferment of syntax, punctuation, grammar, and prosody that induces a kind of spell. A triple repetition recalls the threefold *einmal* of the first stanza:

so that a mouth might thirst for this, later—
a latemouth, like to their own:
bent toward blindness and lamed—
a mouth to which the draught from the depth foams upward.

The first stanza grew around *einmal* ("once"). Now *später* ("later") draws this second stanza toward the fullness of time. Lateness can mean either still accessible or no longer accessible energy, as in Hölderlin's "Bread and Wine": "But my friend! we come too late. True the gods live, / but over our heads up there in another world." After the Third Reich, however, German song can cite Hölderlin only as "The Vintagers" does, sifting "Bread and Wine" and "Patmos" and "Remembrance" in an unprecedentedly "destitute time." The "latemouth" or *Spätmund* in "Die Winzer" I hear as the poet's own. And *Spätmund* plays on *Spätlese*, a "late gleaning" of grapes before they rot, to make the richest wine. Thirsting for utmost speech, he had said "Speak as the last" (1:135).

Answering that thirst, the syntax in "Die Winzer"'s longest line delivers a marvelous verb, *emporschäumt,* and wants a strong pulse in English too: "a mouth to which the draught from the depth foams upward." Another high Romantic chance arises, if only Celan's line could be rendered by this from Keats: "O for a draught of vintage! that hath been / Cool'd a long age in the deep-delvèd earth." Or from Hölderlin's "Remembrance": "But pass me, / Someone, the fragrant cup, / Full of the dark light." Celan's vintagers spoke through muteness "down / into the mineshaft." Now a drink foams up *aus der Tiefe,* as it were *de profundis.* We could say "out of the depth," echoing the King James Bible, because Celan echoes Luther's and Buber's German from Psalm 130, a cry of hope for Israel. But his phrase needs more speed: "the draught from the depth."

Meantime another voice can be heard behind Celan's—namely, that of Amos foreseeing grape harvests so abundant they compress time: "Behold, the days come, saith the Lord, that the plowman shall overtake the harvester,

and the treader of grapes him that soweth seed; and the mountains shall
drop sweet wine . . . And I will turn the captivity of my people Israel . . .
and they shall no more be pulled up out of their land which I have given
them" (9:13–15). "The Vintagers" resonates with Scripture—with Amos and
with Moses, whose stick struck the rock and water gushed forth.

Celan's closing lines push that resonance as far as it can go. Literally:

> *der Himmel hinabsteigt ins wächserne Meer,*
>   the sky/heaven descends into the waxen sea,
>
> *um fernher als Lichtstumpf zu leuchten,*
>   in order from afar as a candle-stub to shine,
>
> *wenn endlich die Lippe sich feuchtet.*
>   when at last the lip moistens itself.

When "heaven descends into waxen seas," is this catastrophe à la Icarus or
theophany of God in the world or simply sunset? Or the Havdalah ceremony
closing the Jewish Sabbath, when a candle is doused in wine to symbolize
abundance? Celan's 1953 poem to his mother, "In Front of a Candle," used
that same phrase "heaven descends."[23] And later he titled a poem "Havdalah"
(1:259). Maybe "The Vintagers" envisions a day brought in and seen out by
candles and wine.

This final couplet turns on the Sabbath's pivotal force: Creation ends, and
rest anticipates redemption.[24] Celan's lyric, with light shining over the face
of the waters, ends in the beginning. A saying favored by Walter Benjamin—
"Origin is the goal"[25]—holds for this poem and for translation too.

"Die Winzer" closes with the meter that began it, and the season consum-
mates: an even couplet holds the poem's only rhyme.[26] After "heaven descends
into waxen seas," Celan's recorded voice balances both lines in equal parts:

um fernher	*als Lichtstumpf*	*zu leuchten*
˘ / ˘	˘ / ˘	˘ / ˘
wenn endlich	*die Lippe*	*sich feuchtet.*
and far off,	as light-stub,	it brightens,
when just at	long last the	lip moistens.

But will that really do, "brightens / moistens" for the near-rhyme *leuchten /
feuchtet* touching a transcendent light to human lips? Moments like this bring
to mind Benjamin's 1923 essay "The Task of the Translator" (*Die Aufgabe des
Übersetzers*),[27] for the word *Aufgabe* also means "relinquishment": "The Translator's Giving Up."

What's needed, then, is a dissonance, as from *leuchten* to *feuchtet*. Somewhere from the mineshaft of musings comes another possibility:

heaven descends into waxen seas, and
far off, as a candle-end, glistens,
at last when the lip comes to moisten.

This roughens the rhyme, as in German, and puts off the redemptive light a little, timing it to when the lip may moisten.

The Talmud holds that "Whoever says a word in the name of its speaker, brings redemption to the world."[28] And to quote Benjamin again: "Translation kindles from the endless renewal of languages as they grow to the messianic end of their history."[29] These are grandiose expectations for a secondary act and art. Yet with lyric verse as charged as Celan's, the translator enters its evolution. Hölderlin knew this vis-à-vis Sophocles, Rilke vis-à-vis Valéry, to name the German poets whom Celan prized. In *After Babel,* George Steiner writes about translation at its fullest, saying that the process culminates in restitution: something is given back to the source in return for what was lost.[30] After all, the act of translation repeats an original poem with a difference: each line of verse in English, reflecting backward toward its origin, is scrolling one line closer to the future.

Celan's poem could not end in a perfect rhyme. No such rounded closure is in order here, no reconciling of early with late. Muteness, blindness, and lameness have intervened. Grave and night and stone offer the silence of answers. No perfect rhyme, but something beyond that: a differencing, *leuchten* to *feuchtet,* repetition pressing toward restitution.

Why does the lip at last come to moisten? Wine pressed from grief for the toast to life, and something simpler, like any of us briefly wetting our lips—to begin to speak.

6

Words That Will Not Heal
(1954–57)

"And there is ourselves, we who look at these ruins and sincerely believe that race-madness was buried in them forever, we who see this image fading and act as if we had cause for hope again, as if we really believed that it all belongs to only *one* time and only *one* country, we who overlook what's happening around us and do not hear that the scream never falls silent [*der Schrei nicht verstummt*]" (4:97).

This sentence by Paul Celan both is and is not a quotation from him. In 1956 he translated Jean Cayrol's French narration for the Alain Resnais film

Night and Fog, the first documentary on Nazi death camps, which ends with that alarm, as the camera pans over the present-day remains of Auschwitz in color. Celan's version of the script inevitably speaks for him as well. "Todesfuge" springs to mind, for instance, when he has this to translate from *Night and Fog:* "An orchestra plays cheerful tunes during the march out to factories and stone-pits" (4:82). Or this: "Goethe's oak at Buchenwald. They build the camp, they respect the oak" (4:86). The film's closing sentence resonates in Celan's own voice, telling us we "do not hear that the scream never falls silent."

In making a German translation, did Celan take into account that this film would circulate with his subtitles in the Bundesrepublik?[1] He dealt specially with the word *Rasse* ("race"). In his own verse he never used it, preferring *Geschlecht* ("species," "generation") or *Stamm* ("stem," "lineage") to a term corrupted by anti-Semitism. When he came upon the French word *race* in translating a poet-friend, even then he declined to say *Rasse* in German.[2] But, surprisingly, he uses it in the narration to *Night and Fog,* where Cayrol's French does not even call for it: *Il y a nous qui regardons sincèrement ces ruines comme si le vieux monstre concentrationnaire était mort*—"We look at these ruins as if 'the old concentrationary monster' were dead," as if *Rassenwahn* ("race-madness") were dead, Celan says, and a new compound strikes German ears.[3]

Translations took up much of the 1950s for Celan, on top of his studies, teaching, marriage, fatherhood, readings in Germany, and the writing of poetry. Many were merely paid jobs, but others drew on his own concerns.[4]

After translating Jean Cocteau's *Letter to the Americans* (1949), Celan worked on three books of Yvan Goll's poetry during 1950 and 1951 and also on French and Romanian surrealist lyrics. In 1952–53 he translated poems by Moore and Apollinaire, then in 1954 a wartime farce by Picasso. In August 1954 he abandoned "with shame and sadness" a project of translating the French correspondence between Rilke and Gide.[5] Meanwhile he produced translations of two Georges Simenon mysteries and some essays by the Romanian-born E. M. Cioran and started on a novel by Cayrol.[6] For months in 1956 he worked as a translator for Geneva's International Labour Office.[7] In teaching German language and literature at the École Normale Supérieure, he regularly set translation exercises for students.

Celan sometimes undertook translations for both love and money. Early in 1954, he found a way to let translation speak for him—not as soulfully as with Apollinaire but more gainfully. Picasso's play *Le désir attrapé par la queue* ("Desire Caught by the Tail") had both historical and literary appeal for him (4:8–63). Only months after the Germans occupied Paris, Picasso had composed this six-act farce, a gesture of resistance, and in 1944, still under occupation, the artist's friends put on the play in Michel Leiris's apartment.[8]

Albert Camus did the staging, and roles were taken by Simone de Beauvoir, Jean-Paul Sartre, Raymond Queneau, Dora Maar, and others. Celan's own kind of resistance throughout the war years, holding fast to a poet's calling, allied him to this job of translation, as did his French surrealist leanings. The result was an agile rendering of Picasso's exact absurdities.

Yet it took work, he told his publisher: "I've been back in Paris a long time now and have been translating industriously. A first draft is now finished. A first draft: that is, Picasso's text has to be not only translated, but also—if I may misuse a term of Heidegger's—translocated [*übergesetzt,* "carried across"]. You see: for me what's involved sometimes is a sort of ferry service. So may I hope that for the payment of my work, not only the lines but also the oar-strokes will be counted?"[9] He used that term again a few months later, in explaining to an editor why he had failed at "translocating" Rilke's French into German. Rilke's letters to Gide daunted him, since he saw that he would have to rewrite them in Rilkean German and thus risk pastiche, if not *lèse-majesté.*

The breadwinning jobs along with the vital encounters as a translator show Celan's polyglot genius, but also an unfortunate cosmopolitanism—and "cosmopolitan" sounds too elegant. Czernowitz had hosted diverse languages and cultures. Then the poet lost all that, emigrated, fled, and resettled. Although he acquired French citizenship in the early 1950s, "stateless" would be an apt description.[10] He said once to Yves Bonnefoy, "You are at home within your language, your reference points, among the books, the works you love. As for me, I am on the outside."[11] Coming from a homeland that hardly existed anymore, writing for a German audience that he did not live among or trust, residing in France yet unvalued there, Paul Antschel-Celan's native tongue itself was the only nation he could claim. "I've become neither European nor western," he wrote to Petre Solomon in 1957. "Friends—I have scarcely any. The 'praise' you speak of—you can safely put that in quotes."[12] And this letter uses what Solomon calls "an astonishingly correct and lively Romanian," considering Celan's decade-long absence from Bucharest.

Stranded, Celan was alert to Germany's reception of his work and France's neglect. Possibly he was aware of the first notices in Britain and the United States, which had trouble placing him. In 1955 London's *Jewish Quarterly* published a translation of "Todesfuge" by Michael Bullock, with a note saying that Celan had "spent the war years in the Soviet Union," which suggests Siberian exile.[13] Also in 1955, *Commentary* in New York carried Clement Greenberg's translation of "Todesfuge," plus a note with more misinformation: Celan was born "in 1912" (rather than 1920) in Czernowitz, "now Rumania" (by then the Ukraine); he is "a survivor of the concentration camps" (as if he had been deported to Poland) who "has lived in Paris since 1945" (not 1948); and "Todesfüge" (with an unneeded umlaut) comes from *Poppies* (rather than

Poppy) and Memory.[14] These misperceptions have to do with the emergence of a world-class poem from an obscure corner of the Old World rather than from London or New York. Though the British and American versions lacked a fine ear for Celan's rhythm and tone, the poem's uncanny force came through.

Meanwhile in France, save for an early and somewhat faulty translation of "Todesfuge" in January 1952,[15] recognition was tardy. No collection of French translations appeared until after Celan's death.[16] But in Marseille's *Cahiers du Sud* (April 1956), Jean-Pierre Wilhelm translated four lyrics and added thoughtful paragraphs on this migrant spirit.[17] Coming from the "ethnic and linguistic polymorphism" of central Europe, "a poet imbued with German culture in the purest sense must find himself isolated. . . . His true native land is *his language,*" Wilhelm said—a point that some German critics had trouble making. Wilhelm singled out "Todesfuge" as doing more than anything since 1945 "to seize the conscience and purify the spiritual landscape."

This is headier stuff than most poets could hope for. Yet Celan still told Petre Solomon that any praise he had received needed quotes around it: "Now and again they invite me to Germany for readings. Even the anti-Semites have discovered me."[18] Celan's readings in the Bundesrepublik suggest otherwise: Munich—"an Orphic singer"; Esslingen—"something seldom experienced: we believe him"; Frankfurt—"these dreamlike images bring one closer to the reality of the world."[19] And in 1956, the Cultural Circle of the Federal Association for German Industry awarded Celan their prize: his voice "reaches us from those fairytales of Chagall-country and the poet's youth in southeast Europe."[20]

When Celan gave a reading in Stuttgart in June 1957, "Count up the almonds" and other poems were well received, according to clippings he kept. But the city's leading paper commented on "so much talent . . . sometimes getting caught in the underbrush of its own metaphor-forest."[21] This (not altogether invalid) judgment seems insufficient cause for his saying a month later that the anti-Semites had discovered him. More likely, Celan was still smarting from the critiques of Curt Hohoff. In 1954, on the heels of Claire Goll's open letter accusing Celan of plagiarizing her husband, Hohoff had written this: "In Celan, the late student of Yvan Goll, one can hardly see one's way through the ambitious high-literary gesticulation."[22] He had called his article "Flutings from the Void." Then a year later Hohoff publicly renewed his charge, setting lines by Goll above similar ones by Celan, whose "diction and imagery are hand-me-down, at times poetically hackneyed."[23] No amount of serious enthusiasm for *From Threshold to Threshold* (1955) could offset denunciations coming, as it were, *aus Deutschland.*

Celan's interests also come through in the books he was acquiring.

A Romanian-Jewish friend gave him Trakl's poems in 1950. In 1952 Celan bought Gerard Manley Hopkins in English, in 1953 Karl Kraus's *Last Days of Mankind,* and in 1954, Else Lasker-Schüler's volumes, as well as Buber on the Baal Shem Tov. Heidegger first presented his work to Celan in 1956. From 1957 there was more Buber, Hermann Cohen, and Gershom Scholem's booklet *The Secrets of Creation.* Celan's library included German philosophy: Hegel in 1952, much Nietzsche, Schlegel and Fichte in 1957, and Curtius and Ortega. He was given Hölderlin in 1956 and 1958, bought a new Russian edition of Mandelshtam in 1957, Isaak Babel in 1958, first editions of Rilke and was reading Walter Benjamin in 1959. All along, he kept a variety of reference works: numerous German and other wordbooks, the big two-volume Muret–Sanders English–German dictionary and a superb Brockhaus English–German dictionary, which he bought on his birthday in 1953, plus volumes on zoology, geology, mineralogy, crystallography, physics, botany, anatomy, birds, and especially roses. It is a richly mixed bag, German and Jewish and German-Jewish.

Occasionally a purchase led to a poem. Celan's marginalia fed into his own writing, and often an item he came upon had figured—or been pre-figured—in something he himself had written. Such findings animated him, and he would pencil the relevant words from his own work into the book he was reading. Experience for Celan was legible, first and last.

An incident from the 1950s offers another glimpse behind his poetry. He spotted two menorahs in a bookstall on the Seine, Celan's widow told me, bought one and brought it home. They talked about it: Where does this candlestick come from? What has it survived? Does a non-observant Jew have a right to it? The two menorahs were identical—should he have separated them? Celan went back to the stall and bought the other. Eventually he and his wife kept one in their Paris apartment, the other at their Normandy farmhouse.

Celan once noted Emily Dickinson's phrase "Real Memory" (which is "shod with Adamant"), then copied out her verse "You cannot make Re-membrance grow."[24] But this is what his lyrics from the mid-1950s attempt to do—make remembrance grow. A March 1955 poem entitled "Confidence," the earliest for his third book, *Speech-Grille,* originally began:

> There will be yet one eye,
> a strange one, next to ours:
> mute under stony lid.[25]

Later he reset the lines:

> There will be yet one eye,
> a strange one, next

to ours: mute
under stony lid.   [1:153]

With the phrasing cropped, the colon dislodged, and "mute" left gaping at a
line break, this verse now makes vision chancier than ever.

There will be an eyelash,
turned inward in the rock
and steeled by unweptness . . .

This is more severe than "The Vintagers," where tears foam up as wine to
moisten the lips. Celan had spoken about the essential "questionableness" of
his poems.[26] This one ends in the subjunctive: "as if, because stone is, there
were still brothers." Stone is the matter in which No does not split off from
Yes, in which muteness forms the medium of speech.

Stone—and always snow, as in another lyric from 1955 with the overly
promising title "Homecoming." Already in 1939, returning from Tours to
Czernowitz, Paul Antschel had called a poem "Homecoming," thinking of his
mother. Celan's 1955 "Homecoming" says this:

Snowfall, denser and denser,
dove-colored, like yesterday,
snowfall, as if you still slept even now.   [1:156]

Addressing his mother, these words form a medium for re-entering the past.
(In June 1955 a son was born and named Eric after Celan's mother Fried-
erika.) The possibility—or rather, the necessity—of "denser and denser" snow
conveying us along "the sleigh track of what's lost," as "Homecoming" goes
on to say, springs from a pun in the phrase "denser and denser": *dichter und
dichter* suggests the concentrate of poems, since *Dichter* also means "poet."

Words such as "mute," "stone," "snow," "crystal," "lost," "remembered,"
"forgotten," "dark," "eye," "voice," and "silence" sound obstinately in the mid-
1950s. For his poems Celan borrowed a definition from Rilke: "Enclosures
around the limitlessly wordless."[27] If not quite wordless, his verse was growing
more reticent and strange. "Streak" (1956) was already puzzling when it
ended thus:

Streak in the eye:
so as to guard
a foreboded sign,
livened by the sand—or ice?—of
an alien time for a more alien always
and tuned as
a mute harp.[28]

Later Celan changed "a foreboded sign" to "a sign carried through the dark," and the "mute harp" became "a mutely vibrating consonant" (1:159). By that time, he had said that language went through "muting" and "darkness" during the war. The "harp" of early sorrow was giving way to minimal speech.

Celan's longest poem to date—begun in 1956, finished in 1958, and placed first in *Speech-Grille* (1959)[29]—admits no title, being known by its initial word:

> *Voices,* nicked into
> the green of the water's surface.
> When the kingfisher dives,
> the second whirrs:
>
> What stood by you
> on each of the banks
> steps
> mown into another image.   [1:147]

This arose from a moment in July 1956 when Celan, walking with a friend by a stream, saw a small bright bird dive into the water.[30] He knew the bird's name in French, *alcyon,* but not in German. Back home, they looked it up in a new edition of Brehm's four-volume animal encyclopedia that Celan and his wife had just acquired and found the name *Eisvogel.* And discovering the name released a poem.

The bird Celan glimpsed becomes voices nicking the surface, or scribing it—Gisèle Celan worked in etching. Then the kingfisher's dive in and out of time brings news that "what stood by you," what you relied upon, can change in the twinkling of an eye, "mown into another image"—a metaphor which itself presents the action of metaphor, of breakdown and rebirth.[31] For Celan the harvest metaphor, like the bird's kill, comes out both deathly and life-giving.

That paradox persists in the poem's next section:

> *Voices* from the nettle path:
>
> Come on your hands to us.
> Whoever is alone with the lamp,
> has only his hand to read from.

Celan later recalled this "little quatrain" as one where "I encountered . . . myself" in "a kind of homecoming," via "paths on which language gets a voice . . . paths of a voice to a perceiving Thou" (3:201). These "*Voices* from the nettle path" are seeking out the poet, telling him from their pain to come toward them painfully too. In a letter Celan said that "Only true hands write true poems," the hands of someone "who with his voice and his muteness seeks a way" (3:177).

A few lines later, the voices focus their demand:

Voices from which your heart
shrinks back into your mother's heart.
Voices from the gallows tree,
where latewood and springwood
change and exchange their rings.

In a tree that became a gallows, the past ingrains the present. Genocide—though Celan's poem resists abstraction—alters the natural order, making memory work against human comfort:

Voices, guttural, in the rubble,
where unendingness also shovels,
(heart-)
slimy streamlet.

Then the refrain abruptly changes:

Jacob's voice:
The tears.
The tears in the brother's eye.
One stayed clinging, grew.
We dwell inside.
Breathe, that
it come loose.

Celan (or his publisher) changed *Jaakob* to *Jakob,* for the sake of the rhythm or to follow German usage. Whether Celan is deploring or accepting the primal deception—"The voice is the voice of Jacob, but the hands are the hands of Esau" (Gen. 27:22)—the quietest possible German asks for an old grief to be resolved: "Breathe, that / it come loose" (*Atme, dass / sie sich löse*). Originally *lösen* was in the indicative, then Celan made it subjunctive—exact and tentative.

Still in a Judaic vein, the sequence closes:

Voices in the bowels of the ark:
It is only the mouths are sheltered.
You sinking ones,
hear us too.

Celan wrote the lines this way on a café pad. In the published poem he staggers them, unsettling the voices:

Voices in the bowels of the ark:
It is
only the mouths
are sheltered. You
sinking ones, hear
us too.

If the only thing saved is the power of speech, whose mouths are they? Perhaps "vintagers" from the end of his previous book, reaching toward "a latemouth like to their own." And who are "You / sinking ones"?

Here Celan's poem ended, as of July 1956, but while publishing poems written after "Stimmen," he held onto it for two years. During that time he carved and cracked and chipped and scraped and hammered too many words, in both composing and translating, to let *"Voices"* rest. In November 1958, just before his new collection went to press, he added a section:

No
voice—a
late-noise, alien to hours, for your
thoughts a gift, here, at last
waking near: a
carpel, large as eyes, deeply
nicked; it
resins, won't
scar over.

In reciting this upended sentence, Celan lurches as if struggling to keep No and Yes unsplit. No voice, but a late noise, late but alien, alien but a gift for your thoughts. "No / voice" does not annul but supersedes the earlier voices. The latemouth at last awakens, and what is it? A "fruit-leaf" (*Fruchtblatt*) or "carpel," a flower's minute ovary-bearing leaf—the nub of life. It is eye-sized because, like the "almond eye of the dead" in "Remembrance," it sees us, and vice versa. And "deeply / nicked," it points back to *"Voices* nicked" into the water. This fruit-leaf, like the nettle path and gallows tree, bears a wound but still lives: it oozes resin and "won't / scar over," will not forget.

In nomenclature Celan found a way to deal with those wounds inflicted by Nazi namings. Already in *"Voices"* we start with the kingfisher, then wood tissue formed early and late in a growing season and "fruit-leaf." Words dull if they lack exactness for this poet, who used to reel off botanical terms in several languages.[32] So even if Nazi-Deutsch abused the body of German speech, it could not contaminate the clean terminology of the natural world that Celan loved.

While "*Voices*" was awaiting its second ending, from 1956 to 1958, Celan's poetry grew unforgivingly dark and mindful. "Tenebrae," dating from March 1957, is a stunning case in point, a study in understated bitterness. Yet, just after writing it, Celan told a Catholic friend, Otto Pöggeler, a scholar of Hegel and Heidegger, that this was "one of his favorite poems": it came to him on the street, then he wrote it right down at home.[33] It was provoked partly by François Couperin's Passion cantata *Leçons de Ténèbres,* a lucid setting of the Lamentations of Jeremiah, Judaism's principal elegy for the fall of Jerusalem and all subsequent misfortune.[34] In draft, Celan even adopted Couperin's French title, installing his poem under the rubric for Matins and Lauds of Holy Week in Roman Catholic liturgy, during which candles are extinguished one by one to symbolize the Crucifixion: *Tenebrae factae sunt,* the Gospel says—"there was darkness over all the earth" (Matt. 27:45). A few months later, Celan retitled his poem "Tenebrae,"[35] telling Pöggeler that he preferred the Latin's priestly character.

"Tenebrae," true to its title, traces a prayerlike curve: *Nah sind wir, Herr, / nahe und greifbar . . .*

Near are we, Lord,
near and graspable.

Grasped already, Lord,
clawed into each other, as if
each of our bodies were
your body, Lord.

Pray, Lord,
pray to us,
we are near.

Wind-skewed we went there,
went there, to bend
over pit and crater.

Went to the water-trough, Lord.

It was blood, it was
what you shed, Lord.

It shined.

It cast your image into our eyes, Lord.
Eyes and mouth stand so open and void, Lord.
We have drunk, Lord.
The blood and the image that was in the blood, Lord.

Pray, Lord.
We are near.   [1:163]

Bete, Herr. / Wir sind nah. A Christian poem? Yes, by definition. Celan was swayed by Christ's crucifixion, and this lyric grips onto Christian faith. But does it enhance Holy Week? That would be something quite different.

Celan's word *Tenebrae* ("shadows," "darkness") does not need or even want translating. One of his few titles in a foreign tongue, it has ritual currency throughout Christendom. Yet it bears pondering a moment. The title "Tenebrae" does not stand over a poem like Yeats's "Easter 1916," reconsecrating the sense of Easter. For the Jewish survivor-poet, something has "changed utterly," but no "terrible beauty is born."

In opting for "Tenebrae" rather than "Leçons de Ténèbres," Celan opens our ears to other Scriptural turning points that bring "darkness" or חוֹשֶׁך (*Choshech*) or *Tenebrae* or *Finsternis*. There was "darkness upon the face of the deep" in Genesis (1:2) and "darkness in all Egypt" in Exodus (10:22). God speaks "out of the midst of darkness" at Sinai (Deut. 5:20), and Job (3:4) laments, "Let that day be darkness" wherein he was born. A cross-purpose of Crucifixion and chosenness, of Catholic and Judaic mysteries, stays in mind as we read "Tenebrae."

Other layers turn up in the poem's opening:

Near are we, Lord,
near and graspable.

To the peeled ear, these few syllables evoke the opening paradox of Hölderlin's 1802 hymn "Patmos," on the apostle John banished to an Aegean island:

Nah ist	Near by
Und schwer zu fassen der Gott.	And hard to grasp is the God.
Wo aber Gefahr ist, wächst	Yet where danger is, grows
Das Rettende auch.	What rescues as well.

Strangely, in Celan's poem it is "we" who are near, not "the God," we who may be grasped and maybe not rescued. Thus "Tenebrae" starts out by inverting and really subverting Hölderlin's hymn. "Patmos" makes its way from Saint John, Christ, and the disciples to Scripture and God's care for "German song." That made Hölderlin a precursor for Paul Celan, but also an impossible example. No saving grace of a God "Near by / And hard to grasp" was to descend upon the speakers in these postwar verses, who are "grasped already" and "clawed into each other."

At an even deeper layer than Couperin and Holy Week, than Hölderlin and John and Patmos, stands the word *nah* ("near" or "nigh")—signaling mercy throughout the Psalms. "The Lord is nigh unto them that are of a broken heart" (34:18). "We give thanks, and Thy name is near" (75:2). "The Lord is nigh unto all them that call upon Him" (145:18).[36] Yet "trouble is near" in the crucial Psalm beginning "My God, my God, why hast Thou forsaken me?" (22:12). And, as Celan had written in 1944, "God's as nearby as the vulture's nail" (*F* 140).

During the Tenebrae service Psalms are chanted, and they also came to the lips of Jews struggling for breath inside "shower rooms." Shortly before writing "Tenebrae," Celan had translated the narration for *Night and Fog,* which says as the camera pans upward in a gas chamber: "The only sign—but you have to know about it—is the ceiling dug into by fingernails" (4:94). So the question is: what reconcilement starts when this poem's speakers liken themselves to Jesus?

> Grasped already, Lord,
> clawed into each other, as if
> each of our bodies were
> your body, Lord.

Buckling "our bodies" to "your body, Lord," the image of excruciation brings a mythic authority to bear. Yet this likening occurs only "as if," in the subjunctive, the mood reserved for what is doubtful or contrary to fact. The speakers are not suffering in Christ's name. To see these lines as "Judeo-Christian" is to vitiate their force.[37]

Their source was an all but unknown phrase. Just before Celan composed "Tenebrae," Gerald Reitlinger's ground-breaking study *The Final Solution* came out in German translation.[38] There, at the end of an already horrifying paragraph, a cluster of Jews pressing against the gas chamber door, suffocating, is described as "even in death clawed into each other" (*ineinander verkrallt*). Now Celan's line says *ineinander verkrallt, als wär . . .* ("clawed into each other, as if . . ."). It passes understanding: the poet, being who he is and knowing what he knows, absorbing such a paragraph, folding the crude fact into verse whose pruned, rhythmic clarity ("one of his favorite poems"!) came to grace anthologies, conferences, and scholarly studies.

Not Golgotha now, but the Polish countryside sees human life so broken that it bows down divinity:

> Pray, Lord,
> pray to us,
> we are near.

This "we" of Easter supplication and suffering cedes to the God-forsaken "we" of "Deathfugue." Maybe Celan also remembered that cry of the first modern Hebrew poet Bialik after the Easter 1903 Kishinev pogrom: "Heavens . . . You pray for me!"[39]

Ecumenical minds have taken up the analogy of crucifixion and the triplet following it. Criticizing "pray to us" as "sacrilegious," Pöggeler in April 1957 advised the poet against "rebellious subjectivism." A few days later, Celan agreed that his line was "a mere empty gesture" and dropped it.[40] When "Tenebrae" came out that fall, the passage simply read: "Pray, Lord, / we are near," just like the closing couplet. But by the time his poem reached book form a year later, Celan had restored the triplet's middle line. Even so, Pöggeler maintains, "Whoever does not see that the blasphemy is missing at the end, is really missing the dynamic of the poem." In other words, when "pray to us" disappears as the poem closes, its blasphemous indictment of God and Christianity is dissolved.

But it was not from Paul Celan in 1957, before Vatican II, that conciliation had to come. His poem's middle section, "Wind-skewed we went there . . . ," evokes the terrain where *Einsatzkommandos* did their job. A touch of animality, "Went to the water-trough," jars against the twenty-third Psalm's shepherded soul beside still waters whose cup runneth over. What is more, the eucharistic "body" and "blood" in this poem are hinting—not all that darkly—at anti-Jewish blood libels, claims of desecrating the Host and killing Christ. Celan's "Tenebrae" taps into an ancient mind-set, set down by Matthew (27:25): "His blood be on us and on our children." It is one thing for Isaiah to speak of "the people that walked in darkness [*in tenebris*]," but quite another for prewar Catholic encyclopedias to say that the Tenebrae service involves "the darkness of the Jewish people who knew not our Lord and condemned Him to the gibbet of the cross."[41]

In Celan's "Tenebrae" the Jews see Christ reflected when they drink "what you shed, Lord," but that image looks like their own. Though "It shined" (*Es glänzte*), Celan on both recordings of the poem says *Es glänzt* ("It shines"), making the past present. "Eyes and mouth stand so open and void, Lord": through Celan's strong verb "stand," these belong to mortally emaciated faces. "We have drunk," they say, as in "Todesfuge" "we drink and we drink."

To bind the Crucifixion into Jewish agony was no interfaith gesture for Celan—or for Marc Chagall, whose Russian-Jewish scenes he admired.[42] In Chagall's crucifixions, the martyr is an East European Jew in a tallit, amid burning scrolls and synagogues, and there is no salvation, suffering goes on.[43] To imagine their death throes "as if / each of our bodies were / your body, Lord," reclaims the Jewish Jesus' suffering from an ecclesiastic ideology that used it against Jews.

German readers who recognize the poem's reversal of Passion motifs still cannot always pull free of the Christian schema.[44] "In 'Tenebrae,'" says one, "human beings watch with Jesus in Gethsemane and then go the Way with Him to Golgotha."[45] Another says that when the body and blood of men, not of Christ, are sacrificed in Celan's poem, this "extends the meaning" of the Eucharist.[46] The vision of universal suffering finds its grandest advocate in the philosopher Hans-Georg Gadamer, who derives a Christian existentialism from Celan's "Tenebrae."[47] "In dying," he says, "each of us is as alone and forsaken as the dying Jesus on the cross." And he speaks of "this commonality between Jesus and us." But the subversions in "Tenebrae" do not support an idea of commonality; nor does the poem's "we" migrate into Gadamer's "us." "Eli, Eli, lama sabachtani?" we hear in the Gospel account of Jesus' final hour, "My God, my God, why hast Thou forsaken me?" (Matt. 27:46). That that cry sounded originally in Psalms or that the Lamentations of Jeremiah form part of the Tenebrae service does not signify a continuity, as far as Jewish history is concerned.

"Tenebrae" closes in quiet entreaty: "Pray, Lord. / We are near," with "Lord" now invoked eleven times. "In the ever-repeated 'Lord,'" Gadamer says, "the person speaking for us recognizes finally that the Jesus who died on the cross remains our Lord." Again that word "us" uproots this poem from the poet's history and religion. Litany, even on the term "Lord," can have an emptying rather than a cumulative effect, as Celan tonelessly reiterates *Herr* . . . *Herr* . . . *Herr* and echoes it in *leer* ("void"). By the end this "Lord" may even be Jewish blasphemy: "Pray, Lord. / We are near"—because dead.

When the poem's first *Nah sind wir* ("Near are we") finally returns as *Wir sind nah* ("We are near"), a prayer has come round by way of language.[48] Celan's title word, *Tenebrae,* has all along had linguistic as well as theologic point for the mother tongue's fatal darkness.

At the same time as "Tenebrae," another lyric emerged, differently inspired but bound to the darkness of tenable words. Eric, the son of Paul and Gisèle, was twenty months old in early spring of 1957 when he spoke his first word, *fleur* ("flower"). This became a poem's working title which Celan then shifted to the German, "Blume."[49] For new speech had to happen in the mother tongue.

The stone.
The stone in the air, which I followed.
Your eye, as blind as the stone.

We were
hands,
we scooped the darkness empty, we found
the word that ascended summer:
Flower.

Flower—a blindman's word.
Your eye and my eye:
they look
after water.

Growth.
Heartwall by heartwall
adds on petals.

One more word like this, and the hammers
will be swinging free.   [1:164]

That sudden turn, from the title "Flower" to "stone" in the first line, hardens
the medium for speech and vision. This logic also links "The stone in the
air" to "Deathfugue"'s "grave in the air." In drafts for "Blume," after "The
stone in the air," Celan wrote: "The shining of the stone, the extinguishing."
Later he cut this, but its tension persists: "Your eye, as blind as the stone."
Celan's "you" may be his mother witnessing the first word of her grandchild,
her namesake.

If "Blume" opens by speaking to the poet's mother, its "we" then speaks
for his wife and him:

We were
hands,
we scooped the darkness empty, we found
the word . . .

Early drafts say "we found each other," which lends a parental sense to
scooping the darkness empty. (They also contain an intimacy later dropped:
"Close to [his] temples you hear him babble: Flower.") Cognate with Celan's
schöpften, "scooped"—rather than "drained" or "baled"[50]—suggests delivering
a birth. The German verb also yields *Schöpfung* ("creation"). And for "darkness" Celan revised *Dunkelheit* to *Finsternis,* bringing Genesis within earshot,
scooping darkness for the advent of speech.

"Every word is a name of God": Celan welcomed this idea a few months
later, reading Gershom Scholem's *The Secrets of Creation.*[51] Visionary tradition
told him that "Flower—a blindman's word" was a speaking blindness, like
that of Tiresias, Oedipus, and the vigilant dead. For the poet orphaned young,
growth by way of language became an open question. Now in 1957, when
"Heartwall by heartwall / adds on petals," "the word" grows from the same
cause as our organ of life and love.[52]

Reaching a buoyant, colloquial tone at the end,

One more word like this, and the hammers
will be swinging free,

"Blume" sounds close to celebration, if also to violence. Behind it, as happens
more and more with Celan, earlier poems set a somber backdrop: "It is time
the stone consented to bloom" (1:37), and for his mother's name, "the

hammers swung free in the belfry of your silence" (1:78). Now a brave word lifts the last moment of "Flower," where hammers "will be swinging free."[53]

Words matter—and the word "word" itself occurs more than any noun except "eye" in Celan's work.[54] A poem such as "Blume" looks like a mosaic of key words: "Flower . . . stone . . . stone . . . air . . . eye . . . blind . . . stone . . . hands . . . darkness . . . word . . . flower . . . flower . . . blind . . . word . . . eye . . . eye . . . heart . . . heart . . . word . . . free." Finding such stringency, Theodor Adorno thought Celan the only authentic postwar writer to stand with Samuel Beckett and made copious notes in his copy of Celan's *Sprachgitter* (1959).[55]

"Speech-Grille," as Celan said of his book title, "voices both the difficulty of all speaking (to one another) and at the same time its structure."[56] The grate in a door keeps persons separate yet permits speech between them, and this was Celan's situation: the more alienated, the more articulate, as in "Speech-Grille," his title poem. "Eyes-round between the bars": in this opening line a German fourth grade saw a prisoner forlornly gazing out at the world.[57] Celan might not have rejected that picture, but an actual *donnée* exists. When he married Gisèle de Lestrange in 1952, her family could not wholeheartedly accept him. In 1955 her mother, then a widow, entered a Breton convent. When the Celans visited, they saw her only through a grille. This may have prompted "Speech-Grille": the French Catholic marquise vis-à-vis an East European Jewish poet, with all the otherness involved in this encounter.

Just at the time he composed "Speech-Grille," Celan wrote to Petre Solomon that his wife was "a truly exceptional human being" to whom "I owe very much."[58] The poem involves her, a Lestrange, as much as her mother:

> (If I were like you. If you were like me.
> Did we not stand
> under *one* trade wind?
> We are strangers.)   [1:167]

Subjunctives, a question, the word "strangers"—all hedge inside parentheses. Still there's a saving element, a pun just audible in German but effaced in translation: that favorable "trade wind," *Passat,* resembles *Passah,* German for Pesach or Passover, the Jewish festival of deliverance. Then "Speech-Grille" ends on an estrangement—

> zwei   two
> Mundvoll Schweigen.   mouthfuls of silence.

—that almost suggests communion.[59]

This poem marked his farewell to "the game of hide-and-seek behind metaphors," Celan claimed years later, and its line "If I were like you. If you were like me" used "for almost the last time" the "deceitful" preposition *wie* ("like").[60] "No one person is 'like' another," he said; "only 'distanced' can my reader understand me . . . always grasping only the grilled bars between us." What separated Celan from his wife's mother alerted him to the grillwork between poet and reader.

Though Celan did not abandon metaphor in 1957, he was trying to fuse its two halves, outer and inner reality. That way, words would not refer but would themselves act and suffer:

Chants:
Eyevoices, in chorus,
read themselves wounded.   [1:169]

As Celan said at the time, "that which happened" in the middle of his European youth left him "wounded by reality and seeking reality"—seeking it through the paradox of "No / voice," God praying "to us," and "two / mouthfuls of silence."

Part Two
Seeking

7
Only Language through Memory
(1958)

"The German lyric is moving, I believe, along other paths than the French," Paul Celan wrote in Paris for the Flinker Bookshop's 1958 almanac, and his words were meant to admonish German listeners while reporting on his own practice. "With the most dismal things in its memory, and dubiousness all around it," Celan said, German poetry "can no longer speak the language that many a ready ear even now seems to expect. Its language has grown more sober, more factual, it mistrusts 'Beauty,' it attempts to be true. Thus it is . . . a 'grayer' language, a language whose 'musicality' has nothing more in common with that 'euphony' which more or less untroubled still tripped tunefully alongside the most frightful things" (3:167).

The pressures of history had impinged on Celan's verse for years, but before 1958 he had not drawn a program from them. He must also have had in mind Gottfried Benn's *Problems of the Lyric* (1951), accounted "the *ars poetica* of the present generation."[1] Benn's early (and temporary) attraction to National Socialism would have prompted Celan's suspicion of this influential document. In it, Benn plumped for "the absolute poem, the poem without belief, the poem without hope, the poem directed at no one." Worse yet, in light of Celan's need to reach through his poems toward a thou, Benn insisted on the modern poem's "undoubtedly monologic impulse."

Prone to anxiety over the "dismal" and "dubious" state of things for a German-speaking Jewish poet, Celan in 1958 wrote to Nelly Sachs (who had fled Germany in 1940 to Sweden) about some poems she had sent: "I thank you, I thank you from my heart. All the unanswerable questions in these dark days. This ghastly mute Not-yet, this even ghastlier, muter No-longer and Yet-again, and in between, what cannot be overcome, even tomorrow, even today."[2] This ghastly mute "No-longer" may refer to the Third Reich, "Yet-again" to a remnant and recrudescent Nazism. His letter added a post-script: "Our three-year-old boy is outside scattering breadcrumbs for the birds: 'Venez moineaux! Venez pigeons!' [Come sparrows! Come pigeons!]."

"Beauty," Celan found, excludes truth, so the language in German poetry must constrict and harden, as his statement for the Flinker almanac goes on to say:

> This language, for all its inalienable complexity of expression, is concerned with precision. It does not transfigure, does not "poetize," it names and posits, it tries to measure the realm of the given and the possible. To be sure, it is never language itself, mere language at work, but always an I speaking from a particular angle of inclination, its own existence, and concerned with outline and orientation. There is not ipso facto reality, reality must be sought and won.

Just at this time, Celan wrote "Sketch of a Landscape":

> Round graves, below. In
> four-beat the year's pace
> on steep steps around them.
>
> Lavas, basalts, worldheart-
> red-heated stone.
> Wellspring tuff,
> where light grew for us, before
> breath.   [1:184]

By hardening language with terms such as "tuff," a rock made of volcanic ash, these lines find a primal speech in geologic space and time.

Celan's austere idiom, mindful of horror, is rooted in his struggle to realize—by way of uninnocent language—"that which happened," *das was geschah*: for years I've relied on this understatement to designate events of 1933–45. The forum in which he struck this quiet note was granted him in January 1958, which saw his first major speech on poetry. A Bremen official had written offering the city's literature prize, and Celan had immediately answered "your so extraordinarily friendly, your so gratifying letter. That I . . . am to receive the prize of the Free Hanseatic City of Bremen: For me this news counts among the finest that has ever reached me! And so, with such a thing bestowed on me now, I must put myself the question: Have you earned this? And tell myself: You must earn it, tomorrow and after."[3]

This effusive gratitude for the Bremen prize has a touch of pathos, given Celan's remark a few months earlier that "Now and again they invite me to Germany for readings. Even the anti-Semites have discovered me."[4] His acceptance speech, given on 26 January 1958, urged harsh truths through an exquisitely ironic tact.

After honorifics to his hosts, Celan starts with a lesson in roots but converts it to a lesson in Jewish memory: *Denken und Danken,*

> Thinking and thanking in our language are words from one and the same source. Whoever follows out their meaning enters the semantic field of: "recollect," "bear in mind," "remembrance," "devotion." Permit me, from this standpoint, to thank you. [3:185]

Celan knew Heidegger's *What Does Thinking Mean?* (1954), which explores this semantic field. But his verbal tour lets his listeners know that thinking entails remembering certain others who also spoke "our language"—*unsere Sprache,* a finely tuned sarcasm as uttered by a Jew in postwar Germany. These others—if, like Celan, they survived—now hold gingerly to the mother tongue. "Erlauben Sie mir," he says politely, "Permit me, from this standpoint, to thank you."

From this standpoint, the Bremen speech goes on to recall the alien origins of the poet being honored in Germany. Each sentence works a barely audible irony:

> The landscape from which I—by what detours! but are there such things: detours?—the landscape from which I come to you might be unfamiliar to most of you. It is the landscape that was home to a not inconsiderable portion of those Hasidic tales which Martin Buber has retold for us all in German. It was, if I may add to this topographic sketch something that appears before my eyes now from very far away—it was a region in which human beings and books used to live.

Self-interruption and understatement veil a grief at origins brutally effaced. The actual "detour" in Celan's sentence covers not only his own migrations but his parents' deportation. His question—"but are there such things: detours?"—invites the audience to recognize persecution and homelessness as integral to a Jewish poet's stance toward postwar Germans. And the gambit of acquainting these Germans with an unfamiliar region points to the Third Reich's usurpation of Eastern Europe.

To name this strange terrain, Celan tells his listeners: "It is the landscape that was home to" Hasidism, and his phrase *zu Hause war*—"was housed," "was born and bred in"—implies the Jewish spirit's onetime rootedness and later eradication from an ancient homeland. What is more, he specifies the movement's legacy: "those Hasidic tales which Martin Buber has retold for us all in German." This may even embed a memory of Celan's mother, who was born in the seat of a Hasidic dynasty that Buber once devoutly visited.[5] It took a bitten-back tact to say "retold for us all in German"—to presume "us all," a Germany-with-Jews now destroyed, if indeed it ever truly existed.

This "landscape from which I come" takes doubly the past tense: "It was . . . —it was a region in which human beings and books used to live." That final verb *lebten* could be "lived," but "used to live" transfers "human beings and books" even further into the past. Jews had lived in Bukovina since the thirteenth century, so Celan's remark that *Menschen* lived there, human beings, seems obvious unless the word *Mensch* suggests what several million Yiddish speakers once meant by it: a real human being. And the fact that books used to live there also points up the loss of an entire culture.

Celan calls this charged reminiscence a "topographic sketch," as if he were simply reminding his audience that the Danube flows east. He doesn't name his Bukovina homeland, implying that they wouldn't recognize the name; and anyway it's gone from postwar maps, "this erstwhile province of the Hapsburg monarchy, now fallen into historylessness." The landscape "might" be unfamiliar, though it fostered a "not inconsiderable" part of Hasidic legend, and he asks "if I may" augment this sketch. A rhetoric anxious not to belabor or presume leaves its listeners exposed. A bottomless understatement—"used to live"—only deepens the void of what cannot be stated. Above all, Celan leaves unspoken the rude words "Jew" and "Nazi."[6]

The loss of homeland, joined to the dilemma of "our language," leads into an itinerary:

Reachable, near and not lost, there remained amid the losses this one thing: language.

It, the language, remained, not lost, yes in spite of everything. But it had to pass through its own answerlessness, pass through frightful muting, pass through the thousand darknesses of deathbringing speech. It passed through and gave back no words for that which happened; yet it passed through this happening. Passed through and could come to light again, "enriched" by all this.

So much purpose moves these words that Celan's listeners could hardly have grasped it in thirty seconds. But certainly they felt the force of "pass through" used again and again, three times in the doubled form *hindurchgehen durch*. Someone or some thing has been *through* too much, day in, day out, as in "Todesfuge"—language itself has. After the "thousand darknesses" that ring of the "Thousand-Year Reich," language could "come to light" again, like ore cropping up from the depths, "enriched."[7] Celan uses quotes to highlight both the irony and the mineralogical sense of the word: that certain ores concentrate their yield while buried with others. Even the word *angereichert* ("enriched") buries Hitler's *Reich* within itself.

Throughout his remarks Celan speaks only of "language" or "speech" (*Sprache*). The adjective "German" never occurs. He is, after all, among fellow-speakers.

> In this language I have sought, during those years and the years since then, to write poems: so as to speak, to orient myself, to find out where I was and where I was meant to go, to sketch out reality for myself.

This view takes after Celan's 1946 sketch, where a slate pencil "skips across the blackish earth . . . looks around, spots nobody, goes on wandering, writes" (F 191). The search for where to go "was event, movement, being under way." These words of Celan's in Bremen, which Heidegger had used since *Being and Time* (1927), claim more than Heidegger did for poetry's penetration of history:

> For a poem is not timeless. Certainly, it lays claim to infinity, it seeks to reach through time—through it [*durch sie hindurch*], not above and beyond it.

Yet doubt intrudes:

> A poem, as a manifestation of language and thus essentially dialogue, can be a message in a bottle, sent out in the—not always greatly hopeful—belief that somewhere and sometime it could wash up on land, on heartland perhaps. Poems in this sense too are under way: they are making toward something.

In a speech on "remembrance" and violent "loss," this hope for a hearing emerges as unappeasable need. "*Voices* in the bowels of the ark" cry out "hear us too" (1:149), and it's those voices as well as German listeners that Celan's poems are moving toward.

A few in his audience may have recognized someone else he was saluting when he called a poem "a message in a bottle." Celan took this image from the silenced poet Osip Mandelshtam and in effect gave it back to him. He had recently bought an edition of Mandelshtam's works, including his essay "On the Interlocutor" (1913), which imagines walking along the dunes and finding a bottle with the name and fate of some shipwrecked poet inside it.[8] In 1958 Celan still believed that Mandelshtam had died in Hitler's 1941 Russian campaign, rather than earlier in Siberia. So adopting this image brings Mandelshtam in reach of the Bremen address.

Celan says that poems are "making toward something":

> Toward what? Toward something standing open, occupiable, perhaps toward an addressable Thou, toward an addressable reality.

Under cover of "perhaps," he intends a poem to seek and even regenerate its hearer. Buber's *I and Thou* (1923) made "Thou" the greeting between human spirits. Now Celan aligns "an addressable Thou" with "an addressable reality," fusing two aims for poetry. His speech ends:

> And I also believe that such lines of thought attend not only my own efforts, but those of other lyric poets in the younger generation. They are the efforts of someone who, overarced by stars that are human handiwork, and who, shelterless in this till now undreamt-of sense and thus most uncannily in the open, goes with his very being to language, stricken by and seeking reality.

Celan feels exposed in a technologic universe (three months before, Sputnik had gone into orbit)—"shelterless," as he did in "l'univers concentrationnaire," another "undreamt-of" cosmos. A flurry of terms—"most uncannily in the open, goes with his very being to language"—adapts Heidegger's sense of the "uncanny" (*unheimlich*) as pure dread at having no true home (*Heim*).

A powerful philosophy stands implicated here. The poet who "goes with his very being to language," with his *Dasein,* is doing what Heidegger postulated (*Dasein* occurs over two thousand times in *Being and Time*[9]). But that language passed through something which Heidegger never brought himself to mention. He referred publicly only once to Nazi genocide, in a 1949 speech in Bremen that he never published: "Agriculture is now a motorized food industry, in essence the same as the manufacturing of corpses in the gas chambers and extermination camps."[10] As Philippe Lacoue-Labarthe comments, this sentence was "scandalously inadequate."

In a way that chastens Heidegger, Celan ends his speech by getting behind language, disclosing himself "stricken by and seeking reality." A double bind in this phrasing grasps the truth patented by Celan's life and work. "Wakening or wound?" he had asked in 1943. Now he knows. The reality that wounded

Celan at Bremen, 1958, with Rudolf Alexander Schröder (Deutsche Verlags-Anstalt)

him he has to pursue. Celan's final German phrase shows this better than English can: *wirklichkeitswund und Wirklichkeit suchend*—"reality-wounded and Reality-seeking."

The 1958 Bremen speech was Celan's first full profession of poetic doubt and faith. How he felt about it, though, is hard to know. Some photographs show him standing shyly next to a hefty Rudolf Alexander Schröder, the German Christian poet whose eightieth birthday the Bremen occasion also celebrated.[11] Celan's wan, thin face has a constrained smile. Next day, an interviewer noticed the poet's "wariness" about how his work might be mistaken. "Celan remains sunk down in the easy chair" at his lodgings, "staring pensively toward his visitor and concentrating solely on the words.

And he is especially on the lookout . . . for misunderstandings. 'I'm prepared for that,' he says with a melancholy smile."[12]

The week after Celan's speech, a Bremen high school class studied an early lyric of his. At first the poem was "completely incomprehensible, we found no coherence," their teacher wrote to Celan, inquiring "whether you didn't want it interpreted at all and we should just let ourselves be guided by the feeling we get in skimming through it."[13] Celan promptly replied that "skimming through" is no way to grasp the sense of a poem. He rehearsed some points from his Bremen speech, using the word "reality" over and over. "Reality for a poem is in no way something that stands established, already given, but something standing in question, that's to be put in question. In a poem, what's real *happens* . . . The poem itself, insofar as it is a real poem, is aware of the questionableness of its own beginning."

The day he wrote this, Celan began a long poem in which "what's real *happens.*" It was his follow-up to "Todesfuge" and moved deeper into inaccessible terrain.[14] "Engführung" (1:197–204) pushes his earlier title further, denoting a fugue's *stretto,* the intense, overlapping entrances of themes, literally a "leading narrowly" or "leading into the straits"—which describes this poem's form and content alike. An English title might be "Straitening," but when a French translation was prepared, Celan approved *Strette* for *Engführung.*[15]

He composed this nine-part "stretto" between February and May 1958, but its genesis reaches further back. By the time Celan wrote "Engführung," he had for years experienced the notoriety of "Todesfuge." One instance of that notoriety gave him a lead for the title of his 1958 poem.

A German journal of socially conscious pedagogy published in 1957 an account of teaching "Todesfuge" to high school seniors.[16] The teacher thanked Celan for permission to reprint his poem, so maybe Celan saw the article. It makes an exceptionally fair effort for its time, yet he could easily have sensed something amiss. To begin with, the journal's editor regretted that "just now Göttingen's city fathers have spoken out against students seeing the film *Night and Fog.*" This item alone, since it was Celan who translated the film's narrative for German audiences, would be disquieting news. What's more, the teacher treated his poem "like a Bach fugue." Her students' quite intelligent responses feature "theme . . . countertheme . . . motif . . . repetition . . . variation . . . modulation . . . coda." When, finally, she asked them, "Do you feel the poem to be an accusation?," in "unanimous protest" they replied: "just the opposite—forgiveness and reconciliation." They saw this poem's pain "raised to the higher level of art, and thus purified, shaped, objectified." No wonder Celan insisted that in poetry, "what's real *happens.*" He saw "Todesfuge" helping German youth to "grasp, master, and surmount" the "shadowy force of our history," as the journal's editor put it in 1957. Yet what happened in

Nazi Europe was not to be mastered and surmounted. Celan closed his Bremen speech with "seeking," and his statement for the Flinker almanac with "reality must be sought and won."

If "Todesfuge" was getting appropriated, he must now write something resistant, working beyond the early form. Curiously enough that 1957 teacher's account, in analyzing "Todesfuge"'s fugal complexities, resorted three times to the uncommon term *Engführung* ("stretto"). Its existential along with its musical sense gave Celan exact incentive, since *eng* is cognate with "angina" and "angst" (and the Hebrew is *tsar,* whence *Mitsrayim,* Egypt, the place of oppression).

This poem's opening, lacking any antecedent, is as stringent as its title:

Verbracht ins	Taken off to the
Gelände	terrain
mit der untrüglichen Spur:	with the unerring track:

Who or what has been *verbracht,* "transferred," "removed"? How and where? Celan once told someone that he had "spent" (*verbracht*) the war years in labor camps.[17] Does *verbracht* have a technical sense too? A French translation of his poem that Celan "guided" begins with *Déporté* ("Deported"),[18] but German documents regularly used the word *deportieren,* and Celan translated *déporter* in *Night and Fog* by *deportieren, verschleppen, aussiedeln* (4:79, 81). For his word *Verbracht,* then, in "Engführung," "Deported" would let in euphemism. Instead, from the victims' standpoint, a German émigrée interned in a French camp recalls: "We knew that Hitler tore Jews from their homes and had them *verbracht* somewhere."[19] In everyday idiom, a whole population and anyone entering this poem is "Taken off to the / terrain / with the unerring track" to find

Grass, written asunder. The stones, white,
with shadows of the blades.

"Surely the people is grass," cries Isaiah from exile (40:7). "My days are like a shadow that declineth, and I am withered like grass," says the Psalmist (102:11). Celan's Biblical resonance has a real basis, for *Night and Fog* begins with color footage of "a strange grass that has sprouted and covered the earth worn down by prisoners' trampling" (4:76). At the end of the film, where there was once roll call, "the grass has resettled again" (4:97). So with "Grass, written asunder," "Stretto" exposes and reclaims, pushing back what has grown over.

We are led into straits of language that will constitute the reality to be explored. On 17 February 1958, the day he began "Engführung," Celan wrote to Petre Solomon: "I've written a certain number of poems, a bit different, I think, from those I've published till now."[20] "Engführung" displaces reality into a text, making the poem into real time, place, and event. Its 171 lines, many only a monosyllable or two, follow an "unerring track" or "trace"— "unerring," because for those "taken off," it led straight to their end, and "trace," because for us this poem forms the only evidence we have:

> Read no more—look!
> Look no more—go!

Mere reading or even witnessing won't do anymore:

> Go, your hour
> has no sisters, you are—
> are at home.[21]

For an exile it catches on the lips to say "you are— / are at home" in a "blackish field," where "the night needs no stars." The first part of "Stretto" ends: "nowhere / are you asked after."

An asterisk (in German *Sternchen,* "little star") occurs between parts 1 and 2:

> . . . nowhere
> are you asked after.
> *
>
> Nowhere
> are you asked after—

This is the first time that Celan marked a poem this way.[22] An asterisk, meaning nothing in itself, breaks yet binds our going. And "nowhere / are you asked after" occurs before, then after, the asterisk, set far right as if overlapping in a fugue, altered—though only slightly—to regulate our pace and to pass from telling to acting. Language in this poem will not be describing much.

> The place where they lay, it has
> a name—it has
> none. They did not lie there. Something
> lay between them. They
> did not see through.
>
> Did not see, no,
> spoke of
> words. None
> awoke,
> sleep
> came over them.

Whoever "they" are (the same people as in "The Vintagers"?), we know that in 1942 Czernowitz Jews were taken off to a place in the Ukraine that the Romanians simply called "Cariera de Piatră" (Stone Quarry).[23] Hence "it has / a name—it has / none." The contradiction jolts us into the grip of language itself. There "they lay" and "did not lie," and only "spoke of words."

And "sleep / came over them." At Celan's hands, sleep is no time-honored metaphor, the little death, but euphemism, exposed on a line of its own:

> sleep
> came over them.
>   *
>
>   Came, came. Nowhere
>   asked after—
> I it is, I,
> I lay between you, I was
> open, was
> audible, I ticked toward you, your breath
> obeyed, I
> it is even yet, you
> still sleep.

Suddenly out of nowhere an "I" insists sixfold that it was present, ticking toward the sleepers—metronome, alarm clock, time bomb.[24] Then after "Years. / Years, years," "a finger" replaces the "I," groping along

> Sutures, palpable, here
> it gapes wide asunder, here
> it grew back together—who
> covered it up?
>   *
>
>   Covered it
>   up—who?

That finger, pointing "here . . . here" to an unhealing wound, splits open a question and exposes "a word." It may be Christ the light that the Jews rejected and/or a language that passed through darkness—these two histories converge:

Kam, kam.	Came, came.
Kam ein Wort, kam,	Came a word, came,
kam durch die Nacht,	came through the night,
wollt leuchten, wollt leuchten.	would lighten, would lighten.
Asche.	Ashes.
Asche, Asche.	Ashes, Ashes.

Nacht.	Night.
Nacht-und-Nacht.—Zum	Night-and-Night.—Find
Aug geh, zum feuchten.	that eye, the moist one.

At its nadir "Stretto" has no "I," "you," "they," or "we," but a single word: "Ashes." And then, both expanding and emptying the sense: "Ashes, Ashes." A decade earlier, Celan had felt the struggle for "ashes of burnt-out meanings and not only that!" (3:157). "Stretto" enacts that struggle. When actuality dumbfounds speech, one repeats, with no hope or with hope in this word only:

Night.
Night-and-Night.

Stripped of the narrative role they had in "Todesfuge," "ashes" and "night" now move toward an eye moist with life and grief. It is hard to carry over Celan's imperative—

Zum	Find
Aug geh, zum feuchten.	that eye, the moist one.

—and still match *leuchten / feuchten,* the rhyme that closed "The Vintagers." Quoting himself, the poet tries for tenable speech.

Celan began this poem on 17 February 1958, resumed work on 20 April, and completed it on 12 May (around the time that Elie Wiesel's *La Nuit* ["Night"] came out in Paris).[25] Maybe the poem's first half came in February. Some letters he wrote during the break in his work display a temper of mind behind this poem being "written asunder." "Inside me there is—may I say this to you?—much laceration," he told a German woman friend in March 1958.[26] Then in mid-April he wrote to a German-Jewish acquaintance about the impossibility of communicating "experiences like ours." Our common "threads to the past," Celan says, "lead into the depth, down to the center . . . where bits of them appear in words." He notes "the slenderer terrain on which German poetry is trying to orient itself," but perhaps "what is past, passing, and vanishing will become more addressable."[27]

To lead into that past, the second half of "Stretto" grows more specific:

Hurricanes.
Hurricanes, from all time,
particle flurries, the rest,
you
know, we've
read it in the book, was
opinion.

This passage compacts sources so hidden that Celan (this once) informed scholars about them.[28] Dante's Paolo and Francesca, reading of Lancelot and Guinevere, became enflamed, and "that day we read no further." But Celan had also read Democritus: "Nothing exists but atoms and empty space, everything else is opinion."[29] He called this "a frightful remark," in which mechanistic forces deny human bonding. "Who isn't alone?" he wrote to Petre Solomon. "Who isn't tormented by anxieties, atomic and otherwise?"[30] At the height of cold war and nuclear threats, can a Paul Celan (Lan-celot) and his French wife Gisèle (Guinevere) hold onto love any more than Paolo and Francesca did? Celan said he "cited" the words of Paolo and Francesca, but "Cited? No, these words *come forth*."

With *Inferno* in mind, "Stretto" feels like a journey to and from the hellish past. After a parody of God's creative *fiat*: "Spoke, spoke. / Was, was," we are led "once again"

above the
bullet trap on
the crumbled wall:

visible, once
again: the
grooves . . .

Resnais' *Night and Fog* showed the yard of Block Eleven at Auschwitz with its infamous black wall "shielded against the ricochet of bullets." To translate that, in 1956, Celan had used *Kugelfang* ("bullet trap" [4:87]), the same word that juts up in "Engführung." Those "grooves," too—bullet scorings in the backstop? channels for the victims' blood?—cinematically come into focus "once / again," now.

Having named this wall, "Stretto" forces across line and stanza breaks:

. . . the
grooves, the

choirs, back then, the
Psalms. Ho, ho-
sanna.

"Hosanna" shouts welcome and praise, like the glorious *Osanna in excelsis* in Bach's B Minor Mass. But in Psalms the Hebrew term means "Save [us] please!" (118:25). Celan's "Ho, ho- / sanna" reduces to a stammer or derisive laughter, with echoes of the German marching song "For we are Hitler's brown-clad host—Huzza, ho-ho!"[31]

All these traces have become present. And "So" (or "Thus") the poem goes on, using a term that Celan has never used before, *Also / stehen noch Tempel*:

So
temples still stand. A
star
may still have light.
Nothing,
nothing is lost.
Ho-
sanna.

By a logic rooted in "Todesfuge," these sanctuaries still stand, if anywhere, at the killing wall. And that verb "stand," throughout Celan's writing, signals perseverance against all odds. Now "A / star / may still have light"—not the sparkling in "Deathfugue" but the Star of David sewn on how many million coats, an extinguished star whose light still reaches us:

Nichts,
nichts ist verloren.

"Nothing" stands on its own, more substantive than negative: "Nothing, / nothing is lost." Possibly "Nothing" itself, our lack of traces and signs, is now gone, thanks to this poem.

In many ways "Stretto" responds to Rilke's tenth Duino elegy, which "sings jubilance and praise" and traffics with "the endlessly dead," especially "the Mothers." Celan's elegy has no such Orphean power. Ending this journey, we come on "groundwater traces." Then an asterisk, and in parentheses those words repeat and overlap. But no new words are spoken. On both recordings of "Engführung,"[32] at the poem's overlaps, Celan's voice after the asterisk becomes slower, softer, sadder—two voicings of the same perception, except that one comes later (like the survivor himself) and takes more pains.

Still in parentheses, nothing other than this poem's beginning brings it to a close, but with a difference:

Taken off
to the terrain
with
the unerring
trace:
Grass.
Grass,
written asunder.)

The poem's opening words recur at the end in split time, a terrain spaced over twice as many lines and thus strange, to be seen anew. "Grass"—the overgrown past—has been "written asunder."[33]

Though work from before and after "Engführung" appears chronologically in *Speech-Grille,* Celan let this poem conclude the volume. The book's "cycles," he said, "are not only structural (but also that); also and above all they're the years, the hours, the (may I say it to you? I may: the frightful) caesuras. These words, these *voices* I have really led narrowly [*enggeführt*]—have let myself be led narrowly by them—into the inexorableness of the last poem (timewise it was not the last, yet I knew it was the last)."[34]

"Stretto," by far Celan's most demanding poem, came just after the Bremen speech, which ends with the poet "stricken by and seeking reality." He told an interviewer in Bremen: "In my first book I was still transfiguring things—I'll never do that again!"[35] "Engführung" reconceives the manner and matter of "Todesfuge," going beyond the pathos of black milk, exploring memory itself as a dimension of the original trauma.[36] The poem's close melds into its opening, the way memory almost coincides with reality. And there is something else here, easy to miss. Not only does an asterisk come after each section, but there is also an asterisk between the title and the first line—a mark devoid of purpose unless we are to link "Stretto"'s last line to its first and set out again, *da capo*. Repeat this to the six-millionth degree, and "Nothing is lost."

8
The Other Voice Your Own
(1958–59)

"Whether the spirit stands on the left? Would that it (still) stood there! But what is spirit? And where, after everything that's happened, is the left? I believe the spirit stands—insofar as it can still maintain its 'verticality'—by itself."[1] In this 1958 letter, Celan condemned the "prettily rhymed banalities" in *Doctor Zhivago* and Boris Pasternak's celebrity: "All this testifies most tragically to the isolation of the spirit in Russia. Do you know about the fate of Mayakovsky? Esenin? Isaak Babel? Boris Pilnyak?" Here he names two poets not at home with Bolshevism who committed suicide and then two writers of Jewish origin who perished in Stalin's purge.

"One of the greatest Russian poets of this century, Osip Mandelshtam," Celan added, "after coming back from Siberian deportation, was murdered by Germans (he was a Jew, like Pasternak)." Then another parenthesis: "(I myself as a Jew was in a camp during the war; later I also had a chance to encounter anti-Semitism Soviet-style.)" And a postscript: "Recently in an auditorium at Bonn University a re-encounter with Nazism took place, on the occasion of a reading." A caricature had been left at his lectern, with the caption: "There's the Jew at the Wailing Wall again. Just look how he bites at his chains!"[2] This was bound to rub wounds that "won't scar over," as Celan's new ending of "*Voices*" had just said.

By naming Pasternak, Esenin, Mandelshtam, and others, Celan was orienting himself. Despite growing recognition in Germany and a wife and child in France, "you are— / are at home" only in a ruinous history (1:197). Ill at ease with the lack of conscience in postwar Western Europe, he began to find his needs someway met by interwar Russian poetry. "When my homeland, the Bukovina, went Soviet," he told the Slavist Gleb Struve, "I learned Russian (under circumstances familiar to you . . .), but only now, years later, have I gladly and gratefully found my way back to this language."[3] What Russian offered was easterly, homeward, counter-Germanic, a memory of revolution, and a purer lyric medium.

When Soviet troops occupied Czernowitz in 1940, Paul Antschel had tried his hand at translating Sergei Esenin (1895–1925), the poet of a lost peasant countryside, of brief hope after October 1917, and ultimately of suicidal despair.[4] Early in 1958 Celan again took up Esenin, choosing lyrics of nostalgia and disillusion. One of them says: "Within my homeland I'm no more at ease" and has the poet revisit his father's house to hang himself (5:173). Another starts out wistfully:

> Near to yellow nettles, near a
> worn-out wattle fence,
> cottages stand lonely—willows
> give them some defence.   [5:167]

Celan made other Esenin translations "to re-establish an image of the poet close to the October revolution."[5] Most of these lyrics ring hollow and hectic, but one speaks of

> Fleeings, fleeings—on toward a
> darkness with no voice.
> Nothing left to us and nothing
> yielding any trace,   [5:179]

and of "wandering between East and West."

Celan once said he "grew up with the writings of Peter Kropotkin and Gustav Landauer" (3:190), revolutionists who impassioned interwar East European Jewry—as did Alexander Blok (1880–1921), whose notorious poem "The Twelve" sprang from a few rapt days in January 1918. Blok got the revolution's brutal wind and wild music into this poem about a Red Guard marauding in Petrograd's snowy streets to purge the old bourgeois world. In his translation, Celan gets all that chaotic energy, a mélange of street talk, slang, slogans, ballads, cursing, crackling onomatopoeia, and Christian vision. He once called attention to the poem's centerpiece:

O thou grief and misery,
Drear thou, deathly
Dreariness!

I've got time I've got a while,
Pass it here, pass it there . . .
Got a knife with blade so thin,
Snap it open, stick it in!

Fly, bourjie, fly . . .
Lord, grant rest and peace to your servant's soul . . .
Dreariness!   [5:35]

Blok's translator was moved by the Russian's last hard years. "He died" in Petrograd, Celan said, "renowned and solitary" (5:623).

In 1958 Gisèle made an etching which speaks for that time and which, like all her work, defies description. His wife's art was, "quite frankly," Celan told someone then, "a bit abstract."[6] This gray oblong, 12 inches by 16 inches, shows a scattering of slender strawlike needles oriented diagonally from the top left. V-shapes thrust their points down toward the right, and splinters move against this. The effect is of a magnetic pull with fragments contrary or converging. This etching was titled (by Celan[7]) "Rencontre—Begegnung" (Encounter), counterpoising the artist's French with the poet's German.

Paul Celan in 1958 had as vital an encounter as any he ever experienced—one he soon began distinguishing with the term *Begegnung*. In May 1957 he had bought the collected works of Osip Mandelshtam (1891–1938),[8] and in October he joined a gathering of German writers which discussed Mandelshtam's image of the poet as a shipwrecked sailor: "The letter sealed in the bottle was addressed to its finder. I found it. That means, then, that I am its secret addressee."[9] At Bremen in January 1958, he said that a poem may "wash up . . . on heartland perhaps" (3:186).

Celan undertook to be that "secret addressee" of his Russian predecessor in 1958. The day before completing "Stretto," 11 May, he began translating

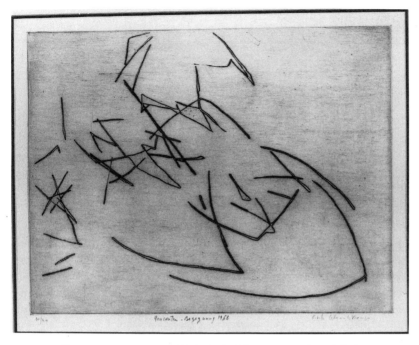

"Rencontre / Begegnung," 1958, Gisèle Celan-Lestrange (Eric Celan)

Mandelshtam, then scarcely known in the West, and finished fourteen lyrics within a week. Among them was "Silentium," whose poet aspires to "a tone, crystalline, from the depth"—except that "from the depth" is wholly the translator's invention (5:57).[10] Many things occasioned this "shock of recognition" (Melville's phrase[11]) in Celan. Mandelshtam—the name means "almond stem," which to Celan meant "Jewish stock"—had worked as a translator and had once attempted suicide. Each grew up close to his mother and because of his father harbored ambivalence toward Judaism. Both underwent political and literary persecution not unrelated to their origins. And after a groundless plagiarism charge, Mandelshtam embraced the "proud title of Jew."[12] This nexus may account for Celan's saying that Mandelshtam "was murdered by Germans" rather than lost in Siberian exile, as was generally believed.

Celan early on translated an elegy which Mandelshtam wrote in 1916 after his mother's funeral. The Russian poem begins:

[This night is not remediable,
but with you there is still light.

At the gates of Jerusalem
a black sun arose.]

Celan translates:

Diese Nacht: nicht gutzumachen,
bei euch: Licht, trotzdem.
Sonnen, schwarz, die sich entfachen
vor Jerusalem.

(This night: not to be made good,
with you: Light, nonetheless.
Suns, black, that kindle
before Jerusalem.)   [5:95]

With a colon after "This night" breaking the original verse movement, Celan takes over Mandelshtam's elegy. Across the break in his German line he transforms "night" into the night his own mother was taken off: *nicht gutzu-macchen* ("not to be made good") refutes postwar Germany's *Wiedergutmachung* ("making good again"), the reparations recently agreed to for Jewish survivors.

Celan could not make a move without transmuting Mandelshtam, while still respecting the Russian 4/3/4/3-beat stanza. A blunt *trotzdem* ("nonethe-less") rhymes with *Jerusalem*; then, by reversing Mandelshtam's last two lines, Celan goes straight from "Light, nonetheless" to "Suns, black" (for the Russian "black sun"). *Sonnen, schwarz*: only a slight shift from the original, yet by multiplying "Suns" and giving "black" its own status in the present rather than the past tense, Celan turns a symbol into a perennial presence.

"At times when an era is ending, the sun turns black," wrote Mandel-shtam's widow, Nadezhda. Mandelshtam's mother died just before Russia's revolution, and "black sun" could attach to both events. During the war Celan saw "black flakes" around his own mother and "black milk" in victims' mouths. Reality, he knew, could preempt the surreal: for one woman in Auschwitz, summer dawn "was not like the sun . . . It was always black to me."[13]

Celan's self-election as addressee persists throughout the elegy. Where Mandelshtam's Jews are "lacking grace and priesthood," Celan calls them "no longer priestly, grace- and holiness-bereft." A year later, reading Walter Ben-jamin on Kafka's characters who "have lost the Holy Writ," Celan penciled a note: "Cf. Mandelshtam, 'They, no longer priestly.'"[14] Kafka's and Mandel-shtam's disaffection tugged at him across the mid-century catastrophe.

At the elegy's end, Mandelshtam's translator takes possession of the "I" entering then:

[And over my mother rang out
voices of the Israelites.

I awoke in the cradle,
lit by a black sun.]

Judenstimmen, die nicht schwiegen,
Mutter, wie es schallt.
Ich erwach in meiner Wiege,
sonnenschwarz umstrahlt.

(Jewish voices, not gone silent,
Mother, they resound.
I awake inside my cradle,
sunblack beams all round.)

Wanting a primary stress in each verse, Celan promotes the "voices" of Mandelshtam's (standoffishly named) "Israelites" to the first line and opens with *Judenstimmen* ("Jewish voices"). And he adds a new thought: they have "not gone silent." Then he takes Mandelshtam's "mother," mentioned with a past tense, and in the present tells his own mother how the Jewish voices resound. Nadezhda said that the mother's death threw Mandelshtam back to his origins: "I awoke in the cradle, lit by a black sun." As at Jesus' crucifixion, she says, the sun darkened, signaling the doom of Jewry in our era.[15] Celan says "I awake inside my cradle," and the "Suns, black" of stanza one are now *sonnenschwarz* ("sunblackly"), which translates Mandelshtam but itself resists translation, making the poem peculiarly Celan's.

True poems, Celan said in Bremen, are "making toward . . . something standing open, occupiable." So are true translations. Mandelshtam himself (Clarence Brown says) turned Petrarch and Racine "not into Russian, but into Mandelstam."[16] Celan's copy of Mandelshtam's works, its introduction closely read and German phrasings written in, along with datings of when Celan translated each poem, is a deeply entered text.

Just as revealing is a lyric that Celan never finished translating, from 1932, one of the Mandelshtams' difficult years.[17] Trying only one line, which in Russian says "And I am alone on all roads," he found a rueful cadence and idiom: *Und bin allein und bins auf allen Wegen* ("And am and stay alone on every pathway"). The alienation Celan shared with Mandelshtam and Kafka made them into alter egos. The Russian poet, he once said, offered "what is brotherly—in the most reverential sense I can give that word."[18]

After the first spate of translations, Celan made no more for two weeks. "All the unanswerable questions in these dark days," he wrote Nelly Sachs in May 1958. Four days later he took up Mandelshtam again, with a poem from 1917, just after the Bolshevik takeover. In it a "young Levite" (the poet himself, says Nadezhda) foretells Jerusalem's (St. Petersburg's) apocalyptic fall. Mandelshtam sees Bolshevism overturning Christian spirituality, with Judaism somehow involved.

Celan copiously marked his copy of this Russian text, and again a trifocal view shows why:

[Among the priests as a young Levite
he stayed on the long morning watch.
Jewish night grew thick over him
and the ruined temple rose up gloomy.]

Die Priester. Und inmitten er. Er wacht,
der junge, der Levit. Es tagt, vor offnen Lidern.
Dicht stand die Nacht um ihn, die Judennacht,
und der zerstörte Tempel stand—stand wieder.

(The priests. And him in the midst. He stands on watch,
the young one, the Levite. It gets light, before open lids.
Thick stood the night around him, the Jewish night,
and the ruined temple stood—stood again.) [5:101]

Curiously enough, in draft Celan began by saying not *Die Priester* but *Die Leuchter,* "the light-bearers," looking toward a "seven-armed candelabra" later in the poem. And where the Russian has no stop, the German fragments every few syllables. Likewise, Celan's penchant for repetition, his ingrained need, shows up when he translates. First "him" and "he," then "the young one, the Levite," stress this prophet's vigilance. Celan's pentameter makes room twice for Jewish "night," which "stood" thick around the Levite, then that verb comes twice more: "the ruined temple stood—stood again." In excess of the Russian, this line recalls "Stretto," completed a few weeks before: "So / temples stand." Celan's "stood—stood again," extending Mandelshtam, builds its own hope against hope.

The young Levite, spotting night and yellow heavens, warns the priests to flee, but they welcome "this black-yellow light, this joy of Judea":[19]

[It was with us, when on the banks of the stream
we wrapped the Sabbath in precious linen
and with the heavy seven-armed candelabra lit up
Jerusalem's night and the fumes of nonbeing.]

Es stand mit uns am Wasser, der Sabbath kam, und wir,
wir hüllten ihn in Linnen, in kostbarstes, der grosse,
der Siebenleuchter flammte, erhellte dieses hier:
die Nacht Jerusalems, den Qualm des Wesenlosen.

(It stood with us by the water, the Sabbath came, and we,
we wrapped it in linens, the choicest, the great one,
the menorah blazed, brightened this here:
the night of Jerusalem, the fumes of nonexistence.)

Celan's "by the water," like Mandelshtam's "banks of the stream," echoes Psalm 137's "By the waters of Babylon." Though true to the Russian, in his fashion, Celan advances "Sabbath" to the first line, and his menorah abandons the Russian grammar to activate its own main clause with an extra verb— "the menorah blazed, brightened." Finally, where Mandelshtam's candelabra lit up "Jerusalem's night and the fumes of nonbeing," Celan has "the night of Jerusalem, the fumes of nonexistence," equating a people with an existence lost in smoke.

Has Celan Judaized the Russian poem? Heidegger, for one, may have had that impression. In reading Celan's Mandelshtam translations, he came upon this one and "brusquely whisked it off the table"—he had only rudimentary Hebrew, he said, and the Old Testament was not his field.[20] Nor, we might add, was "the night of Jerusalem."

Mandelshtam's widow thanked Celan for his work and its closeness in tone, but years later she linked his and Robert Lowell's "very free" versions as "a very far cry from the original text."[21] Expert Slavists have certified Celan's skill.[22] "Can Mandelstam's poetry be translated into another language?" Simon Karlinsky asks. "His verbal splendors, his deliberate ambiguities, the multiple levels of perception which his Russian conveys would seem to make the task of translating him almost superhuman. Yet Paul Celan has managed to transpose Mandelstam into German almost intact."[23] Intact, through Celan's idiosyncrasy—he had said as much in a 1948 love poem: "Only faithless am I true. / I am you, when I am I" (*Ich bin du, wenn ich ich bin* [1:33]). In love or translation, identifying with an other demands truth to oneself.

Celan kept turning to Mandelshtam during 1958, and by January 1959 he had thirty-four translations with ten more planned. He wrote modestly to Gleb Struve, who had edited Mandelshtam's works (and from whose brother in Paris Celan bought all the Mandelshtam he could), making a confession, really a surrogate creed:

> May I say even here, right away, that Osip Mandelshtam lies closest to my heart? . . . I know scarcely any other Russian poet of his generation who *was in time* like him, thought with and out of this time, thought it through to its end, in each of its moments, in its issues and happenings, in the words that faced issues and happenings and were to stand for them, at once open and hermetic. I'm simplifying—I know. Please just see in these lines . . . the impression of my encounter with Mandelshtam's poems: an impression of inalienable truth.[24]

Eager to convey his own *bona fides,* Celan asks whether Mandelshtam (and by implication himself) isn't someone who "wanted to make the Word 'thing-fast,' so to speak—whether in that sense we may not often understand the Word under the sign of a 'last' thingliness.—But where in great poetry is it *not* a question of last things?" Then, like any translator (except perhaps Saint Jerome or Martin Luther), he asks for critique, having only now "gladly and gratefully found my way back to this language. Yet I think I may say that my translations testify to my steadfast effort at philologic exactness. . . . Of course my chief concern, staying closest to the text, was to translate what's poetic in the poem, to render the form, the timbre of speaking." Finally, to explain two slim volumes he is enclosing: "May I also mention here that I myself write poems?" The afterthought confirms a blood-brotherhood between one poet and the other.

"I consider translating Mandelshtam into German to be as important a task as my own verses," Celan once said.[25] One task could even displace the other, for in 1958 and 1959 he composed very little of his own, while taking on Mandelshtam's poems. How he handled them bears out his bond with the writer who said "The word is flesh and bread. It shares the fate of bread and flesh: suffering."

Alongside Mandelshtam's longest poem, "The Horseshoe Finder," written in free verse, Celan's version reads literally, not spurred to invention by formal constraints (5:130). Still, one can hear him seconding this poem's concerns:

> (Human lips
>   with nothing more to say
> keep the shape of the last word they said,
> and a hand still senses the full weight of the jug
> it half
>   spilled,
>   carrying it home.
> What I'm saying now isn't said by me,
> it's dug from the earth, like petrified wheat grain.)

The close of Mandelshtam's poem has Celan writing lines whose bitterness he himself would soon underwrite:

> (Time saws me like a coin, and I—
> I don't suffice, not even for myself.)

At one moment, though, Celan as translator finds a wholesome thought and renders it cleanly:

> (Thrice blessed, whoever brings a name into his song!
> A name-adorned song
> lives longer amongst the others.)

That exclamation mark was added by the translator, who had written his own naming poems. It anticipates Celan's lines of 1962: "The name Osip comes toward you, you tell him / what he already knows . . ." (1:284).

Tell him what he already knows: a bold idea of conversation between poet and translator. When Celan wrote his 1946 sketch about a wandering slate pencil, I wonder if he already knew Mandelshtam's "Slate Ode." In 1959 he came primed to translate it, covering his Russian text with notes. This ode traces a river of time that teaches flint stone to speak. Mandelshtam's

[Language of flint and air,
flint with water, ring with horseshoe,]

becomes more vocal in translation:

(Flint speaks and air, horseshoe speaks
to the ring, water speaks to the flint.)   [5:139]

With Mandelshtam's other great poem, "1 January 1924," Celan did something unusual, besides compressing, repeating, and activating (5:144). These stanzas cry out against the "lying times"—"Oh pain, oh seeking the lost word." To endorse Mandelshtam's focus on a certain date, "1 January 1924," Celan in the Russian text dates his own translation pointedly: "Easter Sunday '59 28.3.59." This ties a later to an earlier poet's thinking "*in time,*" as Celan said, and "through to its end."

When he wrote an afterword for the Mandelshtam selection, he dated that too—"9 May 1959 P.C.," again witnessing his own affidavit. He takes a circuitous approach:

> As for scarcely any of the poets who share his time and destiny in Russia—and these poets, who in Roman Jakobson's not-yet-fathomed remark were "wasted" by their generation, are Nikolai Gumilev, Velimir Khlebnikov, Vladimir Mayakovsky, Sergei Esenin, Marina Tsvetaeva—for OSIP MANDELSHTAM, born in 1891, a poem is the place where what can be perceived and attained through language gathers around that core from which it gains form and truth: around this individual's very being, which challenges his own hour and the world's, his heartbeat and his aeon. All this is to say how much a Mandelshtam poem, a ruined man's poem now brought to light again out of its ruin, concerns us today.   [5:623]

Celan's Bremen speech also used that mining term for language "brought to light" after the thousand darknesses.

Although Celan's work, which also "challenges his own hour and the world's," was not suffering anything like the fate of Mandelshtam's, empathy shadows his afterword:

In Russia, the homeland of this poetry, Osip Mandelshtam's volumes . . . still figure as suppressed, long forgotten, at best mentioned in passing. . . . What was inscribed innermost in the poems, a deep and hence tragic corroboration of his time, also designated his path for the poet.

Swayed by his own sense of things, Celan surmises the poet's ultimate fate:

In the course of Stalin's "purges," in the thirties, Mandelshtam was deported to Siberia. Whether he met his death there or, as even the *Times Literary Supplement* has asserted, after his return from Siberia had to share the fate of so many other Jews in that part of Russia occupied by Hitler's armies: to answer this conclusively is not possible at present.

Just after he began translating, Celan had seen a May 1958 *TLS* review which said that Mandelshtam was "murdered by the invading Germans because he was a Jew" (and which also cited the poet's "stubborn courage . . . he never wrote an unworthy line").[26] It mattered to Celan to keep open the date of Mandelshtam's death.[27]

Since Mandelshtam was little known outside Russia in 1959, we sense an urgency when Celan calls his translations "the first major foreign-language selection in book form" and says that it "will above all be given the chance which among many remains paramount for any poetry: that of mere presence." Celan himself hoped for that much. "The chance my verse has," he had said not long before, "is its presence."[28]

When his selection came out, Celan sent it to Gleb Struve and must have received an enthusiastic reply. He thanked Struve: "Mandelshtam: rarely have I had, as with his poetry, the sense of making my way—making my way alongside the Irrefutable and the True, and it's *thanks to him*. (Again recently, in translating [Valéry's] *La Jeune Parque,* I felt on its heights a nostalgia for that more harsh climate, more ours . . .)."[29] Celan then prepared a March 1960 radio broadcast on Mandelshtam, putting forward the idea of poetry as "*actualized* language" and declaring that "Poems are sketches for existence: the poet lives up to them."[30]

"Poems are sketches for existence," and so are translations, as Celan showed in desiring Mandelshtam's harsher climate. By 1959 he had worked on numerous French, British, American, and Russian poets. But not until he engaged with Osip Mandelshtam did he find himself moving "from darkness to darkness" (1:97), as he put it, likening the "translation" between lovers to that between poets.

Translating, like his own writing, set Celan "under way . . . making toward something." Rimbaud's "Bateau ivre" drew on characteristic energies:

Et dès lors, je me suis baigné dans le Poème
De la Mer . . .

[And since then, I have bathed in the poem
of the sea . . .]

Des Meers Gedicht! Jetzt konnt ich mich frei darin ergehen . . .

(The Sea's Poem! Now I could freely go about in it . . .)   [4:102]

"It's the first *true* German translation," Celan said, composed "in a trance."[31]
He befriended René Char in 1954 and later worked with him on his
wartime Maquis notebooks, which mattered to Celan (4:436–561). When
these translations came out, the Frenchman gave his translator an offprint,
inscribing it "À Paul Celan, à qui je pensais" (To Paul Celan, of whom I was
thinking)—the perfect tribute, as though a Resistance testament had been
looking ahead to its (German-speaking!) translator.

From a less political, more personal impulse, Celan returned to Apollinaire
in 1959, choosing "Les Colchiques" (Meadow Saffron, Autumn Crocus
[4:792]).[32] Before the first line has gone by, the translation declares itself a
revision, erasing the key word "but" from this "poisonous but pretty" flower:

Le pré est vénéneux mais joli en automne
[The meadow is poisonous but pretty in autumn]
Der Herbst lässt seine Wiese so schön, so giftig blühen.
(Autumn makes its meadow bloom so beautiful, so poisonous.)

For Celan, what is beautiful *is* poisonous: the issue arose in "Todesfuge"—
"he shouts play death more sweetly." Where Apollinaire starts with a meadow,
Celan makes autumn the primary force, his *idée fixe*. In the next lines as well,
poison comes first for Celan, and autumn, though gone from the French,
persists as an "it" strewing death:

Les vaches y paissant	*Ein Gift, das schleicht*
Lentement s'empoisonnent	*Streut er den Kühen.*
[The cows grazing there	(Poison that creeps
Slowly poison themselves]	It strews for the cows.)

"Translation" and "transference," after all, share the same root.

Along with Apollinaire, Robert Desnos' "Epitaph" and last poem (he died
in Terezín), Antonin Artaud's "Prayer," lyrics by Nerval, Éluard, Mallarmé,
Baudelaire, as well as Andrew Marvell and Emily Dickinson, all made their
way into Celan's German. "To His Coy Mistress" by Marvell keeps its four-
beat couplets, though not without Celan's punctuations:

But at my back I always hear
Time's winged chariot hurrying near.
Doch hör ich's sausen hinter mir:

Die Zeit! Im Flügelwagen! Hier!
(But rushing at my back I hear:
Time! In its winged chariot! Here!)   [5:377]

Elsewhere Marvell's "ashes" and "grave" do not touch off an allergic reaction as do images of mortality when Celan translates Shakespeare. But he alters "coy" to "mute" (*stumm*), and overcharges these lines:

Now let us sport us while we may;
And now, like am'rous birds of prey,
Rather at once our Time devour,
Than languish in his slow-chapt pow'r.

Lass uns zwei rasche Falken sein,
Verliebt und mördrisch. Dein und mein
Gemeinsam Opfer: diese Zeit,
Die uns den Lähmungen geweiht.

(Let us as two swift falcons fly,
Beloved and murd'rous. Thy and my
Victim in common shared: this Time,
Who cripples us by his design.)

Something essential is lost, if something is also gained, when Celan's verse roughens in dealing with "Time."

More complex motives made Celan attempt the first German translation of Paul Valéry's *La Jeune Parque* ("The Young Fate" [4:114]). Composed during the Great War after a twenty-year silence, this "exercise," said Valéry, was "perfectly useless and released from time."[33] That alone would not have drawn Celan. "My concern is not euphony, it's truth," he had said recently.[34] But Rainer Maria Rilke, for Celan an essential poet, had encountered Valéry as Celan had Mandelshtam.[35] Though he translated Valéry's "Cimetière marin" "rapidly and with a joyous rapture," Rilke maintained until his death that the "wondrous" *Jeune Parque* was "untranslatable at present: (if only someone could convince us otherwise!)."[36]

Celan took up this challenge. Breaking Valéry's first line into six pieces, twice as many as in French, stamped the rendition as his own. He worked from a fine-press copy of *La Jeune Parque,* annotating it thoroughly, and his German version itself came out in a sumptuous bibliophile edition.[37] It was a sizable commitment, over five hundred rhymed alexandrines. With *La Jeune Parque,* Celan did not feel at home "on its heights," he told Struve. Later, after a speech distinguishing poetry from "art," he said he had translated Valéry "so as to earn the right to say something *against art.*"[38]

Just as Celan's Valéry and Mandelshtam books were coming out, he sent friends his *Sprachgitter* (1959). A warm response came from Nelly Sachs, exiled in Stockholm. Celan had written to her in 1957, saying that her books "stand side by side with the truest books of my library" and inviting her to contribute to the Roman journal *Botteghe Oscure*.[39] Because he prized her work, she said "I have a homeland," and she sent him some quite Judaic lyrics, elegies on her mother's death.[40] Celan replied: "You cannot know how much it means to me to receive poems from you yourself, accompanied by such kind words, and to be permitted to disseminate these poems."[41] Though addressing her formally, he closed with a greeting in Hebrew script: "Shalom u'vracha!" (Peace and Blessing!). Sachs's poems appeared in *Botteghe Oscure,* placed—doubtless by Celan—just ahead of his Rimbaud translation.[42]

"Your Book of Radiance, your Zohar is with me," Sachs wrote to Celan about *Sprachgitter*. "The crystalline alphabet-angels transparent to spirit . . . I went out to kneel on the doorsill full of dust and tears."[43] Telling Celan that his book was like the Zohar, the germinal thirteenth-century text of Kabbalah mysticism, struck with special force, as they had both read Scholem's edition of the Zohar.[44] For Celan to hear an older Jewish poet speak of *"Voices,"* "Tenebrae," and "Stretto" in the same breath with the Book of Splendor and Secrets shed a keen light on dark days.

The summer after Celan's book came out, his connection with another older German Jew inspired a new kind of writing. In July 1959, with his wife Gisèle and four-year-old son Eric, he went to Sils-Maria in the Engadine region of the Swiss Alps. There he was to have met the sociologist Theodor Adorno. But Celan returned early to Paris, and so—"not accidentally," he said—missed seeing Adorno.[45] A month later, out of this missed encounter, Celan wrote his only prose fiction, if that term can describe the talky yet poetically cadenced "Gespräch im Gebirg" (Conversation in the Mountains), a sort of folktale where Jew Little meets Jew Big—Klein and Gross—and they schmooze for a while (3:169–73).

How was it that Adorno, or a failed encounter with him, gave rise to this little tale? In March 1959 Celan had bought a volume by Adorno and had marked up a sympathetic essay on Heine's alienation within the German language.[46] Further, Adorno had said in 1955, "After Auschwitz, to write a poem is barbaric,"[47] which was taken to refer to "Todesfuge"—a stricture that pained and angered Celan (though Adorno, when he made it, probably did not know Celan's poem). Inscribing an offprint of "Gespräch im Gebirg," Celan mentioned Sils-Maria, "where I was to meet Herr Prof. Adorno, who I thought was a Jew."[48] With this dig he had in mind that Theodor Wiesengrund had suppressed his Jewish father's name and adopted his Catholic mother's name, Adorno. When the two did meet later, Adorno said that Celan should have stayed longer in Sils, then he would have met "the real Jew

Gross, Gershom Scholem," whose recovery of the Jewish mystical tradition was beginning to influence Celan.[49]

"Conversation in the Mountains," brief yet gabby, humorous yet fateful, reflects on selfhood, language, perception, God, and nature by way of a journey into the mountains. What Celan wrote resembles, if anything, a cross between Ingmar Bergman and Samuel Beckett.

A prototype for "Gespräch im Gebirg" was the novella Lenz, by Georg Büchner (1813–37): "On the 20th of January Lenz went walking through the mountains [durchs Gebirg]," where he wanders in search of something, wrestles with lightning "like Jacob," and "hears a voice in the mountains," till madness overcomes him.[50] "I am the Wandering Jew," Lenz cries, and "Don't you hear the horrible voice . . . that we customarily call silence?" Celan later recalled Lenz and his own "little story" with its "roundabout paths from thou to thou . . . paths on which language gets a voice, these are encounters" (3:201).

Another possible source was Nietzsche, who in Sils-Maria conceived the idea for Also sprach Zarathustra: "When Zarathustra was 30 years old, he . . . went into the mountains." Under morning and midday sun, Zarathustra announces the death of God—a paradox not lost on the survivor-poet working out his own transvaluation of values. In Heidegger's Nietzsche (1961) Celan lit on a saying of Zarathustra—"Not only one sun had gone down for me"[51]— that jibed with the opening of his own 1959 story: "One evening the sun, and not only that, had gone down" (Eines Abends, die Sonne, und nicht nur sie, war untergegangen). The mere aside "and not only that" opens up Celan's tale to the European Jewish catastrophe, or Untergang. Since Nazism co-opted the creator of the "Superman," Celan felt some sympathy with Nietzsche and inscribed a copy of his story: "In memory of Sils Maria and Friedrich Nietzsche, who—as you know—wanted to have all anti-Semites shot."[52]

Also hovering behind "Conversation in the Mountains" was Franz Kafka, whose "Excursion into the Mountains" (1904) Celan translated into Romanian after the war. "I'd gladly—so why not—go on an excursion with a group of pure nobodies," runs this monologue. Besides semantic links to Celan's "Conversation," which calls God "No One" and laments a language made of "pure It," Kafka's tone—"Our throats become free in the mountains!"—sounds a little like Jew Klein's garrulous voice.

Above all, "Gespräch im Gebirg" owes to Martin Buber, whose philosophical writings and retellings of Hasidic tales Celan was reading during the late 1950s. Buber's "Gespräch in den Bergen" (Conversation in the Mountains, 1913) expounds the I–Thou encounter that concerned Celan.[53] On his birthday in 1959, Celan bought a book about Buber and underscored his speech philosophy: "Creatures stand within the secret of Creation, of Speech . . . We can say thou, because thou is also said to us."[54] And this: "Spirit is not in the I, but between I and Thou." These principles underpin Celan's "Conversation in the Mountains," which turns on dialogue: "I who can say to you" . . . "because I'm asking you" . . . "I, who can say, could have said, all that to you" . . . "do you hear me, you hear me."

A visceral presence in the "Conversation" must surely be Mandelshtam. When Celan wrote it, his translations of Mandelshtam were about to come out, and in Mandelshtam's essay "On the Interlocutor," poetry is the search for an other and oneself—as Celan's translations make clear. In his "Gespräch," "It was . . . myself I encountered," Celan said (3:201). "Conversation in the Mountains" goes from evening until night, through interruptions, self-corrections, contradictions, and questions answered with questions, "on the way to myself."

One evening the sun, and not only that, had gone down, then there went walking, stepping out of his cottage went the Jew, the Jew and son of a Jew, and with him went his name, unspeakable, went and came, came shuffling along, made himself heard, came with his stick, came over the stone, do you hear me, you hear me, I'm the one, I, I and the one that you hear, that you think you hear, I and the other one—so he walked, you could hear it, went walking one evening when something had gone down, went beneath the clouds, went in the shadow, his own and alien— because a Jew, you know, now what has he got that really belongs to him, that's not borrowed, on loan and still owed—, so then he went and came, came down this road that's beautiful, that's incomparable, went walking like Lenz through the mountains, he, whom they let live down below where he belongs, in the lowland, he, the Jew, came and he came.

Came, yes, down this road, that's beautiful.

And who do you think came toward him? Toward him came his cousin, his kin and first cousin, older by a quarter of a Jew's lifetime, he came along big, he too came in his shadow, the borrowed one—because I'm asking you, I'm asking, who, if God's made him be a Jew, comes along with something his very own?—, came, came big, came towards the other one, Gross came up to Klein, and Klein, the Jew, bade his stick be silent in front of Jew Gross's stick.

So the stone was silent too, and it was quiet in the mountains where they walked, himself and that one.

So it was quiet, quiet, up there in the mountains. It wasn't quiet for long, because when one Jew comes along and meets another, then it's goodbye silence, even in the mountains. Because the Jew and Nature, that's two very different things, as always, even today, even here.

So there they stand, first cousins, on the left is Turk's-cap in bloom, blooming wild, blooming like nowhere, and on the right, there's some Rampion, and *Dianthus superbus,* the superb pink, growing not far off. But they, the cousins, they've got, God help us, no eyes. More precisely: they've got eyes, even they do, but there's a veil hanging in front, not in front, no, behind, a movable veil; no sooner does an image go in than it catches a web, and right away there's a thread spinning there, it spins itself around the image, a thread in the veil; spins around the image and spawns a child with it, half image and half veil.

Poor Turk's-cap, poor Rampion! There they stand, the cousins, standing on a road in the mountains, the stick is silent, the stone is silent, and the silence is no silence, no word's going mute and no phrase, it's merely a pause, it's a word-gap, it's a vacant space, you can see the syllables all standing around; tongue is what they are and mouth, these two, like before, and the veil is hanging in their eyes, and you, you poor things, you're not there and not blooming, you do not exist, and July is no July.

The babblers! They've got, even now, with their tongues bumping dumbly against their teeth and their lips going slack, something to say to each other! Alright, let them talk . . .

"A good ways you've come, you've come all the way here . . ."

"So I have. I've come like you."

"Don't I know it."

"You know it. You know and you see: Up here the earth has folded over, it's folded once and twice and three times, and opened up in the middle, and in the middle there's some water, and the water is green, and the green is white, and the white comes from up further, comes from the glaciers, now you could say but you shouldn't, that that's the kind of speech that counts here, the green with the white in it, a language not for you and not for me—because I'm asking, who is it meant for then, the earth, it's not meant for you, I'm saying, and not for me—, well then, a language with no I and no Thou, pure He, pure It, d'you see, pure They, and nothing but that."

"I know, I know. Yes I've come a long way, I've come like you."

"I know."

"You know and you're still asking: So you've come anyway, you've anyway come here—why, and what for?"

"Why and what for . . . Because maybe I had to talk, to myself or to you, had to talk with my mouth and my tongue and not just with my stick. Because who does it talk to, the stick? It talks to the stone, and the stone—who does *it* talk to?"

"Who should it talk to, cousin? It doesn't talk, it speaks, and whoever speaks, cousin, talks to no one, he speaks, because no one hears him, no one and No One, and then he says, he and not his mouth and not his tongue, he and only he says: D'you hear?"

"You hear, says he—I know, cousin, I know . . . You hear, he says, I'm there. I'm there, I'm here, I've come. Come with my stick, I and no other, I and not him, I with my hour, undeserved, I who was touched, I who was not touched, I with my memory, I feeble-memoried, I, I, I . . ."

"Says he, says he . . . You hear, he says . . . And HearestThou, of course, HearestThou, he says nothing, he doesn't answer, because HearestThou, that's the one with the glaciers, the one who folded himself over, three times, and not for humans . . . The Green-and-White there, the one with the Turk's-Cap, the one with the Rampion . . . But I, cousin, I, I'm standing here, here on this road I don't belong on, today, now, when it's gone down, it and its light, I here with my shadow, my own and alien, I—I, I who can say to you:

—On the stone is where I lay, back then, you know, on the stone slabs; and next to me, they were lying there, the others, who were like me, the others, who were different from me and just the same, the cousins; and they lay there and slept, slept and did not sleep, and they dreamt and did not dream, and they did not love me and I did not love them, because I was just one, and who wants to love just one, and they were many, even more than those lying around me, and who wants to go and love all of them, and—I won't hide it from you—I didn't love them, those who could not love me, I loved the candle that was burning there, to the left in the corner, I loved it because it was burning down, not because *it* was burning down, for *it* was really *his* candle, the candle that he, the father of our mothers, had kindled, because on that evening a day began, a certain one, a day that was the seventh, the seventh, on which the first was to follow, the seventh and not the last, I loved, cousin, not it, I loved its burning down, and you know, I've loved nothing more since then;

nothing, no; or maybe what was burning down like that candle on that day, the seventh and not the last; not the last, no, because after all here I am, here, on this road which they say is beautiful, well I'm near the Turk's-cap and the Rampion, and a hundred yards further, over there, where I can go, the larch climbs up to the stone-pine, I see it, I see it and don't see it, and my stick, it spoke to the stone, and my stick, it's keeping silent now, and the stone, you say, can speak, and in my eye the veil is hanging, the movable one, the veils are hanging, the movable ones, you lift one and the second's already hanging there, and the star—oh yes, it's above the mountains now—, if it wants to go in, it will have to get married and soon not be itself anymore, but half veil and half star, and I know, I know, cousin, I know, I met you, here, and we've talked, a lot, and the folds there, you know, for humans they're not and not for us, who went walking and came on each other, we here under the star, we, the Jews who came here, like Lenz, through the mountains, you Gross and me Klein, you, the babbler, and me, the babbler, we with our sticks, we with our names, unspeakable, we with our shadow, our own and alien, you here and I here—

—I here, I; I, who can say, could have said, all that to you; who don't say and haven't said it to you; I with the Turk's-cap on the left, I with the Rampion, I with what burned down, the candle, I with the day, I with the days, I here and I there, I, companioned perhaps—now!—by the love of those not loved, I on the way to myself, up here."

Whatever gave rise to it—missing Adorno, mulling over Büchner, Nietzsche, Buber, Kafka, translating Mandelshtam—this tale voices long-held concerns about language, speech, and naming, all in a talky vein.

To move into speech is to meet stumbling blocks: a Jew's "unspeakable" name (for Nazis, or like the ineffable divine name); the "stick" and "stone" of blindness and muteness (or of a deeper vision); a road still "beautiful" for those who made Jew Klein live "down below where he belongs"; the Jew fallen from Nature which God made "not for you and not for me"; a "language with no I and no Thou."

Jew Klein speaks to a "No One" God he calls "HearestThou" (*Hörstdu*), who "says nothing, . . . doesn't answer." "HearestThou": Celan's invented name for God stems from the watchword of Judaism, the *Sh'ma*: "Hear, O Israel . . ." This God became a No One whom Jews prayed to, a HearestThou who didn't answer when "One evening the sun, and not only that, had gone down."

What matters throughout "Conversation in the Mountains" is how things are voiced and heard. To begin with, "the Jew" is not the proper term *Jude*; it's *Jud,* "Yid." Though this smacks of anti-Semitism in Germany, in Yiddish mouths it has a homey sound. It's *the* Jew we're presented with, the type, as in centuries of propaganda. Yet the full naming, *der Jud und Sohn eines Juden* ("the Jew and son of a Jew"), goes behind racial stigma to Jewish custom, which always identified a boy as his father's son. Celan's "Conversation" starts with a semiotic flip, the tag of shame a mark of pride. Likewise "the star— oh yes, it's above the mountains now"—marks the onset of the Sabbath and, as the Star of David, forms a shield as well as a badge of persecution.

One word points up the problem of human speech: *Die Geschwätzigen!* "The babblers! They've got, even now, with their tongues bumping dumbly against their teeth and their lips going slack, something to say to each other!" That word crops up again: "the Jews who came here . . . you Gross and me Klein, you, the babbler, and me, the babbler." *Geschwätz*—a common enough word. Kafka liked it, and for Heidegger it meant everyday talk cut off from true being. To translate the word as "babble" (rather than "prattle," "chatter," or "gossip") hints at Babel and the loss of original language. For in Walter Benjamin's essay "On Language in General and on the Language of Man," *Geschwätz* designates empty speech after the Fall, speech without Adam's power of naming (which emerges only when Jew Klein names certain flowers and trees).[55] The "babbling" of Celan's Jews is a comedown—via the cataclysm that ruined Benjamin—from God-given speech.

This talk of theirs, it's halting, doubled back, dividing and divided against itself, like the self it speaks. A translation ought not to smooth out the idiom, the accents I've absorbed, again and again, in Celan's reading of "Gespräch im Gebirg."[56] His voice finds supple rhythms and soft or sad inflections quite different from the enunciation heard in his recordings of poems. Sometimes in this dialogue you catch the shrug behind it, elusive yet vital. Celan said the "Gespräch" was "actually a *Mauscheln*" between him and Adorno—that is, a sort of jabber that Germans overheard between Jews, *Mauscheln* being an old slur coined from Moishe, Moses.[57]

Above all, this talk will not be made *judenrein,* as the Third Reich wanted Europe: "pure of Jews," who had used Yiddish there for a thousand years. The "Conversation" tastes of spoken Yiddish—and here I think of Kafka surprising himself with a love for that language. Celan reaffirms the Jewish mother tongue by livening up the cognate German tongue.[58] The Yiddishisms and Judeo-German throughout his "Gespräch," the repetitions, run-ons, contractions, inversions, diminutives, interrogatives, and idioms such as *Gott sei's geklagt* ("God help us")[59]—all these merit care in translation precisely because they incurred contempt in Europe (as even in Celan's proudly "Austrian" upbringing) and because Yiddish was obliterated along with its speakers.

With these "cousins," as Jew Klein calls them, meaning everyone "gone down" in the catastrophe, he ponders his kinship, and the conversation contracts into monologue. He tells "you" (who have by now become his cousin too) that *damals,* "back then," he did not love his kin, "who were like me, the others, who were different from me." "On the stone is where I lay . . . and they lay there and slept." Owning up to his apartness, Jew Klein finds a voice and something to love. "I loved the candle that was burning there" and "a day that was the seventh, the seventh, on which the first was to follow." These words virtually name the Sabbath. When candles are kindled (by a mother) at the close of the week, what seems a burning down, the last of something, turns into a beginning. "I loved its burning down," says Jew Klein, "and you know, I've loved nothing more since then." Celan's recorded voice here has a plaintiveness, that of loss within survival—"because after all here I am."

It's "goodbye silence" I hear Celan saying in this tale from the summer of

1959, drawing a communal self from a mortally wounded Yiddish-German. Recalling those others who lay around him, Jew Klein walks along "paths on which language gets a voice" (as Celan later put it), saying "I here and I there, I, companioned perhaps—now!—by the love of those not loved, I on the way to myself."

9
With and Against the Pain
(1959–60)

"Oh you can hardly imagine how things really look again in Germany," Celan wrote in a headlong hand to Nelly Sachs in 1959.[1] "You see—oh, I know how much I'm burdening you with this, but I must let you know about it— my latest experience." After signing himself warmly, he adds: "And nobody answers these fellows! Even that—the answering—is left up to the Jews. The others write books and poems 'about' it. . . ." As for those "others" failing to answer insults, Celan has in mind well-meaning German authors who wrote on anti-Semitism. And one word needs no explanation between survivors: "how things really look *again* in Germany."

With the promptness of a fellow-sufferer, Nelly Sachs answered this letter the day she got it: "Paul Celan, dear Paul Celan—blessed by Bach and Hölderlin—blessed by the Hasidim."[2] Celan in turn wrote back at once: "Now here is the letter this Blöcker addressed to me . . . You know the 'old story': naturally he has 'his Jew,' naturally he rejects my 'imputations' etc. . . . Only he can't find that single, so simple word: 'I'm sorry, I see what I've done.'"[3] Then the letter takes up "Blöcker's anti-Semitism."

What touched off this anguish and anger can be identified, on the face of it. Günter Blöcker, a prolific literary critic, published a brief review of Celan's third book, *Sprachgitter,* in a Berlin daily.[4] In it, he said: "Celan's lyrics only seldom correspond to an object. As a rule, they develop their verbal filigree like cobwebs out of the glands of language itself, so to speak. Without exception, Celan's store of metaphors is not won from reality nor serves it." Did Blöcker follow "Stretto" to the "bullet trap at the crumbled wall" only to arrive at verbal filigree?

Blöcker's letter to Celan referred to Jewishness, and that rankled, because the insult had occurred on (larger) literary ground. Blöcker had called Celan's verses "odorless," "graphic images" with a chiefly "combinatory" quality. "Nor is their want of concrete sensuousness completely made up for by musicality. The author does work willingly with musical concepts: the much-praised 'Todesfuge' from *Mohn und Gedächtnis* or, in the present volume, 'Engführung.' Yet those are really contrapuntal exercises written on music paper or by wordless touch—eye music, optical scores." But "Engführung" drove far beyond "Todesfuge." The critic cancels this by labeling Celan's major poems "contrapuntal exercises."

Another notion of Blöcker's may have been meant innocently, but stood little chance of being taken that way: "Celan has greater freedom vis-à-vis the German language than most of his poet colleagues. That may owe to his origins. Language's capacity for communication hinders and burdens him less than others. Indeed this often induces him straightaway to operate in the void." For someone dedicated since 1945 to purifying his mother tongue, someone just appointed Lecturer in German at the École Normale Supérieure, this pointing at "his origins" must have galled Celan's Jewish and authorial selves alike.

Not surprisingly, Blöcker omitted this review from a 1962 collection that contains everything else possible, including sympathetic pieces on Joseph Roth, Else Lasker-Schüler, and Gertrud Kolmar.[5] Was Celan's reaction to Blöcker excessive? Many other reviews of *Sprachgitter* had appeared, some by distinguished German poets and critics deeply attuned to the book. Celan's vehemence exposes a wound that will not heal—will only, from now on, deepen.

Witness him at cross-purposes even with Johannes Bobrowski (1917–65), an East Prussian Christian poet sympathetic to Jewish experience, a sworn anti-Fascist. In March 1959 Bobrowski told Peter Jokostra he disliked Celan's phrase "A word—you know: a corpse" (1:125), because it sounded charnel and denied the "efficacy" of poetry.[6] Jokostra then took it upon himself to seek clarification from Celan, who replied tersely, citing the rest of his phrase: "Come let us turn / its eye heavenward."[7] Celan also linked his faith in poetry to "Kafka's statement, 'The fact that there is nothing but a spiritual world, takes away our hope and gives us certainty!' I've always read that as if it gave grounds for being here, living, breathing." Bobrowski stiffened against Celan, calling him (to Jokostra) "at best a perfume factory," then relented. Celan sent Bobrowski the Mandelshtam translations and in November 1959 wrote warmly to him.[8] But when Bobrowski later wanted to dedicate to Celan a poem in the spirit and very idiom of the Jewish poet, Celan brushed it off— "that's no concern of mine."

A *contretemps* with Heidegger in 1959 had more obvious cause. Patent Heideggerisms marked Celan's 1958 Bremen speech, and that year he also sent Heidegger poems by his friend Klaus Demus.[9] "They are the poems of one who esteems you," Celan said, signing himself "In sincere gratitude." But soon afterward Heidegger "had a curious wish," as Ingeborg Bachmann described it. "For a Festschrift on his seventieth birthday he requested his publisher to get a poem from Paul Celan and one from me. And we both said no"—though Celan's friend René Char, among others, agreed.[10] Evidently the philosopher's 1935 Rectoral address welcoming Nazism, plus his long failure to recant after the war, was more than Celan and Bachmann could overlook.

Alert to Germany's use of his work, Celan recorded "Todesfuge" around 1958 but never again. The poem became too notorious. He did write one lyric, though, that focused on the core action of his early poem—digging earth. This was his first publishable piece after the year of working on Mandelshtam.

"There was earth inside them" dates from late July 1959, just after the Sils-Maria trip that prompted "Conversation in the Mountains." "Es war Erde in ihnen," which headed Celan's next collection, is one of his first untitled poems, so avoiding any single tag of meaning:

THERE WAS EARTH INSIDE THEM, and
they dug.

They dug and dug, and so
their day went past, their night. And they did not praise God,

Celan, 1958, photograph by Gisèle Celan-Lestrange (Eric Celan)

who, so they heard, wanted all this,
who, so they heard, witnessed all this.

They dug and heard nothing more;
they did not grow wise, invented no song,
devised for themselves no sort of language.
They dug.

There came then a stillness, there came also storm,
all of the oceans came.
I dig, you dig, and the worm also digs,
and the singing there says: They dig.

O one, o none, o no one, o you.
Where did it go, when it went nowhere at all?
O you dig and I dig, and I dig through to you,
and the ring on our finger awakes. [1:211]

Because *graben* ("dig") is akin to *Grab* ("grave"), the terrain of "Deathfugue"
lies nearby, where day and night pass as Jews shovel their own graves. "They"
still pull at Celan's pen.

These diggers who "did not praise God" stem from a Psalm: "The dead
praise not the Lord, Neither they that go down into silence" (115:16).
Immediately after the war, Jacob Glatstein began a Yiddish poem:

We received the Torah in Sinai
and in Lublin we gave it back.
Dead men don't praise God.[11]

Celan's laconic lines belong to a new psalter and its defunct covenant with
God,

who, so they heard, wanted all this,
who, so they heard, witnessed all this.

der, so hörten sie, alles dies wollte,
der, so hörten sie, alles dies wusste.

I've touched up *wusste* ("knew") to "witnessed," to get Celan's rhythm and
alliteration, his psalmlike incremental repetition.

Agelong instruments of praise and lament, Psalms also set off Celan's line
"they did not grow wise, invented no song." In Psalm 107:43, "Whoso is
wise, let him . . . consider the mercies of the Lord," and in Psalm 98:1, "Sing
unto the Lord a new song, For He hath done marvelous things." As in
"Deathfugue" with its command to "sing up and play," song—and even
language—goes under when the order to dig is intoned twelve times over.

Some grace still flows from Celan's hymnal cadence—"There came then a stillness, there came also storm"—as when, in Psalms, "they cried unto the Lord" and "He made the storm a calm" (107:29), or when Elijah beholding wind, earthquake, and fire then heard "a still small voice" (1 Kings 19:12). But with a flood ending it all for Celan, grace is reversed.

His new order impinges on language itself, as the voice jumps to a present-tense "I dig, you dig" (*Ich grabe, du gräbst*). Since "no song" and "no sort of language" were devised while "they dug," they (and we) must relearn language, conjugating *graben*. The paradigm in Western civilization has always been one of love: *amo, amas, amat*. Now another verb takes over: "I dig, you dig, and the worm also digs."

"O one, o none, o no one, o you"—or better, in the German's waltzing rhythm, *O einer, o keiner, o niemand, o du*: the voice cries to a company of pronouns with open-mouthed *o*'s, ciphers in search of someone. Celan's "Conversation in the Mountains" deplores "a language with no I and no Thou," and speaks to the "No one" God (3:172). The grammar of survival requires personal pronouns.

"There was earth inside them" ends with a lift as its speaker goes straight to *du*:

> O you dig and I dig, and I dig through to you,
> and the ring on our finger awakes.

Now the digging leads to a ring and an awakening: is it the Nibelungs' ring of buried gold? If so, what of the rings pulled from the fingers of Jews about to be slaughtered? Celan's ring seals a bond with those who dug. In French, for instance, instead of *anneau* for "ring," *alliance* would mean "wedding ring" and also "covenant."[12]

The day after finishing "There was earth inside them," Celan bought *Aufruf zum Sozialismus* by Gustav Landauer, the German-Jewish anarcho-socialist murdered in 1919 when the Bavarian revolution was crushed. A few days later he got Jakob Wassermann's book on Hofmannsthal. Also in late 1959, Celan was reading Walter Benjamin on Kafka and Hölderlin. In September he bought a French translation of Blok's "The Twelve" and two books by the Russian-Jewish philosopher Lev Shestov. When Celan's Mandelshtam collection came out in November, he wrote in it to his wife, Gisèle: "Near our seven-branched candlestick, near our seven roses." And for Nelly Sachs, he inscribed his Mandelshtam in Hebrew: "If I forget thee, Jerusalem, let my right hand forget her cunning"[13] (Ps. 137:5). That December he underlined in Martin Buber, "Every name is a step toward the consummate Name, as everything broken points to the unbroken."[14] Twice Celan noted Buber's words: "All of time is immediate to redemption."

At the Librairie Levy in Paris, on 30 January 1960, Celan bought several volumes: Buber's *Three Talks on Judaism*, Franz Rosenzweig's translations from

Judah Halevi, a 1905 monograph on the Jew in German literature, and one book that afforded a way, he later said, into understanding his poetry. *Vom Judentum* ("On Judaism"), published by Kurt Wolff in 1913 for Prague's Zionist Bar Kochba circle, gathered contributions from twenty-five leading figures.[15] Kafka owned a copy.[16] Celan in his own copy marked up only "The Sanctification of the Name," by Kafka's friend Hugo Bergmann. He scored many sentences in the margins, and above the opening paragraph Celan wrote the Hebrew of Leviticus 22:31–32: "And ye shall keep My commandments, and do them: I am the Lord. And ye shall not profane My holy name, but I will be sanctified among the children of Israel: I am the Lord who sanctifies you." What is even more surprising: where Biblical Hebrew has the unpronounceable letters יהוה ("Yahveh") for the name of God, and we would say "the Lord" or *Adonai,* Celan omitted any letters at all, inserting three dots—this, from someone who since his bar mitzvah had scarcely entered a synagogue. Do not profane the holy name: the poet observed that literally.

Elsewhere in Bergmann's essay on the naming of God, Celan underlined a Talmudic saying: "Whoever pronounces the Name, loses his share in the world to come." In hundreds of sources that interested him, Celan read to discover or prove his own insights. Here he had in mind "Conversation in the Mountains," where Jew Klein babbles of "No one" and "HearestThou." If language had any point after "that which happened," it was to name the eclipse without profaning it.

The strain of Jewishness came home to Celan in a startling way at this time. Among his reference works he kept a copy of the *Philo-Lexikon* (Berlin, 1935), a "Handbook of Jewish Knowledge." (Its issuance alone was a form of resistance, like the Schocken Bücherei series of Jewish writings published in Berlin from 1933 to 1939.) Stuck into this small volume, which teems with information and illustrations, I found a clipping torn from the *Frankfurter Allgemeine Zeitung* of 16 February 1960, with this headline:

CRIMINAL OFFICIALS CARRIED OUT EXECUTION ORDER
A TRIAL FOR THE MURDER OF 300 JEWS BEFORE THE WEST BERLIN JURY

The article concerns a sixty-eight-year-old legal counselor, Alois Hülsdünker, who in 1942 was sent to the Ukraine because he refused to leave the Catholic Church and join the SS. There, in Berdichev, he was ordered to "liquidate" some four hundred Jewish prisoners, "with women among them." "He had the order carried out" by SS men. "'I knew that I was taking part in a crime,' said Hülsdünker, but troubled in conscience he thought of his wife and six children. Had he refused to carry out the order, he would have come before a court-martial and himself been shot."

What must have caught Celan's attention, besides the newspaper's sympathy for religious and familial scruples, was that these murders occurred in

July 1942, 80 miles north of where his own parents were deported at that time. Hülsdünker eventually received a light, three-year sentence. After all, the jury reasoned, he was very Catholic; it had been his "misfortune" to be sent where a camp existed; and for seventeen years since then he had been a law-abiding citizen.[17]

By 1958, West German papers had begun reporting Nazi criminals in the government, Nazis in South America and Arab countries, and flagrant anti-Semitic slander, vandalism, and violence in Germany.[18] On Christmas Eve of 1959 Cologne's reconsecrated synagogue was daubed with swastikas and slogans. Then followed a wave of neo-Nazi outbursts. In this atmosphere Celan clipped the February 1960 article on Hülsdünker's trial and a few days later wrote to Nelly Sachs: "What can I say to you? Every day, baseness comes into my house, every day, believe me. What is in store for us Jews? And we have a child, Nelly Sachs, a child!"[19]

Are these *Menschen*?, he asks Nelly Sachs, human beings? "Some of them even write poems. These men, they write *poems*! What all don't they write, the liars! Oh if only I could be near you, talk with you often! God protect you!" Celan's angry stress on "poems" reveals his expectation: poetry should have a moral basis.

That expectation was crushed early in 1960. While Celan was preparing a broadcast on Osip Mandelshtam and assuring Gleb Struve that Mandelshtam's poetry led him to "the Irrefutable and the True," suddenly the plagiarism charge dormant since 1953 was revived. A new magazine in Munich strung together excerpts from glowing reviews of *Sprachgitter,* undercut by an editor's note refusing to "lick Herr Celan's ass."[20] That alone was more cutting than anything ever printed about him. But then the widow of Yvan Goll, who had befriended Celan in 1949, wrote to the Munich magazine. The March–April 1960 issue carried her letter under the title "Something Unknown about Paul Celan."[21]

Claire Goll recounted Celan's visits to her dying husband in 1949 and how moved they were by the young poet's "sorrowful legend" of parents killed by the Nazis, which he "related so tragically." Her word "legend" hit a nerve in one who could barely bring home to himself, much less to others, the reality of his parents' death.[22] She also said that Celan made "cursory and inept" translations of Yvan Goll's French poetry and that his "burning ambition" could not tolerate a Swiss publisher's rejecting them. These unprovable claims stung Celan on both ethical and literary grounds. In fact, he believed that Claire Goll later used his versions in translating her husband's poems herself.

What hurt most was the plagiarism charge disseminated in Germany. Claire Goll cited "parallel passages" along with hearsay about this "master plagiarist." Her charges were not simply groundless, they involved misquotation and specious chronology. Examples from Celan's 1952 *Mohn und Gedächtnis* said to "rely wholly" on passages in a 1951 volume by Yvan Goll actually stem from Celan's first collection, *Der Sand aus den Urnen,* which he had given to Goll in 1949. Still, the damage was done.

The earliest evidence of Celan's reaction is a letter of May 1960 to the editor Hans Bender: "Craft—that is a matter of hands. And these hands belong in turn to *one* person only. . . . Only true hands write true poems. I see no basic distinction between a handshake and a poem" (3:177). The letter closes in a less detached manner: "We live under dark skies, and—there are few human beings [*Menschen*]. This is probably why there are also so few poems." Then Celan "expressly" asks Bender, should he wish to publish this letter, "to present it as what it is: a letter directed to you under today's date." A dossier is already building up.

"You're acquainted with the machinations of neo-Nazism in the Federal Republic," Celan wrote to his old Bukovinan mentor Margul-Sperber.[23] "Clearly connected to these machinations there has now resulted for some time an attempt to destroy me and my poems." Celan recounts his connection with the Golls, the "theft" of his translations, and the "pillorying" of him as "swindler, legacy-hunter and charlatan . . . duping the so *good* people of Germany by . . . depicting in such a tragic fashion the *legend* of my parents murdered by the Nazis." He locates all this "in the middle of a Hitlerism risen again" and resents it that no one has spoken up for him. "As for me, I shall not do this obvious infamy the courtesy of entering into it: I don't converse with the—Jewish or Aryan—Goebbels aftergrowth." He closes this letter: "Oh you know, I've often asked myself if I'd have done better to remain among the beechtrees of my homeland. . . ."

Meanwhile the literary community was nearly unanimous in refuting any plagiarism. Germany's Academy of Language and Literature met in late April 1960, commissioned an analytic defense of Celan, and informed him that he would receive their prestigious Büchner Prize later that year.[24] Marie Luise Kaschnitz, Ingeborg Bachmann, and Klaus Demus wrote a reply, as did Peter Szondi, Hans Magnus Enzensberger, Walter Jens, and the Austrian PEN Club, under headlines such as "Frivolous Slurs against a Poet" and "Celan is Rehabilitated." The Stuttgart weekly *Christ and World* issued a retraction from the journalist who first picked up Claire Goll's charge, and another magazine compared it to the Dreyfus affair. But so grave an insult had loosed too much anxiety about the war years, exile, Germany, and poetry itself. Celan would never get over it.[25]

One spell of light did come to this otherwise grim spring: Paul Celan and Nelly Sachs met for the first time. As early as 1953 he had seen her "Chorus of the Orphans" and had responded to "Chorus of the Stones" ("We stones . . . Whoever lifts us / lifts millions of memories") with his own harsher lines:

"Whichever stone you lift— / you lay bare / those who need the protection of stones" (1:129).[26] From 1954 on they were in contact, but Sachs was reluctant to travel from Sweden. In 1959 she greeted Celan's *Sprachgitter* as "a Book of Radiance" and commiserated over an insensitive review: "Dear Paul Celan . . . Between Paris and Stockholm runs the meridian of grief and of comfort."[27] He inscribed his Mandelshtam translations "To Nelly Sachs the sister," and she replied "Dear Brother."[28]

Germany's Droste Prize was awarded to Nelly Sachs in 1960. Twenty years after her last-minute flight from Berlin, she still could not bear to pass a night on German soil and opted to stay in Zurich, crossing the Bodensee to Meersburg for the ceremony. "Of course I'll come to Zurich, whenever you wish," Celan wrote on 3 May; "please just name the day and hour!"[29] Sachs had begun suffering from a terrifying persecution mania (aggravated by Eichmann's capture), in which she heard vicious electronic voices. This could have been worsened by visiting a German-speaking country, but she went anyway. "A fairytale here," she wrote on 26 May from Zurich's Hotel Zum Storchen ("Hotel at the Stork").[30] "At the airport the *Celan* family from Paris, their little son with a giant bunch of roses . . . Everything in glorious harmony, even *Max Frisch* came. How ever shall I grasp it all, after so much darkness." Celan made notes on their meeting. On hearing Nelly Sachs's "Yes, I'm a believer," he said he "hoped to be able to blaspheme up till the end," and she replied: "One really doesn't know what counts."[31] That day Sachs and Celan sent a postcard together: "Unforgettable time with Paul Celan," she said, and he added a greeting, then two more lines, the germ of a poem: "It is a bright and storks' day. From the cathedral comes sun."[32]

Sachs received her award on 29 May 1960. On 30 May, back in Paris, Celan wrote "Zürich, Zum Storchen," evoking their conversation of a few days earlier, when (on the day marking Christ's ascent into heaven) they saw Zurich's great church, its minster, mirrored in the Limmat River.

Zurich, at the Stork

For Nelly Sachs

Our talk was of Too Much, of
Too Little. Of Thou
and Yet-Thou, of
clouding through brightness, of
Jewishness, of
your God.

There-
of.
On the day of an ascension, the

Nelly Sachs, 1960 (R. Piper & Co. Verlag, Munich 1983)

Minster stood over there, it came
with some gold across the water.

Our talk was of your God, I spoke
against him, I
let the heart that I had
hope:
for
his highest, death-rattled, his
wrangling word—

Your eye looked at me, looked away,
your mouth
spoke toward the eye, I heard:

We
really don't know, you know,
we
really don't know
what
counts.   [1:214]

Nelly Sachs, a generation older than Paul Celan, had also carried her mother tongue into exile. But, more than Celan, she devoted her poetry to "the suffering of Israel." While he could not share her faith in an answering God, his lines cast the two poets in a tentative dialogue. We hear them beginning to say *du,* the intimate "you," and when they speak of *Du / und Aber-Du,* we get their sense of "an addressable Thou" (as Celan put it in Bremen). Translations of this poem say "Thou / and thou again," since *aber* can mean "again." Yet *aber* ("but") also points to a problematic God. Celan himself once approved "Pseudo-Thou" for *Aber-Du.*[33] Given his strong line break, I try for both rebuttal and renewal in *aber:* "Thou / and Yet-Thou."

Celan's opening sentence gives a nod to Margarete Susman, who lived in Zurich and whose 1946 *Book of Job and the Fate of the Jewish People* says that vis-à-vis the catastrophe, "every word is a Too Little and a Too Much."[34] In light of Nelly Sachs's award, Celan's phrase also suggests the "too much" and "too little" of German philo-Semitism.[35] Then ambivalence gives way to the heart of this encounter. *Am Tag einer Himmelfahrt,*

On the day of an ascension, the
Minster stood over there, it came
with some gold across the water.

The day Celan met Sachs, 26 May 1960, was Ascension Day in the Christian calendar. Yet, by speaking only of "an" ascension, he opens this moment to other ascents besides Christ's: "You'll rise then as smoke in the sky," said "Todesfuge," and in 1945 Sachs saw "Israel's body in smoke through the air."[36] In 1957 she used the term *Himmelfahrt* rudely: "This is the . . . ascension made of screams."[37]

"From the cathedral comes sun," Celan had said on the card they sent. In verse four days later, "some gold across the water" comes as a different miracle of ascension: a shining that two survivors witnessed together (and remembered for the rest of their lives). This vision gives way to bare hope

for
his highest, death-rattled, his
wrangling word—

It comes down to *haderndes* ("wrangling"), a word used when the people "strove" against Moses (Exod. 17:2) and—crucially for Celan—when Job urged God, "Make me know wherefore Thou contendest with me" (Job 10:2). Nothing like Moses' faith or Job's grit stirs this poem:

"We
really don't know, you know,
we
really don't know
what
counts . . ."

Originally Celan had these quotation marks and three dots, for Sachs in her acceptance speech had said that "Everything counts" in God's eyes.[38] His final version removed them, leaving both poets in doubt over "what counts" (*was gilt*).

Celan had invited Sachs to stay in Paris, though he lived "five alas quite steep floors up," and maybe "you dread this sort of Alpinism."[39] She visited with her friend Eva-Lisa Lennartsson on the way back from Zurich in mid-June 1960.[40] The Celans were loving, generous hosts; Sachs called them "the Holy Family." But the two Jewish poets' anxieties proved mutually contagious, and a *contretemps* only made things worse.

Out walking on the Boulevard St. Germain, they spotted at a café the painter Max Ernst, who had known Lennartsson's husband. Lennartsson went over to him and was invited to join him with her companions. Celan in those days, during the onset of the Goll affair, could trust no one. He even had his wife walk their son to school for fear that he would be kidnapped by Nazis because his father was a Jew. At the thought of joining Max Ernst, though, "a glimmer of hope came into Paul's eyes," says Lennartsson. But when Ernst saw that it was Celan and Sachs whom she was with, "he stiffened, turned away and made as if we did not exist. We left without a word." Did Ernst remember Celan's skeptical elegy for Paul Éluard, Ernst's closest friend? Was he behaving in solidarity with his fellow-surrealist Yvan Goll? The snub (from a painter who had himself been exhibited in Hitler's 1937 "Degenerate Art" show) hurt Celan. "You see how it is," he said right away and suggested to Nelly Sachs that they go and visit Heine's grave in Montmartre. This recoil has a meaning of its own—this homage to Heine, another German-speaking Jewish poet destined to die in exile. The two friends laid flowers on Heine's grave and for a long while stood there silent.

After the joyous encounter in Zurich and the golden light, their days together in Paris proved a mixed blessing. In Celan's apartment they experienced a second shining of sunlight, but he was in no condition to do Nelly Sachs much good. The evening before her visit ended, Celan confided to Lennartsson a story of "betrayal" in 1942, when he had let go of his father's hand through barbwire and run away. "Paul couldn't keep back his tears," and she urged him not to foist his anxieties on Sachs. The next day, on the way to Orly, Celan passionately encouraged his sister-poet.

"It was wonderful in Paris and painful," Nelly Sachs wrote after returning to Stockholm. As her fears of "this frightful radio traffic above my house" were becoming intolerable,[41] Celan began sending jocular, heartening letters. "And you?," he wrote from Brittany on 20 July 1960. "You certainly can't bicycle as well as Eric—only a few can do that!—that's probably why you write poems. Which, I'll have you know, is far less difficult."[42]

Beneath this tender humor, Celan's own malaise persisted, as in a poem one week later:

It goes dumb, it goes deaf
behind my eyes.
I see the poison bloom.
In every word and shape.   [1:220]

Then the next day, writing to Sachs again, he tried to pull her up by his own bootstraps: "*You're getting better—I know.* I know it because I sense that the evil haunting you—which haunts me too—is gone again, retreated into the unreality where it belongs. . . . So now you're free, once and for all. And— if you'll allow me this thought—I along with you."[43] He enclosed a piece of plane-tree bark with orders to grasp it between thumb and forefinger and think of something good. And "*poems,*" he said, "especially yours, are even *better* plane-tree bark. So please, write again. And let it find its way into our hands."

Two days later he was writing to Margul-Sperber about neo-Nazi machinations against him.[44] Celan then took his family to Vienna, probably to seek friendship in a German-speaking milieu. On 9 August, having bought two books by Buber that morning, he returned to Paris and, finding a letter from his friend in Stockholm, wrote to reassure her again: "It's going well for us, Nelly, really well. . . . Yes, it's bright again—the net, the dark one, is pulled away—isn't that right, Nelly, you see it now, you see you're free, in the clear, with us, among friends? . . . And I even see the words waiting for you, Nelly, the words you give life to with your new brightnesses—to all our joy."[45] After only two days he wrote again, describing five-year-old Eric galloping through their apartment on the backs of horses and camels and mountain goats.

But "I so long for my beloved dead," Nelly Sachs replied, whereupon Celan's tone turned urgent: "You still know, don't you, when we spoke about God a second time in my house, how the golden gleam stood on the wall? . . . Look, Nelly: the net is pulled away! . . . Look: it's getting light, you're breathing, you're breathing free!" Sachs, undergoing a nervous breakdown, hospitalized herself amidst what she called "all Dante-hells" and "Hieronymus Bosch-images."[46] "Come as quickly as possible," she wrote to Celan but then wired him: "Don't under any circumstances come."[47] Celan went by train to Stockholm during the first week of September 1960 and stood at the door of her room, but either she did not recognize him or else would not admit him.[48] Maybe it was herself she was shielding, maybe him. For his whole family, Nelly Sachs said, she had "death anxieties."[49]

He returned to Paris, only to suffer another blow. Since his youth he had read and revered Martin Buber—for the recovery of Hasidism, the spiritual constitution of dialogue, and his translation of the Bible.[50] Celan's 1958 Bremen speech identified Bukovina as "home" to Buber's Hasidic tales. "Conversation in the Mountains" affiliated with the author of *I and Thou*, and, reading him in 1960, Celan found Buber's thought worth underlining. In one book: "the Eternal is brought forth out of contradiction . . . Judaism is not simple and single-minded, but imbued with antithesis."[51] Then in August, from Buber's *Daniel*: "the poet . . . drinks eternally from both springs: Lethe and Mnemosyne" and knows "all the tensions" of the human soul.[52] Clearly it counted to see contradiction vouched for by the reigning Jewish philosopher, an emigrant to Jerusalem who bridged the war years with his *Muttersprache*. Celan "venerated Martin Buber to the point of rapture," said a lifelong friend.[53]

Buber came to Paris in September 1960, having lectured in Munich on "The Word That Is Spoken"—language grounded in the truth of dialogue— and been given a prize for renewing the bond between Germans and Jews.[54] Celan, just back from his comfortless visit with Nelly Sachs in Stockholm, telephoned and went to Buber's hotel on 13 September. He took his copies of Buber's books to be signed and actually kneeled for a blessing from the eighty-two-year-old patriarch.[55] But the homage miscarried.[56] How had it felt (Celan wanted to know), after the catastrophe, to go on writing in German and publishing in Germany? Buber evidently demurred, saying it was natural to publish there and taking a pardoning stance toward Germany. Celan's vital need, to hear some echo of his plight, Buber could not or would not grasp. This encounter, or failed encounter, left the poet even more vulnerable.

The day he met Martin Buber, Celan wrote an explicitly Judaic lyric, addressed to himself and to Nelly Sachs, his "sister."[57]

The Sluice

Over all this
grief of yours: no
second heaven.

. . . .

To a mouth
for which it was a thousandword,
lost—
I lost a word
that was left to me:
Sister.

To
polygoddedness
I lost a word that sought me:
Kaddish.

Through
the sluice I had to go,
to salvage the word back into
and out of and across the salt flood:
Yizkor.   [1:222]

With no remedy for god-forsakèn grief, Celan's dots after "no second heaven" insert a silence before any appeal to history or memory.

Translating a poem that already spells out the loss of certain words risks further loss. Celan's *Tausendwort* has been translated "myriad-word," but his "thousandword" was lost to the "Thousand-Year Reich."[58] Along with countless sisters wasted, that precious word "sister" speaks for the sister Celan never had, for a beloved, for a lost mother, all embodied by Nelly Sachs. In saying that this word "was left to me," Celan means against all the odds. When the Goll trouble broke, he had said to a German editor: "The hopes I still have are not great: I shall try and hold onto what is left to me" (3:178).

The harshness of *Tausendwort* attaches also to *Vielgötterei*: "polytheism" will do, but "polygoddedness" sounds barbaric, hinting at Wagnerian *Götterdämmerung* ("Twilight of the Gods"). Now a lost word, *Kaddish,* issues not in the mother tongue but from the holy tongue—an archaic word used in mourning loss itself. By converting from German to Hebrew, Celan's stanzas literally repossess what was lost: *Kaddish,* Aramaic for "holy," is a prayer for the dead, actually a praise of God, traditionally recited by the surviving child.

Celan's last sentence barely translates, as prepositions in time and space put off the final verb *retten* ("salvage"):

das Wort in die Salzflut zurück-

the word into the salt flood back-

und hinaus- und hinüberzuretten:

and out-of- and across-to-salvage:

Then, as climax, comes the word that this process has salvaged: *Yizkor,* Hebrew for "May He remember," identifying a memorial service—another ritual term preserved in italics, strange to most German ears but free of the need for translation because native to Jews everywhere.

"The Sluice" came out of resistance to Claire Goll's plagiarism campaign, mischance with Martin Buber, and painful solidarity with Nelly Sachs. From May to October 1960, Celan was also preparing to receive Germany's premier literary award, the Georg Büchner Prize. Such recognition, from the nation that gave him such cause for despair, gave rise to a manifesto on poetry in the form of an acceptance speech (3:187–202). Some 314 pages of notes and drafts accumulated as he looked for words, turns of speech, metaphors, memories, precedents, and citations that might release the truth of poetic experience. "It was a dark summer," he wrote to a friend. "And the Büchner Prize was, up to the last minute, an ordeal, i.e. it was both temptation and affliction. Really. Now it's been gotten through, I even managed—at the very last moment—to write down a (sort of) speech."[59] Celan composed "The Meridian" in three days.[60] Yet this nuanced, layered, elaborately qualified, covertly and overtly allusive speech has nothing hurried about it, forming with all its questioning Celan's authoritative statement on poetry.

Here is a sentence from his notes, written hastily but densely thought: "Whoever takes up a poem enters the sphere of that most-strangeness which—voiceless and thus close to speech—it is addressing; in an encounter, as in the resultant poem, *language strikes up,* language becomes *free.*"[61] The phrase between the dashes Celan added later, deepening his already complex sense of poetic process. Although this sentence shows up nowhere in the Meridian speech, its key words do, and its root idea: a poem, encountering what is most strange, sets language free.

The word "encounter," occurring ten times toward the end of Celan's speech, points to someone without naming him, in a speech that is not shy of naming. Celan once remarked that "a couple of formulations from the Mandelshtam broadcast" made their way into "The Meridian."[62] His broadcast of March 1960, before he was even slated for the Büchner Prize, fed into his acceptance speech because Mandelshtam touched the core of his poetics.

Celan's broadcast said of Mandelshtam—and "The Meridian" makes it an axiom—that the poet speaks "*actualized* language, at once voiced and voiceless, set free under the sign of a radical individuation, which at the same time stays mindful of the limits set by language, the possibilities opened by language."[63] The broadcast insisted on poetry as *Gespräch,* "conversation" or "dialogue"—and "often it is despairing dialogue," he adds in "The Meridian."

It is astonishing how many authors Celan brings into "The Meridian" to orient himself: Mallarmé, Kafka, Büchner, Pascal, Landauer, Kropotkin, Malebranche, and Benjamin. And he does something else with names. Four times during the speech, in seemingly gratuitous fashion, he makes an essential point by way of some intermediate source. In citing a comment on Büchner's drama, Celan interrupts himself: "—if I may be allowed to give voice here to a phrase coined by Moritz Heimann about *Danton's Death*." Both the deference and the insertion of Moritz Heimann (1868-1925), a minor German-Jewish author, are part of a design.

Celan again frames a key quotation in treating the "darkness" or "obscurity" of poetry: "Allow me here, abruptly—but hasn't something suddenly come open—allow me to cite a phrase of Pascal's, a phrase I read some time ago in Leo Shestov: 'Ne nous reprochez pas le manque de clarté puisque nous en faisons profession!' [Don't reproach us for a lack of clarity, because that's what we profess!]." Celan had recently bought a work of the philosopher Lev Shestov (1866–1938) and had marked this quotation from Pascal.[64] "Allow me," Celan says in effect, to refract Western thought through this Russian Jew who died an exile in Paris.

The third time Celan takes a detour—"but are there such things: detours?" he had asked in the 1958 Bremen speech—we hear not one but two Jewish authors interposed. He is speaking of poems as "lonely and under way," standing "*in the mystery of an encounter.*" Then he defines "'Attentiveness'— allow me here to quote a maxim by Malebranche from Walter Benjamin's Kafka essay—'Attentiveness is the natural prayer of the soul.'" Reading Benjamin in December 1959, Celan had underlined this maxim.[65] Just as Benjamin on Kafka differs from Kafka alone, so Celan seeing Kafka through Walter Benjamin, a German Jew exiled in Paris who committed suicide in 1940, asks more attentiveness than any audience was likely to "allow."

Celan introduces one more interpreter he might have done without. He has been recalling his earlier work: first, some lines from 1956, "Voices from the nettle path: / *Come on your hands to us.*" And "a year ago," he adds, "I wrote down a little story" ("Conversation in the Mountains"). Both times "It was . . . myself I encountered," and the ellipsis is Celan's. He calls poems "paths on which language gets a voice; they are encounters, paths of a voice to a perceiving Thou." (Though speaking German, he must have liked the French homonyms *voie*, "path," and *voix*, "voice.") These are paths "in the search for oneself . . . a kind of homecoming." Having ventured this meridianlike notion of poetry, Celan turns to Büchner's first editor, Karl Emil Franzos (1848–1904), a Jewish writer who grew up in Czernowitz. Though Franzos stood for assimilation to German culture and against Zionism, his compassionate stories made East European Jewish life visible in the West.[66] For Celan, assimilation had become a more loaded option—hence his italics: "*my here rediscovered fellow countryman Karl Emil Franzos.*" Heimann, Shestov, Benjamin, and Franzos make up a lineage, exposing to postwar German listeners the particular/universal condition of their honored poet.

Not that "The Meridian" makes any outright Jewish statement. Instead, Celan quotes from *Danton's Death*—"ach, die Kunst!" (alas, art!)—and says that he himself has "no other choice" than to put an "acute accent" on this phrase, "the acute of the present." What he means remains unclear until a few minutes later, when he distinguishes *Kunst* from *Dichtung,* art from literature (or poetry), urging a "radical calling into question of art . . . to which all present-day literature must return." The reason for this questioning "lies in the air—in the air that we have to breathe."

Such explanation would still mystify his audience. A gloss helps, from Celan's letter thanking someone for solidarity in the plagiarism trouble: "it's a question of the breathable air that's still left for us all."[67] That air, the German political climate, resembles the *Luft* which his listeners may remember from "Todesfuge": "you'll rise then as smoke in the air." By 1960 Celan saw "Todesfuge" passing as a "work of art" into German pedagogy. One journal advised analyzing a Bach fugue, then having students underline the poem's voices in various colors "to make the polyphony audible" and to show how "what actually happened" can be "artistically mastered."[68]

Against such mastering, "The Meridian" poses its "radical calling into question of art" with that staunch word *eng* ("narrow"). Is the point "to enlarge art?" Celan asks. "No. But with art go into your very selfmost straits. And set yourself free" (*geh mit der Kunst in deine allereigenste Enge. Und setze dich frei*). It takes a new word to say this, *allereigenste* (literally, "most own of all"): your "very selfmost straits." Here only, Celan's Meridian speech uses the intimate *deine* and *dich* for "you," turning toward himself and anyone with ears to hear.

Through these "straits," toward what is "most strange," a poem speaks "*in the cause of an Other*—who knows, perhaps in the cause of a *wholly Other*." Just before his speech, Celan had bought Rudolph Otto's *Das Heilige* ("The Holy," 1917). From it he took this theologian's name for a God we cannot grasp—"the wholly Other"—to set the aim of poetry.

"But with art go into your very selfmost straits. And set yourself free." *Frei,* the last word, sounds like a tocsin throughout Celan's Meridian speech, especially in the verb *freisetzen* ("set free").[69] A poem, "setting free an Other," moves toward "the vicinity of something open and free. And finally the vicinity of utopia." Apart from Heidegger, Celan had evolved his own usage of *frei.* When his mother found a name, "the hammers swung free in the belfry of your silence" (1:78). He told her, "I speak you free / of the Amen that deafens us" (1:111). He called the dead "strange and free" (1:141). His baby son spoke—"Another word like this, and the hammers / will be swinging free" (1:164). Death, it seems, and language break us free. The word even caps some witty couplets of June 1960:

With the spaces, with the straits,
with those gone down to their fates.

With me alone, and with us three,
half in bonds, half in the free. [1:216]

And when Nelly Sachs began suffering from persecution mania, her fellow-poet's letters (while he was preparing his speech) rang with that same word: "So now you're free"; "Nelly you see it now, you see you're free, in the clear"; "Look: it's getting light, you're breathing, you're breathing free!" A week before the speech, Celan told her "it's so uncommonly freeing" to hear that she's emerged from her agonies.[70]

To tell his audience what springs a poem free, Celan recalls an eighteenth-century visionary poet who ended up going mad. Büchner's 1836 novella *Lenz* begins, "On the 20th of January Lenz walked through the mountains . . . only it sometimes troubled him that he could not walk on his head." Celan comments: "Whoever walks on his head, ladies and gentlemen, . . . has heaven as an abyss beneath him." Then he cites "heaven as an abyss" as grounds for poetry's "obscurity."

The prize-winning poet is himself obscure in bringing up a 20th of January, for it was at the Wannsee conference on 20 January 1942, over breakfast, that Heydrich, Eichmann, and others settled on the "Final Solution." After a passage that uses the word "perhaps" nine times, Celan goes on: "Perhaps one may say that every poem has its '20th of January' inscribed? Perhaps what's new for poems written today is just this: that here the attempt is clearest to remain mindful of such dates?" Tentatively—how many in his 1960 audience would "remain mindful" of the Wannsee conference?—Celan sets an agenda. Poetry ought to speak in view of Europe's murdered Jews.

That massive though tacit agenda returns as Celan's speech closes, recalling his earlier work, "Voices from the nettle path" and "Conversation in the Mountains": "In both instances I began writing from a '20th of January,' from my '20th of January'"—the date when he lost "the place of my own origin. I am seeking all of that with an inexact because restless finger on the map—on a children's map, I must admit. None of these places is to be found, they do not exist, but I know where, especially now, they would have to exist, and . . . I find something!" Celan says, "I find . . . a *meridian*." Again the ellipsis connotes being under way, traversing nadir and zenith to arrive at an origin—a "u-topia" (or "no-place"—he divides the word for its root sense). Celan omits saying why these places on a children's map do not exist.

More and more questions draw in his listeners, abetted by remarks such as "I'm just asking," "So I must ask now," and direct appeals: "you'll remember," "you see it," "you know this already," "as you see." Meanwhile a motif of doubt enlists the audience in his search: "but . . . but . . . but," "who knows?," "perhaps . . . perhaps . . . perhaps." Along with the pervasive "Allow me," Celan studs his talk with *Meine Damen und Herren* ("Ladies and Gentlemen") eighteen times over, with a spate toward the end. While this honorific keeps the poet conversant with his listeners, it also impugns their honor, as Jerry Glenn suggests, and even—who knows?—evokes the politeness the SS used.

Behind such gestures stands the speech's simplest dictum: "Poetry: that can signify a breath-turn," an *Atemwende*. Like "heaven as an abyss," "breathturn" has to do with "an old mystical motif," Celan once said:[71] through its strangeness, a poem breaks open new reality. On the model of *Sonnenwende*, meaning "solstice," Celan's *Atemwende* speaks for a turning, a revolution of the spirit in him and in us.

Shortly after the speech, Celan demonstrated that breath-turn in "Psalm."[72] Nothing of his except "Todesfuge" has attracted so much attention, with its bluff title and paradoxes.

Psalm

No one kneads us again out of earth and clay,
no one incants our dust.
No one.

Blessèd art thou, No One.
In thy sight would
we bloom.
In thy
spite.

A Nothing
we were, are now, and ever
shall be, blooming:
the Nothing-, the
No One's-Rose.

With
our pistil soul-bright,
our stamen heaven-waste,
our corolla red
from the purpleword we sang
over, O over
the thorn.   [1:225]

The psalm, benediction, doxology, and prayer which this poem sounds like are undercut in breath-turnings, abysses opened beneath those ritual forms. Throughout the Christian West, words for "psalm" are alike. Identical in

German and English, they need no translating—whence the snare of Celan's title. As with his "Tenebrae," we assume we know what is meant. But "Psalm" can never, for this poet, purely and simply line up with the hymns of lament and praise that have comforted generation unto generation.

"No one" (*Niemand*) makes that clear right away, as the opening words annul not only comfort but Creation itself:

No one kneads us again out of earth and clay,
no one incants our dust.
No one.

With a bonus pun on "kneads" (in English), "Psalm" speaks in the aftermath of destruction, co-opting "earth" and "dust" from Genesis. Even worse, the verb I translate as "incants," *bespricht,* can also mean "speak about." Thus no one—not today's bystanders and not, above all, God, as George Steiner puts it—will speak about the dust unto which God's people were returned.[73] "No one": isolated in the third line, this pronoun speaks the name of One who is not to be named.

With the poem's formula of praise, *Gelobt seist du,* I've taken a free hand. The literal "Praised be thou" resembles the end of André Schwarz-Bart's *The Last of the Just* (Paris, 1959): "And praised. Auschwitz. Be. Maidanek. God. Treblinka." But in a German prayer book which some refugee friends had saved, I found the Ashkenazi rite using *Gelobt seist du* for the basic Hebrew benediction *Baruch ata* (and Israeli versions of "Psalm" say *Baruch ata*[74]). "Blessèd art thou" sounds closer to Celan's pitch, a souvenir from childhood.[75]

"Blessèd art thou, No One." This benediction invokes *Niemand* head-on, capitalizing the word in mid-sentence like Jew Klein: "no one hears him, no one and No One" (3:171). In that story and this poem, the absent "No One" of the catastrophe masks the unknowable "No One" of Jewish mysticism.

"No One," the proper noun for God, is of course addressed as *Du*:

Dir zulieb wollen	For thy sake would
wir blühn.	we bloom.
Dir	Toward
entgegen.	thee.

But *entgegen*'s double sense—both "toward" and "against"—requires something sharper. Borrowing a Biblical idiom ("A thousand ages in thy sight": Ps. 90:4), then framing a contradictory rhyme, gives:

In thy sight would
we bloom.
In thy
spite.

If this seems to go too far, Celan himself has gone beyond his Meridian speech, where God is the "wholly Other." What is more "Other" than "No One"? Yet denial, by countenancing what it denies, still affirms it. *Ein Nichts* again merges mystical with historical nothingness:

A Nothing
we were, are now, and ever
shall be . . .

Besides capitalizing "Nothing" (with a nod to German), I've drawn on a traditional formula. To some ears, Celan's threefold conjugation of time will evoke the Christian doxology: "As it was in the beginning, is now, and ever shall be." Others will hear a more ancient liturgy, the Hebrew hymn "Adon Olam" (Lord of the World): "For He has been, for He is now, for He shall be, in radiance, For He is One, no Other is." Both legacies press upon a poem that travels from Creation to Crucifixion.

When "Psalm" joins "Nothing" and "No One" to the vitality of a rose, ambiguities boost the odds against translation. In the rose's soul-bright "pistil," besides a flower's seed-bearing organ, *Griffel* also means a stylus: the rose blossoms with writerly energy. In "our stamen heaven-waste," *Staubfaden* for "stamen" compounds "dust" and "thread," while "heaven-waste" replaces the earth of Genesis—"waste and void"—with a wasted heaven. In "our corolla," *Krone*'s botanical sense matches the regal "crown," a potent Judaic symbol, which then yields Jesus' crown of thorns. And "our corolla red / from the purpleword" calls up a bleeding King of the Jews in his purple robe, tying Christ's agony back into Jewish suffering. As in "Tenebrae," Celan will not let the New Testament supersede the Old.[76] He himself warned against fixing on Christian resonance in "Psalm."[77]

Singing "over, O over / the thorn" ends up eloquent and broken, like "the / choirs, back then, the / Psalms" in "Stretto."[78] Celan turns most Jewish in struggling with Jewish faith and most lyric in singing "over / the thorn."

10
Wrestling with the Angels
(1961)

"You ask about language, about thought, about poetry; you ask in concise terms—permit me to give my answer in just as concise a form" (3:175). Paul Celan was responding to a 1961 inquiry about the "Problem of Bilingualness" from Martin Flinker, a Czernowitz-born bookseller transplanted to Vienna and Paris. He went on: "I do not believe in bilingualness in poetry. . . . Poetry—that is the fateful uniqueness of language." This fatefulness of German led Celan to strain, admix, invade, and undo that same language. His writing collected in *Die Niemandsrose* ("The No One's-Rose," 1963) reveals a Jacob's struggle with the German lexicon. Jacob wrestled with the angel until he obtained a blessing and a name, but in the struggle he "was strained" (Gen. 32:26). "And must I still wrestle with Ya'akov's angel?," Celan had asked years before in Czernowitz. The poems from 1960 to 1962 are astir with that question—whether words hold good and whether Jewishness does, with all its past and present riches and agonies. His verse practically crackles with polyglot, heterogeneous formations, and it turns repeatedly on Jewish themes. We hear Celan's odd compounds and fractures, disruptive syntax, repeated or truncated syllables, and his arcane, archaic, technical, playful, or neologized German, along with quotes from his earlier work. We see three poems with French titles and more with Villon's, Baudelaire's, and Verlaine's French in them, and others with Latin, Spanish, English, Russian, Hebrew, and Yiddish. We find *baobab, menhir, Pneuma,* a Mozart motet, Hölderlin's babbled word *Pallaksch,* the sixteenth-century slang word *Kannitverstan,* a nonsense title "Huhediblu," poems called "Radix, matrix," "Havdalah," "Mandorla," "Anabasis," and "Benedicta." People's names crop up all over the poems— Hölderlin, Nelly Sachs, Paul Celan, Heinrich Heine, Marina Tsvetaeva, Osip Mandelshtam (and Mandelbaum and Bandelmaum and Mandeltraum and Trandelmaum and Machandelbaum and Chandelbaum), Abadias, Berenice, Petrarch, Abraham, Jesse, Jacob, Rabbi Loew, Orion—and the names of places: Zurich, Paris, Eden, Tübingen, Czernowitz, Sadagora, Edom, Friuli, Siberia, Brest, Kermorvan, Huesca, Petropolis, Tuscany, Warsaw, Vitebsk, Cracow, Russia, Karelia, Moravia, Prague, Normandy, Bohemia, Tarusa, Pont Mirabeau, Niemen, Elbe, Rhine, Oka, Colchis, and one proper noun that is both a person and a place—Babel.

The semantic explosion within *Die Niemandsrose* lands Celan's reader (and his translator) in questions of poetic intelligibility. Take the proper names: a translator can only ferry them across and let the reader make something of them. Yet with these names Celan was not dealing in a universal currency, like Yeats's Byzantium, Pound's Cathay, Eliot's Augustine, and Lowell's Ahab, to which we all (we're told) have access. His poem "To one who stood before the door" calls up the legend of Prague's Rabbi Loew, who created a golem that served the Jews, but also shows elusive traces of Kafka. And what is quite tacit, *Loew* or *lev* means "lion," or "Leo," which was Celan's father's name.

What relates this explosion in Celan's writing to Jewish consciousness? More and more he was seeking out new resources in German, because he felt its lyric vocabulary to be exhausted, mendacious. The idiosyncratic quotes from his reading or his memory, the people and places bridging Western and Eastern Europe, the eight other languages migrating into his verse, all testify to Celan's experience of wandering and exile—as Eliot might have put it: "Czernowitz Semite Parisian." During Eichmann's trial, Claire Goll's plagiarism campaign, and the anti-Semitic aftermath that he sensed, Celan in 1961 was one of those who, as the Psalmist says (84:6), "going through the vale of misery use it for a well, And the pools are filled with water."

Visiting Tübingen in January 1961, he wrote a poem involving Hölderlin's vision and last deranged decades. Celan's "Tübingen, January" half echoes the "20th of January" from his Meridian speech, and his poem's hard articulations share the baffled, sometimes brilliant darkness into which Hölderlin descended.

Eyes talked in-
to blindness.
Their—"a
riddle, what is pure-
ly arisen"—, their
memory of
floating Hölderlintowers, gull-
enswirled.

Visits of drowned joiners to
these
plunging words:

Came, if there
came a man,
came a man to the world, today, with
the patriarchs'
light-beard: he could,
if he spoke of this
time, he
could
only babble and babble,
ever- ever-
moremore.

("Pallaksch. Pallaksch.")   [1:226]

These lines bear the imprint of actual speech: eyes "talked" into blindness, Hölderlin's Rhine hymn quoted brokenly, his "plunging words," "babble," and deranged utterance.[1] Each instance throws in doubt the chances for truth telling.

Hölderlin's ode "The Blind Singer," his notes to Sophocles' *Oedipus*, and his Rhine hymn where "the blindest are the sons of gods," all support Celan's belief that only some seeing blindness, some inward counter-vision, could lay claim to truth anymore. He displays his precursor's genius—"a riddle, what is purely arisen"—yet splays that heady line over three of his own. A riddle of sacred purity, which Celan underscored in his edition of Hölderlin, now breaks apart in the river waters near where Hölderlin lived out his days in a carpenter's house.

"Naming occurs in the depth of language," Celan once said. "'Baptise' and 'plunge' [taufen and tauchen] are closely related."² Whatever Gospel renewal "these plunging words" should bring about, it comes to pieces:

Käme,	Came, if there
käme ein Mensch,	came a man,
käme ein Mensch zur Welt, heute,	came a man to the world, today,
mit	with
dem Lichtbart der	the patriarchs'
Patriarchen: er dürfte,	light-beard: he could,
spräch er von dieser	if he spoke of this
Zeit, er	time, he
dürfte	could
nur lallen und lallen,	only babble and babble,
immer-, immer-	ever-, ever-
zuzu.	moremore.
("*Pallaksch. Pallaksch.*")	("Pallaksch. Pallaksch.")

Celan's clipped verse demands some mimic ingenuity. Michael Hamburger catches the repeated subjunctive—"Should, / should a man, / should a man come"—but nothing in English has the torque of the German umlaut, carried on from the title words *Tübingen, Jänner* to the subjunctives *käme* ("came"), *dürfte* ("could"), *spräch* ("spoke"). So much doubt touches this advent—"if there came a man . . . he could, if he spoke . . . he could only"—that prophecy reduces to babble.³

Plunging down the page toward "babble and babble, / ever, -ever- / moremore," this nonsense still has a runic charm, revealing the nucleic doubleness of truth—of saying Yes and No, or merely of saying and not saying. The patriarch's odd *zuzu* ("moremore") even has a forebear in the stammering prophet Moses, who told the Lord, "I am heavy of mouth and heavy of tongue" (Exod. 4:10).

Finally, in parentheses, seeming to come from elsewhere, we hear a strange voice: "*Pallaksch. Pallaksch.*" A senseless term that Hölderlin was given to uttering in his late years, sometimes it meant Yes, sometimes No.⁴ Lacking any gist or nuance in German, this gibberish (like any silence in a text) loses little in transit to English: here, as with *Yizkor* in "The Sluice," poet and translator enjoy a moment's unison. With "Pallaksch," Hölderlin's towering voice has gone under, but we remember Celan saying "Don't split off No from Yes" (1:135). Maybe "Pallaksch. Pallaksch," for a Europe where the Big Lie reigned, says all that can and need be said.

"There would have to be *readers* again" (Celan remarked shortly after "Tübingen, January") to recognize his lyric "encounters," where "I have gone with my very being toward language."[5] One week later he composed a bizarre ballad whose readers might recognize traces of Villon, Buber, Heine, Isaiah, Mandelshtam, and Camus. The title itself, set as four lines, needs teasing apart:

A ROGUES' AND SWINDLERS' DITTY
SUNG IN PARIS EMPRÈS PONTOISE
BY PAUL CELAN
FROM CZERNOWITZ NEAR SADAGORA   [1:229]

Ganoven ("swindlers") is cognate with *gonifs* in Yiddish—and by now English. *Paris emprès Pontoise* comes from a sardonic Villon quatrain on being sentenced to hang: "I am François, which on me weighs, / Born in Paris près-de-Pontoise. / When on a rope my body sways, / My neck will learn what my ass weighs." Paul Celan's name occurs only this once in his work. *Czernowitz bei Sadagora* reverses the priority of metropolis over nearby town, because Celan's mother was born in Sadagora, also known for its thieves, and because it was a Hasidic center until the war—in fact Martin Buber, in a book Celan owned, told of an illuminating experience he once had in "Czernowitz not far from Sadagora."[6] Clearly a poet's self-definition is under way.

Before this poem can begin, though, another voice intervenes, in an epigraph—Celan's first—from Heinrich Heine's caustic lines "To Edom!" (the Jews' Biblical name for their enemies). "Now and then only, in dark times," says the epigraph, leaving us to recall the rest of Heine's poem about Gentile "tolerance," broken each time "your pious claws / you color with my blood." We may also recall Heine's saying, "Where they burn books, they'll end up burning people."[7] The SS in 1937, besides declaring Heine's "Lorelei" anonymous, accused him of having taken French payment in Paris to slander Germany.[8] Celan in 1961 was watching from Paris as the German press considered charges of plagiarism against him.

His ballad begins with gallows humor in these "dark times":

Back then, when they still had gallows,
then—right?—they had
an On High.

Where is my beard, wind, where's
my Jew-spot, where's
my beard you tear out?

Crooked was the way I went,
crooked it was, yes,
for yes,
it was straight.

A colloquial voice hitches old-time religion to SS-style persecution and warps
Isaiah's word of a Redeemer making the crooked straight (40:4). "Hooked,
so grows my nose," Celan adds, and lastly he glances at Camus' Nazi "plague"
by way of *Mandelbaum,* an almond tree. The ballad's *envoi* says that this tree
"stands against / *the plague.*"

Conflict often compacts his syntax, as in Celan's poem ". . . The Well
Rushes," from spring of 1961:

You prayer-, you blasphemy-, you
prayer-sharp knives
of my
silence.

You my words with me go-
ing crippled, you
my straight ones.   [1:237]

Parallel "you"s and hyphens link "prayer" and "blasphemy" in the same space
and the same time. Then returning to "prayer," the next line edges it with
"sharp knives," and "silence" on its own line stops everything said so far. As
the poet's silence contains prayer and blasphemy at once, so only in "going
crippled" do his words go straight.

Softer demands moved an exchange with Nelly Sachs in 1961. She had
sent him a poem, "Man is so lonely / searches eastward," with its refrain "Oh
hear me."[9] On 4 May, the same day that he inscribed an offprint of his
Meridian speech to Sachs, Celan wrote back: "In a loneliest hour: I thank
you. I hear you. Our Jews in Czernowitz, in saying goodbye, would wish
each other: Be well! [*Sei gesund!*] That's no German idiom, it's Yiddish, and
so let me say it yet once more now, in Yiddish and with Hebrew characters:
זײַ געזונט !." He penned those words clearly so that his coreligionist, lacking
much Hebrew or Yiddish, would be able to read them.[10] A good deal of
Celan's purpose distills to this *zay gezunt.*

Reaching back into his personal and mythic past, a healing poem one
week later could not dispel the desolation. Celan's Latin title preempts translation, if only because "Root, Womb" would erase its rhyming equation.
"Radix, Matrix" begins:

As one speaks to stone, as
you,
to me from the abyss, from
a homeland con-
Sanguined, up-
Hurled, you,
you of old to me,
you to me in the nix of a night,
you in Yet-Night en-
Countered, you
Yet-You—:   [1:239]

This probing requires its reader/translator to locate "you" and "me" within a sentence fragment, to array groping words and phrases, and perhaps to find a better term than "con-Sanguined." Celan's *Ver-Schwisterte* ("siblinged") says that his mother, stalled young, is becoming the sister he never had.

The lost mother persists in "you / Yet-You" (*du / Aber-Du*), and then a memory of her verges on infant dada or stammering—

Damals, da ich nicht da war,
damals, da du
den Acker abschrittst, allein:

—until we realize what *damals* ("at that time") must point to:

Back then, when I wasn't there,
back then, when you
paced along the field, alone:

What tempers this loss and its guilt is a hint, in "the field, alone," that binds his mother to Ruth, the grandmother of Jesse, the father of David.

Only a hint, for the covenant ruptures on words such as "murdered," "black," "No One":

Who,
who was it, that
stock, that murdered one, that one
standing black into heaven:
rod and testis—?

(Root.
Root of Abraham. Root of Jesse. No One's
root—O
ours.)

Geschlecht, here translated "stock," could be "race" or "generation," as in Psalms: "One generation to another shall praise Thy works" (145:4). But no amount of ambidexterity can catch the puns that Celan generates. Since *Rute* means "rod" and "penis," and in German the name Ruth is pronounced like the English "root," a triple play between languages unites—without at all reconciling—the murdered mother, the rod of miracle or anger, and a radically threatened people. These puns rebut a lovely German Christmas carol, singable in its English version:

> Lo, how a rose e'er blooming
> From tender root hath sprung!
> Of Jesse's lineage coming,
> As men of old have sung.[11]

And behind this stands Isaiah—"There shall come forth a rod out of the stem of Jesse . . . a root of Jesse"—assuring us that the Lord will "a second time recover the remnant of His people" (11:1, 11). These sources help counter Jewish eradication when Celan's lineage breaks and runs on: "No One's / root—O / ours."

The question of sources worried Celan at the time of "Radix, Matrix," since articles were appearing about the plagiarism charge. Even his defenders troubled him, because any analysis refuting the charge was taking it seriously.[12] When the German Academy of Language and Literature published a thorough acquittal, he called this an "infamy." But it led him to write a revealing letter in mid-May 1961 to the classicist Walter Jens, who was preparing an article on the subject.[13]

"I've often asked myself," Celan says about an animal image he had allegedly copied, "where I might have gotten my 'boar.' Boars, my dear Walter Jens,—such things do exist." He adds that "influences—which are, in the liveliest sense, encounters!"—must be deeply inspected. Then he brings up Yeats, George, Rilke, "or *Celan,*" as well as Hans Christian Andersen and Grimm, because "with my poems, but not only with them, I'm again in my childhood, I'm near the books of my childhood." Celan cites a term for creative recollection—"Anamnesis!"—and closes with this telling formula: "only a re-encounter turns the encounter into . . . Encounter." The ellipsis is his.

Celan's metaphors in "Todesfuge" had been questioned. In this letter he brings up the commandant's snakes, suggesting mythic sources long before Goll and Trakl. But he makes one vital exception: "The 'grave in the air'— my dear Walter Jens, in *this* poem, God knows, that is neither borrowing nor metaphor." "God knows," indeed—in his typewritten letter Celan adds those words by hand. He signs himself "Old-Metaphors Dealer," playing on the Jewish trade of old-clothes dealer.

Old sources provoked new encounters with Latin, German, and Yiddish in a poem from spring of 1961. It sets a title, always flush left in Celan's books, opposite an epigraph to the right:

Benedicta

> *Tsu ken men aroyfgehn in himl arayn*
> *Un fregn bay got tsu s'darf azoy zayn?*

From the Annunciation and the Ave Maria, *Benedicta* ("Blessed art thou among women," Luke 1:42) faces a "Yiddish folk song" (as Celan labels his epigraph) adapted in the Vilna ghetto by a man who perished in Germany: "So will you go up into heaven one day, / And question your God should it all be this way?"[14]

Then Celan's poem begins:

Hast—
thou hast drunk,
what came to me from our fathers
and from beyond our fathers:
— — Pneuma.

Be—
be thou blessed, from afar, from
beyond my
guttering fingers.

Blessed: you that hailed it,
the Tenebrae lamp.

You that heard, when I shut my eyes, how
the voice stopped singing after
's muz azoy zayn.   [1:249]

We know whom the Hail Mary addresses, and the ghetto song, but "thou" and "our"? Celan, we are told, wrote this as a love poem.[15] The phrase "from our fathers / and from beyond our fathers" echoes a Hebrew prayer: "Blessed art Thou O Lord our God and God of our fathers," and it points to a Creation word shared with his Catholic wife: "Pneuma." Celan said a comma belonged after his two dashes,[16] so they may stand for Hebrew *Ruach* from Genesis, which, like Greek *Pneuma,* means "wind," "breath," "spirit." "Pneuma" also figures in the Kabbalah, where "a special pneuma, the 'Sabbath-soul,' enters into the believer."[17]

Having spoken "Benedicta" and "Pneuma" from two Bibles, the Latin Vulgate and the Greek Septuagint, the poem couples Christian and Jewish destinies. The *Teneberleuchter* ("Tenebrae lamp") recalls tortured bodies in Celan's "Tenebrae," along with another sense of *Leuchter,* "menorah." "Benedicta" then turns to its epigraph again, quoting further from the ghetto song latent all along: *'s muz azoy zayn.*[18]

Yiddish had never before featured in a poem by Celan—"At home we always spoke High German only"—but he had heard plenty in the labor camps. His German readers would grasp the Yiddish phrase, though not without sensing a primitive strangeness. To translate it would level things, robbing this song of its undercut, the vulnerability of a language.[19]

If "the voice stopped singing," the poem will not:

> You that spoke it in the eye-
> less ones, the pastures:
> the same, the other
> word:
> Blessèd.

The "eyeless" evoke the Shechinah, God's presence dwelling within the world and weeping over Jewish exile. When Celan echoes these *augenlosen* with *Auen* ("meadows," "pastures"), it is worth choosing "pastures" to resonate with the twenty-third Psalm's green pastures and their comfort in the shadow of death. Also from Luther's Bible, "the same, the other / word"—"Blessèd"— is *Gebenedeiet,* cognate with, yet severed from, a final word this poem has been seeking since its title and epigraph:

Ge-	Drunk-
trunken.	en.
Ge-	Bless-
segnet.	ed.
Ge-	Ge-
bentscht.	bentscht.

"Drunken" (recall "Deathfugue" and "Tenebrae") leads through a Jewish "Blessed" to Yiddish *gebentscht*—derived like its German equivalent *benedeien* from Latin, conjugated as in German, yet untranslatably Yiddish like the Vilna song. "To be sure," Celan said in the Meridian speech, "a poem today shows a strong inclination toward falling mute" (3:197). The verb *gebentscht* holds out after the Yiddish "voice stopped singing." It is a breath-turn, a setting free.

Not every lyric written during spring and summer of 1961 ties language to Jewish destiny as tightly as "Benedicta," but they all show the pressure of history as Celan survived it. "The bright / stones go through the air," says a poem to his wife, "they do not / want to fall" (1:255). His next poems name a "free-becoming tentword: Together" (1:256), and words "wander . . . pitted by time-kernels, by time-dust, orphaned" (1:258). "Havdalah" (the ritual dividing the Sabbath from the secular week) ends with someone setting a table

> for the empty
> chairs and their
> Sabbath radiance in— —
> in honor.   [1:259]

Though Celan's word "honor" corresponds to a powerful Hebrew term, *kavod*, the dashes and the new stanza open a verbal breach, as empty as the chairs.

To steel his language against history, Celan began drawing elements from Jewish mysticism. He bought Gershom Scholem in 1957 and was studying him by 1960. In January 1961, "Psalm" addressed the "No One" God and "the Nothing-, the No One's-Rose." Then in May Celan composed "Mandorla," whose mystical core underlies a medley of personal loss, Nazi racism, earlier poems, longtime keywords, Hebrew, philosophy, and a church visit. The poem reads like catechism:

> In the almond—what stands in the almond?
> The Nothing.
> In the almond stands Nothing.
> There it stands and stands.
>
> In Nothing—who stands there? The King.
> There stands the King, the King.
> There he stands and stands.
>
> Jewish curls, no gray for you.
>
> And your eye—whereto stands your eye?
> Your eye stands opposite the almond.
> Your eye, the Nothing it stands opposite.
> It stands behind the King.
> So it stands and stands.
>
> Human curls, no gray for you.
> Empty almond, royal blue.   [1:244]

The measured couplet sounds odd for a poet struggling with language. To see why Celan needed such euphony, we can start with "mandorla" (Italian for "almond"), the radiant oval aureole around paintings of Jesus or Mary,[20] which right away shifts to *Mandel* ("almond") and its associations: Biblical tree, Levantine eye, and Russian poet. What "stands" in the almond is not *nichts* ("nothing") but *das Nichts*, "Nothingness" or "the Nothing," and in Nothing "there stands the King," a King of glory (Ps. 24:7) antedating Christ.

Back in 1952, reading *What Is Metaphysics?*, Celan had underlined Heidegger's question "How stands it with the Nothing?"[21] He found that paradox of emptiness and pure Being again in Jewish mysticism: "The Righteous stands in the Nothing. . . . The Nothing is the Nothing of God."[22] In "Mandorla," starting with a Christian icon, *Nichts* turns into an annihilated people and their unknowable God. Recalling the side curls of Europe's Orthodox Jews and Celan's mother, whose "hair never turned white," a refrain says: "Jewish curls, no gray for you." And behind the question "whereto stands your eye?" is Celan's "I sought your eye" in "Count up the almonds"; behind the "Nothing," his speakers in "Psalm" who bloomed opposite Nothing.

Poems are "gifts to the attentive," he had said the year before (3:178), and other resonances abound in "Mandorla." *Dein Aug, dem Nichts steht's entgegen* ("Your eye, the Nothing it stands opposite"): like Celan, I've kept "eye" close to "Nothing" because of a pun—the Hebrew for "eye," *ayin* (עין), is sounded though not spelled just like *ayin* (אין), "nothing." For Jewish eyes filled with the nothingness of annihilation or divine absence, *Aug* and *Nichts* unite in Hebrew of all tongues.[23]

In the closing couplet we hear "Jewish curls" transmute to

Menschenlocke, wirst nicht grau.	Human curls, no gray for you.
Leere Mandel, königsblau.	Empty almond, royal blue.

Because Nazism declared Jews *Untermenschen,* subhuman, Celan's move from *Juden* to *Menschen* does not simply universalize the Jewish condition but works against that racist split-off of Jews from their humanity and fills the almond with kingliness.[24]

Judaic paradox drives a more enigmatic poem, "To one who stood before the door," begun the day Celan wrote "Mandorla." It was all very well for Celan in 1961 to advise someone, "Read! Just keep reading, understanding comes of itself."[25] But with these poems we feel like Kafka's Joseph K., who tries to understand the parable "Before the Law" but is told: "The Scripture is unalterable and its interpretations often merely betray bewilderment at this."

Who is speaking in Celan's poem, and to whom? Before what door, and why at evening?

To one who stood before the door, one
evening:
to him
I opened my word—:   [1:242]

"I opened my word": usually in the Bible—in Job and Psalms, for instance—a divine or human speaker opens his mouth or lips, or gates open up. In Celan's poem a word is opened, prompting a broken, almost derisive cadence:

> . . . toward the
> clod I saw him trot, toward
> the half-
> baked
> brother born in a
> doughboy's dung-caked boot,
> him with his god-
> like loins all
> bloody, the
> chittering manikin.
>
> Rabbi, I gnashed, Rabbi
> Loew:

The dialect term *Kielkropf* means a changeling, monster, or dolt. My word "clod" names an earthy, soulless creature, but loses the idea of something misbegotten and also the bite of *Kielkropf,* those *k*'s that cut through again in *Kriegsknecht,* a common soldier—"doughboy," for the fun of it.

Of some guardian "before the door," our speaker asks after a creature, a *golem.*[26] That term first appears when the Psalmist thanks God for "my unformed substance" (139:16). Colloquially for Jews it means a dumbhead, so my word "half-baked" tries for both senses. Rabbi Loew in sixteenth-century Prague is said to have fashioned a golem out of clay by means of Kabbalist incantation, a mute homunculus who defended Jews against persecution and blood libel. Here he's a "brother," for the golem embodies a Jew's creaturely self, awaiting like Adam the touch of spirit. "No one kneads us again out of earth and clay, / no one conjures our dust," said "Psalm" a few months earlier. With blood on his "god- / like" loins, as from circumcision, this clod is painfully inscribed in the Mosaic covenant.

The poem's fulcrum, "Rabbi, I gnashed, Rabbi / Loew," identifies the "one who stood before the door." And just that "gnashed" word "Rabbi" (used nowhere else by Celan) catches the ear. In 1961 he might well have appealed to the rabbi whose golem fought against libel. *Löw* alone evokes the poet's father, Leo, and Jewish tradition, to which Nazism forced Celan back.

Now the speaker intercedes with Rabbi Loew "For this one," the wordless golem, four times over:

> For this one—
> circumcise his word,
> for this one
> scribe the living
> Nothing on his soul,

for this one
spread your two
cripplefingers in the hale-
making prayer.
For this one.

To animate the creature, these difficult petitions draw on a store of ritual, legend, and mystical and Biblical tradition.

First of all, "circumcise his word" gives a poet's turn to that communal mark, for Moses was of "uncircumcised lips" (Exod. 6:12). And Celan gets a pun out of the Hebrew *Brit Mila,* the covenant of circumcision, since *mila* means "word" as well as "circumcision"—a pun audible only in Hebrew overtones and thus not for Aryan ears. After Nazism construed circumcision as a fatal sign, to "circumcise the word" is to take a liberating counterstep, bringing German words within the Covenant.

These words must admit paradox, as in the "living / Nothing." "The Nothing is the Nothing of God," says Scholem, "from which all true creation springs."[27] Here legend also offers a vivid example. The golem wore the word *emeth* ("truth") on his forehead, but when he ran amok, Rabbi Loew tore the first letter Aleph from *emeth,* leaving him *meth,* "dead." In language itself, truth is circumcised, cut down to death.

Paradox also guides the imperative "spread your two / cripplefingers." On Yom Kippur evening during the Priestly Blessing, the priests spread the third and fourth fingers of each upturned hand.[28] Yet Celan has the fingers crippled, much as in another poem—"You my words with me go- / ing crippled" (1:237). He could credit only a wounded reality, and so in his golem poem, the "hale- / making prayer" (*heil- / bringenden Spruch*) of "two cripplefingers" hits a raw nerve: for too long on too many lips, *Heil!* lost its healing sense to another force.

Words with the force of prayer end the poem:

Slam the evening door shut, Rabbi.
. . . .
Fling the morning door open, Ra- —

At sunset on the Day of Atonement there is a prayer: "Open the gates to us when the gates are being closed, for the day is about to set." This echo seemed far-fetched until I noticed that although Celan began his poem in May 1961, he did not complete it until four months later, on 20 September. In that year, 20 September was Yom Kippur. Though he never made any religious profession, as did Franz Rosenzweig returning to Judaism after a Yom Kippur service, Celan's writing cut its own covenant.[29]

At the close of this poem, Celan's early version said "Fling the morning door open, Ra . . ." with three dots trailing off.[30] He changed that to "Ra" with a hyphen and a dash—not only (I think) to accost the Prague rabbi more directly than the Egyptian sun god but also to break off his own voice more abruptly. The hyphen circumcises a word, the dash ruptures ongoing speech. Think again of Rosenzweig, his voice paralyzed for years, dying while dictating "what the Lord has truly granted to me: the point of all points for which there. . . ."[31] Think too of Prague's Kafka, voiceless from tuberculosis at the end of his life.

Kafka's presence hovers over this poem. His parable "Vor dem Gesetz," "Before" or "In Front of the Law," first came into Celan's hands when he was sixteen or seventeen. Later, in Bucharest, he made a Romanian translation and in 1959 endorsed Walter Benjamin's thoughts about it. The parable begins simply: "Before the Law stands a doorkeeper. To this doorkeeper comes a man from the country and asks for entrance into the Law." Stationing himself like the man in this parable, Celan enters into Kafka's radical estrangement. He once marked vigorously the diary passage where Kafka asks, "What have I in common with Jews? I have hardly anything in common with myself."[32] Yet around 1961 Celan said that Kafka's ambivalence about Judaism denied the existential roots feeding his work.[33] Celan also knew that the nameless angst of Kafka's bureaucratic Prague was a far cry from Nazism.

Across the historical rift between these two writers, Celan's poem draws on Kafka's parable, wherein the man waits many years seeking entrance into the Law, growing old and finally almost blind and deaf. "But now in the dark he perceives a radiance that streams inextinguishably from the door of the Law." Gathering all his years of trial into one question, the man asks why, since everyone strives after the Law, no one but himself has come demanding admission. "No one else could obtain admission here," the doorkeeper shouts at the dying man, "because this entrance was meant only for you. I'll now go and shut it."

Prompted by Kafka, Celan's speaker confronts the guardian of the Law to plead for a creature, and Kafka's name itself almost crops up. Possibly the double k's in Kielkropf and Kriegsknecht are hidden signatures: "toward the klutz I saw him trot, toward the half-baked brother born in a kossack's dung-caked boot."[34] For this creature Celan's poem commingles the golem legend with Kafka's parable and ends up crying for entrance. But just as we don't know whether Kafka's doorkeeper ever actually shuts the door, so Celan can only plead for the morning door to be opened. We're never to hear the last word.

The parable holds for Celan, as does a motto from Kafka's notebook: *Schreiben als Form des Gebetes,* "Writing as a form of prayer."[35]

11
Speaking East
(1962)

Pavel Lvovitsch Tselan
Russki poët in partibus nemetskich infidelium
's ist nur ein Jud—

With this trilingual whimsy, Paul Celan signed off a letter to Reinhard Federmann in February 1962.[1] Deciphered, it declares his allegiances. First, the name and patronymic in Russian form, "Paul son of Lev," honor his father and East European origins. Celan was hardly Slavic, but better that than "this so golden West," as he had put it two weeks before.[2] Next, some Russified Latin borrows from the Holy Roman Empire: "Russian poet in the territory of German infidels." Lastly, Celan adapts the jeering ditty from Kafka's "A Country Doctor": "Strip off his clothes, then let him heal, / And if he doesn't, kill him dead! / 'Tis but a doc, 'Tis but a doc."[3] Altogether he signs himself orphaned, misperceived, persecuted like a Russian poet, kin to a Prague storyteller, and mordant—"'Tis but a Jew."

Celan's yearning toward the East had started in 1958 with the Mandelshtam translations. In 1961 he confirmed it, writing to a Russian critic: "Like almost no one else, you've recognized that to me, Mandelshtam means an *encounter,* an encounter such as one may seldom experience. He was, from quite far away, that which is brotherly. . . ."[4] Later Celan found it "Meridian-like" that Mandelshtam's troubles with a plagiarism charge should resurface in his own.[5] And the poem "Siberian" speaks to the Russian whose first book was called *Stone*: "In my / throat too the millennium-colored / stone stands, the heartstone" (1:248).

That summer of 1961 the Celans were spending in Brittany near Gisèle's mother's convent. In Brest one afternoon, some flaming hoops in a circus looped a meridian circle for Celan: "there I saw you, Mandelshtam" (1:261). The moment had a saving impact: "Lost was Not Lost, / the heart a fortress." Also in 1961, Celan's book of Sergei Esenin translations appeared. He sent it to Nelly Sachs: "Years back, first as a schoolboy, later as a student in Czernowitz, I had a lot to do with these verses. Here, in the West, they came back to me, easterly, natively [*heimatlich*]."[6]

With Czernowitz and much of Europe under Soviet influence, one wonders what Celan saw there for himself when he turned east. A ricochet nostalgia kept his youthful socialism and Russian affinities insulated from what he otherwise knew very well. The East holds "everything that remains unforgettably near to my heart," he said when a woman friend from his Bucharest years drowned.[7] Writing to Federmann in March 1962, Celan called himself "an out-and-out *Ashkenazi* Jew," noting that "I have—witness Blok, Mandelshtam, and Esenin—a Russian (read: Jewish) great-grandmother"; a Karaite, he adds, "B'nai Mikra, Children of Scripture." Celan urged his friend to come and visit: "We'll go ahead and make *shabbes,* never mind OASes and palms." He is far from the promised land, that last phrase suggests, but its pun says that such things as the OAS, a French ultra-nationalist army in Algeria, will not hinder him.[8]

Feeling alone in France, Celan wrote a few days later to Petre Solomon in Romanian: "Don't forget how deep the Fascist cancer, clothed or not, has penetrated. I'm trying here to write Romanian, as you see, I'm finding the words—we've got no Romanian friends—only with difficulty."[9] A few lines later, despite the "German language which is mine—and which painfully remains mine," he says, "I am, with my meridian, right there where I began (with my old Communist heart)." By "where I began" he means not only the Bukovina "on a children's map" but a place "not to be found," as his Meridian speech put it, the mind's place where childhood and parents vanished.

A claim on that "old Communist heart" came in the form of Yevgeny Yevtushenko's "Babi Yar," commemorating the 33,771 Jews machine-gunned by SS troops at a ravine near Kiev in 1941. This poem appeared in September 1961, and Celan was stirred when Moscow's Jews rallied to its defense.[10] He translated it, publishing his version twice during 1962. We can hear this Russian elegy through the words of someone whose own parents were killed not far from Babi Yar:

Over Babi Yar no monument stands.
A rough slope—one unhewn gravestone.
I'm in dread . . .
I believe I am now
          a Jew. . . .
Dreyfus, him too,
            that's me.
The citizen
          denounces me,
the philistine
          pronounces judgment. . . .
Hounded.
      And spat on.
            And slandered. . . .
And am—am myself
         a single voiceless scream
over thousands upon
          thousands buried here.   [5:281]

It is not that Celan confuses genocide with his own persecution anxiety by way of a Russian's empathic lines. All these elements make up one mind-set.

"Yes I'm there again, *right* there," Celan wrote in March 1962 to Alfred Margul-Sperber, his old mentor (and father figure) in Romania. "Together with that 'no pasarán' which stands in the 'Shibboleth' poem: that too the gentlemen in West Germany cannot forgive me."[11] He was thinking of lines from 1954 that defy the German marketplace and the flag "I swore no kind of oath to" (1:131). Now in 1962, what German critics could not forgive— Celan's dogged memory—brought about a new poem. "In One" opens with four languages, uniting historical emergencies and dating its own emergence:

Thirteenth of February. In the heartmouth
an awakened Shibboleth. With you,

Peuple
de Paris. *No pasarán.*   [1:270]

The lines require attentiveness—what Celan called "a concentration that remains mindful of all our dates" (3:198): the French at Verdun in 1916, the Viennese workers' uprising of February 1934, the onset of Spain's civil war in 1936, and 13 February 1962 itself, when Parisian demonstrators against the right-wing OAS were buried and the people (as in the communes of 1792 and 1871) marched in the streets.[12] We also remember Celan's poem "Shibboleth," for in saying *No pasarán* again, he frames his own partisan tradition.

History comes close to home as this poem ushers in a "greybeard from Huesca" named Abadias. Besides bearing the name of a Hebrew prophet against Edom, this shepherd was a Spanish refugee and the first person the Celans met when they bought a farmhouse in southeast Normandy in 1962, at Moisville. His "human nobility" leads "In One" toward the 1917 revolution and to "Petropolis" (Mandelshtam's name for St. Petersburg), the "wander-city of those unforgotten," which "lay Tuscanly close to your heart too," Celan tells himself—"Tuscanly" enlisting (Mandelshtam's favorites) Petrarch and Dante. Finally we arrive at Büchner's version of the French Revolution motto, "Peace to the cottages!" (Celan omits its second half, "War to the palaces").[13] What is most tacit here, behind that motto, is a much-favored Psalm about Jerusalem: "Peace be within thy walls, And prosperity within thy palaces" (122:7).

From Edom to Europe, it is a lot to grasp—personally and historically overcharged. Yet in Paul Celan's very moved recital the poem feels right, held "in one" against the drag of history. Petropolis, for instance, was also the Brazilian city where Stefan Zweig, an Austrian Jewish exile, chose suicide in February 1942, as unable to survive where German was not spoken as where it was. However far they reached, Celan thought his poems crystal clear and coherent—not obscure, hermetic, or fantasaic, but fastened to reality.

Another touchstone for Celan's poetry is in Ingeborg Bachmann's "Among Murderers and Madmen" (1961).[14] In this story set in postwar Vienna, a "stranger" (the word she later used for Celan in a novel[15]) hears some beery veterans singing the nostalgic "Heimat, deine Sterne" (Homeland, thy stars), reproaches them, and is shot dead.

The classic stricture against poetry after Auschwitz, Adorno's from the 1950s, resurfaced in December 1961 when the poet Hans Magnus Enzensberger wrote that Nelly Sachs disproved Adorno's "hardest judgment."[16] Adorno replied immediately: "I would not want to modify the proposition that to go on writing lyric poetry after Auschwitz is barbaric."[17] He even elaborated: "Through the aesthetic principle of stylization . . . an unimaginable fate still seems as if it had some meaning: it becomes transfigured, something of the horror is removed." But Celan's *No pasarán* does the opposite of stylizing or transfiguring.

Although Adorno, Jew Gross of "Conversation in the Mountains," did not at all see Celan as barbaric, the poet remained hypersensitive to anything that might even remotely discredit him. He demanded purity from his own German publishers, for instance. When Deutsche Verlags-Anstalt, who had brought out his first two books, reissued the ballads of Börries Freiherr von Münchhausen, who thrived under Nazism, Celan switched to S. Fischer Verlag.[18] In 1962 he had troubles with Fischer too.[19] Even the Büchner Prize, the occasion for his brilliant manifesto, touched off his suspicions of Germany's literary establishment. He said they had chosen him "so that, having gotten this alibi, they could all the better run me down."[20]

Along with letters to friends at this time he sent a "bitter poem":[21]

WHERE the Word, that was immortal, fell:
into the heaven-chasm behind my brow;
led by spittle and trash, there goes
the sevenstar that lives with me.

Rhymes in the night-house, breath in the dung,
the eye servile to images—
And yet: an upright silence, a stone,
evading the devil's stairs.   [1:273]

"An upright silence, a stone": these at least were left him. "The other day," Celan wrote to Petre Solomon, "I sent you a letter accompanied by a poem (which is truly the cry of one who is *abolished*—in the strongest sense of the term—by neo-Nazi German 'human beings' and their tools)."[22]

This rash of letters from 1962 turns again and again to "my case," the plagiarism charge and its aftermath, in which solidarity counted decisively— if you weren't 100 percent with him, you were against him. The letters link perceived insults with a resurgence of "good old Reich-ideas."[23] They lament his exile in the West, and sometimes their sense of betrayal drives Celan to eloquent defense of his vocation. "Poetry, isn'ᵗ it confidence?," he asks, and "Isn't poetry a progression toward the Real, working amid what surrounds and seizes us? To engage oneself—isn't that, above all, to answer back?"[24] Although this can look like persecution mania, we are witnessing an injured survivor injured again by denial of the trust and truth his poetry has struggled for.

"My hope is in the East," Celan writes, linking his homeland to the Zion that Spain's Judah Halevi (1075–1141) longed for in a famous verse: "My heart is in the East, and I in the uttermost West."[25] Outcast, "a 'rootless' Steppenwolf with recognizably Jewish features," he thinks of "Harry Heine—

who had it much better back then than the undersigned Antschel and Ashkenazi."[26] Again he uses the signature "Paul Celan, from Czernowitz near Sadagora" in writing to the cultural historian Erich Kahler (1885–1970), a German-speaking Jew from Prague who had fled to the United States.

Striking up this friendship in April 1962, Celan was stirred by some statements of Kahler's that he found in the Zionist anthology *Vom Judentum* (Prague, 1913): "nothing has power over us that is not power from us." He inscribed these words in a copy of *Mohn und Gedächtnis* that he sent to Kahler, and also a sentence from one of Kahler's books (whose title, *The Responsibility of the Spirit,* must have struck a chord in him): "Eastern Jews were much defamed, and assimilated Jews in western countries greatly contributed to the defamation, wishing to distance themselves from this testimony to their past."[27]

To "try and hold onto what is left me" (3:178), Celan went on speaking to those in his past:

With names, steeped
in every exile.
. . . brimming with your
kingly blood, man—in all the
calyxes of that great
Ghetto-rose from which
you look on us, deathless from so many
deaths that died on morning roads. [1:271]

This poem goes on to name "the Varsovienne" (the nineteenth-century Polish workers' song that suggests Mandelshtam's birth in Warsaw and the 1943 ghetto resistance); "Petrarca" (in Siberia Mandelshtam recited Petrarch to his fellow-prisoners); and finally "Babel" (the confusion of tongues also points to Isaak Babel [1894–1940], a Russian-Jewish writer who perished under Stalinism). In exile and unable to abandon the mother tongue, Celan stamped it strangely his with words like *gebentscht, shibboleth, No pasarán,* Petropolis, Babel.

Far from insulating art against life (which the poet's interpreters often did), Celan's linguistic moves exposed his anxieties building throughout 1962—"a psychological pressure, over the long run intolerable," he said.[28] In a long, convoluted letter of 12 September to Margul-Sperber, Celan commented ironically: "Supposedly there were really war criminals in Germany, I read not long ago, but altogether only five hundred to a thousand of them, and these same have been officially pursued with the expenditure of appropriate federal funds. Meanwhile literature flourishes," he added, and the Press "holds it in front of an alibi-mirror."[29]

Working the outrage behind that letter into a playful lyric, Celan a day
later wrote:

Frugal,
modish and legal,
Schinderhannes goes to work,
social and alibi-elfish . . . [1:276]

Schinderhannes, the eighteenth-century anti-Semitic brigand he met in translating Apollinaire, stands here for contemporary German culture, engaged in
what Celan's letter called "a genealogical cleansing and purification process."
"Something is rotten in the state of D-Mark," he quipped.[30] He saw the Nazi
assault on humanity courteously forgotten and a poet's witness to humanity
defamed. "The thing I should have been able to do was hang it all up," he
wrote to Petre Solomon; "but you know what it means for a German-language
author who has lived through the Nazi terror to be cut off a second time
from his language."[31]

To refresh a poet's German language and free up his voice, wordplay
worked quite well. This pun from a letter of 1962—*Na ja, Sch(m)erz beiseite*
("Well then, all kidding aside")—makes *Scherz* ("joking") include *Schmerz*
("pain").[32] Sense-flips, syllable-reversals, nonsense babbling, coinages and
puns, double allusions, oddments from other tongues—all act to overturn
the ruling order. That September 1962 poem, in which "Schinderhannes goes
to work," plays as eccentrically with language as anything Celan ever wrote.[33]
Its title "Huhediblu" backflips the poem's central question:

Wann,	When,
wann blühen, wann,	when do they bloom, when,
wann blühen die, hühendiblüh,	when bloom the, hoomthebloom,
huhediblu, ja sie, die September-	hoothebloo, yeah them, the September
rosen?	roses?

This stems waywardly from Paul Verlaine's *Ah! quand refleuriront les roses de
septembre!* ("Ah! when will September's roses blossom again!").[34] Celan's poem
quotes but alters the French—*Oh quand refleuriront, oh roses, vos septembres?*
("Oh when will your Septembers, oh roses, blossom again?")—so that Verlaine's exclamation of hope becomes a question, put to the lost No One's-
Roses: Will their autumn bloom again? "September roses" then makes deadly
sense as a "date of the Neverhumansday in September." Everyone knew 1
September 1939 as the day when Hitler invaded Poland. Celan follows this
datum with a singsong word, *Wahnwann*, playing "madness" (*Wahn*) against
"when" (*Wann*) and punning on the 1942 Wannsee conference that planned
the "Final Solution." With wild, cunning words he resisted the crassness of
"economic-miraculous" Germany. One day before beginning "Huhediblu" he

called this "writing myself free from every kind of occident and schlock and contingence."[35]

Autumn of 1962 for Celan, like spring of 1821 for Keats, saw a spate of lyrics driven by malaise. "Tabernacle Window" begins in the spirit of Sukkoth, the Feast of Tabernacles (or Booths), a harvest festival commemorating the Israelites' journey in the wilderness:

The eye, dark:
as tabernacle window. It gathers
what was world, remains world: the wander-
East, the
hovering ones, the
humans-and-Jews,
the people-of-the-clouds.   [1:278]

Yiddish speaks benignly of *luftmenschen,* job-drifters with their heads in the clouds. Writing to Margul-Sperber at the time, Celan recollected how *Mensch* ("human being") during "the Nazi-time" seemed "a rhymeless word calling for rhyme."[36] His compound "humans-and-Jews" provides that rhyme. Tentatively the speaker says "we shall dwell, dwell" (as the Israelites "dwelt in booths"), but now he is beneath

the black hail that
fell there too, in Vitebsk,

—and those who sowed it, they
write it away
with a mimetic bazooka-claw!

Vitebsk, Chagall's birthplace, was mainly Jewish before the war and vulnerable like the hovering figures in his art. Watching postwar Germany write off the Jewish catastrophe, sometimes in reviews of his work, Celan told Margul-Sperber: "These fellows are mimetically more talented than their predecessors."

Against the "black hail" of distortion and oblivion, "Tabernacle Window" unscrolls a forty-eight-line sentence that "goes to Ghetto and Eden" and finally, like some Kabbalist initiate with the Hebrew alphabet,

paces off
the letters and the letters' mortal-
immortal soul,
goes to Aleph and Yud and goes further,

builds it, the Star of David, lets it
flare up, just once,

lets it die down—there it stands,
invisible, stands
near Alpha and Aleph, near Yud,
near the others, near
them all: in
thee,

Bet,—which is
the house, where the table stands with

the light and the Light.

That breath-turn from mother tongue to holy tongue—"in thee, / Bet"—
would vanish in a Hebrew version. Aleph and Yud and Bet are benchmarks
in the Diaspora that ought to sound strange, not at home. Aleph, an unvoiced
letter, begins the alphabet and God's first commandment, and the smallest
letter, Yud, which begins the name Yahveh, in German means "Jew." (Aleph
and Yud are also the initial letters of *Eretz Yisrael,* the Land of Israel.) Bet
means "house" and is also the first letter of Genesis, *Bereshit,* "In the beginning." Celan's verses go through the light of Sabbath evening candles to the
original Light. Gathering a lost world, "Tabernacle Window" traverses the
entire arc of Jewish time: Eden, David, Vitebsk, ghetto, Aleph, Bet, Yud.
Imagine these points of Jewish experience reaching Germany in the early
1960s, in the aftermath of the Eichmann trial.

To keep such points from being written away, to render his language
unimpeachable vis-à-vis a certain history, was a task with no statute of
limitations. In late September 1962 Celan named a poem "La Contrescarpe,"
for the Paris square he frequented as a student in 1938 ("counterscarp" means
a sharp fortifying wall). At one point this poem recalls his November 1938
journey from Czernowitz to Paris, which happened to pass through Poland
and Berlin on Kristallnacht:

Via Cracow
you came, at the Anhalter
Station
you caught sight of smoke
that was already from tomorrow.   [1:283]

Cracow is near Oświęcim. Given that route, Celan closes with a direction to
himself:

Yet again,
there where you must go, the one
exact
crystal.

Simply holding onto the hard word *Kristall,* after 1938, did all the poet could.

He went on looking for "exact crystal" during the fall of 1962, while translating Mandelshtam's newly published exile poems from Voronezh (5:154ff.).[37] Celan's seventy-four-line narrative "Everything is different" actually speaks "the name Osip,"[38] and other guiding spirits are hinted at: Sachs, Heine, Shakespeare, Kafka, Freud, possibly Hölderlin and Isaiah. Vital landmarks turn up: Russia, Karelia, the Bug River, Moravia, Prague, Normandy-Niemen, Bohemia, the Elbe. Entering this verbal landscape the poet has a fantastic encounter:

> The silver shekel melts on your tongue,
> it smacks of tomorrow, of always, a path
> to Russia rises into your heart,
> the Karelian birch
> has
> waited,
> the name Osip comes toward you, you tell him
> what he already knows, he takes it, he takes it off you with hands,
> you undo the arm from his shoulder, the right one, the left,
> you fasten your own in their place.   [1:284]

Whoever "brings a name into his song," Mandelshtam once wrote, is "thrice blessed" (5:133), and here not just "Osip" but "the name Osip" comes toward you.

This bodily encounter dramatizes a translator's intimate, aggressive act of dismembering and remembering:

> —what ripped apart, grows back together—
> you've got them now, so take them now, so now you've got them both,
> the name, the name, the hand, the hand,
> so take them and this pledge will stand,
> he takes that too, and you have back
> what is yours, what was his.

In sealing this blood brotherhood, Celan is remembering a folk rhyme in which children face each other and clap hands:

> My right hand first, my left hand too,
> I give a pledge to you,
> you've got them now, so take them now,
> so now you've got them both.[39]

He had recently made some nonsense couplets for his son (3:134), and a natural affection runs through the lines to Mandelshtam too. Impelled by his fellow-poet, "you're rowing" (Celan tells himself) through canals and ditches "by wordlight," with

> no Why at the stern, no Whither at the bow, a ram's horn lifts you
> —*Tekiah!*—
> like a trumpet blast above and beyond the nights into day.

In the "wordlight" of this voyage, *Bug* ("bow") puns on the Ukrainian river Bug where Celan's parents had no "Whither." And the piercing *Tekiah!* means "blast" but defies translation, being the ceremonial shofar call at the New Year (when these lines were written). Nelly Sachs had used the term in an earlier poem,[40] and now Celan's usage, neither devout nor customary for him, brightens an underworld quest.

For a moment that world with no Why or Whither seems reversed—"love returns . . . the hair of women grows back." Then Celan seeks a name for the place and time he is driven to visit:

> what is it called, your land
> back of the mountain, of the year?
> I know what it's called.
> Like the winter's tale it's called,
> it's called like the summer's tale,
> your mother's Three Year Land, that was it,
> that is it,
> it wanders everywhere, like language,
> throw it away, throw it away,
> then you'll have it again, like the
> flint-pebble from
> the Moravian Basin
> that your thought carried to Prague,
> on the grave, on the graves, into life.

Tentativeness and tenderness prevail, toward himself and this fairytale land. For behind Heine's satiric "Germany: A Winter's Tale" lies Shakespeare's play, in which a mother dies and is reborn in Bohemia. In 1915 Celan's mother had fled to Bohemia (and his grandmother died in Moravia in 1917); he once called her "years of flight . . . decisive for me."[41] In this 1962 poem, wandering is "like language"—the mother and the mother tongue share the same fate. Though Celan may never have seen Bohemia or (Kafka's) Prague, their names possess him. His "thought" follows Jewish custom to lay a pebble on the grave and on all the graves, "into life."

Language is like the pebble, and surprisingly this poem says "throw it away, throw it away, / then you'll have it again," lost and found in the dynamic of memory:

it's
long gone, like the letters, like all the
lamps, you must
seek it again, it's here,
it's small, white,
round the corner, it lies here
at Normandy-Niemen—in Bohemia,
here here here
behind the house, before the house,
white it is white, it says:
Today's the day.

Two particles in these lines sound out like cries of discovery: *fort* ("it's / long gone") and *da* ("it's here"). Freud based his ideas about the recollection of painful experience on a child's game that he observed: a "good little boy . . . greatly attached to his mother" would habitually throw away a toy on a string while uttering the word "gone" (*fort*), then pull it back and say "here" (*da*). This game, a "great cultural achievement," allowed him to master his mother's occasional disappearances (she died several years later, and so did the boy!).[42]

"All things are unforgotten," Celan wrote to Nelly Sachs in September 1962, and though he meant their years of friendship, his phrase also held for the whole past behind him.[43] If his poetry demands an exhaustively retentive reader, that is as he meant it. For instance, seeking the memorial pebble, Celan says: "it lies here / at Normandy-Niemen" (Niemen is in East Prussia). In August he had written from his Normandy farmhouse: "quite near here we recently saw a film on the Normandy-Niemen squadron, which helped in crushing Nazism."[44] That air force squadron, like Heine, Celan's mother, the shofar, a children's rhyme, and the name Osip, all belong here and now, as the poet's voice "finds its way through," ending at a source—not a river so much as a river's name:

White it is white, a water-
stream finds its way through, a heartstream,
a river,
you know its name, the banks
hang down full of day, like the name,
you feel round its shape, with your hand:
Alba.

Alba, meaning "white" in Latin and also the eastern "dawn," suggests the Elbe River where Celan's mother fled.

Still leaning eastward from Parisian exile, Celan obtained a copy of *Tarusskie stranicy* ("Pages from Tarusa," 1961), a bold Russian anthology including forty-one poems by Marina Tsvetaeva and focusing upon a small town frequented by writers on the Oka River south of Moscow.[45] His lengthy, obscure poem "And with the Book from Tarusa" of September 1962 (1:287) again carries an epigraph, like his Heine verse in "A Rogues' and Swindlers' Ditty" and his Yiddish song in "Benedicta." From Tsvetaeva (1892–1941) Celan took a thought that has now become better known than his (or her) poem itself, but one that is always mistranslated. Все поэты жиды (*Vse poety zhidy*), Celan's Russian epigraph, is understood as "All poets [are] Jews," or "Tous les poètes sont des juifs."[46] In Tsvetaeva's "Poem of the End" (1924), she comes upon Prague's ancient ghetto and reflects on the outcast condition of poets: "In this most Christian of worlds / Poets—Jews!"[47] Celan was probably quoting from memory, but the point is that her (and his) word *zhid*, a popular Czarist epithet, is derogatory, and used ironically by Tsvetaeva.[48]

Celan's epigraph really says "All poets are Yids." While he himself heard the slur, his German readers might not, since he printed the epigraph in Cyrillic characters.[49] "But then how very difficult it is to translate Marina Tsvetaeva," Celan had said in 1959,[50] and he never published any translations from this brilliant friend of Mandelshtam and Rilke who married a Jew and after long Parisian exile hanged herself in 1941.

Under such auspices and such an epigraph, Celan's poem on Tarusa has much to do with a poet's possible language in exile. Without grasping every element in this eighty-line rumination, one can feel its drift into "Nonland and Nontime . . . beyond the mute-peoples' zone"—east of Germany? We hear of the

Pont Mirabeau.
Where the Oka doesn't flow. *Et quels*
amours! (Cyrillic, friends, that too
I rode over the Seine,
rode it over the Rhine.)

In Apollinaire, "Neither past time / Nor love will come again / Under the Pont Mirabeau flows the Seine." A bridge from Celan's French exile across Germany to Russia was built up in his verse and in the translations that migrated back east.

These poems, Celan said about his 1963 collection, "went—with me— along a path that was not easy."[51] The last of the seven long poems that close *Die Niemandsrose* is not easy, but at least we know where we are to start with:

IN THE AIR, there your root remains, there,
in the air.

Where what's earthly clusters, earthy,
breath-and-clay.

Looming
up there moves the banned one, the
burned one: a Pomeranian, at home
in the Maybeetle song that stayed motherly, summerly, bright-
blooded at the edge
of all cragged
cold winterhard
syllables.   [1:290]

In der Luft, it begins, citing "Deathfugue"'s "grave in the air" and "Flower"'s "stone in the air," as well as "No One's root—O ours" from "Radix, Matrix." Once again Celan makes heaven an abyss, upending Creation and its life-giving "breath-and-clay." In his play on "banned" and "burned" (*Verbannte . . . Verbrannte*) a Pomeranian (or Bukovinan) whose homeland broke up during the war remains "at home" in a summer lullaby that his mother sang him, but only next to bleak bare syllables.

Catastrophe imprints language itself, so in language (this poem says), "tiny sheaves of hope" are gathered

. . . out of despairs,
a radiance
into which the sundered ones step with their
blinded mouths.

Celan's lines follow these "dispersed . . . tentmakers," "lifelong strangers," and end with

ford-beings, over whom
the clubfoot of the gods comes
stumbling—by
whose
star-time too late?

Why "ford-beings"? The root of "Hebrew" means "crossover," for the Hebrews crossed over the Jordan, and Jacob limped over the Jabbok ford after wrestling with the angel. Here it's over the Jews that "the clubfoot of the gods comes stumbling"—not their one God but the pagan fire god Vulcan, who was lame, or Joseph Goebbels, forever avenging his clubfoot. Celan's poem and book end: "too late?"[52]

"Bitter, yes, so they are, these poems," Paul Celan wrote to his publisher G. B. Fischer in December 1962.[53] The day before, he had complained about "revived anti-Semitism" in Germany, especially among "philo-Semites" and even "self-haters, the Out-with-us-Jews" who "play the role of protégés to so-called 'liberals.'"[54] Celan felt used by Germans, appreciated for an alibi. His poetry after the mid-fifties verged on defiance, and defiance bred more assertion. *Vse poety zhidy.* "Bitter, yes," he said, and added: "But in what's (truly) bitter there's surely the No-more- and More-than-bitter, isn't that true?"

What's bitter and what's more than bitter combined in *Die Niemandsrose* (1963). Celan dedicated his book to Mandelshtam: *Dem Andenken Ossip Mandelstamms*—not to or for him but "In Remembrance of" him.[55] His title "The No One's-Rose," a mind-boggling genitive like *Todesfuge,* tacks absence onto love and beauty such as Dante's celestial white rose and Shakespeare's rose of perishable youth. One of Rilke's Sonnets to Orpheus begins: "Set no memorial stone. Just let the rose / come into bloom for his sake year by year" (I, 5). And Rilke composed his own epitaph: "Rose, oh pure contradiction, desire / To be no one's sleep under so many / Lids."[56]

Deeper than Rilke or Shakespeare or Dante stands the *shoshana* of the Song of Songs, "Like a rose among the thorns" (2:2), which traditionally was seen as the community of Israel among the nations. Celan's early lyrics had roses of erotic and poetic fulfillment. Later, "Your house rode the darkening wave, yet it sheltered a people of roses" (3:42) and "Quiet! The thorn drives deeper in your heart: / it keeps a covenant with the rose" (1:75). In 1962 he wrote of "the great Ghetto Rose" (1:271). So *The No One's-Rose,* gathering his poems from the years 1960–62, speaks for both communal promise and catastrophe, for *zhidy* and "the name Osip" and roots "in the air."

12
Translation Counterpoint
(1961–63)

"Last year, around Christmas [1962], I went through a rather severe depression, but I managed to get a hold on myself again and go back to work in the École at the end of January. Since then, I'm climbing back uphill, there are still highs and lows, not a lot of sleep, but I'm working and I face up."[1] Thinking that Petre Solomon might not have received this letter, Celan wrote again: "I was rather sick last year: a nervous depression (to use the doctor's simplistic formula)."[2]

Simplistic, Celan says, because his illness issued from bitterness at Germany's literary industry, and bitterness grew from anxiety over the plagiarism affair, and anxiety stemmed from what happened in a winter season twenty years before, and how could all this be diagnosed clinically? For an entire year, from the fall of 1962, Celan seems to have written no publishable poems. Early in January 1963, reading a book on the Bible, he put nine scorings next to the Law of the Stranger: "The stranger who dwells among you shall be to you as a home-born, and thou shalt love him as thyself" (Lev. 19:34).[3] One evening around this time, Yves Bonnefoy remembers, Celan burst into sobs at the thought of the Goll plagiarism campaign.[4] In March he could tell Nelly Sachs how happy he was "that it's going better for you, that you've been able to return home, that you're working."[5] But Celan's own distress did not go on working as it had for three years before in poems such as "Radix, Matrix," "Tabernacle Window," "Everything is different," and "In the air."

Some hope still lay in lines like these, which said a great deal for Paul Celan:

who dwelled in Possibility,
a fairer house than Prose,
More numerous of windows,
Superior of doors—

Not Celan's lines but Emily Dickinson's, whose equation of poetry with possibility and openness heartened him. For Nelly Sachs's seventieth birthday on 10 December 1961 he sent some Dickinson he had translated, inscribing the offprint: "these translations from Emily Dickinson, born on 10 December 1830."[6] In English he wrote out for her (and himself) the quatrain about Possibility.

Translating poems remained an option, from French above all, and from Romanian, Russian, Portuguese, Italian, English, and Hebrew. Two huge volumes (1,500 pages) of Celan's collected works contain translations from forty-two poets, in addition to the Picasso play and Resnais' Auschwitz documentary. "All these are encounters," Celan said in 1961; "here too I have gone with my very being toward language."[7] As a translator, he refined and redefined the possibilities of a lyric voice in German.

"Speake-you English?" the thirteen-year-old had asked his aunt in a letter to Palestine.[8] That curiosity led him while in Czernowitz to translate Shakespeare, Housman, Rupert Brooke, and Yeats, including a singable version of "Down by the Salley Gardens."[9] Later he took up Marianne Moore, Andrew Marvell, and Housman again and ingeniously rendered the opening of Lewis Carroll's "Jabberwocky."[10] Celan's impassioned translations of Apollinaire, Mandelshtam, Dickinson, and Shakespeare coincided with his own explorative lyrics during the 1950s and 1960s. The exile of a German-speaker

72

SONDERDRUCK AUS

»DIE NEUE RUNDSCHAU«

HEFT 1/1961

Für Nelly Sachs,

zum 10. XII. 1961

diese Zeilen der am 10.XII.1830

geborenen Emily Dickinson,

who dwelled in Possibility,

a fairer house than Prose,

More numerous of windows,

Superior of doors —

Mit den herzlichsten Wünschen

Paul Celan

8. XII. 1961.

Celan, dedication to Nelly Sachs, 1961 (Kungliga Biblioteket, Stockholm) converged with a translator's inherent alienness. Hearing few kindred voices from Germany itself, Celan brought French, Russian, and English voices into his mother tongue. He did a group of Dickinson's lyrics in 1961 and returned to Shakespeare's sonnets. Both authors stimulated more revealing excesses than anyone else he translated from English.

In the Dickinson translations, her fascination with death and her skepticism about heaven bring out extra stress in Celan. Take the middle stanza of "I reason, Earth is short":

> I reason, we could die—
> The best Vitality
> Cannot excel decay,
> But, what of that?

In responding to this, Celan is also honing his own sense of mortality. Where Dickinson was anything but verbose or abstract, he finds still terser, more concrete things to say:

Ich denk: Sieh zu, man stirbt,	(I think: Look here, we die,
der Saft, der in dir wirkt,	the sap that works in thee,
auch ihm gilt dies: Verdirb—	it too knows this: Decay—
ja und?	so what?) [5:395]

Cannily keeping the off-rhymes (or call them slant rhymes—"Tell all the Truth but tell it slant," Dickinson once said), and cleaving to the original meter, Celan still forces a colon where there was none, prompting an imperative "Look here" to the reader or to the poet herself or *himself*. And Dickinson's discreet conditional "we could die" transmutes into blank fact.

Ordinarily we think of loss in translation, though sometimes of gain, but while both are happening here, they feel more like difference. Dropping Dickinson's deft word "best," Celan makes Vitality concrete ("the sap"), active ("that works"), and intimate ("in thee"). Then, rather than her general noun "decay," *Verdirb* tells the lifeblood: "Decay." The only other time he used that word, he had in mind what his poems cost:

> Whichever word you speak—
> you owe
> to destruction,   [1:129]

Verderben. No wonder Dickinson's shrug of indifference, however ironic— "But, what of that?"—turns clipped, brutal: *ja und?* ("so what?").

Celan's difference takes a theological twist in the closing stanza, where he answers Dickinson's "I reason, that in Heaven" with *Ich denk: Im Garten Eden.* Quite another place from her Heaven, "the Garden of Eden" enrolls a nineteenth-century Protestant in the Hebraic myth of paradise, loss, and possible redemption. It's true that *Eden* makes a catchy rhyme with the other line endings, *eben* ("even") and *gegeben* ("given"). It's also true that *Himmel* ("heaven") came hard to Paul Celan, except as in "The Sluice," from the period when he was working on Dickinson: "Over all this grief / of yours: no / second heaven" (1:222).

One century after Emily Dickinson, Celan shared her solitary, baffled, spiritual yearning and her sense that death dwells close and that poems speak immediate truth if anything can. Here is a perfect lyric whose density, one strophe then the next, Celan concentrates even more:

Let down the bars, Oh Death—
The tired Flocks come in
Whose bleating ceases to repeat
Whose wandering is done—

Fort mit der Schranke, Tod!	(Off with the barrier, Death!
Die Herde kommt, es kommt,	The flock comes in, there comes
wer blökte und nun nimmer blökt,	who bleated and now never bleats,
wer nicht mehr wandert, kommt.	who no more wanders, comes.)

[5:397]

A brusque command already opened Dickinson's poem. The translator is even more brusque—not "Let down . . ." but "Off with . . . !"—and leaves no time for the rhetorical "Oh." Then follows a tour de force, as Celan enacts these comings: *Die Herde kommt, es kommt.* Dickinson's poem dealt with repetition, and Celan bears this out literally. His tense change, "bleated . . . never bleats," incorporates a mortal lapse of time. And where Dickinson ends with wandering "done," Celan keeps going with "comes," making English verse whose shape seemed final molten again. His genius at uncalled-for repetition becomes a symptom proving that translation, a form of repetition, can indeed occur. First *Die Herde kommt*, then *es kommt*; first *blökte* then *blökt*: repetition with a difference—the genetic code of translation.

After his counterpoint in the first stanza, Celan settles momentarily into near-perfect unison:

Thine is the stillest night
Thine the securest fold
Too near Thou art for seeking Thee
Too tender, to be told.

Dein ist die stillste Nacht,	(Thine is the stillest night,
der sichre Pferch ist dein.	the surer fold is thine.
Zu nah bist du, um noch gesucht,	Too near thou art to yet be sought,
zu sanft, genannt zu sein.	too tender, to be named.)

With every word cognate in the first line, either the English or the German could have come first. But Dickinson's soothing parallel— "Thine / Thine"— is inverted by Celan, as if a translation must bear inversely on its source, not just sequentially. Of course, the upcoming rhyme counts here, because Celan's *dein* ("thine") is moving toward *sein* ("to be"). What is lost is Dickinson's odd doubling of Death as subject and object: "Too near thou art for seeking Thee." What is gained is the delay of *sein*, Celan's final verb of being, which almost counteracts death.

Still, it is Dickinson's exquisite versification that has impelled Celan's and released private nuances. "Too near Thou art," *Zu nah bist du*: a fine balance between English and German, and the intimacy of *du*, untranslatable in Celan's own verse, pairs for once with a "Thou." But something else weighs on *nah*: "Near are we, Lord . . . / clawed into each other" (1:163)—a voice from "Tenebrae" unthinkable in Dickinson's prayer to a God-like Death.

One more surprise awaits us in Celan's closing syllables: Death for him is too tender not to be "told" but "named." "Praise the name of the Lord," the Psalmist says. But as Judaism forbids uttering God's holy name, Celan could be rendering "Death" as the ineffable Being of Mosaic law. It takes translation, Celan's voice superimposed upon the earlier poet's, to get a disillusioned sense of twentieth-century death.

With Dickinson and Shakespeare too, the translator's task drew Celan into that time-lapse where poetic language strains under our century's assaults on "Reason" and "Vitality" (Dickinson's words) or on "Beauty" in the Renaissance sonnets. Civil war and religious dissent: these the nineteenth and seventeenth centuries both experienced—but not the genocide and divine eclipse behind Celan's every line.

During his time of psychic distress, Celan translated the author he most esteemed, Shakespeare, whose richness and fluency provoked contraries in German. At moments his versions edge beyond dialogue with the English into argument. In Celan's twenty-one sonnet translations, Shakespeare suffers a sea change into something rich and strange, often very strange.[11] I see no contradiction between the esteeming and the estranging. In sonnet 79, as George Steiner remarks,[12] the poet/lover already sounds like a zealous translator:

> Yet what of thee thy poet doth invent
> He robs thee of, and pays it thee again.

After these lines, Shakespeare's balanced phrasing,

> . . . beauty doth he give,
> And found it in thy cheek: he can afford
> No praise to thee but what in thee doth live,

surges with fresh emphasis in Celan's version:

. . . Er kann dir Schönheit geben:
sie stammt von dir—er raubte, abermals.
Er rühmt und preist: er tauchte in dein Leben.

(. . . To thee he can give beauty:
it stems from thee—he plundered, once again.
He'll praise and prize: he plunged into thy life.)

The added thrust of "plundered, once again" and "plunged," the doubling of "praise" and "prize," plus Celan's new verse breaks, all display translation's reflexive and possessive force.

In his teens, Paul would recite Ophelia and Juliet to his girl friends, and he was aware that Shakespeare had been translated into Yiddish.[13] He began learning English so as to read Shakespeare, tried some sonnet translations, and at eighteen in England went to see the plays performed. Around 1939 Celan may again have tried his hand at the sonnets, since he expressed dissatisfaction with Stefan George's and Karl Kraus's versions. When the Germans invaded in 1941, he recited his Shakespeare translations in the Czernowitz ghetto, I'm told,[14] and during his months at forced labor carried a notebook containing his version of sonnet 57. After the war, in Bucharest, Celan went on rendering Shakespeare sonnets in German. In Paris in 1960 he published translations of sonnets 90 and 137, ones he hadn't dealt with when he was young. Their themes of betrayal and bitterness that "the world is bent my deeds to cross" tallied with his own state of mind.[15] On Shakespeare's four hundredth birthday in 1964, German radio broadcast twenty Celan translations—several strongly reworked from years before—under the title "Die Rose Schönheit soll nicht sterben" (The rose [of] beauty should not die).[16]

Celan never commented, as far as I know, on his translations of Shakespeare's lyrics. Yet what he does to them has the force of commentary, even of confrontation. A Celan translation, no less than his own poetry, is "making toward something," as in the Bremen speech—"something standing open, occupiable, perhaps toward an addressable Thou."

This is not to equate Celan's poems with his translations. Working on Shakespeare in the fall of 1963, he himself had not written a sonnet for twenty years and was at a watershed after his fourth book, *Die Niemandsrose* ("The No One's-Rose"). At that time Celan's own verse, often cut to a word or a syllable per line, had begun to seem chipped off silence, blankness: "stonewrit shadows" (2:14). On the other hand, in translating, his voice resonates against another voice. Celan's versions of Shakespeare reverberate, because the sonnets' main themes—beauty, time, death, memory, regeneration, poetry itself—run disturbedly throughout his own lyrics.

In sonnet 5 a "hideous winter" drives into postwar German:

Those hours that with gentle work did frame
The lovely gaze where every eye doth dwell
Will play the tyrants to the very same,
And that unfair which fairly doth excel:

For never-resting time leads summer on
To hideous winter and confounds him there,
Sap check'd with frost, and lusty leaves quite gone,
Beauty o'ersnowed and bareness everywhere:

Then were not summer's distillation left
A liquid prisoner pent in walls of glass,
Beauty's effect with beauty were bereft,
Nor it nor no remembrance what it was.

But flowers distill'd, though they with winter meet,
Leese but their show: their substance still lives sweet.

Sie, die den Blick, auf dem die Blicke ruhn,
geformt, gewirkt aus Zartestem: die Stunden—:
sie kommen wieder, Anderes zu tun:
was sie begründet, richten sie zugrunde.

Ist Sommer? Sommer war. Schon führt die Zeit
den Wintern und Verfinstrungen entgegen.
Laub grünte, Saft stieg . . . Einstmals. Überschneit
die Schönheit. Und Entblösstes allerwegen.

Dann, blieb der Sommer nicht als Sommers Geist
im Glas zurück, verflüssigt und gefangen:
das Schöne wär nicht, wäre sinnverwaist
und unerinnert und dahingegangen.

Doch so, als Geist, gestaltlos, aufbewahrt,
west sie, die Blume, weiter, winterhart.   [5:325]

(They that, from what's most gentle, formed and framed
the gaze on which all gazes rest: the hours—:
they come again, to do a different thing:
what they did ground, they run into the ground.

'Tis summer? Summer *was.* Already time
leads on to winters and to darkenings.
Leaf greened, sap rose . . . In time past. Oversnowed
is beauty. And a bareness everywhere.

Then, were not summer as summer's spirit left

behind in glass, turned liquid and pent in:
beauty would be not, would be reft of sense
and unremembered and far passed away.

Yet thus, as spirit, formless, still preserved,
it lives, the flower, further, winterhard.)

What, incidentally, do these fourteen retranslated lines have to do with
Shakespeare's and Celan's? Their own (alas, unrhymed) iambic pentameter is
crossbred, sharing in Celan's syntax and diction—his "show"—as well as in
Shakespeare's "substance." My reversion spells out the difference between
Celan's German and Shakespeare's English sonnet.

"Those hours," Shakespeare's protagonist here, remain unnamed for the
rest of his quatrain, whereas in Celan they beget a recurrent pronoun. His
stressed opening, *Sie* ("They"), works through two verbs instead of one, and
only in the last breath of the second line is identified as *die Stunden* ("the
hours"). And where Shakespeare runs almost unbrokenly, Celan's verse stops
nine times. These breaks and short phrase blocks, along with a persistent
"they" and added verbs, make for surplus intensity.

Celan's voluntary doubling—his "gaze on which all gazes rest" and
"formed and framed"—goes on throughout the sonnet, symptomatic of the
doubling action of translation itself. Thus Shakespeare's swift pentameter,
where those hours that framed a gaze "Will play the tyrants to the very same,"
is "unfaired" by *sie kommen wieder, Anderes zu tun.* Not only time but translation itself has "come again, to do a different thing."

Celan's line could be translated "They come again, to do an Otherness,"
taking the radical sense of *Andere* from his Meridian speech (3:196). There,
a poem may, through its own strangeness, set free *ein Anderes,* an Other.
Given Celan's rendering of Shakespeare's tyrannous hours, I see time and
translation working together as agents of change. Facing the Renaissance
sonnet, an estranged postwar German frees the otherness that poetry bears
witness to. "The poem wants to reach an Other," Celan said in 1960, "it
needs this Other, it needs an Over-Against."

Since "never-resting time" leads this sonnet on, difference in translation
can emerge through tense sequence, the grammar of time. Shakespeare's
sonnet urges a youth to breed, because one day those hours "Will play the
tyrants" and will "unfair." Celan's verbs hasten to that future with a present
tense: "they come again . . . they run into the ground." Then when the
English sonnet shifts to the present, and time "leads summer on / To hideous
winter," the German is already looking back: "Summer *was.*" Since the German for "time," *Zeit,* can mean "tense" as well, the fell hand of grammar itself
seems at work. Celan recasts Shakespeare's summer in a spontaneous question
and answer: *Ist Sommer? Sommer* war ("'Tis Summer? Summer *was*"). It's

gone—with the emphatic past tense *war* and Celan's new word *Schon* ("Already"). As *Sommer* abuts *Sommer,* with only a question mark separating them, we hear a moment's dialogue on time and translation: ". . . summer? Summer . . ." The season confronts its loss: high time facing time past.

Responding to Shakespeare's vehement middle quatrain, Celan drops and adds words, deflects and reshapes phrases, alters tense and number and punctuation. His own constraints can be felt when summer cedes to winter (Celan even says "winters"). In fact, his work on the sonnets, in October 1963, colluded with a poem he wrote then:

> FEEL FREE to
> regale me with snow:
> whenever shoulder to shoulder I
> strode through summer with the mulberry,
> its youngest leaf
> shrieked.   [2:11]

Coming upon ruinous winter in the Renaissance lyric, it is hardly surprising to find an outbreak of verbal invention in Celan, as Nazism's darknesses press on his "darkenings" (*Verfinstrungen*) in this sonnet. Or take sonnet 60, where "Nativity" undergoes "crookèd eclipses" (*schiefe Finsternis*), "and Time that gave doth now his gift confound." Celan doesn't simply render that fluent line, he rends it: *und sie, die Zeit, zerstört, was sie, die Zeit, gegeben* ("and it, Time, destroys, what it, Time, has given"). As verse, Celan's overlong line staggers. As translation, it displays Time's confoundings. His versions risk perversion with their willful idiom.

In Shakespeare's ongoing present tense, which sees "Sap check'd with frost, and lusty leaves quite gone," Celan again finds a compelling pastness: "Leaf greened, sap rose."[17] Then his three dots insert a deeper difference with their muteness than does any word or tense change. (His Meridian speech had linked the modern poem's "bent for going silent" to a "quicker slant of syntax" and "livelier sense of the ellipse" [3:197].) Those dots mark a loss, as in "Black Flakes" (1943) where summer is ousted by winter's "darkening suns" and the world "will never green" again (3:25). Opening their line to an eclipse in European time, the dots expose a wound, and it takes a few moments to think through them. "Leaf greened. Sap rose . . . Once upon a time [*Einstmals*]"—a nostalgia already eroded by 1943: "And can you bear, Mother, as once on a time, / the gentle, the German, the pain-laden rhyme?" (3:20).[18]

German rhyme turns harsh where Shakespeare leads "summer on" to "leaves quite gone, / Beauty o'ersnowed and bareness everywhere." Celan forces "snow" before his line break, stepping up the work of time by coupling *Zeit* ("time") with *Überschneit / die Schönheit* ("Oversnowed / is beauty"). Since the word "o'ersnowed" did not appear in English until Shakespeare's sonnet, the older Middle High German *Überschneit* takes primacy—as if an Elizabethan bard had translated a Jewish survivor, relaxing the survivor's "oversnowed" Beauty.

In translating as in creating poems, what is expedient often jibes with what is essential. A rhyme will touch a nerve. Shakespeare has this:

> Then were not summer's distillation left
> A liquid prisoner pent in walls of glass,
> Beauty's effect with beauty were bereft.

For "distillation," Celan's *Geist* ("spirit," "ghost") prompts the compound *sinnverwaist* ("reft of sense"). This delivers more than Shakespeare's "bereft," since *verwaist* denotes orphanhood, folding Celan's personal loss into a sonnet on procreation. Elsewhere he applied *verwaist* to the Jewish people's orphaned wanderings (1:278, 3:100). Adding *Sinn* ("meaning," "consciousness") pushes *sinnverwaist* beyond its text: "orphaned of meaning" describes certain speakers of the German mother tongue.

Hardly an item of Shakespeare's goes innocently into German:

> Then were not summer's distillation left
>
> *Dann, blieb der Sommer nicht als Sommers Geist*
>
> (Then, were not summer as summer's spirit left)

The reflex of *Sommer* upon *Sommer* does what Celan often does: refute a word with the same word made different because repeated. A poet "stricken by reality and seeking reality," he could not defy time. Where Shakespeare repeats the noun, "Beauty's effect with beauty were bereft," Celan shifts to subjunctives, the mood for what is contrary to fact: *das Schöne wär nicht, wäre sinnverwaist* ("beauty would be not, would be reft of sense"). Repetition, which Peter Szondi's fine essay on Celan's translation of sonnet 105 calls the "syntactic realization of constancy," here realizes contradiction instead.[19]

Sometimes it takes a translator's voice-overs to dramatize that radical calling into question which Celan demanded of any poetry. Consider the upshot of Shakespeare's urging beauty to breed—that flowers are crushed to make perfume, that youth dies but its essence lives on in verse. Celan deals hard with this triumphalism. Postwar German poetry, he once said, has to "mistrust the 'Beautiful,' it attempts to be true" (3:167). And truth for Celan required self-exposure. So we expect him to act, when Shakespeare's couplet relents after twelve lines of rich conflict into vapid consolation:

> But flowers distill'd, though they with winter meet,
> Leese but their show: their substance still lives sweet.

Doch so, als Geist, gestaltlos, aufbewahrt,
west sie, die Blume, weiter, winterhart.

(Yet thus, as spirit, formless, still preserved,
it lives, the flower, further, winterhard.)

The German gropes, taking twice as many breaths, breaking down the time of the couplet. Instead of a steady sibilance—"Leese but their show: their substance still lives sweet"—Celan's alliteration has a cumulative tempo: *west . . . weiter, winterhart.* As the syllables augment, they "live further" through alliteration, which itself is translation distilled, a repetition or "asking again" how language goes on.

Repetition—with a difference. Celan could hardly have ended more idiosyncratically.[20] His last line begins with an archaic verb, *wesen* ("exist"), which draws on Heidegger's sense of "come to presence," "endure."[21] Then *sie, die Blume* ("it, the flower")—Celan's anticipatory pronoun is his signature. In sonnet 65, on "sad mortality," he has:

How with this rage shall beauty hold a plea,
Whose action is no stronger than a flower?

Und sie, die Schönheit, soll dagegenstehen?
Sie, eine Blume, soll hier Kraft entfalten?

(And it, beauty, should stand over against?
It, one flower, should unfold power here?)

Fine things do fall by the wayside, such as "rage" and "plea," so it can't simply be that Celan's pronouns are filling out the meter. They are holding up something—both displaying and delaying it—for our attention. They anticipate an act of renaming, if only for a moment: "it, the flower." That commalong delay from pronoun to noun also keeps language going. "It, the language, remained, not lost" (*Sie, die Sprache, blieb unverloren*), Celan said in his 1958 speech.

At the end of sonnet 5 we see that *west* ("it lives") is not all there is to it: *west sie, die Blume, weiter* ("it lives, the flower, further") points forward to the word *winterhart*. In this last word Shakespeare suffers the strangest change of all. His couplet has promised that winter can ruin only the outward flower, for its perfume "still lives sweet." But *winterhart* ("winterhard") says something different. Celan did not coin the word, which the Grimms' dictionary defines as either "hardened *against*" or "*by* winter." Even this ambiguity, poignant enough in a nature lyric, fades against the fact that Celan won't or can't translate "sweet," cannot take Shakespeare's word—not that word, anyway. Beauty lives if it is proof against and proved by winter, *winterhart*.

Celan had used this word in a recent poem tracing the meridian of Jewish survival, remembering a song "that stayed motherly, summerly" next to "cold winterhard / syllables" (1:290). Sweetness is out of the question, even with the safe-conduct of a Renaissance sonnet. That word *winterhart,* startling in his own poem and in Shakespeare's too, claims the translation as Celan's.

In the winter of 1963, telling Petre Solomon of his "rather severe depression" the year before, Celan mentioned that he had "just finished translating a score of Shakespeare sonnets."[22] The two events connect in one small revision to sonnet 116. Just after the war in Bucharest, translating "If this be error and upon me prov'd," Celan had used *Irrtum* for "error," the cognate and perfect equivalent.[23] In 1963 he changed it to *Wahn,* a plausible choice but one with the sense of madness.

"Yes dark and dark," Celan rendered a line from Henri Michaux in 1963, and "Listen, I'm the shadow of a shadow that's sunk in mire" (4:709). But translation kept his hand in. Recovering from a breakdown, waiting for *Die Niemandsrose* to come out and not writing anything of his own, Celan published his versions of Michaux, another translation from Dickinson, two more Mandelshtam lyrics, one by Konstantin Sluchevski, and Housman's "Epitaph on an Army of Mercenaries." After Robert Frost died in 1963, Celan translated "The Road Not Taken"—prosily, but with an eye to lines that spoke for an exile: "Yet knowing how way leads on to way, / I doubted if I should ever come back" (5:404).

Celan also made a generous attempt at "Stopping by Woods on a Snowy Evening." Frost's interwoven rhyme and lucid four-beat rhythm don't carry over, but other gratifying things turn up. Watch what happens to the sweep "Of easy wind and downy flake":

doch, dies noch: leichten Wind, die Flocken, erdwärts, dicht

(yet, this too: easy wind, the snowflakes, earthward, thick)

Did a memory of "Black Flakes" from 1943 fragment Frost's easy line? Did Celan know what "downy" really means and still make a pun with *erdwärts* ("earthward")? At any rate, some otherness happens to Frost's repetition at the end:

And miles to go before I sleep,
And miles to go before I sleep.

Und Meilen, Meilen noch vorm Schlaf.   (And miles, miles yet before sleep.
Und Meilen Wegs noch bis zum Schlaf.   And miles of road yet until sleep.)

What has become of the speaker's "I"? Whether Frost's repetition embodies a death wish or its opposite, or mere drowsiness, Celan opts for a small change, a process, a possibility.[24] He makes his own repetition right away— "miles, miles"—and then shifts "before" to "until," putting off sleep just a shade longer.

Part Three
Reality

13
Etching and Alchemy
(1963–65)

"Next year," Celan said in that 1963 letter about nervous depression and Shakespeare, "I hope to publish a cycle of new (rather short) poems, along with some engravings by Gisèle."[1] The mention of Gisèle announced a life-saving alliance. The cycle came out in a superb yet austere, large-format, black-bound edition, with eight etchings that fortify the poems.[2]

Silent as a poet for almost a year, Celan had not abated his mistrust of Germany. "As a Jew and a German author I've got no easy position," he said in September 1963.[3] Then one October day in a rush came four brief lyrics.[4]

Celan, Paris, 1963 (Lutfi Özkök)

(Wary of the plagiarism charge, Celan was now dating even his drafts.) The first of these, beginning "Feel free to / regale me with snow," originally continued: "I come with seven / leaves from the Seven- / branch." Celan later dropped this menorah image and spoke of striding through summer when the mulberry's "youngest leaf shrieked" (2:11). At his house in Normandy he kept a menorah and planted mulberry trees in the yard.

The tension between hope and pain moves another poem from October 1963, again in a single sentence:

IN RIVERS north of the future
I cast the net that you
haltingly weight
with stonewrit
shadows.   [2:14]

Nothing could be colder or remoter than these rivers or blanker or muter than these shadows, yet between them an "I" casts a net and a "thou" appears to help. In lithography and etching Gisèle worked with gray and black on white, so Celan's poem, meant to be published with his wife's art, shares her somber imagery and severe technique.

These tight-lipped lyrics from the fall of 1963 owe much to graphic art— "etch . . . bite . . . carve . . . groove . . . press . . . copper . . . stone . . . image . . . shade . . . white-gray . . . gray-black . . . wood-song." Celan's alliance with a wordless art sounds salutary, but his illness also impinges and cannot be quarantined from his writing. "Wound" occurs several times, also "pain" and "sleepless," and "Temple-pincers, eyed by your cheekbone" suggests shock therapy (2:21). At this point, the poet digs in with his strongest verb:

To STAND, in the shadow
of the wound-mark in the air.

Stand-for-no-one-and-nothing.
Unrecognized,
for you
alone.

With all that has room in it,
even without
language.   [2:23]

Another poem starts with a dream and its "word trace," cites a horn's "last blast," then shows what going without language might feel like. Here is its closing image, word for word:

The in the vert-
ical, narrow
day-gorge upwards
poling ferry:

it puts
wound-readings across.   [2:24]

This arduous ferrying "puts . . . across"—*setzt . . . über,* roughly the same verb as "translate"—something read (or gleaned) by way of a wound: *Wund-gelesenes.* Only a wounded reading will rise, as if from one language to another, into daylight.

Trying to lay bare the irreducible, Celan one day in late November 1963 composed two small hard credos. The first irrupts without subject or predicate, declaring only allegiance:

WITH THE PERSECUTED in late, un-
silenced,
radiant
covenant.   [2:25]

I say "covenant" for *Bund,* rather than "bond," "league," "union," or "alliance,"[5] because the German word has that sacred sense—and warrants it, after "persecuted," "un- / silenced," "radiant."

Celan's other poem that day often has only its hopeful last clause cited, but the earlier lines hold back that hope.

THREADSUNS
over the gray-black wasteness.
A tree-
high thought
strikes the light-tone: there are
still songs to sing beyond
humankind.   [2:26]

Thin yet tough threads bind the dead to the living. Here, as in an etching of his wife's, tenuous light hovers over the waste and void before Creation. Then a "tree-high" thought—and there is light. "Oh Orpheus sings! Oh high tree in the ear!" Rilke opens his *Sonnets to Orpheus.* For Celan, there is no return from the underworld, but "there are / still songs to sing beyond / humankind [*jenseits der Menschen*]"—not in some afterlife but a step beyond those he kept covenant with.

"Covenant" is not too charged a way of identifying the poet's task, nor is "testimony" or "witness"—*zeugen,* a key word in Celan's 1963 cycle. One poem "witnesses naked for the beginnings" (2:29); another asks the poet's wife: "Where flames a word to witness for us both? / You—all, all true. I— all mad" (2:30).

Responding to that question, the cycle's closing poem finds such witness. Celan's *Weggebeizt* ("Bitten away"), a word related to both geologic erosion and acid etching,[6] has a curative effect just by sharing in his wife's art:

BITTEN AWAY by the
radiance-wind of your language,
the motley gossip of pseudo-
experience—the hundred-
tongued My-
poem, the Lie-noem.   [2:31]

After this exposure of bogus poetry, the last lines pierce through "crevasse" and "ice" to a saving word:

Deep
in the time-crevasse,
by the
honeycomb-ice
there waits, a breathcrystal,
your unannullable
witness.

"In Front of a Candle" (1953) saw his mother "wedded to a crevice in time."
Now, a decade later, Celan binds words the hardest way: glacial "honeycomb-
ice" and "breathcrystal" vital yet vulnerable in each of its halves—*Atemkristall*.
Celan titled his cycle with this "word to witness for us both." "*Atemkristall*
opened the paths of poetry for me," he later told his wife; "it was born from
your etchings."[7] His poems reflect Gisèle's images: fragments, filaments, needles, nervous movement, precise enigmatic forms, white and gray and black.
One etching at the end of the cycle sets Hebrew-like letters against a bed of
white splinters on a gray ground—the graphic equivalent of a threatened yet
"unannullable witness."

Celan's witness to mass death perplexed Rolf Hochhuth, who published
his notorious play *The Deputy* in the spring of 1963. Granting that "Todesfuge"
was "masterly," Hochhuth still thought that its metaphors "screen the infernal
cynicism of what really took place."[8] Whether or not Celan was aware of this
judgment, his poems had long since gone beyond the persuasive rhetoric of
"Todesfuge." Without abandoning figurative language, his metaphors became
barely recognizable or strangely specific, like a "heart-formed" crater or
"honeycomb-ice."

"The truth lies in detail," he remarked in January 1964—an axiom for
making one's way through Celan's idiosyncratic writing.[9] Opening his next
cycle, "the great Eyeless" (God?) scoops up a "six-edged" (Star of David?)
foundling. Then

A blind man's hand, starhard too
from Wandering-through-Names,
rests on him as
long as on you,
Esther.   [2:35]

Since "Names" (*Shemot*) is the Hebrew title for the book of Exodus, this
foundling seems touched (blessed?) by the hand of a blind man (Isaac?) of a
wandering tribe, as is the queen who saved her people from persecution
(along with Esther, Celan in draft had Miriam, Moses' sister).

The more reduced Celan's verse, the more possibilities it releases. One of
his better-known (if less knowable) lyrics also dates from early 1964: "Keine
Sandkunst mehr."

No MORE SAND ART, no sand book, no masters.
Nothing on the dice. How many
mutes?
Seventeen.

Your question—your answer.
Your song, what does it know?

Deepinsnow,
        Eepinnow,
            E - i - o.   [2:39]

Through this experiment, two paths coincide: poetic language and Jewish existence. Recalling his *Sand from the Urns* (1948) with its sense of a desert life running out, this poem turns away from the "art" (*Kunst*) opposed to true poetry in the Meridian speech. To admit no "art," "book," or "masters" is to reject an aestheticism such as that of Mallarmé in "A Throw of Dice." And maybe seventeen mutes lack one for the central Eighteen Prayer of Judaic liturgy, or simply for "18," which in Hebrew spells "alive."[10]

"Question" and "answer," the poles of Celan's lyric effort, themselves get swallowed up by a question: "Your song, what does it know?" Instead of responding, his last lines reach where this poet's imagination has driven him since 1942:

Deepinsnow,
        Eepinnow,
            E - i - o.

No more sand art, a snow art now, contracted to its selfmost straits. Nothing but vowels remain, the heart of a word, the sine qua non. But translated into Hebrew, which has no vowel letters, this poem would verge on silence—a testimony to the literal truth that Celan sought. Ten days later he ended a poem with "sleep grains"

wafting from the true-
stammered mouth
out to the snow-
conversations. [2:42]

In these odd compounds, the word "true-" suspends a promise that "snow-" puts at risk.

If writing crystallized the questions besetting Celan, it still could not heal him. He resigned "irrevocably" from the Austrian PEN club because an elderly member had made anti-Semitic remarks.[11] And in January 1964 he told a friend, "My recent book has been greeted with silence."[12] In fact, *Die Nie-mandsrose* had only just come out, so it was too soon to speak of silence, and favorable reviews did appear in Germany. Though Celan said he missed living "in exclusively German-language surroundings,"[13] his writing had nothing conciliatory about it. "Black, like the memory-wound," he began a poem, adding: "The giving of names has ended" (2:57). A week later he thought up a phrase, "the clinker game against death," and evolved this Beckett-like scene:

LANDSCAPE with urn-beings.
Conversations
from smokemouth to smokemouth.

They eat:
the lunatic-truffle, a piece
of unburied poesy,
found tongue and tooth. . . .

the clinker game against death
can begin. [2:59]

Unlike the intimacy of "The Vintagers" or the pebble laid on Prague's graves, this encounter with the dead occurs somewhere north of the future, in a gray-black wasteness. Two days later Celan thought of changing the title of his first cycle, *Atemkristall* ("Breathcrystal"), to *Wahnspur* ("Madness-trace").[14] Although he didn't stay with that change, it tells us what to look for in these poems of the mid-sixties.

Wahn also enters "In Prague," which has a dreamlike dimension because Celan probably never saw the city that was even more central to him than Vienna.[15] He speaks here to "you"—another writer, such as Bachmann[16] or Rilke or Kafka, or the poet's own Other, his *du*:

In Prague

The half death,
suckled plump on our life,
lay ash-image-true all around us—

we too
went on drinking, soul-crossed, two swords,
sewn onto heaven-stones, wordblood-born
in the night bed,

larger and larger
we waxed through one another, there was
no more name for
what drove us (one of the thirty-
how many

was my living shadow
that climbed the madness-stairs up to you?),

a tower,
the Half built itself into Whither,
a Hradčany
out of pure goldmakers-No,

Bone-Hebrew,
ground down to sperm,
ran through the hourglass
we swam through, two dreams now, tolling
against time, in the squares.   [2:63]

A quintessential autobiography, these lines begin (like "Todesfuge") with a reversal, making death a plump infant "suckled on our life." Then "we too went on drinking." In Nazi slander, Jews were bloodsuckers, so the writers whom death fed on are "wordblood-born."

A landmark shows up midway through, when the poet (in parentheses, questioning) calls himself "one of the thirty- / how many . . . ?" Though he knows well enough the Jewish legend of thirty-six Just Men defending humankind throughout history, perhaps they now number in the millions, among them "my living shadow / that climbed the madness-stairs up to you." Here the poet's mental surgings join, not all that improbably, with the sixteenth-century occult-minded Emperor Rudolf II, who once had a secret conversation with Rabbi Loew of Prague and who set up below Hradčany Castle the Alchemists Lane, where Kafka wrote.[17] These Babel-like "madness-stairs," for a writer raising base metal into gold or earth into spirit, must climb alongside death, whose tower said No to such hopes.

Celan's rude coinage "Bone-Hebrew" rings like the bone-man Death, the skeleton gleaner on Prague's town hall clock tower. Then the charnel sense of "Bone-Hebrew" gets transmuted—not to fertilizer, as in the death camps, but "ground down to sperm." Stirred somehow by "sperm" instead of sand in the hourglass, Celan's lines end up "tolling / against time."

If not to Prague, Celan did go to Amsterdam in May 1964. The old Jewish quarter seemed dilapidated, the Portuguese synagogue too cathedral-like, and at Spinoza's birthplace there was only an empty lot. That month a German critic also rubbed his wound raw. Hans Holthusen compared Celan to Hölderlin and Rilke but again saw only a weakness for "surrealist genitives" in that early line "You grind in the mills of death the white meal of the Promise" (1:35).[18] As it happens, during the Frankfurt Auschwitz trial that spring, Eichmann was quoted on "the mills of Auschwitz." The "surrealist" label stung Celan because he had earlier been accused of taking "mills of death" from Yvan Goll. That summer, traveling south in France to visit friends, he stopped at Oradour, where the SS in 1944 massacred 642 villagers. Then, with his friends, he debated replying to Holthusen. But he could not or would not do it—his poetry already stood for him.[19]

That fall of 1964 brought another mishap, on the occasion of North Rhine–Westphalia's awarding Celan its Art Prize. At the ceremony, spotting someone on the podium who had taken part in Claire Goll's plagiarism campaign, "Paul jumped up with his face flushed, ran from the hall and declared he would not accept the prize." He was persuaded to return but spent that night detailing his "case" to old friends from Czernowitz. He refused to take legal action: "Against them you can't win."[20]

Niemand was his heart cry at the end of "Aschenglorie" (Ashglory, Ash-Aureole):

> No one
> witnesses for the
> witness.   [2:72]

Zeugen ("witness") can also mean "procreate," sharing its sexual origin with "bear witness" and "testify." The urge to witness touches practically every poem around this time:

> WHAT'S WRITTEN goes hollow, what's
> spoken, seagreen,
> burns in the bays.   [2:75]

And that urge puts a verbal strain on tried-and-true religion: "smoke-spent" prayers, "psalm-hooved" stallions, "o-, o-, o- / pen-leaved Bible mountains" (2:81). At the bottom of another painstaking lyric, Celan anchors (or buries) the word *Schrift*:

> by the tinily flaring, by the
> free
> punctuation of the
> toward innumerable to
> be named un-
> utterable names a-
> sunder fled, sal-
> vaged Scripture.   [2:82]

It's scarcely pleasure, in this poetry from 1965, but a doggedness to affirm nothing facilely. Scripture itself is sundered and salvaged to name its unutterable names.

While this poem almost breaks apart (its title "Solve" means "dissolve"), Celan on the same day wrote another one called "Coagula" (2:83), both Latin terms coming from alchemy. Its terse opening—"Also your / wound, Rosa"—

packs together three vital memories. In Czernowitz and Bucharest Paul was in love with a Communist militant named Rosa, and her recent death had deeply affected him.[21] Add to that Kafka's "A Country Doctor" (1917), which has a character named Rosa and uses the phrase "your wound." And in 1917 the revolutionary Rosa Luxemburg wrote from prison of seeing water buffaloes from Romania brutally beaten by German soldiers.[22] Celan's poem catches her compassion:

And the horns' light of your
—also my—
Romanian buffaloes.[23]

In acute need the poet coagulates—drives together—his youth, his kinship with Kafka, and his political solidarity: these form one idea in what the poem calls a "talking, red-ash-potent alembic."

Ash Wednesday 1965 provoked a poem called "Easter Fumes,"[24] merging incense with crematoria and the exodus:

(Never was Heaven.
Yet sea is still, fire-red,
sea.)

We here, we,
glad crossing over, in front of the tent,
where you baked wilderness-bread
out of co-wandered language.   [2:85]

In revising, Celan put "co-wandered" in place of "rescued,"[25] too promising a word for what the poet lived by.

Other lyrics also exposed Judaic tradition to history. An image of phylacteries, for instance, is abruptly broken into:

ON THE WHITE PRAYER-STRAP—the
Lord of this hour
was
a winter creature, for his
sake
happened what happened—
my clambering mouth bit hard, yet again,
as it sought you, smoketrace.   [2:44]

A Jew's *tsitsit* or fringed garment, "show-threads" in German, turns strange:

SHOW-THREADS, SENSE-THREADS, from
nightgall knotted
behind time:

who
is invisible enough
to see you?   [2:88]

Celan's kind of heresy meant calling the believer "invisible" and "smoketrace" an article of faith.

Meanwhile he found himself again at odds with Adorno, who in 1965 republished his essay calling it barbaric to write a poem after Auschwitz.[26] Worse yet, the journal *Merkur,* which promoted the philosopher's thoughts on music and literature, cited Adorno to belittle "Todesfuge" and its motifs, "all of them thoroughly composed in an elegant score—didn't that show far too much pleasure in art, in despair turned 'beautiful' through art?"[27] Then in *Die Zeit,* reacting to a positive review of Celan, a reader deplored "Auschwitz as soil for art, the victims' death-cry in perfectly harmonized verse . . . This beauty of Paul Celan's, wrung from destruction, seems questionable to me."[28] Against these suggestions (from Germany!) that he could batten on Jewish catastrophe, Celan protected himself with sarcasm: "As one newspaper has seen fit to announce in its letters column: what I exhibit by way of my quill owes solely to the murderers of Auschwitz—and now in *Merkur,* which strictly follows Adorno, . . . we finally know where the barbarians are to be found."[29]

Although a distinguished Viennese writer came to the poet's defense, calling "Todesfuge" "far and away the sublimest German poem of the last twenty years," Celan was beyond reach. At the same time, he was irritated with Fischer Verlag for anthologizing him alongside a man whose wartime conduct he disapproved of.[30]

More vulnerable than ever, Celan entered a psychiatric clinic outside Paris for a few weeks in May 1965. There he read Shakespeare's plays and let art hold up the mirror to nature, as it were. Whenever he lit on anything about madness, fools, betrayal, slander, or suicide, he underlined it and noted it in the back of the volume. More desperate than his grasp of the sonnets, this kind of possession has nothing buffering it, no translator's coups to deflect the pain.

While reading Shakespeare so nakedly, Celan wrote the only poem he ever titled with an English phrase: "Give the Word" (2:93)—something the crazed King Lear says to Edgar on the heath (act 4, sc. 6), demanding a password.[31] Later in the scene, Lear tells a gentleman, "I am cut to th' brains," and in translation this image opened Celan's poem. *Ins Hirn gehauner König,* his draft says: "King with your brain hewn into, half as old, / I am already you."[32] Then right away he replaced the personal touch with a gibe, playing the Fool to both Lear and himself: "Hewn into the brain—half? three-quarters?" Cutting into heroic pathos, Celan frees his own anguish. And given the angle he had on Shakespeare, his title loses something in (not needing) translation. "Give the Word" forgoes German in favor of demented speech— a password to truth in poetry.

Celan was not too fastidious to speak of truth: "For a long time I've been carrying on a struggle, that of poetry in solidarity with truth," he said in August 1965.[33] He wrote then to Erich Kahler, voicing the German-Jewish side of that struggle. Kahler in 1964, without at all understating the barbarity of Nazism, had urged Jews as well as Germans to probe their "special interpenetration of dispositions and destinies," so as "to purify their minds."[34] For Celan, such thinking (he told his publisher) recalled "pre-Hitlerite blindness and shortsightedness."[35]

Writing to Kahler of "ourselves who are Jews, trying to be and remain Jews," Celan brought up the anarcho-socialist Gustav Landauer (1870–1919), whom he had mentioned to Kahler before.[36] Landauer's statement of German-Jewish symbiosis—"My Germanness and Judaism do each other no harm and much good"—had once seemed great words. But since the war, Celan thought that Landauer's hope for "new emotional involvement" among Germans was a "most tragic and indeed most childish error." Nonetheless, Celan tells Kahler that Landauer's legacy "lives on in me, not without pain, yet strong . . . together with the oldest Jewishness, a bit isolated yet not cut off from the sources, not without hope for a human today and tomorrow."

Writing poems "not without hope," Celan sees before him "one more sluice" and "a brilliance reaping, as though words were gasping" (2:99). Another lyric adopts a Lutheran hymnal cadence and then erodes it: "REST EASY IN THY WOUNDING, / blubbered and sputtered up" (2:103). Every spiritual certitude can be faulted by language. His fifth book, *Atemwende* ("Breath-turn"), closes with a tribute to divine ambiguity:

ONCE,
I heard him,
he was washing the world,
unseen, nightlong,
really.

One and Infinite,
annihilated,
they I'ed.

Light was. Salvation.   [2:107]

In draft, Celan went back and forth between "Him" and "him," "He" and "he," unsure how to name a God who so washed the world.[37] This cleansing, nightlong flood leaves only more ambiguity: after "annihilated" (*vernichtet*),

Celan's next verb *ichten* could be part of *Licht* ("light") or opposite to *nicht* ("not") or a past tense of *ichen,* "to I"[38]—much as the Hebrew for "nothing," *ayin* (*aleph-yud-nun*), contains "I," *ani* (*aleph-nun-yud*). God who named Himself I AM THAT I AM or, literally, I SHALL BE THAT I SHALL BE, now falls into the past. Like summer in Shakespeare's sonnet, "Light *was.*" This past tense, sprung against the poem's final word, makes it doubtful whether Christian or Jewish salvation has any present or future at all.

14
Crossing into Hebrew
(1965–67)

"'Ride for the Truth' 23 November 1965." On his birthday, Paul Celan wrote this motto and date above a list of poems for a new collection.[1] *Reite für die Treue* could also mean "Ride for the Faith," like Teutonic cavaliers and knights on crusade. Celan at age forty-five took his motto from Psalm 45, in Martin Buber's translation.[2] The Psalmist, having said "My tongue is the pen of a ready writer," was urging his king to ride forth righteously. The poet, for whom certain dates and dates as such held more than natural significance, was marking his birthday with an ancient motto that renewed his task.

Having finished *Atemwende* ("Breath-turn") in summer of 1965, Celan
went on writing. "Frankfurt, September," the first poem for his next collection,
stems from the Book Fair and echoes "Tübingen, January" (1961), where a
Hölderlin "talked into blindness" appeared with "the patriarchs' light-beard."
"Frankfurt, September" begins: "Blind, light- / bearded display wall," updating
the towering poet into an exhibit of Fischer Verlag, which published Freud
and Kafka as well as Celan.[3] After allusions to dreamwork, lamentation,
silence, and "Freud's forehead" opening up, the poem quotes Kafka's remark:

"For the last
time psycho-
logy." [2:114]

Celan's lines sever the psyche from the science of it, as Kafka doubted that
spiritual malaise was curable. Then the poem ends on a jackdaw (Kafka's
father's logo—*kavka* in Czech):

The simulate-
jackdaw
breakfasts.
The glottal stop
sings.

Der Kehlkopfverschlusslaut / singt. Kafka was proofreading "A Hunger Artist"
when he died from tuberculosis of the larynx (*Kehlkopf*), and in his last story
"Josephine the Singer" dies leaving her people in doubt about her artistry.
Against the backdrop of German commerce, Celan meets his precursor with
double *k*'s, hoping that "the glottal stop," at least, "sings."
    That fall the poet kept riding for the truth. Here is an entire lyric:

THE TRACE OF A BITE in Nowhere.

It too
you must combat,
from here out.   [2:117]

And a medley from other poems: "The struggled umlaut in the unword: /
your splendor" . . . "the brick- / mouths / rave. / You burn off a prayer" . . .
"Spasms, I love you, psalms" . . . "The ounce of truth deep within madness"
. . . "even you, with everything / enstranged in you, / enstrange yourself /
deeper." In mid-November 1965 he returned to Mandelshtam, translating the
poem "Unspeakable grief."[4]
    Celan wrote himself a birthday poem whose determined spirit comes
through more clearly than its letter. "All your seals broken? Never," he begins,
and then, as proof, urges himself to "cedar away" an "eleven-hooved perfidy"

so that the wave, honey-
far, milk-
near, when
mettle stirs it to lament,
lament again to mettle,

that it too not
mirror the electron-
idiot, who fabricates
dates for
menetekeling
apes.   [2:134]

If this poet's regal seals, hiding but authenticating what is written inside,
were broken open, they might reveal a (Biblical) cedar's fragrance acting
against perfidy, a land flowing with milk and honey ("wave" was "Jordan
wave" in draft), and the Mene Tekel, the writing on the wall that Daniel
interpreted. Regrettably, it's not always true, as per Franz Rosenzweig, that
"I myself understand a poem only when I have translated it."[5] But these lines
do voice a poet's resistance to crass misreading of his (Biblically rooted)
lament.

A precarious spirit was driving this poem. When Celan hospitalized himself in May 1965, he wrote about Lear "Hewn into the brain." Now in
December he had to go into a clinic again. This time, instead of Shakespeare
as a custom-made commonplace book, Celan took his much-read copy of
Kafka's stories.[6] In the book's endpapers he jotted or scrawled things that are
terribly pained, as well as painful to relate. Yet they belong to the poet's
psychic ground, the dark behind the mirror. For instance: "early afternoon
on the eighth of December 1965: It's still quite clear in my head—If people
would come [Kämen Menschen], I could almost begin anew." Kämen Menschen:
the raison d'être of his poetry. Also, in a distracted hand: "Come Death, come
today!"

On the last endpaper I found in Hebrew שדי שדי (shaddai shaddai, "Almighty"), the ineffable name of God, and below that, with a haste unlike
Celan's usual Hebrew script:

שמע ישראל אדוני אלוהנו אדוני אחד

Shema Yisrael Adonai Elohenu Adonai Echad, "Hear, O Israel, the Lord Our
God, the Lord is One." It is the watchword and the martyrs' millennial cry.

From February to May 1966, Celan's poems are so cryptic as to seem like
signals from another planet.

POUR THE WASTELAND into your eye-sacks,
the call to sacrifice, the salt flood,

come with me to Breath
and beyond.   [3:149]

Some inner listener is roused to vision—scrotumlike sockets filled with Biblical adversity—and led to "Breath / and beyond." Celan thought of entitling the poetry from this period "Scar-true," "Need-song," or "Mad-gait."[7]

Emerging from "nearly seven months in the clinics," as he told a friend,[8] Celan on 11 June 1966 bought books by Anna Akhmatova and Marina Tsvetaeva and began a poem "SLEEPSCRAPS, wedges, / driven into Nowhere" (2:137). It was dedicated "For Gisèle" and later printed with an etching by her—testimony to his wife's "all real" presence, as he wrote once (2:30).[9] Also in June 1966 Celan broke with his publisher after eight years, though G. B. Fischer (to judge from the correspondence) had been loyally attentive.[10] Since the "many bad experiences" Celan mentions refer back a year and more, his illness during 1966 probably brought on this rupture.

Although malaise could stifle Celan, it could otherwise stimulate him. From mid-1966 he wrote many short lyrics, often with crisp cynicism just where earnestness had worked earlier—that is, à propos a murdered people. One poem anatomizes the slaughter industry: "the industrious mineral resources" (buried bodies?), "heated syncope" (cremation of something missing?), "not-to-be-deciphered Jubilee year" (doubtful Biblical renewal?), "glassed-in spider altars" (Auschwitz displays of hair and woven prayer shawls?), "shadow-palaver" (still vocal after death?), "speech-swallowing shower room, / semantically X-rayed," "uninscribed wall / of a standing-cell" (2:151). The death camp documentary *Night and Fog,* in Celan's translation, described "cells where one can neither stand up nor lie down," also a gas chamber that "the newcomer takes for a shower room" (4:93). So this 1966 poem has nothing edifying to say. After his detailed indictment, the poet sets a colon and ends up sentencing himself: "here / live yourself / right through, with no clock."

Celan kept the faith in other ways too. When Elie Wiesel's *The Jews of Silence* came out in the fall of 1966, he bought it and scored various details: that three thousand Moscow Jews gathered on Yom Kippur crying "Next year in Jerusalem!" and that Jews in the West must speak out for Russia's Jews.[11] Then in December, at a Paris celebration of Nelly Sachs's seventy-fifth birthday and Nobel Prize, Celan read her poems aloud, "his trembling voice resonant, somber."[12] Around Christmas 1966 he wrote a long poem called "Aschrei," with an epigraph from Hölderlin's "Homeland": "And no one knows."[13] It began: "When I don't know, don't know, / without you, without you, without Thou" (2:154). After some sarcasm about "the tribe of the Thou-less,"[14] Celan summons the word that tribe sang, transliterated from Hebrew yet still exotic within postwar German verse:

Aschrei,

a word without meaning,
transtibetan,
squirted into
the Jewess
Pallas
Athena's
helmeted ovaries.

Aschrei, "happy" or "blessed," the opening of a familiar prayer, runs throughout the Psalms: "Happy is the man . . ." (1:1), "Blessed is the nation whose God is the Lord" (33:12). But it is now "a word without meaning," because no Jewish community is left in Europe, much less any such happiness, and because Celan's German readers will not recognize *Aschrei* (or they will see the unrelated Yiddish *a schrei*, "a scream"!). What may be remembered, though, is that in prewar Jewish prayer books, the German for *Aschrei* (in the sense of "hale") was *Heil*.

Aschrei offsets the vernacular German around it, like *Shantih* in *The Waste Land*. Leaving Celan's Hebrew intact in English preserves a communal bond against the muting of the Nazi years. But *Aschrei* squirted into "the Jewess Pallas Athena's helmeted ovaries" steps up the sarcasm. Alongside Mary Immaculate and the Greek goddess of war and wisdom, Jewish women who underwent sterilization experiments are now inseminated, blessed by the first word of Psalms.

A few days after writing of *Aschrei*, Celan spoke about his craft. "I don't musicalize anymore, as at the time of the much-touted 'Todesfuge,' which by now has been threshed over in many a textbook. . . . As for my alleged encodings, I'd rather say: undissembled ambiguity . . . I try to reproduce cuttings from the spectral analysis of things, to show them in several aspects and permeations at once. . . . I see my alleged abstractness and actual ambiguity as moments of realism."[15] These hints help in grasping such counter-intuitive expressions as "the Jewess Pallas Athena." Meanwhile most of Celan's readers were still busy absorbing "Black milk of daybreak." A German friend has shown me her high school reader from the 1960s, where she carefully wrote the word *Daktylus* ("dactyl") above "Todesfuge." The poem's fluent meter was probably easier to teach than its abysmal irony.

While Celan's poem was being threshed over in Germany, Theodor Adorno finally recanted his famous dictum. "Perennial suffering has as much right to expression as the tortured have to scream," he wrote; "hence it may have been wrong to say that no poem could be written after Auschwitz."[16] This came rather late, as Celan's verse had exercised that right for some time. Around the turn of the year 1966, tortured phrases came to Celan's pen:

"be-mothered by blinding," "a snakebite before rose-rise," "an ash-huzza," "dust-gorging choirs."

Celan hospitalized himself again in February 1967, and, thinking of the clamps used in shock therapy, he jotted down "Temple-chain" and "Temple-snow" as titles for a new cycle.[17] His writing bruised still more: "Blood falls back into itself," "Love, straitjacket-pretty, makes for the crane couple," and this entire poem:

> YOU WERE my death:
> you I could hold
> while everything slipped from me. [2:166]

From such indrawn spareness, anything can be deduced—mystical encounter or helpless loss. One thing that had just slipped from Celan was his Romanian mentor Margul-Sperber. Learning of the death, he wept and thought about a poet's existence: "a bit anachronous, a bit catachronous"—that is, going back and down into time.[18]

Along his own backward and downward course, Celan in March 1967 found *The Book of Questions* by Edmond Jabès (1912–91) and reacted against this story: "In a central European village, the Nazis one evening buried alive some of our brothers. The earth stirred with them for a long time. That night, the same rhythm connected all Israelites to the world."[19] Instead of assenting to this tragic communion, Celan marked it "Nein!" and crossed out these sentences. Yet his copies of Jabès have underlinings throughout, and Celan considered translating him. He never did: perhaps Jabès's leading idea, that "the difficulty of being Jewish is the same as the difficulty of writing," grounded his own work too deeply for him to rework it in German.[20]

The day he read *The Book of Questions,* in the clinic, he wrote this two-line appeal: "STILLNESS, boat-hag, ferry me through the rapids. / Eyelashfire, light me on" (2:170). Then a week later he began a poem: "THE HEARTSCRIPT-CRUMBLED sight-island / at midnight" (2:174). He also wrote another poem that day "by mother-memorial half-light" (2:176). It took such compulsive word-compoundings to meet Celan's needs.

What his needs dictated, he usually found, or it came his way. During the sixties Celan bought new editions of Mandelshtam, as well as Binswanger's *Schizophrenia* and *Melancholia and Mania,* Bleuler's *Psychiatry,* Jaspers' *Psychopathology,* and much Freud. Self-scrutiny was converging with his passion for precise technical knowledge. He bought two 1966 books on human physiology, and in one of them he penciled the beginnings of a poem: "Come, we'll gobble nerve-cells . . . from the rhomboidal fossa [a brain cavity]" (2:181).[21] Writing the next day, Celan recalled a phrase from Mandelshtam—"that blessed meaningless word" (5:159)—to fill out another X-ray of himself:

"Echo d'une terre / Echo einer Erde," 1967, Gisèle Celan-Lestrange (Eric Celan)

SOULBLIND, behind the ashes,
in the holy-senseless word,
the derhymed one comes striding,
his brain-mantle light on his shoulders.   [2:183]

The word "soulblind" in German also denotes optical loss, and *Hirnmantel,* the cerebral cortex, also includes *Mantel,* a poet's or prophet's cloak.

Whatever his drug and shock therapy were doing for Celan in the spring of 1967, the poems came rapidly, about one a day. They cut away everything easy or comforting: "the Lord broke the bread, / the bread broke the Lord," one of them ends (2:191), and his next poem is nothing but caustic in speaking for the Lord's people:

PROFUSE ANNOUNCEMENT
in a tomb, where
we with our
gas flags are flapping,

we stand
in the odor
of sanctity, yeah.

Burnt
fumes of Beyond
leak thick from our pores,

in every other
tooth-
cavity awakes
an undespoilable hymn.

The two bits twilight you tossed in to us,
come, gulp it down too.   [2:192]

In 1944, the victims could say "we" drink black milk. Now a "we" itemizes gas, odor, fumes, pores, and ripped-out teeth in the same breath as sanctity, the Beyond, and a hymn. "We" may even be telling the poet (imagine this in "Todesfuge"!) to gulp down his own "two bits," his middling poems.

While these poems were occupying him in late April 1967, Celan re-encountered Gershom Scholem (1897–1982) when his new publisher, Siegfried Unseld of Suhrkamp Verlag, gave him *Von der mystischen Gestalt der Gottheit* ("On the Mystical Shape of the Godhead").[22] Celan had known Scholem's work since 1957 and had met him three times in Paris during the sixties.[23] Now he scoured this book over a ten-day period. Many things in Jewish mystical lore engaged him: Kabbalistic speech theory and the names of God, divine hiddenness, Creation and light-apparition, God's self-contraction and nothingness, Sabbath and ensouling, Isaiah's "I will bring thy seed from the east, and gather thee from the west" (43:5), and above all the Shechinah—God's emanation as mother, sister, and bride, symbolized by the rose or crown, in exile with the people of Israel.

Lighting on terms that tallied with something he had written years before, Celan often noted such reassuring "meridians." On 1 May he began three poems, each primed by what he had read that day. Two summon up the divine radiance that only Moses beheld, the "glimmer of primal Light" (2:195, 197). The third is a tissue of Scholem's terms, blending erotic and spiritual rebirth:

OUT OF ANGEL-MATTER, on the day
of Ensouling, phallically
united in the One
—He, the Enlivening-Righteous, slept you toward me,
Sister . . .   [2:196]

Celan hungered for archaic prooftexts. A later line in this cryptic poem—
"scattered from the East, to be gathered in the West"—makes Isaiah witness
to his own plight.

Sometimes Celan's verse seems to be assembling fragments of a shattered
vessel. On 7 May a poem beginning ". . . STILL NO KIND OF / peace" took
terms from Freud's *Beyond the Pleasure Principle* to traverse his own "gray-
nights" of "consciousness-gravel" (2:201). Celan's closing lines, "Repetition
compulsion / Camaïeu," let the Old French behind "cameo" suggest that art
can carve reliefs out of memory's damaging recurrence.

Celan carved all his past and present pain and hope into the astonishing—
and astonished—poem he wrote next. It was 10 May 1967 in the clinic,
where he was perusing his new handbook of human physiology with its
detail on various organs and functions. A section on the heart describes the
coronary arteries, speaks of *hellrotes Blut* ("clear" or "bright red blood") in the
aortic arch, and tells how to put an *Umschnürung* ("tourniquet") on a wound.
At the same time, things that Celan had marked in Scholem's chapter on the
Shechinah jumped to mind: her "unearthly brilliance" and the image in
Jeremiah where, as Scholem says, "Mother Rachel weeps for her children
going into exile."[24]

Something clearly sparked between the technical matter of vital organs
and the stuff of spirituality. Inside the front cover of the paperback physiology
handbook, Celan wrote a poem, made a few small but telling changes, and
had this:

NAH, IM AORTENBOGEN,	NEAR, IN THE AORTA'S ARCH,
im Hellblut:	in bright blood:
das Hellwort.	the brightword.
Mutter Rahel	Mother Rachel
weint nicht mehr.	weeps no more.
Rübergetragen	Carried across now
alles Geweinte.	all of the weeping.
Still, in den Kranzarterien,	Still, in the coronary arteries,
unumschnürt:	unbinded:
Ziw, jenes Licht.	Ziv, that light. [2:202]

Nah, "nigh," "near" in space or time, not distant, not long to await: the poem
opens here and now in a poised syllable countervailing everything that till

now has been not near but displaced, estranged. *Nah* harks back ten years to the nearness in "Tenebrae"—"Near are we, Lord . . . clawed into each other"—and thence to Hölderlin's "Patmos," where God is "Near by / and hard to grasp." We know that a Word became flesh and blood, but Celan's *Nah* reaches farther back than this, to what could be his poem's epigraph: "For the word is very near to you, in your mouth and in your heart, that you may do it" (Deut. 30:14).

Blood from the lungs recirculates "in the aorta's arch" to the body. This heart's pulse in Celan's next two lines holds me to their steady beat:

> in bright blood:
> the brightword.

Though we haven't heard that "brightword" yet, *Hellblut* ("bright blood") recalls (as Celan once did) a children's song that "stayed motherly, summerly, bright-blooded [*hellblutig*]" (1:290).

Both the private and the collective past come forward now. Thanks to the kindredness of English and German, Celan's lines carry across rhythmically:

Mutter Rahel	Mother Rachel
weint nicht mehr.	weeps no more.

At the poem's midpoint this present-tense *weint,* changed from past tense in draft, balances the poem at an ever present turning point: we will always need to know an end to weeping. This is ambiguous news, touching first on the New Testament, the Gospel according to Matthew on the slaughter of the innocents, where it is said: "Then was fulfilled that which was spoken by Jeremy the prophet, saying, In Rama was there a voice heard, lamentation, and weeping, and great mourning, Rachel weeping for her children, and would not be comforted, because they are not" (2:17–18). But the Christ child is saved. "Prefiguring" this event, in the Old Testament (as Matthew sees it), six centuries earlier, we find Jeremiah lamenting Israel's Babylonian exile: "Thus saith the Lord, A voice is heard in Ramah, Lamentation, and bitter weeping, Rachel weeping for her children . . ." (31:15). But the people return to Zion, for God renews His covenant with Jacob, husband of Rachel, the matriarch of the tribes of Israel, as recounted in Genesis. So "Mother Rachel / weeps no more": this prepares quite another fulfillment from the one the Gospel imagines.

Tradition, the receiving and that which is received, in Hebrew *Kabbalah,* speaks of Mother Rachel as a figure of the Shechinah, God's luminous presence dwelling in the world. Wherever the tribes of Israel are suffering, she weeps and entreats God's mercy. Commentators point out that Celan's Judaic sources came by way of Scholem and Buber. But that is only partly true, and what of it? Tradition gave him what he needed or knew already, often to his grief. Long before adopting the image of Rachel lamenting her children, he had written an elegy to his own mother. "Aspen Tree" (1945) has this couplet:

Rain cloud, do you linger over the well?
My soft-voiced mother weeps for everyone,   [1:19]

Meine leise Mutter weint für alle. So Celan's 1967 poem, "Near, in the aorta's arch," makes for continuity ("Mother Rachel") and redemption ("weeps no more").

I was startled, one cold night in Normandy, to find in Celan's copy of Scholem on the Shechinah, at the bottom of the page that speaks of Mother Rachel weeping for her exiled children, some penciled lines in Yiddish script:

Vet di mamme Rokhl veynen
Vet Meshiekh nit mer kenen
Dos geveyn aribertrogn.

The rhyme and beat don't translate easily, though the longing does:

Mama Rochl starts her weeping
Then Messiah can't bear keeping
Far away from such lamenting.

Scholem's discussion touched off in Celan the memory of a song, originally a sardonic 1919 pogrom lullaby by Moyshe-Leyb Halpern, later adopted in the wartime ghettos.[25] Heard now beside the middle stanza of "Nah, im Aortenbogen," these Yiddish lines attune Celan's lyric to messianic longing. As the Yiddish *aribertrogn* ("endure") transmutes into German *rübertragen* ("carry across"), whatever was wept is now something not to bear with but to bear across—even to transform.

This turning point acts out a metaphor at the root of "meta-phor" (and "trans-late" as well): "carry across." Celan called such a critical moment an *Atemwende,* a "breath-turn." Here the breath turns as the blood returns in a moment of renewal.[26] And carrying across befits a people: Abraham out of Ur to Canaan, Moses through the Red Sea to Sinai, Joshua across the Jordan into the promised land, the Israelites back from Babylon to Zion. As the Lord says in Jeremiah, comforting Rachel, "Thy children shall come back to their own border" (31:17).

Here especially Celan's verse needs close rendering to convey a "bright-word" waiting to be pronounced and a messianic legend.[27] He has made translation itself of the essence, since *übertragen* ("carry across") also signifies a creative mode of literary translation (and can mean "transfuse" as well). Celan even cites himself—*alles Geweinte* ("all that's been wept")—from "The Vintagers." And *Geweinte* echoes Yiddish *geveyn* ("lament"), from the song about Rachel that his poem transforms. To keep Celan's rhythm, a slightly freer version can say "now":

Rübergetragen   Carried across now,
alles Geweinte.   all of the weeping.

From then to now, translation carries across in time as well as space. Celan's ending renews his opening:

Near, in the aorta's arch,
in bright blood:
the brightword. . . .

Still, in the coronary arteries,
unbinded:
Ziv, that light.

Both stanzas lead to their third line, announcing something that is not clear until the "brightword" is finally spoken: *Ziw*, or, phonetically in English, "Ziv." The last stanza fulfills the first.

Although my word "Still" adds a temporal sense—"now as before"—to the German *Still* ("motionless," "silent"), Keats's Grecian urn and Eliot's music in *Four Quartets* vouch for that sense. Am I really adding something, though, when Celan's poem speaks of weeping "no more," of a word "unbinded"?[28]

The word moves in twenty seconds from "near" to "still." Physiologically, freshened blood pumps first through the aorta and then into the coronary arteries that wreathe and sustain the heart. We have, not stasis, but a vivified stillness in the *Kranzarterien*. As so often with Celan, the technical term engenders something extra through its literal sense. Although "coronary" drags out the rhythm, it does suggest a wreathlike corona of light that helps bring home the circle moving through the poem.

What's unbinded is *Ziw, jenes Licht* ("Ziv, that light"). But then what does *Ziw* mean? Where did Celan find it? Why not italicize it? Should one translate it at all? Does "Ziv" really correspond to "light"?

In Zurich with Nelly Sachs, hoping for God's highest "wrangling word," Celan had seen "some gold across the water" (1:214), but that summer Sachs broke down. "Look, it's getting light [*hell*]," Celan wrote.[29] Then in May 1967 he found "Ziv" in Scholem's chapter on the Shechinah, where God's indwelling presence "can reveal itself in an unearthly brilliance—this is often called the light (*Ziv*) of the Shechinah."[30] Celan underlined this, wrote "Ziv" at the bottom of the page, wrote "p. 143 Ziv" on the book's endleaf, and finding "Ziv" missing in Scholem's index, inserted it with its page number, in all these ways marking the salience of a word that for years he had been waiting for and that had been waiting for him. Later in 1967, Celan wrote to Sachs about the light they had seen together: "Once, in a poem, there also came to me, by way of the Hebrew, a name for it."[31] And when she recalled it again, he said, "Yes, that light," and in his poem she will find it "named—denominated with a Hebraic name."[32] This déjà vu of *Ziv* told him the language had been holding a spiritual reality in store for him. "Poetry is mysticism," he once remarked.[33]

Whatever "Ziv" means—for Celan's poem will not really say—it must be the "brightword" announced at first. But this esoteric term is not set in italics like Celan's other Hebrew and Yiddish words.[34] Maybe the word now felt at home in his writing, not strange. His whole poem takes the same typeface, so we read along expecting to understand "Ziv" in its turn. Most of us do not. We know we're now hearing the "brightword" but still expect a final clarity. To translate would dissipate that sense of half-concealed revelation. And nothing could render this unearthly brightness anyway—not the usual bulky "divine effulgence," or even "radiance" or "splendor."

Because we cannot translate *Ziv*, we must not. Having emerged from a people's experience of exile, it has no Christian equivalent. For Judaism, what's more, "Speech reaches God because it comes from God."[35] In a word like *Ziv*, letter and spirit are not separable, as they must be for translation to occur. Especially in the Kabbalah, God's speech created the world—"Let there be light"—and as that speech was Hebrew, the "brightword" *Ziv* names what no other word can. So let it be.

In the aftermath of Nazism's "Final Solution" to the "Jewish problem," Celan's poem surprises us by breaking into Hebrew—or is it that Hebrew breaks into the poem? Jews uttered Hebrew at the cost of their lives (and at the moment of their deaths), so this word stands fast. German (or, with less historical point, English) gives way to Hebrew. Celan's German audience held only a handful who would recognize any Hebrew term. Thus, he let his poem go dark for a moment. He let his readers, for whatever good it might do them, stumble on the Hebrew and fail to understand. Then why not use a Hebrew font? This would not have strained the resources of Suhrkamp Verlag. Possibly Celan wanted *Ziw* refractory but not totally baffling. Or possibly, having shunned his father's Zionist leanings, he was reluctant to make use of Hebrew, the old–new language reclaimed on its native soil. "Nah, im Aortenbogen" had not carried him quite that far across.

Taking this thought further, I have wondered what would become of the poem in an Israeli version.[36] Readers would recognize *Ziv* but lose that sudden breath-turn from German to Hebrew. We commonly lament the "loss in translation," and here an invisible loss would occur, an effacement. Celan's poems with Hebrew in them, especially with Hebrew ending them, trace a meridian of Diaspora yearning.

Yet the Hebrew does not bring this poem to its end. If Celan had simply said *Ziw, das Licht,* he would only be translating a "brightword": "Ziv, the light." Instead, "Ziv, that light" throws us back to the pure word and gestures at something ineffable—not Saint John's *logos* which was "In the beginning . . . the light of men," but *Ziv haShechinah,* a radiance attending Israel even in dark exile.

By the date of this poem, 10 May 1967, Syrian raids and shelling had been met by Israeli air attacks, terrorists had struck the Galilee, and Nasser's Egypt was threatening in the south. Celan was still in the clinic. Maybe some acute nervous crisis had become "unbinded." Yet wasn't it, after all, sheer gratitude at encountering the Hebrew word that moved Celan's poem?

This poem's earliest commentary may have come from the poet himself, two days later. His key word is *Notscherben,* a "necessity-" or "privation-shard":

BECAUSE YOU FOUND THE NEED-SHARD
in a wilderness place,
the shadow-centuries relax beside you
and hear you think:

Perhaps it's true
that peace conjured two peoples here
out of clay vessels.   [2:204]

In the Kabbalah, divine light at Creation shattered its vessels, leaving to humanity the *tikkun,* or restoration, of these shards. Celan found *Ziv,* a "need-shard." The "two peoples" here may be Jews and Arabs, and possibly *Not* ("need"), reversed by *Ton* ("clay"), moves a language written from left to right toward another written the other way: German and Hebrew.[37]

Along with Celan's probings of mysticism in May 1967, other writing became his daily therapy. Then war broke out, stirring him to an unambiguous poem. Starting on 7 June, when Jerusalem's Old City was regained, he worked closely on it for two days in the clinic.[38] His title "Denk dir" (Just [you] Think) registered the jolt that Jews everywhere felt:

Just think:
the Peat-Bog Soldier of Masada
makes a homeland for himself . . .

A piercing thought, at a time when Israeli troops were regaining the Temple wall—to name Masada in the same breath with the Peat-Bog Soldier. During the 1930s a protest song, the Song of the Peat-Bog Soldiers, had spread through the camps in Germany:

Here we've no lamenting voices,
Not for ever winter's reign.

Come the day when each rejoices:
Homeland, you are mine again.[39]

At the ancient fortress of Masada above the Dead Sea, Jewish zealots once resisted a Roman siege then took their own lives rather than surrender. Celan's verse connects a history of resistance to his own need for "homeland":

Just think:
the Peat-Bog Soldier of Masada
makes a homeland for himself, most
ineffaceably,
against
every barb in the wire.

Just think:
the eyeless ones without shape
lead you free through the tumult, you
strengthen and
strengthen.

Just think: your
own hand
has held
this piece of
habitable earth,
again suffered
up into life.

Just think:
this came toward me,
name-awake, hand-awake
for ever,
from the unburiable.   [2:227]

The "you" inhabiting Celan's stanzas is a people, led by those who wept their eyes out. Now free, they go from strength to strength, as the Psalmist says (84:7). "Just think": it's "toward me," the poet, that all this came. In draft, "name-awake, hand-awake" was "handname-awake," closer to the *yad vashem* ("hand and name"—monument and memorial) that God promised His people in Isaiah (56:5) and that names Israel's Holocaust memorial. Finally, Celan's word "unburiable" fuses the two halves of one idea: Jewish victims who *could* not be buried and their spirit that *will* not.

Celan published "Denk dir" right away in Zurich, and it came out twice in Israel's German-Jewish press.[40] He also sent it to the German-born Israeli poet Natan Zach, who translated it, checked his version with Celan, and published it in Israel's chief daily.[41] Later that year, "Denk dir" appeared in Germany[42] and then as the culminating poem in Celan's next collection, *Fadensonnen* ("Threadsuns," 1968). Yet the Six-Day War had not swept him up on a wave of enthusiasm. Celan was, after all, a sick man, sometimes violent and even suicidal. He and his wife had decided that he should live apart. When Petre Solomon visited Paris from Bucharest that summer, he found his old friend, at forty-six, "profoundly altered, prematurely aged, taciturn, frowning . . . 'They're doing experiments on me,' he said in a stifled voice, interrupted by sighs . . . Paul wasn't depressed all the time, sometimes he had moments of great joy—very brief, it's true, and punctuated by a nervous laugh, shrill and broken."[43]

15
Prophecy out of Exile
(1967)

"Into the hut-book, looking at the well-star, with a hope for a coming word in the heart. On 25 July 1967 Paul Celan."[1] To inscribe these lines in the guest book at the Black Forest retreat of Martin Heidegger, the philosopher who had recently declared that Being speaks German, shows a bit of nerve.[2]

This first meeting with Heidegger took place after Celan left the clinic and traveled to Freiburg for a reading. For years he had read Heidegger closely. His poems show numerous Heideggerian traces, and his Bremen and Meridian speeches find in poetry the truest path toward Being—though only under history's acute pressure. Heidegger, for his part, had sent his books to Celan and wanted to meet him. "I know everything of his," he said in 1967.[3] But if even some journalist's insensitive review could disturb Celan, or his publisher's reissue of a tainted writer, it is clear that an encounter with the man who under Hitler was Rector at Freiburg in 1933–34, who in 1935 declared Nazism's "inner truth and greatness," who in 1936 still signed his letters *Heil Hitler!*, had his classes give the salute, and sported a swastika pin, and who paid party dues until 1945—an encounter with this man had to be fraught, especially given Heidegger's silence about it all since the war.[4]

At the University of Freiburg on 24 July 1967, well over a thousand people, Celan's largest audience, overflowed the hall.[5] He chose his poems carefully, articulated them with unrelenting precision, and refrained from commentary. Presenting a decade's worth, from "Count up the almonds" (1952) to "Bitten away" (1963), he ended his recital "Deep in the time-crevasse" with

> . . . a breathcrystal,
> your unannullable
> witness.

Heidegger attended this reading, and though Celan shrank from having a joint photo taken beforehand, the philosopher gave him a copy of his book *Was heisst Denken?* ("What Does Thinking Mean?") and invited him for an outing the next day. "I know about his difficult crisis," Heidegger had told a colleague. "It would be salutary to show P.C. the Black Forest."[6] Doubtless the high Schwarzwald's clear air, so conducive to philosophy, would be good for what ailed this wretched survivor.

"Heidegger told me," says Hans-Georg Gadamer, "that in the Black Forest, Celan was better informed on plants and animals than he himself was."[7] They also talked about contemporary French philosophy, but Celan's attention was elsewhere. Years before, Martin Buber had met Heidegger, which to Celan seemed uncalled for.[8] Recently, in an interview with *Der Spiegel*, Heidegger had spoken of the Nazi years and of his later silence. He mentioned this interview to Celan but forbade its publication until after his death.[9]

The Jewish *Dichter* accompanied the German *Denker* to his mountain retreat at Todtnauberg, noticed midsummer blossoming along the way, took a drink from Heidegger's much-photographed well with its star-shaped wooden cube on top, and signed the guest book "with a hope for a coming word in the heart." Later, because the high moorland was too wet, they broke off their walk.

We have a record of this visit, as Celan experienced it, in his poem "Todtnauberg," written a week later.[10] It begins:

Arnica, Eyebright, the
drink from the well with the
star-die on top,

in the
hut,

into the book
—whose name did it take in
before mine?—
the line written into
this book about
a hope, today,
for a thinker's
(un-
delayed coming)
word
in the heart.   [2:255]

In simply noting things, Celan ekes out an autobiography. During the war in Czernowitz he had astonished friends by using botanical terms in several languages.[11] Now, like Jew Klein in "Conversation in the Mountains," he names the natural world, and these particular flowers signify healing—arnica for bruises, eyebright a balm he remembered from childhood. While the poet comes as a pilgrim and drinks in conciliation, Heidegger's well touches off a memory of Bukovina, the "Land of Wells" (1:59). Its star (along with arnica's color) signals the yellow badge; and the hut echoes "Hüttenfenster" ("Tabernacle Window," 1962), which "gathers . . . the wander-East." Things done or spoken in the past become present for Celan. Thus his line is "written into / this book," giving "a hope" scriptural force.

The inscription his poem records adds only a little to what Celan actually put in Heidegger's guest book, but—as we're warned by the abrupt "whose name did it take in / before mine?," which looks back to the 1930s—that little means a lot.[12] The hope in "Todtnauberg" holds "today," every today, like the "hope for a human today and tomorrow" that Celan declared to Erich Kahler.[13] This is hope for the word of "a thinker" who has seemed unable to rethink the unconscionable past. And, may one add (the parentheses say), let this word be "un- / delayed coming."

The word "coming" mattered to philosopher and poet alike. In a 1936 essay, Heidegger described Hölderlin's sense of "a new time": "It is the time of the fled gods *and* of the coming God."[14] Hölderlin's hope still awaits a heartfelt word, Celan implies. Again his poem challenges Heidegger, noting the "half- / trod log- / paths" of their aborted walk. Heidegger's *Holzwege* ("Woodland Paths"), showing poetry "under way" toward truth in language, convinced Celan. Yet, in an explosive wordplay, Celan's term for "log" (*Knüppel*) also means "bludgeon." Translating *Night and Fog* he had used that word for death camp prisoners "bludgeoned awake" at 5 a.m. (4:83). Along the paths of German language, Celan could only go halfway with Heidegger.[15]

Still hoping for the thinker's word, Celan took an unusual step. He had his Paris printer do a bibliophile edition of "Todtnauberg"[16] and sent the first copy to Heidegger. The response was a letter empty of anything but conventional thanks. How, after all, could the seventy-eight-year-old philosopher respond? He knew what troubled Celan, but his silence on the Nazi years was tied up in a lifetime's search for human Being, not human beings. When Celan readied "Todtnauberg" for his next book, he made one change, taking out "un- / delayed." He was still waiting for the coming word.

From June through December 1967 Celan wrote constantly—eighty-one poems, making up a collection he again titled with a hard-sprung compound: *Lichtzwang*. "Light-Compulsion" suggests being forced by or toward light. It recalls forced labor and resettlement and coins an opposite to "compulsory blackout." The resonant poems of *Die Niemandsrose* have been left far behind. "Just Think" and "Todtnauberg" run smoothly compared with the poems that follow. Celan's late poetry "stands its ground on the edge of itself" (3:197).

> KNOCK the
> light-wedges away:
>
> the floating word
> is dusk's.   [2:268]

That is an entire poem. But sometimes Celan's constraints on language give off a little more light:

> WAN-VOICED,
> flayed from the depths:
> not a word, not a thing,
> and of both the single name . . .
>
> wounded gain
> of a world.   [2:307]

It takes a moment to hear Psalm 130 in this voice from the depths. Then another moment to see that the Hebrew *davar*, meaning both "word" (sacred or secular) and "thing," must be that single name.[17] Whereas the Gospel offers Christ's wounds, without which one may gain the whole world but lose one's soul, Celan puns "wounded" (*wunder*) into its own wondrous gain.[18]

He might have taken heart from enthusiastic, empathic reviews of his last book, *Atemwende,* in October 1967. But a few months earlier, the German Academy of Language and Literature had evenhandedly (and belatedly) published some "corrections" to its 1961 acquittal of Celan in the Goll plagiarism charge.[19] This alone was enough to offset a dozen good reviews. In late October Celan began a poem, as in "Wan-voiced," with a cry from the depth: "ALSO ME, one born like you, no hand holds," yet it ends: "the almond-testicle / thunders and blooms" (2:311). His next poem opened: "THE BACKWARDS-SPOKEN / names, all of them" (2:312). "I'm thinking about our trip to the Carpathians more than twenty years ago," he wrote to Petre Solomon in November 1967.[20] "Lia, Lia, drowned, drowned, drowned. Vanity of writing." Celan's forty-seventh birthday had come round, and he was living alone in a one-room flat. "It's the 23rd again, nine in the evening . . . I've just written a poem ending with the words: 'cold start, despite everything, / with hemoglobin.'" Ending with a "start" and a word in the blood, this poem has begun in rupture and loss:

LEAP-CENTURIES, leap-
seconds, leap-
births, novembering, leap-
deaths . . .   [2:324]

Celan also speaks of "the menorah poem from Berlin"—I wish I knew what that refers to—and finds a rubric for all his lyrics now: "Reading-stations in the lateword."[21] Along his own *via dolorosa*, these are ways to station himself in the Word that was, like *Ziv*, long ago, with God.

The later his time came to be, the more lateness grew full, expectant, yet desperate. Nothing enacts this process better than "Du sei wie du," from 3 December 1967.[22] Intervoicing Celan's lines with Meister Eckhart's medieval German version of Isaiah and then closing with Isaiah's words themselves, this lyric is proof of (and against) translation:

Du sei wie du, immer.	YOU BE LIKE YOU, ever.
Stant vp Jherosalem inde erheyff dich	*Ryse up Ierosalem and rowse thyselfe*
Auch wer das Band zerschnitt zu dir hin,	The very one who slashed the bond unto you,
inde wirt erluchtet	*and becum yllumyned*
knüpfte es neu, in der Gehugnis,	knotted it new, in myndignesse,
Schlammbrocken schluckt ich, im Turm,	spills of mire I swallowed, inside the tower,
Sprache, Finster-Lisene,	speech, dark-selvedge,
kumi	*kumi*
ori.	*ori.* [2:327]

Short of doing justice to the original, we can at least see what that would require by thinking through this poem's eight phases.

Du sei wie du, immer.   You be like you, ever.

A tensile arc moves between *Du* and *du,* though we can't yet tell who is addressed—God, the poet himself, or some other auditor. Celan's first version of the line, "Nothing is like you, nowhere," suggested divinity.[23] Replacing it with "You be like you, ever," brought his poem (as one Hebrew translation does) near to God's naming: *ehyeh asher ehyeh,* "I shall be that I shall be" (Exod. 3:14).[24] Celan's taut grammar urges identity, perseverance, renewal.

Stant vp Jherosalem inde   *Ryse up Ierosalem and*
erheyff dich   *rowse thyselfe*

Just who is being exhorted becomes clearer with these imperatives, whose antique strangeness and italics have fended off translators. French, Italian, and English versions merely retain the original as is, but that begs a question.[25] For in translation the lines should sound as they do to German listeners.

But that depends on who is speaking them. They come from the mystic Meister Eckhart (1260–1328), in whose heretical "negative theology" God is unknowable, unspeakable, a fullness of *Nichts.*[26] Eckhart always began his German sermons with a Biblical text in Latin, then spoke it in the vernacular as here, then went on to speculation. Having become acquainted with Middle High German in 1944, Celan in 1967 was studying Eckhart, and one sermon caught his eye[27] with its rubric from the Latin of Isaiah 60:1: *Surge, illuminare, iherusalem.* (From the King James Bible comes a soaring aria and chorus in Handel's *Messiah:* "Arise, shine, for thy light is come.") The preacher's Middle High German version made its way verbatim into this poem—a way that had passed from the prophet Isaiah's pre-Christian Hebrew to Saint Jerome's fourth-century Latin to Meister Eckhart's medieval German and then into Paul Celan's lyric voice, the messianic word translated through time.

Unlike Eckhart, Celan does not adjust the old words for his listeners. Most Germans would grasp them and at the same time feel displaced, conversing backward in time. Although there was rabid persecution of Jews in Eckhart's Germany, his language precedes Nazi-Deutsch by seven centuries. Long before "Juden raus!" (Jews out!), Germans had heard "Stant vp Jherosalem inde erheyff dich" (which has been taken for Yiddish—a plausible yet ironic mistake[28]).

Consulting Bible translations from around the time of Eckhart, such as John Wycliffe's, I formed an amalgam with the help of fourteenth-century English mystical writings[29] and Isaiah 51:17 ("Awake, awake"): "*Ryse up Ierosalem and / rowse thyselfe.*" The verbs exhort a people returning from exile to Zion.

Auch wer das Band zerschnitt	The very one who slashed the
zu dir hin,	bond unto you,

Isaiah's prophetic word has been cut into, interrupted by someone who slashed *das Band,* the "cord," "strap," or "bond." One Hebrew translation hears *Band* as *brit,* meaning "covenant" (as in German *Bund*), and cutting a bond signifies breaking a covenant. But it can also mean breaking free, as in Isaiah, "Loose thyself from the bands of thy neck, O captive daughter of Zion" (52:2). To paradox and ambiguity Celan was no stranger. In his puzzling *zu dir hin* ("to thee thither"), a bond was cut not away from but toward Jerusalem.

inde wirt	*and becum*
erluchtet	*yllumyned*

The dialogue resumes in another imperative, because the prophet's voice has been working all along behind the poet's.

knüpfte es neu, in der Gehugnis,	knotted it new, in myndignesse,

In draft Celan went from *knüpfte* to *knüpft* and back again—from past to present to past. Both tenses fit: to speak of renewing a bond is to do so. Through God's word to Isaiah, persisting via Eckhart into Celan's own voice, the covenant holds good. "There remained amid the losses," he said in Bremen, "this one thing: language," so his poem knots a bond anew and says where: *in der Gehugnis,* in an archaic, arcane term for "memory," whose root meant "be in mind of," "long for." Eckhart's sermon called it the soul's "secret hidden knowledge." For *Gehugnis* I tried "memoraunce," dating from 1320, but it came to seem too Latinate and, worse, too comprehensible. The point is that Celan is leading his listeners to something they cannot know yet need to know. To dig for *Gehugnis* is to perform remembrance itself. Early Middle English "myndignesse," akin to "mindedness" and meaning the faculty of memory, may be just obscure enough.

Schlammbrocken schluckt ich,	spills of mire I swallowed,
im Turm,	inside the tower,

Saying "I," the speaker now activates his own memory. To regularize the verse—"I swallowed bits of mud in the tower"—would drain it of revulsion, the pull of *Schlamm* ("mud") into *schluckt* ("swallowed"). But what then—"hunks of muck," "bits of swill"? As Yeats said, "Difficulty is our plow."[30] Our own mindedness will turn up *Schlamm* in dire scenes: Jeremiah prophesying Jerusalem's fall was put in a dungeon and "sank in the mire" (38:6). Psalm 69 fits Celan only too well: "I am sunk in deep mire, where there is no standing, I am come into deep waters, and the flood overwhelmeth me. I am weary with my crying, my throat is dried . . . Deliver me out of the mire" (69:3,

15). Or this: "He brought me . . . out of the miry clay . . . And he hath put a new song in my mouth" (Ps. 40:3). For the poet A.D. 1967 *Schlamm* sounds with *schluckt* and then (in a tower like Hölderlin's) with the next line's *Sprache*: "Spills of mire I swallowed . . . speech."

Sprache, Finster-Lisene,   speech, dark-selvedge,

Sprache is also "language," but a thick sibilance here prompts "speech," as in the "speech-swallowing shower room" of a 1966 poem (2:151). Then *Finster* ("dark") joins *Lisene,* a pilaster strip buttressing or bordering the corner of a building, which comes from *lisière,* "selvedge," a woven edge that keeps fabric from unraveling, thus also a frontier. So we have language to buttress, or maybe only edge, the darkness. Celan cherished the uncommon, unspoiled names of things—they in themselves withstood darkness. Reluctantly, I drop the architectural sense of *Lisene* in favor of "selvedge," derived from "self" and "edge" and with overtones of "savage" and "salvage": "Speech, dark-selvedge." And here endeth the German.

kumi   *kumi*
ori.   *ori.*

In this case, German and English here transliterate identically from Hebrew. But ultimately they converge only in .he Hebrew itself: קוּמִי אוֹרִי. Original and translation reach an endpoint where they began, in Isaiah, whose "Arise, shine" we know already from Eckhart's "*ryse*" and "*becum yllumyned.*" Yet the Hebrew keeps a last glint hidden. With the suffix -*i* of *kumi* and *ori,* Isaiah is calling to a female "thou": Jerusalem, home of exiles, a woman, as in Lamentations. Celan's memory would also harbor the Sabbath hymn "Lecha dodi" (Go, my beloved), which sings the words *kumi ori.* With this joyful hymn, Kabbalists in the Galilean town of Safed used to beckon the Sabbath bride as the Shechinah, God's presence returning from exile.[31]

Oriented the way it is, Celan's whole poem seems to invite translating into Hebrew. But Hebrew can hardly manage the phasing between medieval and modern. For Eckhart's "Stant vp . . . ," one translator ingeniously draws on the early Aramaic version of Isaiah for a semi-strangeness.[32] With *kumi ori,* in Hebrew versions of Celan's poem, the Biblical resonance is audible, but not the sudden release from mother tongue into holy tongue.

Like *Yizkor, Kaddish,* and *Ziv,* the words *kumi ori* knot a bond anew, binding the speaker to a people that stayed like itself chiefly through the spoken word. Just before *kumi ori,* Isaiah says: "This is My covenant with them, saith the Lord. My spirit that is upon thee, and My words which I have put in thy mouth, shall not depart out of thy mouth, nor out of the mouth of thy seed, nor out of the mouth of thy seed's seed, saith the Lord, from henceforth and for ever" (59:21).[33] Then chapter 60 begins, like the end of "You be like you," *kumi ori.*

If, as Scholem told Buber, his translation of the Bible from Hebrew to German was "the tombstone of a relationship that was extinguished in unspeakable horror,"[34] then Celan in his way has turned that loss around with *kumi ori.* For those who recognize it, his poem traces a meridian from modern German to Eckhart to Isaiah, reversing the process of translation as if of history itself. Again, as with Walter Benjamin reflecting on history and revolution: "Origin is the goal."

For guidance I go back to Franz Rosenzweig, who once made a German version of the Hebrew Grace After Meals. He said he would hide his translation from a guest who knew any Hebrew, because "the least comprehended Hebrew word gives him more than the finest translation."[35] Rosenzweig calls the need for translation "our predicament" and accepts it: German-speaking Jews "cannot avoid this path that again and again leads us out of what is alien and into our own."

Even Rosenzweig, painstakingly translating the Bible up through Isaiah before he died in 1929, could scarcely have imagined the path of someone like Paul Celan. The poems ending in *Ziv* and *kumi ori* act under "light-compulsion" (as Celan titled his work from late 1967). Those Hebrew words, for a moment, break the mired voice free.

16
An Embabeled Tongue
(1968–69)

"Not in the least hermetic" (*Ganz und gar nicht hermetisch*), Celan insisted to an English translator,[1] because if his poetry was seen as magically sealed off from understanding, that would relieve its readers of responsibility. In "Du sei wie du," though the word *Gehugnis* seems inaccessible, recovering this archaic term for memory engages memory. A few days after writing the poem, in a *Times Literary Supplement* review of *Atemwende,* Celan saw his poetry called "mysterious" and "hidden" and one of his neologisms taken differently from what he intended.[2] Yet this article made fine observations, evoked the mystics' *mysterium tremendum,* and dubbed Celan "one of the few great religious poets of our time."

That Celan's was a cryptic, private craft is proved for some readers by a poem dating from his Christmas 1967 visit to Berlin. "Of course Celan's poetry is 'hermetic,'" a Berlin daily reported, and two days later he composed some verses in the teeth of that notion.[3] From Berlin's snowy weather, from the room he stayed in, the walks he took, the places he visited, and a recent book that he had read, there emerged a sort of sonnet concatenating all these data (without the explanation I provide here). Celan's poem involves meat hooks (used to hang Hitler's would-be assassins in 1944), Berlin's (Christmas) festiveness, the "Eden" (luxury apartments built on the site where in 1919 a revolutionary couple was shot), a man (Karl Liebknecht) and a woman (Rosa Luxemburg) bullet-riddled, and the canal (where her body was thrown, near the railway station through which Paul Antschel had passed in 1938 on Kristallnacht).[4] All this generated a poem that "turns around an Eden."

> The man became a sieve, the Frau
> had to swim, the sow,
> for herself, for no one, for everyone—
> The Landwehr Canal makes no murmur.
> Nothing
>   stops.   [2:334]

Nothing, that is, except Celan's poem, holding onto its data. To grasp them all asks too much of the reader—but what is too much, given this history?

Celan looked mainly backward, with glimpses now and then into a possible future. Before leaving Berlin he wrote another poem, on Christmas Day, that had less to do with birth and blessing than with crucifixion and a year's end that "hurls back December, November, it digs up its wounds" (2:336). At his lowest ebb, the poet calls on time only to rehearse his own pain. For New Year 1968, he wrote this ten-second lyric:

> THE BROACHED YEAR
> with its rotting crust
> of madnessbread.
> Drink
> from my mouth.   [2:337]

A stifled voice still voices its predicament. What concerned Celan was not his poetry's but the world's obscurity and the language which that called for:

> ILLEGIBILITY of this
> world. Everything doubled. . . .

You, clamped in your depths,
climb out of yourself
for ever.   [2:338]

His next poem opens in an even fiercer Biblical vein:

WHORISH OTHERTIME. And eternity
bloodblack embabeled,   [2:339]

blutschwarz umbabelt. Metaphor and myth are not defunct, but at Celan's
hands they are bent to breaking point. His unheard-of verb *umbabelt* has our
high hopes Babeled round by hubris. And *blutschwarz* ("bloodblack") compounds the mortality of human language.

Like one of Samuel Beckett's survivors, Celan goes on writing:

I HEAR, THE AXE HAS BLOOMED,
I hear, the place is not nameable . . .
I hear, they call life
the only refuge.   [2:342]

For paradox to show more than uncertainty, we have to hear wounded speech
as a reality no less primary than things or deeds:

WORLD TO BE STUTTERED AFTER,
in which I will have been
a guest, a name
sweated down from the wall
where a wound licks up high.   [2:349]

Three months before, in a voice "flayed from the depths," Celan had ended
his poem: "wounded gain / of a world" (2:307). Now, as if already posthu-
mous in a strange land, he is named at a wall—a wall, Celan said in draft,
"at which a fugitive shot himself dead."[5]

One day before beginning the cycle that includes all these lyrics, in
December 1967, Celan had written: "I desire that an edition of my poems
and my translations from English, Russian, and French poetry appear with
Suhrkamp."[6] It sounds like a last will, addressing the world "in which I will
have been a guest." Then in the months to come, beneath each of these
poems he deliberately added its date and place of composition.[7] His poems
were "stations in the lateword," or as he once said, "an I clarifying itself in
the process of writing"[8]:

Un-
sung, un-
wrung, un-

wreathed, in
front of tents astray planted

soul-bearded, hail-
eyed whitegravel-
stutterer.   [2:357]

Such lines were his only possible autobiography.

However wounded his speech, Celan kept a translator's commitment. In Bucharest he had become aware of Henri Michaux (1899–1984) and during the 1960s valued him almost as much as Kafka.[9] Given Michaux's uncompromising vision and the poets' friendship, Celan's versions respond directly, as in "*Contre!*":

Death-, Death-, Deathknell over you all!
And nothingness over the living!
Yes I believe in God! He surely knows nothing of this! . . .
In the dark we'll see clear.   [4:679–81]

Celan worked at length on a German edition of Michaux and asked his co-translator for "concessions to the literal sense."[10] In 1966 he dedicated to Michaux an enigmatic poem of "sundered thought-music" (3:135). The next year, Michaux's "Toward Completeness" impressed Celan, who thought it untranslatable—

Nothing
only Nothing
"Nothing" rises from the shipwreck   .

Greater than a temple
purer than a god

—which may have meant that it cut too close to translate.[11] When they were together, Michaux reports, "We spoke, so as not to have to speak."[12]

Taking a safer poet than Michaux, Jules Supervielle, Celan made a straightforward version of "God's Sadness" in 1967: "God survives you, he alone survives you, surrounded by a huge massacre / Of men, of women, of children" (4:403). In 1968, his book of Supervielle poems included one, "Paris," that attracted excess energy:

O Paris, ville ouverte	*Du offne Stadt, du wunden-*
Ainsi qu'une blessure,	*offene Stadt Paris,* [4:413]
[O Paris, open city	(You open city, you wound-
Same as a wound]	open city Paris)

Recalling the "open city" under German occupation, Celan's line break then opens the wound of his own experience there.

Drawn also to Giuseppe Ungaretti's late work, with its disillusioned tone and "memory crumbs,"[13] Celan translated *The Promised Land,* finding passages he could tune to his own voice:

A mute, endarkened,
you stride over the seedless land.   [5:441]

And from *Notebook of an Old Man:*

Death-rattled away,
there, there again . . .
clearer, inwarder, more cherished, frightful:
your word, extinguished.   [5:527]

This driven cadence might well have been written—it was, in fact—by the "whitegravel-stutterer" himself.

Translation took Celan out of himself a little. In 1967 he once again renewed his touch with Shakespeare, publishing the twenty earlier sonnets and a complex rendering of "Not mine own fears" (5:349). He also returned to Mandelshtam:

In Petersburg we shall meet again
as though we had buried the sun in it.   [5:159]

Celan now joined the new Parisian magazine *L'Éphémère.* Probably at his suggestion, they published—just in front of his own "Engführung" in German and French—Mandelshtam's essay "On the Interlocutor," whose image of a letter in a bottle with its "secret addressee" had figured in Celan's Bremen speech.[14] Later he became a co-editor of *L'Éphémère* and translated poetry, always quite faithfully, by the magazine's French contributors who themselves had translated him—evidence long overdue that he had some standing in his adopted land.

Events in the other land, the one he could not adopt, continued to affect Celan. Answering an inquiry by *Der Spiegel,* "Is a Revolution Unavoidable?," Celan said "I still hope" for anti-authoritarian "transformation . . . It begins, in Germany, here and today, with individuals. May we be spared a Fourth," he adds, thinking of the Third Reich (3:179). Celan's political skepticism was borne out in April 1968. Visiting London, he heard about Martin Luther King's murder on the 4th; then a week later came the near-assassination of Rudi Dutschke, a German opposition leader. Both events registered right away in a poem that noted the poet's "sharply heavened . . . gulps of co-air" (2:365).[15] Two days later, in Paris, Celan's next poem ended: "come with your reading-shimmer, / it is / the barricade" (2:366).

In May 1968 the French student uprising aroused Celan's political sentiment and his personal staunchness as well. He was living apart from his family, and when his son Eric, just turning thirteen, visited him, they walked through the streets, Celan singing the Internationale and other revolutionary songs in Russian, Yiddish, and French. Eric felt proud of his father. At the same time Celan bridled when students mimicked the Hitler salute or proclaimed "We are all Jews," or when wall posters equated Paris security police with the SS or De Gaulle's logo with the swastika. "It's not all that simple," he was heard to say.[16] And he saw in Paris the dangers of revolutionary fanaticism. Trying to weigh past and present, he wrote the poem "For Eric":

> Illumined
> a conscience rams through
> on this side and that
> the Plague-ish leveling . . .
>
> just like you, son,
> my (with you) arrowing
> hand.   [2:372]

"Illumined" and "rams through" are tinged with misgiving, and "Plague-ish leveling" hints at oppressive Nazi conformism, against which the poet's "arrowing hand" (he was a Sagittarius) will hold straight. On the same day, an intricate poem wove Marlowe's persecuted Jew of Malta into Kristallnacht and Celan's childhood (2:374). Two days later he titled another poem "For Eric," ending it, "We stand" (2:376).

Celan's private needs did not let up during the turbulence of May 1968. He turned to Kafka's diaries, sometimes noting next to an entry the date he himself was reading it—as if Kafka's feeling "terribly abandoned" on 24 January 1922 now applied to "13.5.68." And still threading his own way, the day after students occupied the Sorbonne on 14 May, he went with Gisèle to an exhibit at the Petit Palais called "Israel through the Ages."[17] He also seized upon a new friendship—with Edmond Lutrand, a German-Jewish refugee who in June 1967 had gone immediately to Israel as a volunteer.[18]

Interviewed by Israeli radio for Independence Day, May 1968, Celan read "Just Think," his Six-Day War poem, and wrote to a former Czernowitzer in Tel Aviv about a prewar friend whom this poem had "sustained in a difficult time." Celan also recalled Gustav Landauer's words, "My Germanness and Jewishness do each other no harm and much good": "*Perhaps* they held good" once for Landauer (who was brutally murdered by Bavarian soldiers in 1919), but "they do not and may not hold for any of us, and will never again hold for anyone."[19] Meanwhile "Todesfuge," in anthologies and textbooks, had its true effect on some German readers while persuading others that Shulamith and Margareta "once again extend their hands to each other" in reconciliation.[20]

Celan kept traveling to Germany, which may seem perverse in one who held no brief for German–Jewish symbiosis. Yet these visits answered a need. He made a reading tour in June and July 1968, meeting students and also presenting his translations from Russian. "Celan was a restrained, almost hesitant reader," says one report, and another describes his stance: "One hand held the book or manuscript, the other supported his head. Now and then the reader looked up and addressed single verses to his listeners. Otherwise no movement." His "monotone, penetrative, imploring voice" sometimes "cast a spell."[21] Even in recordings one senses an aura of concentration, heightened by the merest rustle of paper being carefully turned between poems—everything possible vested in the reality of words.

The range of Celan's "spareness, clearness" (2:391) comes out in the summer of 1968. On 19 July, for instance, he started nine poems, the next day seven more. One of these has "Sabbath candles standing upwards" from a moor; another plays on *Erz* (both "ore" and "arch-") to begin a poem "ORE-GLITTER, deep in the / uprising, arch-fathers" (2:390–91); and a third also questions spirit through the matter of geology.

"IN-EDGER: Rembrandt," it begins, stemming from the late self-portraits and from a painting Celan saw in London, the "Bearded Man in a Cap" (1655). He sent Nelly Sachs a postcard of this painting,[22] whose model was probably an Amsterdam Jew—Celan's poem even speaks of a "beardlock, templed," the side curls worn by the Orthodox. Rembrandt, who lived in the Jewish quarter of Amsterdam, used a young Jew in portraits of Jesus and older Jews in studies of the human countenance:

handlines cross the forehead,
in desert boulders, on
the table-rocks
there glimmers at your
mouth's right corner the
sixteenth psalm.   [2:392]

An insight into suffering, into their wandering, drew Rembrandt to Jews such as those reaching Amsterdam after Poland's 1648 massacres. And that drew the poet to the painter. Self-portraitists, they cut into their medium. Celan's word *Einkanter* ("In-edger") resonates with *Kantor* ("cantor"), as if Rembrandt, who painted David playing before Saul, were a Jewish singer. "Keep me, O God . . . For Thou wilt not leave my soul in hell . . . In Thy right hand bliss for evermore" (Ps. 16). This is one of Christianity's messianic Psalms, putting the poet's and painter's religions for a moment on speaking terms.[23]

One critical event in August 1968 shook Celan badly. During the night of the 20th, Soviet and Warsaw Pact troops invaded Czechoslovakia, ending the Prague Spring. His poem the next day does not longingly summon Rabbi

Loew, Kafka, Rilke, or his mother's years in Bohemia. Instead, an animality
breaks out, in the vein of Mandelshtam's Stalin epigram or Pablo Neruda's
Spanish civil war satire. Celan sees the liberal experiment as a new-hatched
chick "slipping into the octopus-nerve for a cure":

> a tentacle clasps
> the jute sack full of
> decision-murmuring from
> the CC . . .   [2:402]

The German here for Central Committee (CC) is *ZK*. Reversed to *KZ*, it
designates a concentration camp. Celan's anagram makes communism the
mirror image of fascism.

Another poem that week speaks defiantly of a "capital city, unoccupiable,"
and a third begins, "Lime crocus," covering that too early spring flower with
the caustic which German troops used to throw into mass graves. But it ends:
"in the rich mines / the Moldau rises" (2:404, 406). Celan for years had
wanted to go to Prague,[24] and "In Prague" (1963) imagines the poet there,
"tolling against time." In 1968, the violation of this Central European city
aroused the protest he still had in him.

With these poems written in late summer of 1968 Celan closed the
collection he had been assembling, called *Schneepart* ("Snow-part"). At one
point he gave it an epigraph from Kafka about raising the world "into the
Pure, the True, the Immutable."[25]

One lyric written on 2 September, though within the time frame of
Schneepart, he did not include, maybe because it was too personal a communication. *Mandelnde*, a new word, starts this poem. From *Mandel* ("almond"), Celan has turned the obsolete verb *mandeln* ("to yield almond
kernels") into a participle *mandelnd* ("almonding") so as to form the noun
Mandelnde, "almonding woman." Since 1952, in "Count up the almonds,"
that oval-eyed sweet or bitter fruit had signaled Jewishness—his mother's or
his people's.

MANDELNDE, *die du nur halbsprachst,*	ALMONDING ONE, you half-spoke only,
doch durchzittert vom Keim her,	though all trembled from the core,
dich	you
liess ich warten,	I let wait,
dich.	you.
Und war	And was
noch nicht	not yet
entäugt,	eye-reft,
noch unverdornt im Gestirn	not yet enthorned in the realm
des Lieds, das beginnt:	of the song that begins:
Hachnissini.	*Hachnissini.* [3:95]

These lines address someone Celan first knew as a young woman in Czernowitz. Her survival in Israel came to embody a deferred yet saving possibility. And the poet's mother, who spoke and sang him into language, also hovers near this almonder, along with the Shechinah, the female presence of God. So the poem confesses to an old-new friend and a germinal spirit whom the exiled poet turns to at last: "you / I let wait, / you."

In letting his *Mandelnde* wait, the poet was "not yet" *entäugt,* "un-" or "dis-" or "de-eyed." Yet *enäugen* (as in the word *entkeimen,* "sprout forth") can suggest the opposite of "de-eyed." Both senses feed into a blinding which is visionary truth, as the Shechinah in exile wept out her eyes and as in "Benedicta" a woman blesses "the eyeless ones." With "eye-reft" I try for Celan's raw diction. His "enthorned" also wrests a Jewish destiny out of Jesus' crown of thorns. Whatever the poet has "not yet" become—"eye-reft," "enthorned"—ties pain to hope.

About that final *Hachnissini* the translator need do nothing. Identified easily enough, it reverberates endlessly: a Hebrew imperative to a feminine singular, "Bring me in." This word, which closes Celan's poem, opens a popular 1905 lyric by the first modern Jewish poet, Chaim Nachman Bialik (1873–1934). *Hachnissini tachat knafech,*

> Bring me in under your wing,
> and be mother and sister to me,
> and let your breast shelter my head,
> a nest for my thrust-out prayers.[26]

Celan had no sister, had lost his mother, and sought them both in a beloved. This song draws on the Psalms: "Hide me in the shadow of Thy wings" (17:8). With erotic yearning, as in the Song of Songs, and with "thrust-out prayers," Bialik's lyric urges a return from homelessness. Someone converting to Judaism is said to come "under the wings of the Shechinah."[27]

Songs leave a trail of their own through Celan's work. Spontaneous and popular, songs in a poem stamp it genuine: the Zionist Song of the Cedar, the Yiddish *Es mus azoy zayn,* the one about Mama Rochl, the Varsovienne, the Maybeetle's song, the Peat-Bog Soldiers. There is singing in "Deathfugue" and "A Song in the Wilderness"; Celan says "I sing before strangers," "There are still songs to sing beyond humankind," and in "Psalm": "We sang over O over the thorn." His 1968 "almonding woman" evokes "Raisins and Almonds," a favorite Yiddish lullaby from Goldfaden's *Shulamis,* and East European Jews learned by heart "the song that begins: *Hachnissini.*"

What Celan expected from Germans as they came on the closing word of "Mandelnde" was nothing . . . and everything. Let them call him hermetic. With *Hachnissini* his verse turns mute yet audible to people with ears to hear.

"My recent book is everywhere seen as encoded," Celan complained in the fall of 1968. "Believe me—every word was written in direct relation to reality. But no, this they just will not and will not understand."[28] The question is: What reality do his poems relate to, and how directly? Celan more and more needed a "darkened splinter-echo" (2:414), as he wrote just after "Mandelnde."

Such a state of mind had its pitfalls. After the flow of poems for *Schneepart,* Celan wrote nothing for six weeks from early September, then one poem in October, and nothing again for more than four months. He broke this silence, in late February 1969, with ambiguous force:

> if one who
> smashed the canticles
> spoke now to the rod,
> his and everyone's
> blinding
> would be gone.   [3:69]

For Celan to point to Moses breaking the tablets and working wonders or Hölderlin going mad or Oedipus blind is not hubris but a crushing sense of tradition and vocation.[29]

"Poetry no longer imposes, it exposes itself" (*La poésie ne s'impose plus, elle s'expose*), Celan wrote in March 1969 (3:181). His lyric trail through spring and summer of 1969 bears out that axiom with a "tongue uprooted" (3:73) and a "raging for silence" (3:76). In other lines—

> a motherstump
> leads a budding face
> through a pain,
>
> its God
> mows past, reviewing images
> on the crests
> of the highest
> cradle   [3:91]

—we hear an anchorite struggling with the language left him.

The poems from mid-1969 have an overall title in Celan's papers, "Zeit-gehöft," an elusive compound of "Time" with "homestead" or "farmyard." It stems partly from earlier uses of *Gehöft,* as in 1964: "Hollow homestead of life" (2:42). He had recently used *Zeithof,* too, where *Hof* means an enclosed space or court, as in the Psalmist's "courts of the Lord" (2:297, 365; 3:76). Celan also underscored *Zeithof* in a Heidegger lecture: "The now-point gives consciousness a *time-court,* borne out in what memory continually apprehends."[30] A decisive instance of *Gehöft* may be Rilke's breathtaking passage:

Exposed on the mountains of the heart. Look, how small there,
look: the last village of words, and higher,
but again how small, yet one last
farmstead of feeling. Can you make it out?[31]

For Celan's *Zeitgehöft,* my "Homestead of Time" tries for a sense of poems as
places where time is at home.

During 1969 Celan was teaching Rilke's *Malte Laurids Brigge,* translating
the futurist Velimir Khlebnikov, and still buying Mandelshtam. In April he
clipped an article from *Le Monde* about Mandelshtam, this "forgotten Russian
poet" who "has been very well rendered by Paul Celan."[32] Reading Gustav
Landauer in July, he noted questions of Jewish versus universal humanity
and even entered his own date next to a 1913 letter denouncing anti-
Semitism.[33] In August Celan wrote to his publisher: "Adorno's death: I am
struck, dismayed"—not quite his strongest words.[34] In one poem from around
that time he called himself "a drowning man" (3:82).

"Excuse my silences—they're involuntary, due above all to troubles with
my health. I am very much alone."[35] Celan was writing from his office to
Petre Solomon in Bucharest on 26 September 1969. "I'm flying in three days
to Israel, for a fortnight," he added, and the letter ends: "J'ai d'assez grosses
difficultés, mon cher Pierre." So a poem he dated 29 September may come
from the very day of departure. "Ambidextrous dawn," it begins, and it closes
darkly:

one more gate swinging with stonerage,
concede it
to the forced-ripe night.   [3:152]

In "rather great difficulties" and "very much alone" Celan journeyed at last
to Israel, possibly to find "the realm / of the song that begins: / *Hachnissini*"—
"Bring me in."

17
To Name Jerusalem
(1969)

I have come to you in Israel because I needed to.

As seldom with such a feeling, I have the strongest sense, after all I've seen and heard, of having done the right thing—not only for me alone, I hope.

I think I have a notion of what Jewish loneliness can be, and I recognize as well, among so many things, a thankful pride in every green thing planted here that stands ready to refresh anyone who comes by; just as I take joy in every newly earned, self-discovered, fulfilled word that rushes up to strengthen those who turn toward it—I take that joy during this time of growing self-alienation and mass conformity everywhere. And I find here, in this outward and inward landscape, much of the force for truth, the self-evidentness, and the world-open uniqueness of great poetry. And I believe I've been conversing with those who are calmly, confidently determined to stand firm in what is human.

I am thankful for all that, and I thank you.   [3:203]

Paul Celan's talk to the Hebrew Writers Association, in Tel Aviv on 14 October 1969, shows one essential difference from his 1958 Bremen speech. In Germany he told his audience: "the language remained, not lost, yes in spite of everything. But it had to pass through . . . deathbringing speech." In Israel he enjoys "every newly earned, self-discovered, fulfilled word that rushes up to strengthen those who turn toward it." Celan took care with those adjectives for the Hebrew word. At first he called it "self-felt" and "self-aware," then made it *selbsterfühlte erfüllte,* something like "self-felt-out fulfilled."[1] He prized the revived Hebrew language no less than the land. Yet I sense in his earnestness—"I needed . . . I hope . . . I think . . . I recognize . . . I believe . . . I am thankful"—an undertow of ambivalence.

Israel's 1967 war had quickened the thought of going there. Finally, in late September 1969, Celan made the journey—without his fourteen-year-old son, whom he had wanted to bring.[2] His time in Israel was given over to people, places, and poetry, all of this surcharged with being in a free Jewish collectivity in the promised land he himself had not chosen. Friends and family whom he hadn't seen since Czernowitz were astonished at how lighthearted he seemed. And Gershom Scholem (who claimed to be baffled by Celan's writing) gave a party for him.[3]

Celan's Hebrew was surprisingly resourceful. "He remembered quotations," says a friend, "and came up suddenly with difficult words and sentences." Visiting Yehuda Amichai, he recited Bialik—possibly that stanza of "Hachnissini."[4] And the German-born Amichai, Israel's leading poet, translated some Celan into Hebrew. "Celan sat and listened. From time to time he surprised us by commenting that we could be more precise. He would suggest some other root, which was stored in his memory."[5] Amichai, on 8 October, gave a volume of his work to Celan, inscribing it in Hebrew "with much love," and Celan read the poems attentively.[6]

He visited Bethlehem, the Church of the Nativity, Rachel's Tomb, Mount Scopus, the Mount of Olives, the Western (or Wailing) Wall, and the Mosque of Omar, where he said, "Let's move along, too much holiness."[7] He saw Yad Vashem and may have visited a kibbutz. At the windmill across from Mount Zion he was struck by Moses Montefiore's motto on a crest: "Think and Thank." The same words *Denken* and *Danken* had opened his Bremen speech,

DU SEI WIE DU, IMMER.

Stant up Jherosalem inde
erheyff dich,

auch wer die Band geschnit zu dir hin,

inde wunt
gemachtet,

knüpfte es wir, in der Gehägnis,

Schlammbrocken schluckt ich, im Turm,
Sprache, Finster-Lisene,

קומי
אורי

Celan, "Du sei wie du," autograph copy, 1969 (Ilana Shmueli)

insisting on remembrance. Above all, Celan wanted to perambulate the gates of Jerusalem's Old City. He sent Nelly Sachs a postcard of the Damascus Gate on 8 October, and other sites appeared later in his poems. One day, for Ilana Shmueli, the "almonding woman" of that 1968 poem, he wrote out "Du sei wie du" from memory, putting Isaiah's *kumi ori* ("Arise, shine") not in transliterated form—why should he?—but in fluent Hebrew script, knotting the bond anew.

To speak his poems in Jerusalem meant something different from doing so in Germany, and Celan feared that few people would attend his reading. But a crowd overflowed the hall, not all native German-speakers.[8] Amichai and Manfred Winkler, a former Bukovinan, presented some Hebrew trans-lations. Then Celan read poems from 1948 through 1967, including "Count up the almonds," "The Vintagers," *Voices*, "Stretto," "Mandorla," and "In Prague." A listener described his "musical tone, pure diction, simplicity, sureness and strength."[9] Celan closed with his Six-Day War poem, "Just Think." His Czernowitz admirers "clamored at the end for 'Todesfuge,'" but the poet refused.[10] "It was a good reading," he said later, "a good listening."

To an even larger audience in Tel Aviv, Celan a week later read "with calm accents and careful articulation . . . without raising his voice, almost whispering."[11] People who had known his parents greeted him afterward, and one woman gave him a kind of cake his mother used to bake. At this, he wept.[12]

The meridian originating in Czernowitz seemed to have come full circle. Celan was given a recent Israeli reprint of a 1939 Czernowitz booklet of Yiddish lullabies, among them that ghetto song about Mother Rachel weeping and Messiah giving in.[13] But the meridian had not really come round: 1969 was not Bukovina. Celan knew the European-born German-speakers who in Israel had become Hebrew poets—Amichai, Winkler, Dan Pagis, Natan Zach, David Rokeah, and Tuvia Ruebner. His joy in their "newly earned . . . fulfilled word" came alloyed with doubts about his own choice, as he had told his Israeli relatives in 1948, "to live out to the end the destiny of the Jewish spirit in Europe."

Israel, and being in Israel, brought the perennial Jewish dilemma of identity into sharp new focus for Celan. Giving an interview to Israel Radio in the Amichais' kitchen, he settled on a low-keyed yet stubborn word for that identity: *selbstverständlich,* "understandable of itself," self-evident, ob-vious, a matter of course.[14] "I think I may say that I am of course a Jew. Questions about Jewishness always meet up with this self-evidentness." Celan then went on to a vital distinction. "Of course Jewishness has a thematic aspect. But I think the thematic alone doesn't suffice to define what's Jewish. Jewishness is so to speak a spiritual [*pneumatisch*] concern as well." This odd term comes from Greek *pneuma,* equivalent to Hebrew *ruach* ("wind," "breath," "spirit")—*pneuma* was his word in "Benedicta" for "what came from our fathers to me / and from beyond our fathers" (1:249). Celan meant that people should not simply expect Jewish themes in his poetry—it is also Jewish in spirit. "Jewishness anyway is interwoven in everything that someone like me writes, someone who grew up in a Jewish environment." Maybe Celan saw the dense fabric of life in the land of Israel as a thematic Jewishness not accessible to him. In the interview he stressed his Germanic culture too: "I myself grew up in and with this tongue. . . . Rilke was very important to me, and afterwards Kafka."

Celan left Israel three days earlier than planned. He did not make one trip that would have been expected, down to the Dead Sea and then up to Masada, the fortress where a few Jews held out against the Romans and finally chose suicide over surrender. He felt he hadn't earned that pilgrimage.[15]

Back in France, he wrote to an old friend in Tel Aviv: "I'm no longer a Parisian, already I'm struggling against these hardships here. . . . I'm happy now to have been in Israel . . . happy to have lived so intensively, more intensively than for a long time . . . I'm already thinking of coming back, of carrying on further, of completions, consummations. So much not seen yet, so much not heard."[16] And to other friends: "It was good, just a short time ago, to make my way past Denmark Square to your . . . hospitable home. Instead I'm again going the ways of this cold city Paris . . . But maybe one day soon you'll come here, or I'll come again to Jerusalem. I'll definitely come again, and not only because I still have so much to see. I need Jerusalem, as I needed it before I found it."[17]

Celan's awakening to this need in himself lasted intermittently for weeks. "So many Jews, only Jews, and not in a ghetto," he remarked,[18] yet he spoke of the "anonymity" Paris granted him. A friend at Tel Aviv University tried to get him a post there.[19] Celan was also struck by the memoir a veteran Israeli writer had given him and by how, during Arab attacks on Jews in pre-state Jerusalem, Christians put crosses on their doors for immunity.[20] "In disquiet and peace," Celan wrote to this writer of his "anxiety for Israel." Yet "Jerusalem lifted and strengthened me," he told Ilana Shmueli. "Paris presses me down and empties me. Paris, through whose streets and buildings I've dragged such a burden of madness, of reality, all these years."

A spate of short lyrics followed Celan's return to Paris in mid-October 1969.[21] They name Israeli sites, and though no Hebrew terms appear, these "Jerusalem" poems—some elated, some not—breathe the *pneuma* that Celan had sworn by.

In the first of them, written the day he got back, a loving encounter with his friend Ilana from Czernowitz frames messianic and historical moments:

Es STAND	THERE STOOD
der Feigensplitter auf deiner Lippe,	a splinter of fig on your lip,
es stand	there stood
Jerusalem um uns,	Jerusalem around us,
es stand	there stood
der Hellkiefernduft	the bright pine scent
überm Dänenschiff, dem wir dankten,	above the Danish skiff we thanked,
ich stand	I stood
in dir.	in you. [3:96]

Not the almond here, but the autumn fig gives to a sensuous moment the

Biblical overtones of abundance and peace (while echoing the elegy for Celan's son and father, "Nourished by figs" [1:121]). To translate "there stood / Jerusalem around us," both Hebrew versions say the same—*amda /yerushalayim saviv lanu*—because Celan's few words are calling up favored Psalms: "Our feet are standing within thy gates, Jerusalem" (122:2) and "Jerusalem, mountains are around her as the Lord is around His people" (125:2).[22]

A fine story is told about Else Lasker-Schüler, who ended her days in Jerusalem during the Second World War. One day she read her German lyrics to a Hebrew writer, who later asked if he might translate them. "But they *are* written in Hebrew!" she exclaimed and would not have them translated.[23] Surely Celan's verse "there stood / Jerusalem around us" is already "written in Hebrew" with a messianic savor.

Another kind of comfort comes from "the Danish skiff." The year before Celan's visit, a monument was placed in north Jerusalem to commemorate the Danes' 1943 rescue of their Jewish population, and there are pines above this sculptured metal rowboat. Under the sensuous but risky "splinter of fig," his stanzas line up survival with an embracing city. Then *stand,* voiced a fourth time, adds more than erotic energy: "I stood / in you." Whether in translating Mandelshtam, whose "ruined temple stood" (4:101), or in "Mandorla," where "Your eye stands opposite Nothingness" (1:244), or in telling himself "Stand . . . for you alone," Celan relied on this verb for staunchness (2:23).[24]

Staying close to his experience in Jerusalem, Celan from Paris asked his friend for a diagram and notes of where they had walked. His next poem, "The heat," moves around several sites, noting them diary-wise. At the same time it brims with that charge he could find in things. This poem starts with a Hamsin, the season's hot dry wind, which carries passion too:

THE HEAT
counts us together
in the shriek of an ass at
Absalom's Tomb, here as well,

Gethsemane, yonder,
circled around, whom
does it overwhelm?

At the nearest gate nothing opens up,
through you, Open one, I bear you to me.   [3:97]

It is a long way from "Count up the almonds," which numbers the poet among the Jewish dead; a still longer time since Jesus entered Jerusalem on an ass, and even longer since the beloved son Absalom on his mule was slain for rebelling against his father. In simply affirming the matter of fact—the Kidron valley, hot in October, with animals grazing—Celan's lines take everything as present: a messianic shriek, a defiant son who erected his own tomb. The merely practical decision to bypass Gethsemane does not evade the garden's agony.

"At the nearest gate nothing opens up": near Absalom's Tomb, the city wall has what Christians call the Golden Gate and Jews call the Gate of Mercy where Messiah will enter—walled up centuries ago by the Moslems. (In a letter with this poem, Celan spoke of "the gates of all futility.") To this closed gate, an I and a thou bring not messianic but erotic consummation: "through you, Open one, I bear you to me." Or is that a needless distinction? In the Song of Songs: "I rose up to open to my beloved" (5:5).

Still drawing root truths from the fact of things, Celan next wrote about his last night in Israel, when he was staying near Tel Aviv (a city founded on sand dunes): "We, like the dune grass steadfast" (3:98). This takes a sense of transience from Psalm 103 and Isaiah—"All flesh is grass" (40:6)—yet dune grass also grips the land. Celan puns on *Wahren* to make the lovers steadfast—both "true" and "preservers." They share "the unkissed / stone of a lament" from the over-memoried Wailing Wall that in Jerusalem he had passed by quickly. Finally, this last night forces them to hard truths:

the night—watch out—under sway
of the sand,
exacts all it can
from us two.

Over twenty years before, "sand from the urns" gave Celan a symbol of Jewish wandering and mortality. Now in 1969 the sand comes home to him, or he to it.

Another moment from the days "lived so intensively" in Israel came back as an ambivalent one-sentence lyric composed "before evening" on 7 November, Celan said, at the Café Royal. This moment occurred on the way back from Bethlehem, outside Jerusalem's walls near an Arab neighborhood overlooking No Man's Land—or, in ancient topography, the hell of Gehenna.

THAT SHINING, yes, the one that
Abu Tor
saw riding toward us, as we
orphaned into each other, with living,
our hands holding on from the roots—:

a goldbuoy, up from
Temple depths,
marked out the danger that fell
still beneath us.   [3:100]

With sun catching the roofs of the Arab village, two Czernowitz friends orphaned by history (like Celan and Sachs in Zurich) bond with what life they possess. The "shining" becomes a precious buoy bobbing up, marking the haven of Zion but also the danger—Israel's peril, the lovers' obligations—that briefly succumbed for them. Hours after Celan finished "That shining," its vision gave way to other lines, images of a "blinding," a "tumor-daughter," an "abyss" (3:101).

"That Jerusalem would be a turning, a caesura in my life—that I knew," Celan wrote. The city seemed a possible "homestead of time" after the catastrophe, an end and a beginning for Celan as for Judaism. From Paris he kept sounding this question, sending poem after poem to Ilana Shmueli in Israel. One of them, on 16 November, keeps the question open by leaving its author and reader alike with an imperative—*hör dich ein / mit dem Mund*—that subtly resists translation. The verb here is unusual in German: "hear yourself in / with the mouth," though correct, loses the threefold pulse of the German *hör dich ein*, while "listen in" and "tune in" are idiomatic yet inexact. A French version says "insouffle-toi l'écoute" (inspirit your listening)—a Godlike resuscitation.[25] English can find a sound and rhythm to overlay the German:

hör dich ein	hear deep in
mit dem Mund.	with your mouth.

I overhear Celan's lines as demanding a translator's response too, a deep hearing that turns into speech.

Here then is "Die Posaunenstelle," both thematically and spiritually Jewish, yet nonetheless open to countless responses:

DIE POSAUNENSTELLE	THE TRUMPET PLACE
tief im glühenden	deep in the glowing
Leertext,	text-void,
in Fackelhöhe,	at torch height,
im Zeitloch:	in the timehole:
hör dich ein	hear deep in
mit dem Mund.	with your mouth. [3:104]

What place do the first five lines locate? Citing Martin Luther's use of *Posaunen* for the apocalyptic "trumpets" sounded by seven angels, Bernhard Böschenstein and others tie Celan's lyric to Revelation 8:10: "And the third angel sounded, and there fell from heaven a great star, burning as a torch" ("torch" is *Fackel,* as in Celan).[26] Christian figurings of Yahveh's wrath may stand behind this poem, which (like Revelation) starkly juxtaposes height and depth. But a very different place, I believe, lies closer to the genesis of "Die Posaunenstelle": those "Temple depths" that Celan had named a week earlier.

"L'veit haTekiah" stone (Israel Antiquities Authority; photograph copyright The Israel Museum, Jerusalem)

Shortly before Celan's visit, the archaeologist Benjamin Mazar had made a major find at the Temple mount in Jerusalem: a large hewn stone lying below the southwest corner on the Herodian pavement, toppled from a parapet when the Romans destroyed the Second Temple.[27] Incised on this ashlar are the words לבית התקיעה, *l'veit haTekiah,* "to the place [or house] of trumpeting" or "place of the shofar blast." Josephus mentions a tower from which the priest would blow a trumpet to signal the beginning and end of the Sabbath, and for rituals and festivals. This finding of *l'veit haTekiah* at the Western Wall, announced in 1969, excited interest because it marked the Temple's flourishing as well as its destruction.

To ascribe "Die Posaunenstelle" to the Revelation of Saint John, then, preempts this other "place of trumpeting," once located high on the Temple above the busiest corner in Jerusalem. Something "unburiable," to cite Celan's June 1967 poem about the war that reopened the Temple mount to excavation, something from "deep . . . in the timehole" emerged on an incised stone.[28]

We can also "hear deep in" another fundamental text beneath Celan's poem. *Posaune* entered the German language via Luther's translation of the Bible, used in Exodus for the Hebrew *shofar,* a ram's horn. Before the giving of the Ten Commandments, there was thunder and lightning "and the voice of a shofar exceeding loud." And as the Lord came down in fire on Sinai, smoke rose and the mountain quaked, "and the voice of the shofar grew louder and louder" (19:16). Then, after God had spoken the Commandments, the people again heard the voice of the shofar—*Posaune*, as rendered by Luther and also by Buber and Rosenzweig. This revelation at Sinai, or at least the passage recounting it, stands behind Celan's trumpet place.[29]

Choosing the word *Posaune* to enter both "text" and "time," his keywords, inevitably takes Celan by way of Martin Luther. Partly Luther's anti-Semitism but mainly the influence of his Bible translation on German language and literature presses upon "Die Posaunenstelle" as it sends a taproot to Hebraic sources. By bringing his Old Testament closer than Saint Jerome's Latin to the Hebrew original, Luther hoped this vernacular Scripture would not only draw Germans but convert Jews to a reformed Christianity. Thus, when Franz Rosenzweig began translating Hebrew hymns and liturgy into German, he remarked to Gershom Scholem that Luther had Christianized the German language.[30] But Celan had direct access to the Hebrew Bible. His term *Posaune* accepts yet implicates Luther's usage and points "deep" toward a founding text.

Another Biblical source lies in store, again from a pre-Christian moment. That the Revelation of Saint John has seven trumpets connects it to Celan's (seven-line) poem, given that number's symbolic value for him. But in the Book of Joshua, seven priests bear seven shofars before the ark of the covenant, circling the city of Jericho seven times, and "when the people heard the sound of the shofar," they shouted themselves into the promised land (6:20).

"The Place of the Shofar" might translate Celan's title, naming the horn blown at a break in time: the Sabbath, New Year, and Day of Atonement. For the Jubilee year a shofar sounds, and it is meant to usher in the messianic age. Whether "shofar" for *Posaune* is too particular depends, as so often with Celan, on how strongly the strain of Jewishness may be felt within his writing.

Sited "deep" in a text, the shofar's place feels beyond our grasp yet fundamental, like *glühenden / Leertext*, which the line break splices, "glowing / empty." How can a text be glowing and empty? Or to rephrase the riddle: What is a text when it is an empty-text? Answer: the Bible. To begin with, Scripture itself originates in a word spoken over emptiness: "The earth was unformed and void [*leer*], and darkness was upon the face of the deep [*Tiefe*], And God said, 'Let there be light'" (Gen. 1:2–3). What is more, since Scripture asks to be fulfilled by believers and interpreters, it starts out "empty." Once given the words of the *Sh'ma*, "Hear, O Israel . . . ," we are commanded to "teach them," "talk of them," "write them" (Deut. 6:4)—in other words, "hear deep in / with your mouth." With Celan's *Leertext* I stress the two ideas equally: "text-void," the presence of an absence that wants filling and that glows with that want.

If as listener you "hear deep in / with your mouth" and speak Celan's word *Leertext*, it makes a perfect homonym with *Lehrtext*. Now *Lehre* means "teaching," like the Hebrew word *torah*, the Mosaic Law, and text-voids, such as the Bible's lean account of Abraham's sacrifice, are essential to Jewish teaching. They draw us in to explore unknowability. "Die Posaunenstelle," devoting a line to pun on "text-void" as Torah, opens up the enigma of Judaic authority, just like Kafka's key parable "Before the Law." There the seeker never gains entrance but before dying sees something like a glowing text-void, a radiance streaming from the door of the Law.

Does Holy Scripture constitute a void, after what "No One" let happen? Celan's writing confronts a near-eclipse of the Word. In 1957 he coined *schriftleer* ("empty of writing," "Scripture-devoid" [1:169]), and in 1961 *leer* could hold divine nothingness—"Empty almond, royal blue" (1:244).[31] So a "text-void" glows with use, however adverse.

The paradoxes framing "Die Posaunenstelle"—"glowing" and "empty," "height" and "hole"—also expose the problem of writing in German. Perhaps Nelly Sachs's book *Glowing Enigmas* (1964) lent its paradox to Celan's poem. A similar strain can be felt in his topography: *Posaunenstelle, Fackelhöhe, Leertext, Zeitloch*. In imitating German compounds, English has several options: "trumpet place," "torch height," "text-void," "timehole."

That last word seems imponderable, given the miraculous descendings and ascendings behind "Die Posaunenstelle." Celan's four-dimensional "timehole" brings to mind a black hole. Earlier, he had formed such words as "time-deep," "time-empty," "time-crevasse" (1:168, 154; 2:31). Now "timehole" sends his late poem downward, backward to an obscure source. *Zeitloch* leaves us facing the stanza break, the void before a final imperative. In a breath-turn these closing words,

> *hör dich ein*
> *mit dem Mund,*

with their triplets moving through a catch-breath, call to the translator as well:

> hear deep in
> with your mouth.

My added word "deep" takes after *dich* and Celan's earlier *tief*, while the three-beat of *te-ki-ah* itself, the shofar blast, leads me to echo the German staccato. Here a common Yiddish command makes itself heard, one used also in Talmudic study—*her dikh ayn*, "pay attention," "listen up." The German *hör dich ein* is standing in for its older, homier cousin tongue that was voided in so many mouths.

What is it to hear "with your mouth"? Sealing the New Testament con-

nection, a German interpreter has cited Revelation 10:10, where Saint John
eats a "little book" the angel gives him "and it was sweet in my mouth like
honey."[32] Yet this derives from Ezekiel in Babylon, whom God commanded:
"Hear what I say unto thee . . . open thy mouth, and eat that which I give
thee," a scroll of lamentations, "and it was in my mouth like honey for
sweetness" (2:8). Celan's text offers a way to "hear deep in / with your mouth"
to the mystery of lamentation and sweetness.[33] "Please write without quotes,"
he once told Ilana. "Just let your own words speak."

With Israel a month behind him, Celan's outlook was already dividing.
"I'd gladly come to Freiburg for a long time," he wrote to a friend. "I'm no
longer up to the city of Paris—and not at all to this world and this time."[34]
Then the next day he composed his most challenging Jerusalem poem.

In "The Poles," all the opposites pulling at him—female/male, sexual/
sacred, present/past, Israel/France, passion/reason, love/loss, free/unfree—
resolve at a layer deeper than consciousness, where Jerusalem's sealed gate
may open.[35]

THE POLES
are within us,
insurmountable
while waking,
we sleep across, up to the Gate
of Mercy,

I lose you to you, that
is my snow-comfort,

say, that Jerusalem *is*,

say it, as if I were this
your whiteness,
as if you were
mine,

as if without us we could be we,

I leaf you open, for ever,

you pray, you lay
us free.   [3:105]

In a lyric whose language has grown simpler than usual, one word stands
out, *Schneetrost* ("snow-comfort"), compacting opposites almost intolerably:
death from 1942's Ukrainian winter with what a mother or a lover gives.
Celan owned a slim book that Schocken had issued in Nazi Berlin, *Die
Tröstung Israels* ("The Consolation of Israel," 1933), where Buber and Rosenzweig's version of Isaiah 40 begins: "Comfort, comfort my people . . . speak

to the heart of Jerusalem." For his ambiguous "snow-comfort," then, the poet had private, historical, and sacred cause.

He had cause, too, for his next verse: "Say, that Jerusalem *is*" (*Sag, dass Jerusalem i s t*). Even his spaced *i s t* lends unusual stress. He used it only once elsewhere, for "a blind *Let there be*": Ein blindes *E s s e i* (1:281). Throughout the Bible it is speech and the command to speak, say, tell, call, utter, shout, cry, proclaim, praise, or sing that makes for authenticity: "O thou, that tellest good tidings to Jerusalem, Lift up thy voice . . . Say unto the cities of Judah, Behold your God" (Isa. 40:9). No less so, a poet's appeal for a spoken word: Tell me it really exists, this place whose spirit held us.

Celan's at once erotic and spiritual impulse merges the beloved with a holy book—"I leaf you open, for ever"—and then ends with a pun verging on crude blasphemy:

du betest, du bettest	you pray, you lay
uns frei.	us free.

To flub the pun on *betest* ("pray") and *bettest* ("bed") loses a jump from sacred to sexual rooted in the "holy wedding" between God and Israel that fascinated Celan. But "you bid, you bed" or "you plead, you breed" won't do, whereas settling for slang, "you pray, you lay / us free," also pictures a mother laying her child to sleep.[36] "As one whom his mother comforteth," says the Lord through Isaiah, "ye shall be comforted in Jerusalem" (66:13).

"Free" and "open," the words in Celan's Meridian speech for what poetry can make us, speak again in his Jerusalem poems. But what the city granted him came mined with uneasiness. On his birthday two days after "The Poles," 23 November 1969, he wrote to Ilana: "The powers I had in Jerusalem have vanished." The verse he wrote then confronts Jewish with Christian and Moslem motifs. Facing the Lions' Gate (where Israelis first entered the city in June 1967), with its crescents overturned above lion figures, he thinks of the Via Dolorosa behind that gate, but in terms of the Jewish Messiah:

THE KING'S WAY behind the false door,

in front, deathed
round by its counter-
sign, the lion sign . . .   [3:106]

This lion (of Judah) leads to a (Moslem) crescent "keeled over, beswamped." Then the poem ends vulnerably—"you, with your / eyelash / fathoming the wound"—like the lovers and their city.

Jerusalem's "outward and inward landscape" presented "the force for truth" of "great poetry" and an end to "Jewish loneliness," Celan had said in Tel Aviv. But in Israel he might again be cut off—though now by Hebrew—from his mother tongue. In Paris in late November, he started a poem in this predicament:

I DRINK WINE from two glasses
and plow away at
the king's caesura
like that one
at Pindar.   [3:108]

Scholars have gone at those two glasses: man and God, life and death, present and past, west and east?[37] Almost all things are possible with Celan, but he may actually have been drinking from two glasses as he wrote, and he was working on two poems. His lines about someone plowing away at Pindar point once again to Hölderlin, who "goes on half mad, plowing away at Pindar" in an 1805 account of him translating Pindar's fragments.[38] Just as Hölderlin drew on Greek myth to infuse German, Celan tapped Hebraic sources. After his stay in Israel the "two glasses," German and Hebrew, sit before him as he writes.

Dividedness acts on the verse itself as he plows away at a "caesura," the break within a line. Caesuras gave Celan a physical sign of every breach affecting him. Where a line in Shakespeare has just one, Celan multiplies them. And Hölderlin's idea of the caesura as a decisive moment in classical drama tallies with Celan's "breath-turn." In "I drink wine" he brings these ideas to a messianic cutting point or "king's caesura" (*Königszäsur,* which also encodes *KZ!*). After Jerusalem, Celan was divided between exile and return: to plow away at the break was to make poetry the scene of decision. Accompanying this poem, he wrote to Ilana about Hölderlin's derangement and quoted "Pallaksch," the poet's Yes/No babble. "There's where we stand now," he said, "in the king's caesura."

So much has emerged from this poem's first sentence that the rest seems to lapse:

God turns in his tuning fork
as one among the least
of the Just,
the lottery drum spills
our two bits.

With God diminished, the lovers' fate falls to chance.[39] A lottery spills out *unser Deut*—our "doit," a coin not worth a farthing, implying *Deutsch* as well as *Deutung* ("interpretation"—our "cents" of things?). My "two bits" gets only a little of all that.

Again Celan's mood shifted. On 13 December a resolute future tense led to rising and wholeness:

THERE WILL be something, later,
that brims full with you
and lifts up
toward a mouth

Out of a shardstrewn
craze
I stand up
and look upon my hand,
how it draws the one
and only
circle   [3:109]

A drink that foamed up to a "latemouth" in "The Vintagers" is met here by
fragments from the vessel of Creation. Celan's poem cuts from future to
present, to madness "shards" and the poet's hand drawing round a meridian
from end to beginning.[40]

His next poem shows the strain of binding that meridian. Beginning with
Das Nichts, it makes and unmakes its hope in every breath:

NOTHINGNESS, for our
names' sake
—they gather us in—,
sets a seal,

the end believes we're
the beginning,

in front of
masters
going silent around us,
in the Undivided, there testifies
a binding
brightness.   [3:110]

A strange ingathering occurs. Instead of God guiding us in straight paths "for
His name's sake," it is Nothingness—a presence both ineffable and eclipsed—
for *our* names' sake. Names are firsthand and sacred, as in an earlier poem:

All the names, all those together burned
names. So much
ash to bless.   [1:227]

Celan felt those names gathering him unto his people, as the Bible has it. But
how to bless them, set a seal on them? Daniel in his vision was told: "The

words are . . . sealed till the time of the end" (12:9). In the New Year, the cycle of Torah readings ends and begins anew, and a prayer asks, "Seal us in the book of happiness." Celan's late poem "Nothingness," where "the end believes we're / the beginning," goes back through the silence of masters (Mallarmé? Hölderlin? Eckhart?) toward "the Undivided," before God divided light from darkness and named them. There we find a *klamme / Helle,* a clammy or gorgelike or "binding / brightness."

Light and the narrow way toward it keep pulling at Celan in his last Jerusalem poem, "Umlichtet die Keime," which moves from sexual opening to spiritual nerve:

CLEARLIT the seeds
I set aswim
in you,

rowed free
the names—they
ply the straits,

a blessing, ahead,
clenches
to a weather-skinned
fist.   [3:114]

This lyric catches up the whole Jerusalem sequence, from the *Keim,* the "core" of an "almonding woman," through straits marked by "night . . . danger . . . timehole . . . snow . . . death . . . wound . . . craze . . . nothingness . . . silence . . . brightness" to "Clearlit," where "names" are rowed free toward a hard "blessing, ahead."

Celan's appeal in "The Poles" to "say, that Jerusalem *is*" occurs "in the light of u-topia," as the Meridian speech put it (3:199). Reaching Israel after years of drinking wine from two glasses only enforced his exile.

18
A Question of Last Things
(1970)

"For me, especially in a poem, Jewishness is sometimes not so much a *thematic* as a *pneumatic* concern"—a concern of the spirit, he wrote in 1970 to Gershom Schocken, editor of the Israeli paper *Haaretz*.[1] "Not that I haven't also articulated Jewishness thematically: it's present in this form too, in every volume of my poetry; my poems imply my Judaism. I'd gladly have gone further into all this with your father; but he must somehow have known it—which explains why he gave me Franz Rosenzweig's Judah Halevi translation. Never, my dear Mr. Schocken, have I set up as 'crypto,' either in Germany or elsewhere." Celan corrects other misimpressions the elder Schocken had: "My parents did not lose their lives in the gas chambers but in a German death camp [*Vernichtungslager*] in the Ukraine," and "I had no sister." He says he would be "delighted sometime to have a longer conversation—in Israel or in Paris."

A need to set things right and keep his footing impelled this letter to the son of the premier German-Jewish publisher. Interviewed in Jerusalem, Celan had fixed on the distinction between theme and *pneuma*, "spirit." Now he adds that his poems imply his Judaism. And it matters to identify that death camp as German. The book he thought an insightful gift was by Franz Rosenzweig, who at incredible physical cost had translated Judah Halevi's Hebrew poems, part of Rosenzweig's effort to mate "the spirits of the two languages" in a "holy wedding," wherein Hebrew would inspirit German Jewry.[2] After his death in 1929, German hands and tongues broke up that bond.

Despite having done "the right thing" in going to Israel, he was still "Your truly lonely Paul Celan" in signing a January 1970 letter to an old German friend, and his poems that February held no hope.[3] "It's gone quiet around me," he told someone, feeling abandoned by readers.[4] Yet he refused to let an American poet publish translations of his work.[5] Nevertheless, the Israeli poet David Rokeah (born in Lemberg) recalls a February meeting: "Hours in conversation about poems, his and mine; about possibilities and impossibilities of translation; about Jerusalem, his and mine."[6] Celan published versions of two Rokeah poems. In one of them, for *Shalom*, he used no equivalent but simply *Schalom*, the Hebraism sounding not quite at home in German (5:603).

The idea of returning to Israel lingered in Celan. "Our last long talks in Paris," a German friend remembers, "were always linked by him to the matter of Israel. He thought finally he'd take up an invitation there."[7] At the same time, he wrote to a childhood friend still in Czernowitz that he would like to see his birthplace again.[8] Meanwhile new occasions arose for revisiting Germany: the bicentenary of Hölderlin's birth, at Stuttgart in March, where Celan would read his poems, and in May a convocation at Freiburg, bringing congenial East European writers to hear him. Celan looked forward to these occasions.[9]

The Hölderlin celebration, where he was the only poet asked to read, honored a long affinity but had its own pitfalls. A glimpse into Celan's state of mind in Stuttgart can be had from friends: "he talked about his flight, his family (his great-grandfather was a very pious man who emigrated to Safed in Israel . . . his grandfather too was a Biblical scribe)."[10] Others who saw him in this period also say that "he talked about his childhood, his parents."[11] Maybe the German ambience, vital to him, threw this "truly lonely" poet back on his past.

In choosing what to present at Stuttgart on 21 March 1970, Celan put himself and his hearers to a test: clipped, cryptic lyrics from *Lichtzwang*. His reading seemed "pressed, dismayed," one reporter said. Another heard lines that seemed symptomatic: "Yet we could not / darken over to you" (2:239).[12] "Philologists precisely informed . . . on particular obscurities in Hölderlin," says Hans Mayer, "shook their heads, rejecting the man up there and his word."[13] Other friends confirm that Celan's poems just did not go over.[14] The "Hölderlin of our time," Nelly Sachs had called him,[15] and that was the trouble—though maybe Celan half-willed this mischance.

Visiting Hölderlin's birthplace the next day, he would not go inside the town's famous Gothic church, and at Tübingen he found "terrifying" some portraits from the poet's last demented years there.[16] He bought a postcard of the tower where those years were spent and sent it to his friend in Israel with a one-word message: *Stehend* ("Standing"), holding firm, hanging on. In Stuttgart, Celan declined to attend a performance of Bach's Saint Matthew Passion. But he did visit the Isenheim Altar at Colmar during Holy Week, and Grünewald's *Crucifixion* put him in mind of his parents' suffering. Then in Freiburg, looking "weighed down, strained" (his host recalls), he read to a small group.[17] During the discussion afterward, Celan at one point reproached Heidegger for inattentiveness. Later the philosopher remarked, "Celan is sick—incurable." Perhaps. But his deeper burden was to be demanding so much from poetry. For instance, to the critic who had first published his Six-Day War poem in 1967, Werner Weber, he gave a copy of the unpublished "Du sei wie du." When Weber's sensitive, informative commentary appeared with the poem on Easter Sunday 1970, Celan read it warily—"gladdened and with cautious agreement."[18] He never developed a tough skin vis-à-vis the fortunes of his poetry in German-speaking Europe.

Once back in Paris, nothing opened up for him. Israel was too problematic, and Paris anything but comfortable. In the Métro one day, Franz Wurm recalls, "Someone jumped out from a group of young people behind us and bellowed down the car, 'Jews to the ovens!' I saw his face tense up and grow sad, his fists clench."[19] Then minutes later in the post office, a clerk noticed Celan's aerogram to Israel and slowly crushed it before tossing it in the outgoing mail. One afternoon at the end of March, Wurm invited Celan to come along and meet Samuel Beckett, but Celan said No—to go unannounced at the last minute wasn't right. When Wurm returned that evening with greetings from Beckett, Celan said sadly: "That's probably the only man here I could have had an understanding with"—with Beckett, whose trilogy proceeds from a mother's death to the end of "The Unnamable": "in the silence you don't know, you must go on, I can't go on, I'll go on."[20]

Although Celan wrote few poems at this time, he kept his hand in by translating. A sequence by Jacques Dupin, his co-editor at *L'Éphémère,* he called "The Night, larger and larger." Close to the original, he could still sound like himself: "it gushes out, the fire's almond . . . behind the dismanteled light." The sequence ends with someone "whose fall deepens him," and with

> this his last self-withdrawal—
> or his sleep
> amid all my
> apocryphal ashes.   [4:747]

Working on a long poem by Jean Daive, who had translated his "Engführung," Celan breaks up and compacts the verse, and three times he refuses to use *Rasse* for Daive's *race,* finding other German equivalents for that tainted word.[21]

April in Paris did not relieve Celan's sense of "this cold city," as he had described it after returning from Israel. Yet on 7 April 1970, staying at Edmond Lutrand's house on the Loire, he wrote a brief lyric discovering early spring in late exile:

> CROCUS, spotted from a
> hospitable table:
> small sign-
> sensing exile
> of a common
> truth,
> you need
> every blade.   [3:122]

The sign says that exiles are only guests. Instead of deploring this, Celan calls it "a common truth" whose every bit is needed because it is, after all, the truth.

During this season of fitful turning toward Bukovina, Israel, and Germany, Celan was reading *La Conscience juive* by André Neher and Buber's *Ekstatische Konfessionen.* In Gustav Janouch's conversations with Kafka, he noted Kafka's interest in the golem legend and also his equation, "Poetry is Disease."[22] Teaching twice a week at the École Normale Supérieure, Celan had his seminar translating Kafka into French, and "The Hunter Gracchus" took hold of him. In this tale a man has died but still lives because his "death-ship" goes astray, perhaps through "a diversion to my lovely native land." So he wanders: "No one will read what I write here, no one will come to help me . . . My ship is rudderless, it's driven by the wind blowing into the nethermost regions of death."[23]

Celan kept returning to Kafka's "A Country Doctor," whose phrase he had adapted to himself in 1962: "'Tis but a Jew." Now it was the story's end that gripped him, where the doctor, out on a winter call, has been stripped and laid down next to a boy with a wound. Trying to leave, he realizes he'll never get back home. "Naked, exposed to the frost of this unhappiest of ages," he regrets the call that brought him out: "Betrayed! Betrayed! Once you've answered the wrong ring of the night bell—it can never be made good."[24] Perhaps he had answered the wrong call, Celan wrote to his friend in Israel, accepted the wrong destiny. On 12 April 1970 he reported that his Kafka seminar was going well and quoted Kafka's diary entry about getting temporary satisfaction from work like "A Country Doctor," "But happiness only if I can raise the world into the Pure, the True, the Immutable."[25]

In a poem the next day, 13 April, Celan turned to words he had always kept by him: "dig," "dark," "hour," "deep," "open," "stone," "eye," "you," "read." Without reaching any ultimate clarity, except possibly in its final word *Sabbath*, this lyric ends up speaking, more simply than ever before, to a *du* who is both the poet and his reader:

REBLEUTE *graben*	VINEGROWERS dig up
die dunkelstündige Uhr um,	the dark-houred clock,
Tiefe um Tiefe,	deep upon deep,
du liest,	you read,
es fordert	the Invisible
der Unsichtbare den Wind	summons the wind
in die Schranken,	into bounds,
du liest,	you read,
die Offenen tragen	the Open ones carry
den Stein hinterm Aug,	the stone behind their eye,
der erkennt dich,	it knows you,
am Sabbath.	come the Sabbath. [3:123]

Turning over soil like time, drawn into straits by God, confronted by stone: for such encounters, the poem tells each of us, "you read" (*du liest*).[26]

That refrain, "you read . . . you read," focuses awareness in the simplest terms, while each stanza deals with a force that could destroy or regenerate: "Vinegrowers dig up / the dark-houred clock," "the Invisible / summons the wind," "the Open ones carry / the stone." Each time, Celan's run-on line breaks the act, at once stalling and preparing what is to happen.

Who then are *Rebleute*? In this archaic word for vintagers, people who cultivate the vine (*Rebe*), one can overhear the Yiddish term *Reb* (like "rabbi") used among East European Jews to address a pious man. Since those were the most vulnerable Jews from 1941 on, Celan's *Rebleute* are digging down into the catastrophe's dark time. But to convey that pun on *Reb* and make the vinegrowers Hasidic—there I'm at a loss.

When it comes to the terse refrain, there seems no problem: *du liest,* "you read." Yet *liest,* besides "read," means "gather." Years earlier, Celan had vintagers "press down on time like their eye." Now *du liest,* coming hard upon the labor of "vinegrowers," tells you to do more than read: it might work to first say "you read," then flip the "d" and the next time say "you reap."

In the next three-line event, some primal force constricts itself as *ruach* or *pneuma*:[27]

> the Invisible
> summons the wind
> into bounds.

And again "you read"—a scriptural response in a text-void. Then

> the Open ones carry
> the stone behind their eye.

Because the Invisible has acted, the vinegrowers are now "open," in the clear.[28] A "stone" for Celan has always meant muteness, danger, or death he cannot bypass. Like the cousins in "Conversation in the Mountains," who had a veil behind their eyes, now "the Open ones carry / the stone behind their eye," hardening their vision.

Finally, *der erkennt dich*—this stone, "it recognizes you," Celan tells himself and also the reader addressed in both refrains. But *erkennen* gives more pause than any word so far. In his 1948 Jené essay Celan "recognized" words rising from the ashes of burnt-out meaning (3:158). Later, this verb spoke in the face of all odds, in "Shibboleth" (1954): "Heart: here too make yourself recognized" (1:131), and in "To Stand" (1963), whose speaker is "unrecognized" (2:23). Now, in April 1970, "recognizes" feels too lengthy for what is happening. An exchange may help: in the Buber–Rosenzweig and Luther Bibles, Adam "knew" (*erkannte*) his wife Eve (and sexual union takes place on the Sabbath). The Torah also says that God "knew" Moses face to face (Deut. 34:10). This stone, then, *der erkennt dich,* it "knows" (or "will know") you, prolonging the *o*'s of "open" and "stone."

Maybe translators, after all, are like the beggar employed to wait on the outskirts of town, watching for when Messiah might come. Asked how he liked his work, he said, "Well, the pay's not so hot, but it's a steady job."

Celan's visionary "stone behind their eye" reminds me of the statue in Rilke's "Archaic Torso of Apollo":

> . . . for there is no place on it
> that does not see you. You must change your life.

And you must change your *line!* Celan's last stanza has an extra line, a bonus: *am Sabbath,* it says, "on the Sabbath." But I like the lift of "come the Sabbath," to hasten that moment of rest and yet keep anticipating it.[29]

One small touch remains in Celan's *Sabbath:* the letter *h.* Until now, this term has occurred only in compounds—"Sabbath radiance" (1:259), "Sabbath candles" (2:390)—and he has spelled it *Sabbat.*[30] But translating Mandelshtam's "The Priests," Celan wrote *der Sabbath kam* ("the Sabbath came"), and only when Fischer Verlag put it in book form did the *h* disappear (5:101).[31] The letter reflects a traditional Hebraic pronunciation and looks antiquated in modern German: though Luther wrote *Sabbath,* twentieth-century editions do not; nor do Buber–Rosenzweig or Heine's *Prinzessin Sabbat* or Celan's German-Jewish encyclopedia. Schocken in Nazi Germany published *Der Sabbat* (1935) for "the rising young generation of Jews."[32]

There's no knowing what sense of "Sabbath" Celan had in mind on 13 April 1970 or whether he thought this poem might "raise the world into the Pure, the True, the Immutable." "Sabbath" in English can stay the same as Celan's *Sabbath*—cognates in two Diasporas. Naturally a Hebrew translation returns *Sabbath* to the source-word *Shabbat.* But in my version, "Shabbat," with its Biblical and Israeli originality, would shortcut the exile of a people nearly lost to deathbringing speech. Years before, Celan's "Conversation in the Mountains" had evoked a candle burning down and "that evening on which a day began, a certain day that was the seventh, upon which the first was to follow, the seventh and not the last" (3:172). All this and more— though it seems extravagant to say so—flows into one silent letter, the last in his poem.

That verse, *am Sabbath,* was Paul Celan's last of all. He was living alone at 6 Avenue Émile Zola, just across the quay from Pont Mirabeau. Even there, as countless times before, his poetry and his life interacted. In 1962 he had quoted Apollinaire's "Pont Mirabeau"—a song of transiency, loss, night—in his poem with the epigraph "All poets are Yids," which also says:

> From the bridge-
> stone, from which
> he bounded over in-
> to life, fledged
> by wounds,—from the
> Pont Mirabeau.   [1:288]

And in 1964 he had written:

> Water needles
> stitch up the split

shadow—he fights his way
deeper down,
free.   [2:80]

About 20 April 1970, around Passover, Celan went from the bridge into the
Seine and, though a strong swimmer, drowned unobserved.[33] He was missed
at the École Normale. Mail piled up under the door of his barely furnished
flat. Gisèle called a friend to see if perhaps her husband had at last gone to
Prague.[34] On 1 May a fisherman came on his body seven miles downstream.

A biography of Hölderlin was found then on Celan's desk, open to an
underlined passage: "Sometimes this genius goes dark and sinks down into
the bitter well of his heart."[35] Celan did not, I noticed, underline the rest of
that sentence in the Hölderlin biography: "but mostly his apocalyptic star
glitters wondrously."

People have said that Celan took his own life at forty-nine because valid
speech in German was impossible after or about Auschwitz. Yet this was the
impossibility that incited him: "Spills of mire I swallowed, inside the tower."
And he did speak—more validly than could ever have been imagined.

Maybe he felt too alone: "No one / witnesses for the / witness." Or maybe
he sensed an attack coming on, another clinical confinement, more suffering
from his medicines and had to free himself from that.[36]

Celan's death desolated friends in Europe and Israel, who cannot forget
what they were doing when the news came by telephone, television, radio,
or newspaper. One of those hit hardest was the emigré historian Erich Kahler.
On his deathbed in May 1970 (as Joseph Frank observed it), Kahler "spoke
not of himself but, with his hands clasped before him as if in prayer, and
with a passion that made his voice tremble and tears come to his eyes, of the
terrible psychic burden—the burden of being both a great German poet and
a young Central European Jew growing up in the shadow of the concentration
camps—which had led to the suicide of Paul Celan."[37] Kahler's last letter
concerned Celan's language, its reduction to "primary-wordness . . . bare
signs and ciphers, stuntedness." Kahler, who had written on "the disintegra-
tion of form in the arts," now said that "*Only* in Celan has this process
attained an inner and paradigmatic necessity."[38]

In Stockholm, the fact of Celan's absence and death reached Nelly Sachs's
bedside. One person says the news was kept from her because of her own
failing health, but other reports say she did hear, was "profoundly shaken,"
and mumbled something about his "going before her."[39] On the day he was
buried in the Thiais cemetery outside Paris, on 12 May 1970, Nelly Sachs
died.[40]

"Paul Celan est mort," said the front-page headline of a leading Paris

literary weekly on 13 May, but added: "In France, he is unknown."[41] Unknown?—after twenty-two years of living, working, teaching, translating
Apollinaire, Rimbaud, Valéry, Char, Michaux, and writing poems that revealed, as Emmanuel Levinas put it, "Insomnia in the bed of Being."[42]

In Freiburg the gathering that Celan had looked forward to took place on
13 May.[43] For the East European writers he had carefully prepared a reading
from early collections. In the event, those awaiting him had his poems alone,
poems already deeply used to absence and death. "But in great poetry," as
Celan said of Mandelshtam, "when is it *not* a question of last things?"[44]

In Israel's German-language press, Bukovinans wrote of their sudden loss
with titles such as "Paul Celan has left us," "Our Paul," "Kaddish for Paul
Celan."[45] They reprinted "The Sluice":

Through
the sluice I had to go,
to salvage the word back into
and out of and across the salt flood:
Yizkor.   [1:222]

And someone quoted the last line of Hölderlin's "Remembrance": "But what
abides is founded by poets."

Scores of memorial poems and articles appeared in Germany, many citing
poetry's "strong bent toward falling silent" from the Meridian speech or how
a poem "constantly calls and hauls itself from its No-longer back into its
Ever-yet." One sympathetic piece nonetheless called "Todesfuge" "all too
rhetorical."[46] Another discovered in that poem a "grief for the hangman . . .
the victim of a system" and suggested that "your golden hair Margareta / your
ashen hair Shulamith" couples German and Jewish ideals in "forgiveness."[47]

Celan was spared this. After his death the German public went on absorbing "Todesfuge" as a virtual institution. At least seven composers set it
for vocal and instrumental combinations, and a German-Jewish dance troupe
performed it in repertory.[48] A book of "poetic testimony on deportation and
annihilation" was titled *Der Tod ist ein Meister aus Deutschland,* as was a major
TV documentary on the "Final Solution."[49] The lines invoking Margareta and
Shulamith figured on several imposing canvases by Anselm Kiefer, which did
not compromise them. And on the fiftieth anniversary of Kristallnacht, an
actress recited "Todesfuge" in the Bundestag.[50]

For many European Jewish survivors, Celan's poem remains the quintessence of whatever understanding they have after the catastrophe. One
phrase has passed into the language: "we shovel a grave in the air"—the
words Celan once insisted were "neither borrowing nor metaphor."[51] In a
1976 preface to his reflections on torture and survival, *At the Mind's Limits,*

Jean Améry described the resurgence of German anti-Semitism as a "playing with the fire that dug a grave in the air for so many."[52] And the partisans' song in Primo Levi's *If Not Now, When?* (1982) says that their slaughtered brothers "have dug themselves a grave in the air."[53] Levi honored Celan's words by giving them to Yiddish-speaking resistance fighters.

It is no coincidence that Jean Améry and Primo Levi also took their own lives. Nor that Celan's loyal younger friend and brilliant critic Peter Szondi, another survivor, drowned himself the year after Celan.[54]

Yet "the end believes we're / the beginning," Celan said. From first to last, his poems stand.

1938	For you are stillness, mother, shimmer from the deep.
1942–43	What would come, mother: wakening or wound—
	If I too sank in snows of the Ukraine?
1943	. . . when snowdrift sifts your father's
	bones, hooves crushing
	the Song of the Cedar . . .
	Then came my tears. I wove the shawl.
1944	God's as nearby as the vulture's nail.
	the gentle, the German, the pain-laden rhyme?
1944–45	there you won't lie too cramped
1945	Oaken door, who hove you off your hinge?
1946	You fill up the urns here and nourish your heart
1948	It's time the stone consented to bloom
1950	seven roses later the well gushes up
1951	This word is your mother's ward
1952	Render me bitter.
	Number me among the almonds.
1953	Whichever word you speak—
	you owe
	to destruction
	Out of beaten gold, just
	as you bade me, mother,
	I formed the candlestick—from it
	she darkens up to me among
	splintering hours:
	your
	being-dead's daughter

1954	Speak—
	But don't split off No from Yes . . .
	Speaks true who speaks shadow
	Cry out the shibboleth
	into the alien homeland:
	February. No pasaran.
1956	*Voices* in the bowels of the ark
1957	Near are we, Lord,
	near and graspable.
	Graspèd already, Lord,
	clawed into each other . . .
	One more word like this, and the hammers
	will be swinging free
1958	. . . the
	choirs, back then, the
	Psalms. Ho, ho-
	sanna
1959	I—I, I who can say to you:
	—On the stone is where I lay, back then, you know . . .
	There was earth inside them, and
	they dug . . .
	They dug and heard nothing more;
	they did not grow wise, invented no song
1960	. . . I
	let the heart that I had
	hope:
	for
	his highest, death-rattled, his
	wrangling word
	Blessèd art thou, No One.
	In thy sight would
	we bloom.
	In thy
	spite.
1961	. . . he could,
	if he spoke of this
	time, he
	could
	only babble and babble

You prayer-, you blasphemy-, you
prayer-sharp knives
of my
silence

the voice stopped singing after
's muz azoy zayn

1962   the black hail that
fell there too, in Vitebsk,
—and those who sowed it, they
write it away . . .

you undo the arm from his shoulder, the right one, the left,
you fasten your own in their place

1963   it lives, the flower, further, winterhard

With the persecuted in late, un-
silenced,
radiant
covenant.

          . . . a breath-crystal,
your unannullable
witness

1964   Your song, what does it know?
Deepinsnow,
               Eepinnow,
                        E - i - o.

Bone-Hebrew,
ground down to sperm,
ran through the hourglass

1967   Near, in the aorta's arch,
in bright blood:
the brightword.

Just think:
the Peat-Bog Soldier of Masada
makes a homeland for himself

a hope, today,
for a thinker's
coming
word
in the heart

speech, dark-selvedge

1968   Illegibility of this
world. Everything doubled.

Almonding one, you half-spoke only

1969   There stood
a splinter of fig on your lip,
there stood
Jerusalem around us

At the nearest gate nothing opens up

deep in the glowing
text-void

say, that Jerusalem is

1970   the Open ones carry
the stone behind their eye,
it knows you,
come the Sabbath.

Notes

The following abbreviations are used in the notes:

GW   Paul Celan, *Gesammelte Werke,* ed. Beda Allemann and Stefan Reichert, with Rolf Bücher (Frankfurt, 1983).

Baumann   Gerhart Baumann, *Erinnerungen an Paul Celan* (Frankfurt, 1986).

Böschenstein   Bernhard Böschenstein, "Gespräche und Gänge mit Paul Celan," in Böschenstein and Giuseppe Bevilacqua, *Paul Celan* (Marbach, 1990).

Briefe   *Briefe an Hans Bender,* ed. Volker Neuhaus (Munich, 1984).

"Briefe"   "Briefe an Alfred Margul-Sperber," *Neue Literatur* 26/7 (1975): 50–63.

"Briefwechsel"   Petre Solomon, "Briefwechsel mit Paul Celan, 1957–1962," *Neue Literatur* 32/11 (1981): 60–80.

Celan/Sachs   *Paul Celan / Nelly Sachs: Briefwechsel,* ed. Barbara Wiedemann (Frankfurt, 1993).

Chalfen   Israel Chalfen, *Paul Celan: Eine Biographie seiner Jugend* (Frankfurt, 1979).

Datum	Datum und Zitat bei Paul Celan: Akten des Internationalen Paul Celan-Colloquiums, Haifa 1986, ed. Chaim Shoham and Bernd Witte (Bern, 1987).
"Der glühende"	"Der glühende Leertext": Annäherungen an Paul Celans Dichtung, ed. Christoph Jamme and Otto Pöggeler (Munich, 1993).
Dimensiunea	Petre Solomon, Paul Celan: Dimensiunea Românească (Bucharest, 1987).
Federmann	Reinhard Federmann, "In Memoriam Paul Celan," Die Pestsäule 1 (Sept. 1972): 17–21, 91.
Fichman	Pearl Fichman, Before Memories Fade (unpub. MS, New York, 1989).
L'Adolescence	Petre Solomon, Paul Celan: L'adolescence d'un adieu, trans. Daniel Pujol (Castelnau-le-Lez, 1990). This is the French edition—lacking the pictures, Celan's letters to Solomon and Margul-Sperber, his Romanian poems and prose, and his four Kafka translations into Romanian—of Dimensiunea.
PC	Paul Celan, ed. Werner Hamacher and Winfried Menninghaus (Frankfurt, 1988).
Silbermann	Edith Silbermann, Begegnung mit Paul Celan (Aachen, 1993).
UPC	Über Paul Celan, ed. Dietlind Meinecke (Frankfurt, 1970).
ZfK	Zeitschrift für Kulturaustausch 32/3 (1982).
"Zwanzig"	Petre Solomon, "Zwanzig Jahre danach," Neue Literatur 33/11 (1982): 23–34.

Introduction

1. GW 3:186. This 5-volume edition is hereafter referred to in brackets in the text by volume and page number. All translations from Celan and other sources are mine unless specified otherwise.
2. Celan, letter to Gleb Struve, 29 Jan. 1959, in Victor Terras and Karl S. Weimar, "Mandelstamm and Celan: A Postscript," Germano-Slavica 2/5 (Spring 1978): 361.
3. Celan, letter to Hans Bender, 10 Feb. 1961, in Briefe, 54.
4. David Young, "Recent Poetry in Translation," Antioch Review 45/1 (Winter 1987): 95; James Dickey, "The G.I. Can of Beets, The Fox in the Wave, and The Hammer Over Open Ground," South Atlantic Review 48/2 (1983): 12.

Chapter 1
Loss and the Mother Tongue (1920–43)

1. Chalfen, illustration 10. References to this first biography are to the German edition. See also the English translation: Paul Celan: A Biography of His Youth, trans. Maximilian Bleyleben, intro. John Felstiner (New York, 1991).
2. Karsten Hvidtfelt Nielsen and Harald Pors, Index zur Lyrik Paul Celans (Munich, 1981).
3. Chalfen, illustration 6.
4. Ibid., 31.
5. Celan, letter in contributor's note, Die Wandlung 4/3 (Mar. 1949): 284.
6. Letter, Hanne Lenz to Ilse Blumenthal-Weiss, 12 Feb. 1971.
7. Celan, letter to Reinhard Federmann, 3 Mar. 1962, in Federmann, 19.
8. Chalfen, 52, 47.
9. Celan, letter to Hans Bender, 18 Nov. 1954, in Briefe, 35.
10. Chalfen, 40.
11. Celan, letter to Walter Jens, 19 May 1961.
12. Cord Barkhausen, "Interview: Moshe Barash über Paul Celan," Sprache und Literatur in Wissenschaft und Unterricht 16 (1985): 99.

13. Hugo Gold, *Geschichte der Juden in der Bukowina* (Tel Aviv, 1962), 1:100, 2:142–43, 163–64.

14. Chalfen, 43.

15. Otto Pöggeler, *Spur des Worts: Zur Lyrik Paul Celans* (Freiburg, 1986), 406.

16. Fichman, 45, 248.

17. Silbermann, 54.

18. Pöggeler, *Spur*, 404.

19. Celan, letter to Robert Neumann, n.d., in *34 x erste Liebe*, ed. Neumann (Frankfurt, 1966), 33.

20. Gerhart Baumann, "Dank an die Sprache: Erinnerung an Immanuel Weissglas," *Neue Zürcher Zeitung*, 2–3 Feb. 1980: 68; Silbermann, 48; Chalfen, 69.

21. Barkhausen, "Interview," 96.

22. Courtesy of Pearl Fichman. This photo has not been published before.

23. Fichman, 64.

24. Celan's early poems are collected in *Gedichte 1938–1944*, ed. Ruth [Lackner] Kraft (Frankfurt, 1985), and *Das Frühwerk*, ed. Barbara Wiedemann (Frankfurt, 1989). My quotations are taken from the latter, hereafter cited in parentheses in text as *F* with page number.

25. David Seidmann, interview by the author, Paris, 16 Aug. 1984; Ilana Shmueli, interview by the author, Tel Aviv, 3 July 1982.

26. Fichman, 62, 65. Another friend remembers Paul in 1941 already reading *War and Peace* in the original language: Dorothea Müller-Altneu, "Erinnerungen an den jungen Paul Celan," *Die Stimme*, Apr. 1990: 4.

27. Interview in the West German documentary *Der Tod ist ein Meister aus Deutschland* (1990).

28. Fichman, 74.

29. Shmueli interview.

30. Gold, *Geschichte*, 2:23, 59–60; Julius S. Fisher, *Transnistria: The Forgotten Cemetery* (So. Brunswick, N.J., 1969).

31. Chalfen, 119.

32. Zvi Yavetz, interview by the author, New York, 11 July 1985; Sigfried Trichter, interview by the author, Paris, 1 July 1988.

33. Fichman, 76–77.

34. Alfred Kittner, "Erinnerungen an den jungen Paul Celan," *ZfK* 218. The other poet was Immanuel Weissglas.

35. Eva-Lisa Lennartsson, "Nelly Sachs och Hennes Vännen. Mina Personliga Minnen," *Fenix* 2/3 (1984): 46–133; unpub. German translation by Olaf Önnerfors, courtesy of Jerry Glenn.

36. Fichman. 213. See S. Meerbaum-Eisinger, *Blütenlese,* ed. Hersh Segal (1976); 2d ed., ed. Adolf Rauchwerger (Tel Aviv, 1979), 72.

37. Arnold Daghani, "The Grave in the Cherry Orchard," *Adam: International Review* 291–3 (1961): 25–26. Chalfen, 42.

38. Celan, letter to Kahler, 25 Apr. 1962. See also "A Tribute to Erich Kahler," *Unicorn Journal* 4 (1972): 99.

39. Celan, *Gedichte*, 5.

40. Chalfen, 122.

41. Ibid., 120.

42. Franz Auerbach, reported in *L'Adolescence,* 14.

43. The reference to gallows humor comes from interviews with David Seidmann and Ilana Shmueli.

44. Celan, letter to Karl Schwedhelm, 6 Nov. 1952, in Theo Buck, *Muttersprache, Mördersprache,* Celan-Studien 1 (Aachen, 1993), 11.

45. Yavetz and Seidmann interviews. See Celan's note about Paşcani in the facsimile of "Schwarze Flocken," *GW* 3.

46. Lenz, letter to Blumenthal-Weiss.
47. Celan, *Gedichte*, 7.
48. On Celan's early poems, see Barbara Wiedemann-Wolf, *Antschel Paul—Paul Celan: Studien zum Frühwerk* (Tübingen, 1985).
49. Chalfen, 130.
50. Celan, letter to Nina Cassian, 6 Apr. 1970, in George Gutu, "Die Lyrik Paul Celans und der geistige Raum Rumäniens" (Univ. of Bucharest, 1990), 253.
51. Chalfen, 129; Silbermann, 64.
52. In the small notebook Antschel used in 1944 to transcribe his work, this is the only poem whose title he wrote in black rather than red: facsimile in Celan, *Gedichte*.
53. *The Oxford Book of German Verse*, ed. H. G. Fiedler (Oxford, 1911), 7.
54. Chaim Nachman Bialik, *Ausgewählte Gedichte*, trans. Ernst Müller (Vienna, 1922), 58. *Philo-Lexikon: Handbuch des jüdischen Wissens* (Berlin, 1935), 306. The Hebraicized form does occur in the titles of Richard Beer-Hoffman's play *Jaákobs Traum* (1918) and in Thomas Mann's novel *Die Geschichten Jaakobs* (1933).
55. Müller-Altneu, "Erinnerungen," 4.

Chapter 2
A Fugue after Auschwitz (1944–45)

1. *Die Wandlung* 4/3 (Mar. 1949): 284.
2. Peter Jokostra, "Ich singe vor Fremden," *Rheinische Post,* 26 Sept. 1970. A similar but more detailed version of this story appeared in Franz Wurm, "Erinnerung an Paul Celan," *Neue Zürcher Zeitung,* 23 Nov. 1990: 40.
3. Fichman gives 4 April as the date on which the Russians reoccupied Czernowitz.
4. Years later, annotating his first volume, Celan wrote "Cz., 44 (after the return from Kiev)" below "Nähe der Gräber." This may refer to his having been sent, as aide in a psychiatric clinic, to accompany a transport of patients to Kiev (according to Meinhard Mayer).
5. Chalfen, 134. Celan himself never published this poem.
6. Celan, letter to Harald Hartung, 4 Dec. 1958, *Park* 14–15 (1982): 7.
7. Ovid S. Crochmalniceanu, "Bruchstücke einer Erinnerung," *ZfK* 213.
8. Celan's usage is all the more interesting in that six years later, settled in Paris, he typed up this poem and respelled the name *Jakob* (F 256).
9. *Nibelungenlied,* sec. 36, stanza 2115.
10. Facsimile of this notebook in Celan, *Gedichte*.
11. Baumann, 24, says that Celan had to care for Soviet soldiers with head wounds or shell-shock.
12. Fichman, 96.
13. Serge Klarsfeld, *Memorial to the Jews Deported from France, 1942–1944* (New York, 1983), 440. Chalfen, 31, indicates that Bruno Schrager was born in 1905, not 1903.
14. Kittner, "Erinnerungen," 218.
15. *Lyrik der Zeit* 2 (Pfullingen, n.d.). The recording was made in the late 1950s, according to Gisèle Celan, and had been issued by April 1959, according to Böschenstein, 9.
16. Kittner, "Erinnerungen," 218. See also Barkhausen, "Interview," 101. Celan's friend Immanuel Weissglas dated "Todesfuge" to 1944: Theo Buck, "Lyrik nach Auschwitz: Zu Paul Celans 'Todesfuge,'" *Datum,* 35.
17. Celan, *Gedichte. Eine Auswahl,* ed. Klaus Wagenbach (Frankfurt, 1962). Celan dated the poems for this school text. When he gave a copy of *Mohn und Gedächtnis* to Erich Kahler in 1962, he noted on the title page: "1944–1952." In his copy of *Der Sand aus den Urnen,* under "Todesfuge" Celan wrote "Buk 45." "Todesfuge" is not among the poems he copied for Ruth Lackner in 1944. She left Czernowitz that year, whereas he left in April 1945;

the poem may stem from early 1945, therefore: Silbermann, letter to the author, Dec. 1993.
18. This remark occurs in the French typescript of Solomon's book-length memoir. In the book itself, Solomon doubted that the poem was written in Czernowitz (Romanian version, p. 56; French, p. 40). But in a letter to the author, 10 January 1984, Solomon says that "when Celan arrived in Bucharest . . . he had the poem with him." And in a later interview he said that in Bucharest, Celan "finished the poems he'd begun in Czernowitz": "Er gehörte nirgendwo hin," *Karpaten Rundschau,* 22 Jan. 1992: 1.
19. Joachim Neugroschel, interview by the author, Seattle, Oct. 1984. Auschwitz was liberated in late January 1945, and some European Jews made their way to Czernowitz then.
20. Konstantin Simonov, *The Lublin Extermination Camp* (Moscow, 1944).
21. *Contemporanul* 32, 2 May 1947. See Exhibition Catalogue, Paul Celan Colloquium in Bucharest (Oct. 1981), in *ZfK* 287. "Tangoul Morţii" is reproduced in *Dimensiunea.*
22. Maybe he had in mind Karl Kraus's poem "Death and Tango" (1913). See Edward Timms, *Karl Kraus, Apocalyptic Satirist: Culture and Catastrophe in Habsburg Vienna* (New Haven, 1986), 226–29.
23. Jewish Black Book Committee, *The Black Book: The Nazi Crime Against the Jewish People* (New York, 1946), 308–09. Sometimes the Janowska musicians, with flute, clarinet, and accordion, also played light classical music under the Germans' balcony (Yehuda Eisman, Tel Aviv, personal communication). "Death Tango" is recorded by Aleksander Kulisiewicz on *Songs from the Depth of Hell,* Folkways FSS37700. Esther Bejarano, who was in the prisoners' orchestra at Auschwitz, remembers: "We had to play while the trains came and the people were driven directly to the gas. The deportees glanced at us happily, because they thought where music's playing it can't be so bad": Eckhard John, "Musik und Konzentrationslager," *Archiv für Musikwissenschaft* 48/1 (1991): 11. At Auschwitz, the SS had prisoners make drums, tambourines, and banjos out of Torah scrolls: *Commitment* (Simon Wiesenthal Center) 4/2 (July 1990).
24. I am grateful to Simon Collier for information on Bianco. See Horacio Ferrer, *El libro del tango,* rev. ed. (Buenos Aires, 1977), 293–94, and Enrique Cadicamo, *La historia del tango en Paris* (Buenos Aires, 1975), 110, 152–54.
25. Szymon Laks, *Music of Another World,* trans. Chester A. Kisiel (Evanston, Ill., 1989), 37–38. Jacob Glatstein, ed., *Anthology of Holocaust Literature* (New York, 1973), 228. Leon Weliczker Wells, *The Janowska Road* (New York, 1963), 135.
26. Mark Rosenthal, *Anselm Kiefer* (Philadelphia, 1987), 95. *New York Times Magazine,* 16 Oct. 1988: 49.
27. Jürgen P. Wallmann, "Auch mich hält keine Hand," *Die Horen* 83 (1971): 83.
28. *L'Adolescence,* 38–39. This collaboration, says Solomon, "helped me understand its nuances and profound connotations."
29. Bullock, *Jewish Quarterly* 2/4 (Spring 1955), 6; Greenberg, *A Treasury of Jewish Poetry,* ed. Nathan and Marynn Ausubel (New York, 1957), 161; Rothenberg, *New Young German Poets* (San Francisco, 1959); Middleton, *Modern German Poetry 1910–1960,* ed. M. Hamburger and C. Middleton (New York, 1962), 318; Neugroschel, in Celan, *Speech-Grille and Selected Poems* (New York, 1971), 29; Hamburger, in Celan, *Poems,* 2d ed. (New York, 1988), 61.
30. Pound, *ABC of Reading* (1934; Norfolk, Conn., n.d.), 29.
31. Dieter Schlesak, "Die verborgene Partitur: Herkunft und Frühwerk von Paul Celan als Schlüssel zu seiner Metapoesie," in *Die Bukowina: Studien zu einer versunkenen Literaturlandschaft,* ed. Dieter Goltschnigg and Anton Schwob (Tübingen, 1990), 344. For Bertram, see Ernst Loewy, *Literatur unterm Hakenkreuz: Das Dritte Reich und seine Dichtung* (Frankfurt, 1966).
32. *Fuge* carries other ironies partly discernible in English. Behind a fugue's running form is the Italian *fuga* ("flight"), a compelling thought in this monologue of imprisonment. In carpentry the verb *fugen* means "join," "fit"—craftsmanship of the "master" who sets death

to music. And medically, *fugue* denotes a prolonged amnesia, which suggests the state of German consciousness that this poem addressed from 1945 on.

33. Donald Hall, *The Pleasures of Poetry* (New York, 1971), 14.
34. Peter Mayer, *Paul Celan als jüdischer Dichter* (Landau, 1969), 12. In 1972 Ausländer said she was honored that Celan had raised her metaphor to the highest poetic expression: Chalfen, 133. Heinrich Stiehler, "Die Zeit der Todesfuge," *Akzente* 19/1 (Feb. 1972): 25–30, points out the many resemblances between the diction of "Todesfuge" and that in a poem written around the same time by Celan's friend Immanuel Weissglas. In 1975 Weissglas described the shared "lyric consciousness" and "comradely counterpoint" he had with Celan, when they would read their work to each other: Stiehler, "Muss ich das wissen, um zu verstehen?," *ZfK* 233. For a discussion of "Todesfuge"'s sources and analogues, see Buck, "Lyrik," summarized in Amy Colin, *Paul Celan: Holograms of Darkness* (Bloomington, Ind., 1991), 42–46.
35. Bettelheim, *Surviving and Other Essays* (New York, 1979), 98–99, 103–05, 110–11.
36. E.Z. (Ezra Zusman?), translation repr. in Hans Tramer, "Der Bestrittene Ruhm," *M.B.* (Tel Aviv), 24 Feb. 1961: 5; Avraham Rimon, in *Haaretz* (Tel Aviv), 15 May 1970: 22; H. Binyamin (Benjamin Harshav), in *Siman Kriah* 7 (1977): 267; Manfred Winkler, in Celan, *Shoshanat Haayin,* afterword by Israel Chalfen (Tel Aviv, 1983), 16. See also Dan Oren's translation in *Proza* 15–16 (June–July 1977): 7.
37. Chalfen, 121.
38. The first and only example I know of not translating a word in a Celan poem occurs with *Deutschland* in Jerome Rothenberg's 1959 version.
39. Celan's translation of Alain Resnais' documentary *Night and Fog* (1956) contains this sentence: "They build the KZ, they respect the oak" (4:86).
40. Celan, letter to Alfred Margul-Sperber, 8 Feb. 1962, in "Briefe," 57. Celan's letters to Sperber can also be found in *Dimensiunea.*
41. Puccini's Tosca, the diva who "lived for art and love," has an artist-lover, Cavaradossi, who (torn between a dark-haired and a fair-haired woman) sings to her from prison, "E lucevan le stelle" (And the stars were shining) when they first meet. Both lovers come to tragic ends.
42. Laks, *Music of Another World,* 53, 84, 112.
43. The name *Shulamith* itself brims with overtones inaudible to most Germans, much less to Americans. The first German-language periodical for Jews was called *Sulamith,* founded in 1806 to promote German-Jewish symbiosis. And many Yiddish authors based works on Shulamith, including the much-loved operetta *Shulamis* (1880) by Avraham Goldfaden, which Kafka saw twice and which played often in Czernowitz: Ruth Rubin, *Voices of a People* (Philadelphia, 1979), 270–71, and *The Jews of Rumania in Modern Times* (Tel Aviv, Beth Hatefutsoth, 1982). Goethe himself translated the Song of Songs.
44. Simonov's 1944 Maidanek report details a procedure used as Jews were pushed into the crematorium: "Two SS men stood at each side of the door armed with short, heavy iron rods. As the person entering the room lowered his head, one of the SS men struck him across the back of the neck with his rod." For Celan's *er greift nach dem Eisen im Gurt*—literally, "he snatches at the iron in his belt"—other translators have "gun," "weapon," "sword," or "steel." But Paul Antschel in Soviet-occupied Czernowitz may have come across those "heavy iron rods" in a version of the report.
45. In the only change that Celan made from an early version (3:64), what had been *Aug* now reads *Auge,* not altering the meaning but sustaining the line's triple beat.

Chapter 3
Song in the Wilderness (1945–48)

1. Reported by Ruth Lackner, in Chalfen, 144.

2. Chalfen, 145, and Fichman, 101, 104. He probably began the journey in a truck, then got to Bucharest by train.

3. Chalfen, 147, credits Ruth Lackner for reporting this remark. But Müller-Altneu, "Erinnerungen," 4, reports an almost identical remark being made to her.

4. Hans Egon Holthusen, "Fünf junge Lyriker," *Merkur* 8/74 (Spring 1954): 386.

5. Jerry Glenn, *Paul Celan* (New York, 1973), 52, was the first to point this out.

6. Fichman, 119. Like Celan, she was born in 1920.

7. Crochmalniceanu, "Bruchstücke," 213. See Silbermann, 56, and Helmut Niemeyer, "Der Tod auf Rappen oder Schimmel," *Die Zeit,* 2 Mar. 1984: 48.

8. *L'Adolescence,* 83.

9. Celan, letter to Solomon, 12 Mar. 1948, in *Dimensiunea,* 210, and Solomon, "Paul Celans Bukarester Aufenthalt," *ZfK* 226. An art documentary on the relationship between Celan and Solomon, entitled (after their wordplay) "Duo for Paoloncello and Petronome," has been made by Solomon's son Alexandru.

10. Keats, letter of 30 Nov. 1820.

11. Pierre Fauchery, *Action* 90 (24 May 1946): 12–13.

12. *Dimensiunea,* 203–08, and *ZfK* 286.

13. Chalfen, 148.

14. *Dimensiunea,* 183–202. For other appearances of Celan's Romanian writings, see Jerry Glenn, *Paul Celan: Eine Bibliographie* (Wiesbaden, 1989); *Halo: Poems by Paul Celan,* trans. Stavros Deligiorgis (Minneapolis, 1991); *Modern Poetry in Translation,* n.s. 1 (Summer 1992): 109–12. For German translations, see F. The translations from Romanian in this chapter are mine, aided by other versions in German, French, and English.

15. Twenty-five German lyrics exist from this period, three of which were published in Bucharest in May 1947, within days of the Romanian version of "Todesfuge." Celan made his debut as a German poet in the first (and only) issue of the multilingual *Agora,* alongside Rilke, Morgenstern, Breton, Michaux, Montale, Quasimodo, Sandburg, and leading Romanian writers. The editor was Ion Caraion; see Caraion, "Über die Anfänge des Dichters," *ZfK* 209.

16. Celan, letter to Max Rychner, 3 Nov. 1946, in Helmut Böttiger, "Paul Celan: 'Mein Ehrgeiz fesselt mir die Hände,'" *Stuttgarter Zeitung,* 15 Apr. 1987: 20.

17. Silbermann, 28.

18. Leonard Forster, "'Espenbaum': Zu einem Gedicht von Paul Celan," in *Wissenschaft als Dialog,* ed. Renate Heydebrand and Klaus Günther Just (Stuttgart, 1969), 383.

19. In *Die Tat,* 7 Feb. 1948: 11; *Plan* 2/6 (1948): 368; Celan, *Der Sand aus den Urnen* (Vienna: A. Sexl, 1948).

20. Thomas Albrich, *Exodus durch Österreich: Die jüdische Flüchtlinge 1945–1948* (Innsbruck, 1987), 153.

21. Celan probably left in early December, since the journey certainly took more than a week, and on 21 December 1947 he wrote a postcard to Margul-Sperber from Vienna apologizing for the delay in sending news of his arrival: see Gutu, "Nur eine Zwischenstation: Zu Paul Celans Wiener Aufenthalt," *Neuer Weg* 41 (23 Sept. 1989): 4. Celan's postcard also contains an intriguing remark: "Unfortunately I had to destroy your letter to Dr. Eder along the way. My journey was very difficult." See also [Albert Emilian], "A. Margul-Sperber und Paul Celan," *Die Stimme* 398 (Apr. 1983): 5; Isac Chiva, interview by the author, Paris, 17 Aug. 1984; Celan, letter to Margul-Sperber, 11 Feb. 1948, in "Briefe," 50.

22. Excerpt published in *Plan* 2/6: 423. Margul-Sperber had also been sending Celan's poems ahead to literary friends in Vienna: Gutu, "Nur eine Zwischenstation."

23. Basil remembered Celan's appearance as occurring in January: Otto Basil, "Wir leben unter finsteren Himmeln," *Literatur und Kritik* 52 (Mar. 1971): 102. However, Celan's card to Margul-Sperber from Vienna, 21 December 1947, says that he had already seen Basil: Gutu, "Nur eine Zwischenstation."

24. Milo Dor, "Paul Celan," in *UPC* 281; English trans. in *Sulfur* 11 (1984): 32–35.
25. Max Rychner, *Die Tat* 37 (7 Feb. 1948): 11.
26. Letter of 11 Feb. 1948, in "Briefe," 50.
27. Letter to Solomon, 12 Mar. 1948, *ZfK* 226.
28. Letter to Margul-Sperber, 11 Feb. 1948, in "Briefe," 50. Uwe Martin, "'Der Sand aus den Urnen': Bemerkungen zu Paul Celans erster Gedichtsammlung," *Text und Kritik* 53–54 (1977; 2d ed., 1984): 76.
29. These appeared in *Surrealistische Publikationen* (1950), and the Césaire poem is also in *GW* 5:757. Jerry Glenn, "Paul Celan in Wien," *Die Pestsäule* (1977), 100–08.
30. Repr. in Glenn, "Paul Celan in Wien." That *Lanze* ("lance") forms an anagram of "Celan" is pointed out, in another connection, by Aris Fioretos, "Nothing: History and Materiality in Celan," in *Word Traces: Readings of Paul Celan,* ed. Fioretos (Baltimore, 1994), 338.
31. *Edgar Jené und der Traum vom Traume,* with thirty illustrations and a note by Otto Basil (Vienna, 1948). See Glenn, "Paul Celan in Wien," 102.
32. Originally this poem was called "Deucalion and Pyrrha" (3:58), after the survivors of Zeus's flood who had the task of repopulating a desolate world.
33. Usually when Celan's poems refer to a time of year, it is when they were composed. But he only spent a winter and a spring in the city. This poem tallies with his season of loss in late 1942, when his parents died.
34. Mary Lowenthal Felstiner, "Alois Brunner: 'Eichmann's Best Tool,'" *Simon Wiesenthal Annual* 3 (1986): 1–41.
35. George E. Berkeley, *Vienna and Its Jews: The Tragedy of Success, 1880s–1980s* (Cambridge, Mass., 1988), 22, 348.
36. Ingeborg Bachmann, *Malina* (Frankfurt, 1971), 68.
37. Chalfen, illustration 16.
38. Alfred Gong, *Early Poems: A Selection from the Years 1941–1945,* ed. Jerry Glenn, Joachim Herrmann, and Rebecca S. Rodgers (Columbia, S.C., 1987), 125–27.
39. Celan, letter of 6 Nov. 1952 to Karl Schwedhelm, in Buck, *Muttersprache,* 16.
40. Letter of 6 July 1948, in "Briefe," 52.
41. Gerhart Baumann, ". . . Durchgründet vom Nichts . . . ," *Études Germaniques* 25/3 (July–Sept. 1970): 277.
42. Letter of 2 Aug. 1948, quoted in Bianca Rosenthal, "Quellen zum frühen Celan," *Monatshefte* 75/4 (1983): 402–03, and "Quellen zum frühen Paul Celan: Der Alfred Margul-Sperber-Nachlass in Bukarest," *ZfK* 230.

Chapter 4
"German" Author in Exile (1948–53)

1. Letter of 2 Aug. 1948, quoted in Rosenthal, "Quellen," 402.
2. *Die Wandlung* 4/3 (Mar. 1949): 241; *Stimmen der Gegenwart 1951,* ed. Hans Weigel (Vienna, 1951), 130; *Surrealistische Publikationen* (1950).
3. Ruth: Ruth Lackner; Miriam: see "Poem pentru umbra Marianei" (*F* 160); Naomi: see dedication of "Tristeţe" (*F* 258). English more than German brings out a latent wordplay between *Fremde,* "stranger," and Lestrange, the family name of Celan's wife-to-be. But Celan dated this poem "beginning of 1949," and Eric Celan told me his father and mother met in August 1950: interview by the author, Paris, 19 July 1993.
4. Surprisingly, Hebrew versions do not bring about the sacred parody that Celan's poem calls for. They of course use "B'mitsrayim" as the title, but his "Thou shalt" has no precise equivalent in Exodus. Nor does either Hebrew translation adopt Scripture's conventional *hine* for Celan's (and Luther's) *Sieh,* "Behold": Celan, *Shoshanat;* Celan, *Davar-ma yihyeh,* trans. Benzion Orgad (Tel Aviv, 1987).

5. Rosenthal, "Quellen," *Monatshefte,* 402.
6. Celan, letter to Margul-Sperber, 11 Feb. 1948, in "Briefe," 51.
7. Glenn, "Paul Celan in Wien," 106; Martin, "'Der Sand,'" 73.
8. Celan, letter to Max Rychner, 24 Oct. 1948, in Böttiger, "Paul Celan," 20.
9. Rino Sanders, "Erinnerung an Paul Celan," in *PC* 312. Another friend from that time, Diet Kloos, remembers Celan's enthusiasm and precise knowledge of the city: Paul Sars, "'Ein solcher Ausgangspunkt wären meine Gedichte': Zu den Briefen von Paul Celan an Diet Kloos-Barendregt," in *"Der glühende,"* 18
10. *Die Wandlung* 4/3 (Mar. 1949): 284.
11. Celan, letter in Böttiger, "Paul Celan," 20.
12. Sars, "'Ein solcher Ausgangspunkt,'" 23–24.
13. Celan, letter to Ruth Lackner, 2 Dec. 1949, in Chalfen, 155.
14. Glenn, "Paul Celan in Wien," 105.
15. Letter of 5 Feb. 1951, in Anton Schwob, "Ein unbekannter Brief Paul Celans," *Karpaten Rundschau,* 6 June 1975: 4.
16. Chalfen, 67; Silbermann, 66.
17. Weigel, *Stimmen,* 168.
18. Claire Goll, "Unbekanntes über Paul Celan," *Baubudenpoet* 5 (Mar.–Apr. 1960): 115–16.
19. *Surrealistische Publikationen* (1950). Glenn, "Paul Celan in Wien," 104, quotes Celan's letter of March 1950 to the Jenés, expressing his distancing from surrealism.
20. This version, which I worked on with Melissa Monroe, still takes in audiences when presented as a Dickinson lyric with "So bist du" as Celan's translation. See John Felstiner, "So you are turned," *Threepenny Review* 43 (Fall 1990): 14.
21. Told to Johannes [Jean] Firges, as reported in Glenn, *Paul Celan,* 58.
22. Winfried Menninghaus, "Zum Problem des Zitats bei Celan und in der Celan-Philologie," in *PC* 172. In Mauthausen, Joseph Drexel was forced to sing "O Haupt voll Blut und Wunden" while the SS whipped him into unconsciousness: John, "Musik und Konzentrationslager," 10. Years later Celan began a poem *Ruh aus in deinen Wunden* (2:103), which adopts the same hymn meter and idiom.
23. Celan, letter to Walter Jens, 19 May 1961, mentions how this tale and others have a voice in his poems.
24. From an early version of the poem, passed on to Jerry Glenn by Erica Jené. Further references to draft versions of Celan's earlier poems, unless otherwise specified, come from this collection.
25. On 25 October 1962 Celan excitedly marked the phrase "And Jeremiah saw nothing but an almond branch" (1:11) in André Neher, *L'Essence du prophétisme* (Paris, 1955), 336.
26. The meeting took place at Niendorf, outside Hamburg.
27. Related by Reinhard Federmann, in Glenn, *Paul Celan,* 24. See Milo Dor, *On the Wrong Track: Fragments of an Autobiography,* trans. Jerry Glenn and Jennifer Kelley (Riverside, Calif., 1993), 157–61.
28. Hans Weigel, *In Memoriam* (Vienna, 1979), 35.
29. Siegfried Mandel, *Group 47: The Reflected Intellect* (Carbondale, Ill., 1973), 100; Friedhelm Kröll, *Die Gruppe 47* (Stuttgart, 1977), 67.
30. Sanders, "Erinnerung," 311.
31. Hans Werner Richter, reported in Dor, *On the Wrong Track,* 160.
32. Hermann Lenz, "Erinnerungen an Paul Celan," in *PC* 316.
33. Reinhard Lettau, ed., *Die Gruppe 47* (Neuwied, 1967), 76; Rolf Schroers, *Meine deutsche Frage* (Stuttgart, 1979), 140; Glenn, *Bibliographie,* T10–12, from 1953. Celan wrote to Erica Jené that his reading was "on the whole a success": letter of 29 June 1952 (courtesy of Jerry Glenn).
34. Letter, Klaus Demus to the author, 12 Sept. 1986.

35. Pöggeler, *Spur*, 251, has a sentence on this background. See Milan Kundera, "A Little History Lesson," *New York Review of Books*, 22 Nov. 1984, and Jean Charles Gateau, *Paul Éluard* (Paris, 1988), 348–49.

36. Robert Kelly discusses this translation in "Retroversion: Marianne Moore's 'A Grave,'" *ACTS*, 8–9 (1988): 119–24. A letter of Celan's to Roditi, 6 April 1952, Leo Baeck Institute, New York, reads: "My dear Edouard Roditi, would it be possible for me to have my fee for the translations of M. Moore's poems before the 19th? I've decided to go to Hamburg [for the Group 47 meeting], and I'll be in great need of this money."

37. Silbermann, 48.

38. In presenting Celan's translations, literal versions of the original verse will appear in brackets, and literal versions of the translation in parentheses.

39. *Neue Rundschau* 65 (1954): 319. The publisher was S. Fischer Verlag.

40. Deutsche Verlags-Anstalt.

41. Karl Krolow, "Zwei neue Lyriker," *Neue Zeitung*, 21–22 Mar. 1953; repr. in Glenn, *Bibliographie*, T17.

42. Paul Schallück, "Schwarze Milch der Frühe," *Frankfurter Allgemeine Zeitung*, 25 Apr. 1953.

43. Rino Sanders, "Ein neuer deutscher Lyriker," *Die Zeit*, 18 June 1953: 6.

44. Karl Schwedhelm, *Wort und Wahrheit* 8 (July 1953): 533–34.

45. Heinz Piontek, *Welt und Wort* 8 (1953): 200–01.

46. Helmuth de Haas, "Mohn und Gedächtnis," *Neue literarische Welt* 4/13 (10 July 1953): 12; also in *UPC* 31–34.

47. Reinhard Döhl, "Geschichte und Kritik eines Angriffs: Zu den Behauptungen gegen Paul Celan," in *Deutsche Akademie für Sprache und Dichtung Jahrbuch 1960* (1961): 101–32. Marie Luise Kaschnitz, Ingeborg Bachmann, and Klaus Demus, "Entgegnung," *Neue Rundschau* 71 (1960): 547–49, refers to Claire Goll's letter.

48. Martin Heidegger, *Holzwege* (Frankfurt, 1950), 250–51, 279. Celan read the Hölderlin essay on 4 July 1953.

49. *Die Vorsokratiker*, trans. Wilhelm Capelle (Stuttgart, n.d.), 163. In Diels's edition, it is Fragment B.I.

50. Buber, *Tales of the Hasidim: The Later Masters* (New York, 1948, 1961), 250. See Rolf Bücher, "Erfahrenes Sprechen—Leseversuch an Celan-Entwürfen," in *Argumentum e Silentio: International Paul Celan Symposium*, ed. Amy D. Colin (Berlin, 1987), 104.

51. Rilke's "Experience of Death" (*Neue Gedichte*) speaks to someone going into death and finding *Grün wirklicher Grüne*.

52. Celan, letter to Petre Solomon, 18 July 1957, in "Briefwechsel," 61.

53. Lasker-Schüler, *Hebrew Ballads and Other Poems*, trans. Audri Durchslag and Jeanette Litman-Demeestère (Philadelphia, 1980), 91.

54. In Assisi on 20 November 1953 Celan bought G. K. Chesterton's *St. Francis of Assisi* (London, 1951). The book is unmarked, but elements from it appear in his poem. See Alfred Kelletat, "Celans 'Assisi,'" *Studi Urbinati* 45/2 (1971): 686–710.

55. In 1953 Celan bought an edition of the pre-Socratic philosophers. Parmenides' fragment on the gates of day and night has "the changing keys" to them guarded by "Dike, the goddess of retribution."

56. Esther Beatrice Cameron, "Paul Celan, Dichter des Imperativs: Ein Brief," *Bulletin des Leo Baeck Instituts* 59 (1981): 58.

57. Heidegger, *Einführung in die Metaphysik* (Tübingen, 1953), 152.

58. Chalfen, 126.

59. Hölderlin, *Sämtliche Werke*, ed. Friedrich Beissner (Kleine Stuttgarter Ausgabe), vol. 2 (1953).

Chapter 5
Saying No To Say Yes (1953–54)

1. Celan, letter to Hans Bender, 18 Nov. 1954, in *Briefe*, 34.
2. Holthusen, "Fünf junge Lyriker," 378–90. Holthusen had written on Trakl, Rilke, and Benn, besides editing an anthology of postwar poetry (including Celan's) that he called *Ergriffenes Dasein* (Munich, 1953), the title declaring Germany now capable of an "emotionally affected" existence.
3. Rosenthal, "Quellen," *Monatshefte*, 403.
4. Holthusen evidently took a liking to his own Yea- and Nay-saying, because he soon published his critical essays (among them the one on Celan) under the title *Ja und Nein: neue kritische Versuche* (Munich, 1954).
5. Michael Hamburger, in Celan, *Poems*, 99.
6. Celan, letter to Federmann, 16 Feb. 1962, in Federmann, 17.
7. Frank H. Simonds, *They Shall Not Pass* (New York, 1916).
8. Walter Benjamin, *Illuminations*, trans. Harry Zohn, ed. Hannah Arendt (New York, 1969), 257.
9. "No passage," as Jacques Derrida points out, also translates "aporia," a philosophical doubt arising from incompatible views of the same matter: *Schibboleth: Pour Paul Celan* (Paris, 1986), 43.
10. *Lyrik der Zeit 2; Paul Celan: Gedichte und Prosa* (2 disks) (Frankfurt, 1975); Celan, *Davar*.
11. Ute Maria Oelmann, *Deutsche poetologische Lyrik nach 1945: Ingeborg Bachmann, Günter Eich, Paul Celan* (Stuttgart, 1980), 391–93; Hermann Burger, *Paul Celan: Auf der Suche nach der verlorenen Sprache* (Zurich, 1974), 63–81.
12. Examples from Tieck and Eichendorf in the Grimms' dictionary and Hölderlin's second "Hymne an die Freiheit" (1792).
13. Kaschnitz et al., "Entgegnung." Demus, who signed the defense of Celan against the plagiarism charge, and his wife were the dedicatees of "Die Winzer." Born in 1927, Demus as a young poet met Celan in Vienna in 1948.
14. Celan found this melancholy in poets before the war, such as Heine, Rilke, George, Trakl, and others. Tears being "pressed out" (*gekeltert*) by a difficult time appear in Jean Paul (*Titan* 3.81), an author important to Celan. Rilke's "Tränenkrüglein" (Jar of Tears), which Celan often recited when he was young, compares wine making to tears; the poem was written on 16 September 1923, thirty years to the day before "Die Winzer." Celan's poem also responds to some autumn poems by Georg Trakl (1887–1914), though their fragile mellowness and somewhat composed melancholy contrast with Celan's more stark, unrelieved diction and syntax. See Trakl's "In Autumn," in which *Sonnenblumen leuchten* ("sunflowers shine") and *Heut keltern sie den braunen Wein* ("Today they crush the brown wine"); or "Autumn of the Lonely," in which "The wine is crushed, the mild stillness / filled with soft answer to dark questions," in Trakl, *Dichtungen und Briefe*, ed. Walther Killy and Hans Szklenar (Salzburg, 1969), 1:31, 109. Klaus Voswinckel, *Paul Celan: Verweigerte Poetisierung der Welt* (Heidelberg, 1974), 123–24, finds another likely source in Trakl's "Song to the Night" (Trakl, *Dichtungen*, 224), whose contradictions, he says, are more facile and composed than Celan's. Celan must have known the Grimms' tale of a "Pitcher of Tears," in which a dead child carries the mother's tears. Finally, Rilke's *Sonnets to Orpheus* envision the poet's generativeness in images like those of "Die Winzer":

> Praising, that's it! One appointed to praise,
> he issued forth like ore out of the stone's
> silence. His heart, oh transitory press
> for humankind of an unending wine.

But this rings bolder than Celan could afford.

15. Heidegger, "Wozu Dichter," in *Holzwege,* 251. On this book's endpaper Celan wrote a page number and a phrase: "250 'dürftige Zeit'" (destitute time).

16. Nielsen and Pors, *Index,* 289.

17. Celan certainly knew the passage in Rilke's ninth Duino elegy where *einmal* occurs six times in four lines. But the drive to transcendence feels stronger in Rilke than in Celan. On *einmal* and uniqueness, see Derrida, *Schibboleth.*

18. Søren Kierkegaard, *Repetition: An Essay in Experimental Psychology,* ed. and trans. Walter Lowrie (New York, 1964).

19. Coincidentally—but is anything merely coincidental in Celan's mature poetry?—the "muteness" (*Stumme*) in "The Vintagers" has an archaic kinship with wine, since the German word is cognate with English "stum," the must or partly fermented juice from which wine is processed. The French call it *vin muet* ("mute wine"). I am grateful to Michael Levine for pointing this out to me.

20. Along with its twelve-monthliness, the number 12 itself had some hold upon Celan. See "Twelve Years" (1:220).

21. Sigmund Freud, "Recollection, Repetition and Working Through" (1914), in Freud, *Collected Papers,* ed. Joan Riviere (London, 1953), 2:366–76. A later poem by Celan, ". . . and no kind of peace" (2:201), quotes from Freud's *Beyond the Pleasure Principle* the word *Wiederholungszwang* ("repetition compulsion").

22. For *kellern* I could try a term other than "cellar" or "store up," since it means to "lay in" a stock of something. But to say that the vintagers "lay in the seepings" risks calling up a scene of rustic torpor.

23. "Vor einer Kerze" (1:110). The verb *hinabsteigt* occurs only in the magazine version of the poem, *Botteghe Oscure* 17 (Spring 1956): 385–86, which appeared later than the published collection that included "Vor einer Kerze" and "Die Winzer." In the collected version, the verb is not *hinabsteigt* but *hinabtaucht.*

24. If heaven "descends," it can resonate with the millennial-sounding "candle-end" rather than "candle-stub" for *Lichtstumpf.* Still, I'm reluctant to give up the abrupt stumpiness of "stub," especially having missed the echo of *Stumme* ("muteness") in *Stumpf.* What is even worse is to lose in the word *Lichtstumpf* the *Licht* ("light") leading to *leuchten* ("shine")—two words that occur blissfully at the end of Hölderlin's "Bread and Wine," as Christ descends and men's eyes grow moist at his light.

25. Benjamin, "Theses on the Philosophy of History," in *Illuminations,* 261. The phrase comes from Karl Kraus, "Der sterbende Mensch," in *Worte in Versen,* vol. 1 (1919); rpt. in *Schriften,* ed. Christian Wagenknecht (Frankfurt, 1989), 9:68.

26. A dactylic (rather than an amphibrachic) meter in "Die Winzer" is argued by Howard Stern, "Verbal Mimesis: The Case of 'Die Winzer,'" *Studies in 20th Century Literature* 8/1 (Fall 1983): 27. One critic does speak of the amphibrach in this poem: Peter Horn, "Rhythmus und Struktur in der Lyrik Paul Celans" (Ph.D. diss., Witwatersrand, 1970), 245. Dieter Breuer, *Deutsche Metrik und Versgeschichte* (Munich, 1981), 70, identifies such verse as amphibrachic.

27. Benjamin, *Illuminations,* 69–82.

28. Babylonian Talmud, Megillah 15a. This saying is based on a Biblical passage in which Queen Esther carries news from Mordechai to the king (Esther 2:22).

29. Benjamin, "The Task of the Translator," in *Illuminations,* 74. For some reason, the translator omits translating the word "messianic."

30. Steiner, *After Babel,* chap. 5. I am also grateful for Steiner's suggestive reference to the passage from Amos which I quoted earlier: Steiner, "Our Homeland, the Text," *Salmagundi* 66 (Winter–Spring 1985): 11.

Chapter 6
Words That Will Not Heal (1954–57)

1. When the Federal Republic's authorities balked, Cayrol's commentary was adapted; but the DDR refused to circulate the film. Elmar Tophoven, interview by the author, Cerisy-la-Salle, France, 21 Aug. 1984; Alfred Grosser, *Germany in Our Time*, trans. Paul Stephenson (New York, 1971), 215.
2. See 1:239, 281; 2:154. Jean Daive, *Décimale Blanche / Weisse Dezimale*, trans. Paul Celan (Frankfurt, 1977), 16, 18, 20.
3. *Wörterbuch der deutschen Sprache* (Berlin, 1974) gives Ludwig Turek, *Klar zur Wende* (Berlin, 1949), 209, or (Berlin, 1956), 244, as the source for *Rassenwahn*.
4. Celan's collected translations are in *GW* 4 and 5.
5. Celan, letter to Renée Lang, 27 Aug. 1954, in Glenn, "Three Letters," *Sulfur* 11 (1984): 27–31.
6. For the mention of Cayrol, see Christoph Schwerin, "Bitterer Brunnen des Herzens: Erinnerungen an Paul Celan," *Der Monat* 33/279 (Apr.–June 1981): 76. When he translated Cioran in 1953, did Celan know of Cioran's nationalist anti-Semitism in 1930s Romania? See Leon Volovici, *Nationalist Ideology and Antisemitism*, trans. Charles Kormos (Oxford, 1991), 74, 78, 82, 107–09, 115–16, 150.
7. Celan, letter to Petre Solomon, 18 July 1957, in "Briefwechsel," 61.
8. Theo Buck, "Zu Paul Celans Übersetzung von Picassos Drama 'Le désir attrapé par la queue,'" part 1, *Celan-Jahrbuch* 2 (1988): 121, 127.
9. Buck, "Zu Paul Celans Übersetzung . . . ," part 2, *Celan-Jahrbuch* 3 (1989): 138.
10. On Celan's citizenship, see Jean-Pierre Wilhelm, "Poèmes de Paul Celan," *Cahiers du sud* 42/334 (Apr. 1956): 401–02.
11. Bonnefoy, "Paul Celan," *Revue de Belles-Lettres* 96/2–3 (1972): 93. English translation in *ACTS* 8–9 (1988): 9–14.
12. Letter of 18 July 1957, in "Briefwechsel," 61.
13. *Jewish Quarterly* 2/4 (Spring 1955): 38.
14. *Commentary* 19 (Mar. 1955): 243.
15. Alain Bosquet, *Le Journal des poètes* 1 (Jan. 1952): 9.
16. Celan, *Strette*, trans. André du Bouchet et al. (Paris, 1971).
17. Wilhelm, "Poèmes."
18. Letter of 18 July 1957, in "Briefwechsel," 61.
19. Glenn, *Bibliographie*, T25, 34, 35. Lenz, "Erinnerungen," 315, says Celan also read in Stuttgart in 1953.
20. *Jahresring* 57/58 (Stuttgart, 1957): 394–95.
21. Oliver Storz, "Die Lyrik Paul Celans," *Stuttgarter Zeitung*, 6 June 1957: 8; repr. in Glenn, *Bibliographie*, T74.
22. Hohoff, "Flötentöne hinter dem Nichts," *Neue Deutsche Hefte* 1 (1954): 69–73.
23. Hohoff, "Die Metaphernsprache des neuen Gedichts," *Jahresring* 55/56 (Stuttgart, 1955): 335–42.
24. Poem #1508, from a 1956 English–German edition of Dickinson.
25. "Confidence" first appeared in *Jahresring* 57/58: 131.
26. Letter to Hans Bender, 18 Nov. 1954, in *Briefe*, 34.
27. Schwerin, "Bitterer Brunnen," 74.
28. *Jahresring* 57/58: 133.
29. Dating in Celan, *Gedichte*, ed. Wagenbach. The poem first appeared in *Jahresring* 58/59 (Stuttgart, 1958): 198–99.
30. Schwerin, "Bitterer Brunnen," 77.
31. In *sirrt die Sekunde* ("the second whirrs"), *die Sekunde* can itself be cut into, metamorphosing

into *diese Kunde* ("this news"): Werner Hamacher, "The Second of Inversion: Moments of a Figure through Celan's Poetry," *Yale French Studies* 69 (1985): 291.

32. In his copy of Insel's *Das kleine Blumenbuch* (Leipzig, 1933), Celan wrote the flowers' names in Romanian, Greek, and Hebrew: Chalfen, 104; Celan, *Gedichte*, 7; Hans Dieter Schäfer, "Die nichtfaschistische Literatur der 'jungen Generation,'" in *Die deutsche Literatur im Dritten Reich*, ed. Horst Denkler and Karl Prümm (Stuttgart, 1976), 487.

33. Pöggeler, *Spur*, 405.

34. Marlies Janz, *Vom Engagement absoluter Poesie: Zur Lyrik und Ästhetik Paul Celans* (Frankfurt, 1976), 225. Information from Jean Bollack.

35. *Jahresring 57/58:* 130.

36. Zephaniah also prophesies wrath: "The great day of the Lord is near" (1:14). See Michael Ossar, "The Malevolent God and Paul Celan's 'Tenebrae,'" *Deutsche Vierteljahrsschrift* 65/1 (1991): 174–97.

37. Already in 1942, Paul Antschel wrote some hymnlike stanzas called "Black Crown," addressing Christ in caustic terms that anticipate "Tenebrae": "Mixed in with the blood from thy torn / Wounds thou drinkest up thy thorns; / So a huddled and a clawing / Anguish rules through all the darkening" (3:129).

38. Gerald Reitlinger, *The Final Solution: The Attempt to Exterminate the Jews of Europe, 1939–1945* (London, 1953); *Die Endlösung: Hitlers Versuch der Ausrottung der Juden Europas, 1939–1945*, trans. J. W. Brügel (Berlin, 1956; 2d ed. 1957). The passage is on p. 151 of the English edition and p. 168 of the German. The phrase from the German translation of Reitlinger occurs in a footnote in Fred Lönker, "'Tenebrae': Discussion," *Revue des sciences humaines* 3/223 (1991): 146. Reitlinger's account is based on eyewitness testimony by a Hungarian doctor, M. Nyiszli. This issue of the journal also contains an analysis of "Tenebrae"'s critical reception.

39. Chaim Nachman Bialik, "On the Slaughter," in *The Modern Hebrew Poem Itself*, ed. Stanley Burnshaw, T. Carmi, and Ezra Spicehandler (New York, 1965), 32.

40. Pöggeler, *Spur*, 405.

41. Glenn, *Paul Celan*, 99.

42. Jokostra, *Die Zeit hat keine Ufer: Südfranzösisches Tagebuch* (Munich, 1963), 175.

43. Isaac Deutscher, "Marc Chagall and the Jewish Imagination," in *The Non-Jewish Jew and Other Essays*, ed. Tamara Deutscher (New York, 1968), 153–62.

44. In a commentary that Celan advised him on, Böschenstein says that "Tenebrae" "breaks through the boundaries of Christian tradition": *A Reader in German Literature*, ed. Robert Spaethling and Eugene Weber (New York, 1969), 223. See also Böschenstein, 8.

45. Ralph P. Crimann, *Literaturtheologie: Studien zum Vermittlungsproblem zwischen Germanistik und Theologie* (Frankfurt, 1978); repr. in Glenn, *Bibliographie*, T1506. In March 1959, Celan bought a biography of Edith Stein (1891–1942), a Jew who became a Carmelite nun and died at Auschwitz. In it, he marked this quote from her: "I spoke to the Savior and said to him, I knew it was his cross that was now laid on the Jewish people": [no author], *Edith Stein—Eine grosse Frau unseres Jahrhunderts* (Freiburg, 1958), 98.

46. Ursula Baltz, "Eucharistie im Gedicht: Zu religiöser Sprache in zwei Gedichten von Paul Celan und Gottfried Benn," in *Literatur und Dichtung*, vol. 2, ed. H. Becker and R. Kaczynski (St. Ottilien, 1983), 903–22.

47. Gadamer, "Sinn und Sinnverhüllung," *Zeitwende* 46 (1975): 321–29. Gadamer also noted closely the relationship between Heidegger and the poet.

48. "In a chiasm [the rhetorical figure of inversion], the cross is nearer than in the theme of the 'cross,'" Celan once said: Renate Böschenstein-Schäfer, "Traum und Sprache in der Dichtung Paul Celans," in *Argumentum*, ed. Colin, 226.

49. The poem was begun toward the end of February and completed, Celan noted, on Easter Monday, 22 April 1957: Beda Allemann and Rolf Bücher, "Synoptische Zeilenzählung in

der Celan-Ausgabe," in *Die Nachlassedition: La publication de manuscrits inédits,* ed. Louis Hay and Winfried Woesler (Bern, 1979), 157.

50. Neugroschel, in *Speech-Grille,* 103; Hamburger, in Celan, *Poems,* 115.
51. Gershom Scholem, *Die Geheimnisse der Schöpfung: Ein Kapitel aus dem Sohar* (Berlin, 1935), 29.
52. A year before, the poet had spoken of *"Voices,* from which your heart / shrinks back into your mother's heart" (1:148). Soon after "Blume" he wrote: "I come, / hardgrowth in my heart" (1:168), and a year later: "No one cut the word from our heartwalls" (1:193).
53. Rilke too kept in touch with a "familiar death," and his tenth Duino elegy sings praise for this on "the hammers of my heart" (here they are piano hammers). But "praise" does not enter Celan's lexicon. On 5 June 1957, six weeks after completing "Blume," he wrote to Karl Schwedhelm: "Everywhere the doors are shutting, and outside, 'in the open' [*im Freien,* the closing words of "Blume"], hands go silent": Buck, *Muttersprache,* 11.
54. Nielsen and Pors, *Index.*
55. Adorno, *Gesammelte Schriften,* ed. Gretel Adorno and Rolf Tiedemann (Frankfurt, 1974), 2:700. Adorno never wrote his projected essay on Celan, much to the poet's distress.
56. Celan, letter to Rudolf Hirsch, 26 July 1958, quoted in Bollack, "Paul Celan sur la langue: Le poème *Sprachgitter* et ses interprétations," in *Contre-jour: Études sur Paul Celan,* ed. Martine Broda (Paris, 1986), 96. *Gitter* also denotes the latticed atoms of a crystal.
57. Dankmar Venus, "Celan im vierten Schuljahr?," *Westermanns Pädagogische Beiträge* 13/10 (1961): 446–50.
58. Letter of 18 July 1957, in "Briefwechsel," 61.
59. A note in Celan's literary remains cites a line from "Speech-Grille"—"By the sense of light / you divine the soul"—in discussing "fateful sense movements toward an Unknown, which can sometimes be seen as Thou": Böschenstein, 15.
60. Hugo Huppert, "'Spirituell': Ein Gespräch mit Paul Celan" (1966), in *PC* 319; translated in *ACTS* 8–9 (1988): 156–62.

Chapter 7
Only Language through Memory (1958)

1. Gottfried Benn, *Probleme der Lyrik* (Wiesbaden, 1951). See Reinhold Grimm, "Die Problematischen 'Probleme der Lyrik,'" in *Gottfried Benn,* ed. Bruno Hillebrand (Darmstadt, 1979), 206–07. Judith Ryan, "Monologische Lyrik: Paul Celans Antwort auf Gottfried Benn," *Basis* 2 (1971): 260–82, argues that Celan's "dialogical" poetry constitutes a radical intensification of Benn's monological poetry. Celan himself, in "Sprachgitter" (1957), subtly revises an image from *Problems of the Lyric.*
2. Letter of 30 May 1958, in Celan/Sachs, 17.
3. Celan, letter of 17 Dec. 1957, in Wolfgang Emmerich, ed., *Der Bremer Literaturpreis 1954–1987: Reden der Preisträger und andere Texte* (Bremerhaven, 1988), 72.
4. Letter to Petre Solomon, 18 July 1957, in "Briefwechsel," 61.
5. Martin Buber, *Mein Weg zum Chassidismus,* in *Werke* (Munich, 1963), 12:970; Leonard Moore Olschner, *Der feste Buchstab: Erläuterungen zu Paul Celans Gedichtübertragungen* (Göttingen, 1985), 55. Celan bought *Mein Weg* in August 1954.
6. To acknowledge his host city, Celan recalls Rudolph Borchardt's 1907 "Ode with a Pomegranate," published by the Bremen press. Borchardt was a baptized Jew who championed Aryan supremacy. Self-hate like this, in Celan's view, gave the lie to prewar German-Jewish "symbiosis"—though his 1958 Bremen audience would take the Borchardt reference as a cultural compliment. Borchardt, *Gesammelte Werke* (Stuttgart, 1957), 3:174, has the poem. See Glenn's translation of the entire Bremen speech in *Chicago Review* 29/3 (Winter 1978): 29–40, and his discussion (*Paul Celan,* 37) of Borchardt's poem and of Rudolf Alexander

Schröder, to whom the poem was dedicated, and who was honored on his eightieth birthday at the 1958 Bremen gathering. Schröder has been called a leader of the German resistance poets during the war: Charles W. Hoffmann, *Opposition Poetry in Nazi Germany* (Berkeley, Calif., 1962), 144. See Sol Liptzin, *Germany's Stepchildren* (Philadelphia, 1944), 184; and Gershom Scholem, *On Jews and Judaism in Crisis*, ed. Werner Dannhauser (New York, 1976), 85, 87.

7. See James K. Lyon, "Paul Celan's Language of Stone: The Geology of the Poetic Landscape," *Colloquia Germanica* 8/3–4 (1974): 298–317.

8. Osip Mandelshtam, *Sobranie Sochinenii*, ed. Gleb Struve and Boris Filippov-Filistinsky (New York, 1955); Mandelstam, *Selected Essays*, trans. Sidney Monas (Austin, Tex., 1977), 58–64.

9. Rainer A. Bast and Heinrich P. Delfosse, *Handbuch zum Textstudium von Martin Heideggers 'Sein und Zeit'* (Stuttgart, 1979), 1:64–68.

10. Quoted in Wolfgang Schirmacher, *Technik und Gelassenheit* (Freiburg, 1983), 25. Cited also in Philippe Lacoue-Labarthe, *Heidegger, Art and Politics* (Oxford, 1990), 34, and Victor Farias, *Heidegger and Nazism* (Philadelphia, 1989), 287.

11. Emmerich, ed., *Der Bremer Literaturpreis*, 69; *Ansprachen bei Verleihung des Bremer Literaturpreises an Paul Celan* (Stuttgart, 1958), 2. Photographs: Rosemarie Fleischer.

12. Harry Neumann, "Wir sprachen mit Preisträger Celan," *Die Welt*, 27 Jan. 1958: 5.

13. Letters of 15 and 17 Feb. 1958, *Hermes* 4/3 (1958): 4.

14. For other relations of "Todesfuge" to "Engführung," see Leonard Moore Olschner, "Fugal Provocation in Paul Celan's 'Todesfuge' and 'Engführung,'" *German Life and Letters*, 43/1 (Oct. 1989): 79–89. Otto Lorenz, *Schweigen in der Dichtung: Hölderlin—Rilke—Celan* (Göttingen, 1989), 198–243, finds connections between "Engführung" and Jean Paul, Dante, Shakespeare, Empedocles, the Bible, Nietzsche's *Zarathustra*, Cayrol's *Night and Fog*, and Rosenzweig's *Star of Redemption*—e.g., in Rosenzweig's last chapter: "In the innermost straits [Enge] of the Jewish heart the star of redemption shines."

15. Hamburger, in Celan, *Poems*, 23; Celan, *Strette*.

16. Charlotte Rumpf, "Die 'Todesfuge' von Paul Celan: Ein Unterrichts Beispiel," *Gesellschaft—Staat—Erziehung* 2/5 (1957): 232–41, with editorial note by "F.M."

17. Celan, letter to Erich Kahler, 25 Apr. 1962.

18. Celan, *Strette*.

19. Barbara Vormeier, *Die Deportierung deutscher und österreichischer Juden aus Frankreich* (Paris, 1980), 17.

20. "Briefwechsel," 62.

21. In Celan's Bremen speech a few weeks before, "those Hasidic tales were at home" in Celan's erstwhile homeland. And "lovers" in Hölderlin's Rhine hymn (stanza 13) are fatefully "at home" (*zu Hause*). Rereading this poem a year later (in Hölderlin's *Sämtliche Werke* [1953 ed.], 2:155), Celan strongly marked the lines about lovers "at home" and wrote in the margin: "17.4.59 cf Engführung!" He also underscored the end of the Rhine hymn, where "at night . . . primeval confusion" returns.

22. His earlier sequence, "*Voices*," which opens the 1959 collection that "Stretto" closes, had no asterisks until it came out in book form, after Celan had devised that usage for "Stretto." Aris Fioretos discusses the asterisk in "Engführung" in "Nothing," 328.

23. Gold, *Geschichte*, 2:75–76.

24. Celan suggested the time bomb: Dietlind Meinecke, *Wort und Name bei Paul Celan* (Bad Homburg, 1970), 177; and *ticken* also means "touch," as at God's touch Adam breathed.

25. Dates courtesy of Rolf Bücher. But I have seen a facsimile of the poem's last stanza dated by Celan "3.XI.58": Gerhard Hoehme, *Engführung: Hommage à Paul Celan* (Neuss, 1991), 61.

26. Celan, letter to Hilde de la Motte, 20 Mar. 1958, in *Autorenkalender '81* (Berlin, 1980), July.

27. Celan, letter to Erwin Leiser, 15 Apr. 1958, in Leiser, *Leben nach dem Überleben: Dem Holocaust entronnen—Begegnungen und Schicksale* (Königstein, 1982), 75–76.
28. Hans Mayer, "Erinnerung an Paul Celan," *Merkur* 24 (Dec. 1970): 1159. The passage from *Inferno* is 5.138.
29. Celan found this citation in Arthur March, *Das neue Denken der modernen Physik* (Hamburg, 1957), 15. See Celan's letter to Walter Jens, 21 Mar. 1959, repr. partially in "Deutsche Literatur heute. Eine Ausstellung, 1968" (Kuratorium unteilbares Deutschland, 1970).
30. Letter of 18 July 1957, in "Briefwechsel," 61.
31. Hamida Bosmajian, *Metaphors of Evil: Contemporary German Literature and the Shadow of Nazism* (Iowa City, 1979), 227.
32. *Paul Celan: Gedichte und Prosa,* and Celan, *Davar.*
33. Written asunder as an anagram, *Gras* gives *Sarg,* "coffin"!: Ossar, "Malevolent God," 174, and Lorenz, *Schweigen,* 207.
34. Celan, letter to Walter Jens, 21 Mar. 1959.
35. Neumann, "Wir sprachen."
36. Because "Stretto" pointedly evokes a fugue, a friend wrote that Celan was disavowing his earlier poem. When the two men later met, Celan said abruptly: "My dear Hans Mayer, I never take back a poem!": Mayer, "Erinnerung," 1158.

Chapter 8
The Other Voice Your Own (1958–59)

1. Letter to Harald Hartung, 4 Dec. 1958.
2. Jokostra, *Die Zeit,* 174. Jokostra reports the caricature's text slightly differently in "Ich singe," 223. Pöggeler also refers to this incident, saying that the caption read: "Hosanna to the son of David": "Die schwarze Sonne der Melancholie," *Die Welt,* 7 Sept. 1990: 19. In Cologne in 1957, when Celan happened to stumble in the street, a heavyset German said, "What's this Jew-pig doing holding up traffic?," and Celan bolted: Mariana Birnbaum, interview by the author, 7 Apr. 1990.
3. Celan, letter to Struve, 29 Jan. 1959, in Terras and Weimar, "Mandelstamm and Celan," 362.
4. Fichman, 65, and Silbermann, 57.
5. Celan, letter to Petre Solomon, 6 Aug. 1962, in "Briefwechsel," 68.
6. Celan, letter to Petre Solomon, 25 Mar. 1958, in "Briefwechsel," 62.
7. "All the titles of my prints that stem from his lifetime originate in him, German as well as French": Gisèle Celan, quoted in Dietmar Grieser, "Ohne Firnis: Im Atelier von Gisèle Celan-Lestrange," *Literatur und Kritik* 153 (Apr. 1981): 233.
8. Mandelshtam, *Sobranie Sochinenii.*
9. Mayer, "Erinnerung," 1151–52; Mandelstam, *Selected Essays,* 59.
10. On Celan's translations of Mandelshtam, I have drawn on the following: Clarence Brown, *Mandelstam* (Cambridge, 1973); Mandelstam, *Selected Poems,* trans. Clarence Brown and W. S. Merwin (New York, 1974); Mandelstam, *Stone,* trans. Robert Tracy (Princeton, 1981); Mandelstam, *Selected Poems,* trans. David McDuff (New York, 1975); Mandelstam, *50 Poems,* trans. Bernard Meares (New York, 1977); Leonard Olschner, "Anamnesis: Paul Celan's Translations of Poetry," *Studies in Twentieth Century Literature* 12/2 (Spring 1988): 163–97; Victor Terras and Karl S. Weimar, "Mandelstamm and Celan: Affinities and Echoes," *Germano-Slavica* 4 (Fall 1974): 11–27.
11. Melville, "Hawthorne and His Mosses," in *The Shock of Recognition,* ed. Edmund Wilson (New York, 1943; 1955), 199.
12. Mandelstam, "Fourth Prose," in *Selected Essays,* 166.
13. Nadezhda Mandelstam, *Hope Abandoned* (New York, 1981), 109–10. Early in 1958 Celan

translated Nerval's sonnet "El Desdichado," calling its Düreresque *soleil noir de la Mélancolie* a "sun of Melancholy, the black one" (4:809). On Auschwitz, see Fortunoff Video Archive for Holocaust Testimony, Yale University, and Geoffrey Hartman, "Preserving the Personal Story: The Role of Video Documentary," *Dimensions* 1/1 (Spring 1985): 16.

14. Benjamin, *Schriften,* ed. Theodor and Gretel A. Adorno (Frankfurt, 1955), 2:228, and *Illuminations,* 139.
15. N. Mandelstam, *Hope Abandoned,* 110.
16. Mandelstam, *Selected Poems,* trans. Brown and Merwin, xvii; Brown, *Mandelstam,* 215.
17. The poem is #165 (1955 ed.), #225 (1964 ed.), #253 (1967 ed.).
18. Celan, letter to Vladimir Markov, 31 May 1961, in Henrik Birnbaum, "Parallels and Contrasts, Traces and Echoes: Some Further Remarks on Mandel'shtam," in *Readings in Russian Modernism,* ed. R. Vroon and J. Mahnstad (Moscow, 1993), 38.
19. From the "Judaic chaos" that Mandelshtam called his upbringing, he is recalling a pious grandfather putting "a black and yellow silk cloth" over his shoulders and making him repeat some obscure (Hebrew) words. A faded prayer shawl, that black and yellow cloth attached to the boy's feeling "stifled and afraid" and rescued only by his mother: Mandelstam, *The Noise of Time,* trans. Clarence Brown (Princeton, 1965), 92.
20. Pöggeler, *Spur,* 249.
21. Nadezhda Mandelshtam, postcard to Celan, 12 July 1962, in Jürgen Lehmann, "Berührung und Dialog: Zu einer unbekannten Mandel'stam-Übersetzung Paul Celans," *Celan-Jahrbuch* 4 (1991): 85. Nadezhda Mandelshtam, Foreword to *Osip Mandelstam,* trans. James Greene (London, 1988), 8. Lowell's poem "Long Summers" is in *History.* On the other hand, Nadezhda had earlier welcomed the "great moment, the meeting of two poets" in Lowell's adaptations: Nadezhda Mandelshtam, letter to Lowell, quoted in Olga Carlisle, *Poets on Street Corners: Portraits of Fifteen Russian Poets* (New York, 1968), xiii.
22. Sidney Monas, Introduction to *Complete Poetry of Osip Emilevich Mandelstam,* trans. Burton Raffel and Alla Burago (Albany, N.Y., 1973), 1. Terras and Weimar, "Mandelstamm and Celan," 356 (in which Vladimir Markov's 1959 review of Celan's Mandelshtam *Gedichte* is also cited).
23. Simon Karlinsky, *New York Times Book Review,* 20 Jan. 1974.
24. Letter of 29 Jan. 1959, in Terras and Weimar, "Mandelstamm and Celan," 361. In the quotation I have restored Celan's sentence "I'm simplifying—I know," which is omitted from the letter as cited in ibid. The original of Celan's letter is in the Hoover Institution, Stanford.
25. Quoted in letter from Emmanuel Raïs to Gleb Struve, 25 Sept. 1975, in Terras and Weimar, "Mandelstamm and Celan," 367.
26. "Soviet Poetry" (review of *Sobranie Sochinenii*), *Times Literary Supplement,* 30 May 1958: 289–90.
27. By March 1960 Celan had revised his view of Mandelshtam's death: he "was seized in the 'purges' of the thirties. The path leads to Siberia, his life trace gets lost": Ossip Mandelstam, *Im Luftgrab,* ed. Ralph Dutli (Zurich, 1988), 81.
28. Quoted, as from 1957 or so, in Christoph Meckel, "Magie des Nichtgesagten: Rede für Judith Herzberg," *Die Zeit,* 7 Dec. 1984: 55.
29. Celan, letter of 29 Feb. 1960, in Terras and Weimar, "Mandelstamm and Celan," 363.
30. Mandelstam, *Im Luftgrab.* See Bernhard Böschenstein, "Celan und Mandelstamm: Beobachtungen zu ihrem Verhältnis," *Celan-Jahrbuch* 2 (1988): 155–68.
31. Celan, letter to Petre Solomon, 17 Feb. 1958, in "Briefwechsel," 62; Olschner, *Der feste Buchstab,* 164–65.
32. This flower was illustrated in the Insel manual *Das kleine Blumenbuch,* which Celan had in Czernowitz.
33. Olschner, *Der feste Buchstab,* 183, 185–86.

34. Celan, letter to Jean Firges, 2 Dec. 1958, in Firges, "Sprache und Sein in der Dichtung Paul Celans," *Muttersprache* 72/9 (1962): 266.

35. Rilke's correspondence with André Gide, which Celan tried translating in 1954, abounds with elation at discovering Valéry: Rainer Maria Rilke and André Gide, *Correspondance: 1909–1926,* ed. Renée Lang (Paris, 1952).

36. Ibid., 153; Olschner, *Der feste Buchstab,* 180.

37. Valéry, *La Jeune Parque* (Paris: Gallimard, Le Club du meilleur livre, 1957). Valéry, *Die Junge Parze,* trans. Paul Celan (Wiesbaden, 1960); unlike Celan's other book-length translations, this edition did not contain the original. Celan had published his translation of lines 1–173 of Valéry's poem in *Neue Rundschau* 70/3 (1959): 499–504.

38. Pöggeler, *Spur,* 121.

39. Letter of 13 Dec. 1957, in Celan/Sachs, 10.

40. Sachs, letter to Celan, 21 Dec. 1957, in Celan/Sachs, 10.

41. Letter of 3 Jan. 1958, in Celan/Sachs, 11.

42. *Botteghe Oscure* 21 (1958): 371–74.

43. Letter of 3 Sept. 1959, in Celan/Sachs, 23.

44. Scholem, *Die Geheimnisse.* See *Briefe der Nelly Sachs,* ed. Ruth Dinesen and Helmut Müssener (Frankfurt, 1984), 125.

45. Otto Pöggeler, "Kontroverses zur Ästhetik Paul Celans (1921–1970)," *Zeitschrift für Ästhetik und allgemeine Kunstwissenschaft* 25/2 (1980): 238. The meeting had been arranged through Peter Szondi, according to Janz, *Vom Engagement,* 115. When Adorno learned of Celan's "Gespräch," he inserted a dedication to Celan in the book version of his Valéry essay (Adorno, *Noten zur Literatur II* [Frankfurt, 1961]).

46. Theodor Adorno, *Noten zur Literatur I* (Berlin, 1958).

47. In "Kulturkritik und Gesellschaft," written in 1949 in the United States, published singly in 1951, collected in *Prismen* (Berlin, 1955).

48. Federmann, 91.

49. Pöggeler, "Kontroverses," 238.

50. Büchner's *Lenz,* based on the life of a contemporary of the young Goethe, the poet J. M. R. Lenz (1751–94), was written in summer of 1836 and published in 1879. See Karin Lorenz-Lindemann, "Paul Celan: Gespräch im Gebirg—Ein Palimpsest zu Büchners Lenz," in *Datum,* 170–82.

51. Pöggeler, "Kontroverses," 238; Martin Heidegger, *Nietzsche* (Tübingen, 1961), 292.

52. Federmann, 91.

53. James K. Lyon, "Paul Celan and Martin Buber: Poetry as Dialogue," *PMLA* 86/1 (Jan. 1971): 110–20; John J. Jackson, "Die Du-Anrede bei Paul Celan," *Text und Kritik* 53–54 (Jan. 1977): 62–68. There are specific traces of Buber's *Gespräch* in Celan's "Conversation," including the evening scene, a stick, and some silver pine: Elisabeth Hense, "Hörst Du Hörstdu?: Mystische Züge im Werk Paul Celans" (Ph.D. diss., Nijmegen, 1985), 90–104. Hense also sees connections with Rosenzweig's *Star of Redemption.*

54. Hans Kohn, *Martin Buber: Sein Werk und seine Zeit* (Hellerau, 1930), 242, 245.

55. Benjamin, *Schriften,* 2:415; English translation in Benjamin, *Reflections,* ed. Peter Demetz, trans. Edmund Jephcott (New York, 1978). Benjamin cites Kierkegaard for this sense of *Geschwätz:* Kierkegaard, *Gesammelte Werke,* ed. H. H. Hagedorn, trans. Emanuel Hirsch (Düsseldorf, 1954), 17:83. The Turk's-cap is illustrated in the 1933 Insel flower manual that Celan had in Czernowitz.

56. Celan, *Gedichte und Prosa.*

57. Janz, *Vom Engagement,* 229. On the term *mauscheln,* see Jacob Katz, "German Culture and the Jews," *Commentary,* Feb. 1984: 59, and Sander L. Gilman, *Jewish Self-Hatred: Anti-Semitism and the Hidden Language of the Jews* (Baltimore, 1986). The derisive term may also be related to English "smouch," meaning a Jew, a usurer, which in turn derived from

Yiddish *schmoose* ("talk"), from Hebrew *shemua* ("rumor," "hearsay"): letter from Paul Haberfield, *Commentary*, June 1984: 16.

58. As a boy, Celan favored the Yiddish fables of Eliezer Steinbarg from Czernowitz, and in 1940 he is said to have recited Steinbarg's rhyme about "Rabbi Leiserl, the Little," who asked himself "What is one? . . . But one is none!" (Chalfen, 101). Perhaps in the 1959 "Gespräch," when Jew Little says "I was just one, and who wants to love just one, and they were many," this renews the question critical to a people of stateless outsiders: solitary alienation versus communal solidarity.

59. Stéphane Mosès, "Quand le langage se fait voix," in *Contre-jour*, ed. Broda, 123.

Chapter 9
With and Against the Pain (1959–60)

1. Letter of 26 Oct. 1959, in Celan/Sachs, 24.
2. Letter of 28 Oct. 1959, in Celan/Sachs, 25.
3. Letter of 31 Oct. 1959, in Celan/Sachs, 25. On 3 November, Sachs wrote to Celan, "I myself struggle desperately against despondency . . . but you dear friend . . . , I wish I could protect you against your own sadness!": Celan/Sachs, 27.
4. *Der Tagesspiegel*, 11 Oct. 1959.
5. Günter Blöcker, *Kritisches Lesebuch* (Hamburg, 1962).
6. Letter to Jokostra, 4 Mar. 1959, in Jokostra, "Celan ist bestenfalls eine Parfümfabrik . . . ," *Die Welt* 253 (30 Oct. 1971) supplement: 5.
7. Letter of 6 Apr. 1959, in Jokostra, "Celan ist bestenfalls."
8. Peter Gehrisch, "Der Wunde Punkt," *Sonntag* 18 (6 May 1990): 7.
9. Celan, letter to Heidegger, 24 Nov. 1958, courtesy of Jerry Glenn.
10. May 1973 interview with Bachmann in Christine Koschel and Inge von Weidenbaum, eds., *Wir müssen wahre Sätze finden: Gespräche und Interviews* (Munich, 1983), 137. See *Martin Heidegger zum siebzigsten Geburtstag: Festschrift* (Pfullingen, 1959).
11. Jacob Glatstein, *Radiant Jews* (1946); *Selected Poems of Jacob Glatstein*, trans. Ruth Whitman (New York, 1972), 68.
12. Neither French translation uses *alliance*, however: Celan, *La Rose de personne*, trans. Martine Broda (Paris, 1979); Celan, *Strette & Autres Poèmes*, trans. Jean Daive (Paris, 1990).
13. In Celan/Sachs, 167.
14. Kohn, *Martin Buber*, 242, 85, 277.
15. *Vom Judentum: Ein Sammelbuch* (Leipzig, 1913). Baumann, 28.
16. Celan may have known this from Klaus Wagenbach, *Franz Kafka: Eine Biographie seiner Jugend* (Bern, 1958), 257.
17. *Justiz und NS-Verbrechen* (1968), v. 16, case 490. I do not know that Celan saw any follow-up article to the original report of the ongoing trial.
18. John Dornberg, *Schizophrenic Germany* (New York, 1961); Rudolph Fischer, "Antisémitisme de brasserie et de salon dans l'Allemagne Fédérale"; and Alfred Grosser, "Mythes et réalités du néo-nazisme en Allemagne," *L'Arche* (Paris) 35, 37 (Nov. 1959, Jan. 1960).
19. Letter of 20 Feb. 1960, in Celan/Sachs, 29, and PC 14.
20. *Baubudenpoet* 1/3 (1959–60): 62–63.
21. Goll, "Unbekanntes."
22. Celan, letter to Margul-Sperber, 30 July 1960, in "Briefe," 54.
23. Ibid.
24. Döhl, "Geschichte." See Lennartson, "Nelly Sachs," 88.
25. Jens, *Die Zeit*, 9 June 1961: 11; *Christ und Welt*, 9 June 1961: 18; Glenn, *Bibliographie*, T165, 193, 150, 202, 228.
26. Celan, letter to Nelly Sachs, 7 May 1960, in Celan/Sachs, 34; and to Ilse Blumenthal-Weiss, 8 Dec. 1966, in Leo Baeck Institute, New York.

. Letter of 28 Oct. 1959, in Celan/Sachs, 25.
28. Celan/Sachs, 167, 28.
29. Letter, in Celan/Sachs, 33.
30. *Briefe der Nelly Sachs,* 247.
31. Celan/Sachs, 41.
32. Rudolf Peyer, "Andenken," *Neue Zürcher Zeitung,* 29–30 Sept. 1984: 66.
33. Alvin Rosenfeld, *A Double Dying: Reflections on Holocaust Literature* (Bloomington, Ind., 1980), 101.
34. Thomas Sparr, "Das Gespräch im Gedicht," *Neue Zürcher Zeitung,* 23 Nov. 1990: 39. Susman's book, which Celan knew, was published in Zurich.
35. Ruth Dinesen, *Nelly Sachs: Eine Biographie* (1991), trans. Gabriele Gerecke (Frankfurt, 1992), 299–300.
36. "O the Chimneys," in Sachs, *O the Chimneys* (New York, 1967), 2.
37. Sachs, *O the Chimneys,* 128.
38. *Nelly Sachs zu Ehren* (Frankfurt, 1961), 32. Sparr, "Das Gespräch." Inscribing a book to Celan on 26 May 1960, Sachs said: "It counts Paul it counts": Celan/Sachs, 157.
39. Celan, letter of 3 May 1960, in Celan/Sachs, 33.
40. Lennartsson, "Nelly Sachs," describes this 13–16 June 1960 visit. Celan's notes on these days show the visit to Heine's grave occurring a day before the Ernst incident: Celan/Sachs, 46.
41. Sachs, letters to Gisela and Alfred Andersch, 23 June 1960, and to Hilde Domin, 5 July 1960, in *Briefe der Nelly Sachs,* 249, 251.
42. Celan/Sachs, 51, and *PC* 15.
43. Letter of 28 July 1960, in Celan/Sachs, 53, and *PC* 16.
44. Letter of 30 July 1960, in "Briefe," 55.
45. Letter of 9 Aug. 1960, in Celan/Sachs, 55–56, and *PC* 17.
46. Sachs, letter of 16 Aug. 1960; Celan, letter of 19 Aug. 1960, in Celan/Sachs, 57, and *PC* 18; Sachs, letter to Enzensberger family, Oct. 1960, in *Briefe der Nelly Sachs,* 252.
47. Letter of 29 Aug. 1960, telegram of 31 Aug. 1960, in Celan/Sachs, 61–62.
48. Ehrhard Bahr, *Nelly Sachs* (Munich, 1980), 54; Dinesen, *Nelly Sachs,* 310. Another report says that Celan had sent Sachs a recording of Martin Buber (and that in Stockholm he witnessed her confusing Buber with the Baal Shem Tov): Pöggeler, letter to the author, 8 Nov. 1993, and "Der Gang ins Moor," *Neue Zürcher Zeitung,* 2 Dec. 1988: 46. Celan arrived in Stockholm on 1 September and left for Paris on 7 September.
49. Letter to Enzensberger family, Oct. 1960.
50. Chalfen, 175.
51. Buber, *Drei Reden über das Judentum* (Frankfurt, 1920), 37.
52. Buber, *Daniel* (Leipzig, 1913; 1922), 117–18.
53. Edith Silbermann, "Paul Celan und die Bukowina: Von der Wirkung der Herkunft," *Pannonia* 14/1 (1986): 12.
54. Buber, "The Word That Is Spoken," in *The Knowledge of Man,* trans. Maurice Friedman, ed. Alan Udoff (Atlantic Highlands, N.J., 1988), 100–10; Maurice Friedman, *Martin Buber's Life and Work: The Later Years, 1945–1965* (New York, 1983), 383–84.
55. Jean Bollack, interview by the author, 22 Aug. 1984, Cerisy-la-Salle; Silbermann, "Paul Celan," 12. For the date 13 September 1960, see James K. Lyon, "Judentum, Antisemitismus, Verfolgungswahn: Celans 'Krise' 1960–1962," *Celan-Jahrbuch* 3 (1989): 195.
56. Celan brought his copy of *Ich und Du,* which he had reread on 25 August 1960. Buber signed it, but for some reason Celan later gave the book to Klaus Demus: James K. Lyon, interview with Demus, 2 July 1962.
57. Peter Horst Neumann, "Was muss ich wissen, um zu verstehen?: Paul Celans Gedicht 'Die Schleuse', ein Gedicht für Nelly Sachs," *Celan-Jahrbuch* 4 (1991): 27–38, notes that the first version of this poem was titled with a Stockholm place-name.

58. Neugroschel, in Celan, *Speech-Grille*, 181.
59. Letter to Pöggeler, 1 Nov. 1960, in Pöggeler, *Spur*, 407.
60. Bollack, interview by the author. Celan gave the speech in Darmstadt on 22 October 1960.
61. *Der Georg-Büchner Preis 1951–1978: Eine Ausstellung des Deutschen Literaturarchivs Marbach und der Deutschen Akademie für Sprache und Dichtung, Darmstadt* (Marbach, 1978), 129.
62. Letter to Pöggeler, 1 Nov. 1960, in Pöggeler, "Kontroverses," 240.
63. Dutli, *Im Luftgrab*, 70–71; *GW* 3:197.
64. Léon Chestov, *Le Pouvoir des Clefs*, trans. B. de Schloezer (Paris, 1928), xxxvii. Celan has slightly altered the quote.
65. Benjamin, "Franz Kafka," in *Schriften*, 2:222.
66. Martha Bickel, "Zum Werk von Karl Emil Franzos," in *Juden in der deutschen Literatur*, ed. Stéphane Mosès and Albrecht Schöne (Frankfurt, 1986), 152–61; Colin, *Paul Celan*, 12–14.
67. Letter to Jürgen P. Wallmann, 25 Jan. 1961, in Wallmann, "Auch mich," 81.
68. Wolfgang Butzlaff, "Zwei Bemühungen um ein Gedicht, Paul Celans Todesfuge II," *Deutschunterricht* 3 (1960): 42–51.
69. At first he identifies an "act of freedom" in *Danton's Death*, when Lucile Desmoulins near the guillotine cries out "Long live the" King!"—a suicidal utterance which Celan calls a "counter-word . . . bearing witness to the human present through the majesty of the absurd." Then he pursues the idea of "actualized language, set free."
70. Letters of 28 July, 9 Aug., 19 Aug., 13 Oct. 1960, in Celan/Sachs, 53, 55, 58, 64.
71. Letter to Pöggeler, 30 Aug. 1961, in Pöggeler, "Kontroverses," 242.
72. Written 5 Jan. 1961.
73. Steiner, "The Long Life of Metaphor: An Approach to 'the Shoah,'" *Encounter* 68/2 (1987): 61.
74. Winkler, in Celan, *Shoshanat*, 68; Natan Zach, "HaMeshorer baMigdal Bavel," *Moznaim* 57/3 (1983): 5.
75. Joachim Schulze, "Mystische Motive in Paul Celans Gedichten," *Poetica* 3/3–4 (1970): 485, called attention to the use of *Gelobt seist du* in German-Jewish benedictions. One translator has—unwarrantably, I think—turned *Gelobt seist du* into ecclesiastical Latin, *Laudamus te*: Katherine Washburn, cited in Paul Auster, "The Poetry of Exile," *Studies in Twentieth Century Literature* 8/1 (Fall 1983): 109.
76. Perhaps this helps to explain the only revision Celan made to an early version of "Psalm," which spoke of the purpleword we "exchanged" (*tauschten*): S. Fischer Verlag, *Almanach* (Frankfurt, 1962), 48.
77. Böschenstein, 8.
78. A Grimms' tale, "The Jew in the Thornbush," has a strong anti-Semitic streak, calling an old Jew a swindler and thief.

Chapter 10
Wrestling with the Angels (1961)

1. Martin Anderle, "Sprachbildungen Hölderlins in modernen Gedichten (Celans 'Tübingen, Jänner' und Bobrowskis 'Hölderlin in Tübingen')," *Seminar* 8/2 (June 1972): 101.
2. Meinecke, *Wort und Name*, 189.
3. Hölderlin's elegy "Bread and Wine" had asked what use poets are in a "destitute time" (*dürftiger Zeit*). Celan plays with *dürfte* ("could") and *Zeit* to expose his own destitute time.
4. Friedrich Hölderlin, *Sämtliche Werke*, ed. Ludwig von Pigenot and Friedrich Seebass (Berlin, 1923), 6:444.
5. Letter to Bender, 10 Feb. 1961, in *Briefe*, 54.

6. Buber, *Mein Weg zum Chassidismus*, in *Werke* 3:970.
7. From Heine's drama *Almansor* (1821). See Jeffrey L. Sammons, *Heinrich Heine, the Elusive Poet* (New Haven, 1969), 92.
8. Lionel Richard, *Nazisme et littérature* (Paris, 1971), 149.
9. Celan/Sachs, 75. This poem appeared in "Death Still Celebrates Life," a section of *Fahrt ins Staublose: Die Gedichte der Nelly Sachs* (Frankfurt, 1961). Celan's inscription on the offprint of his Meridian speech, which he didn't send in the end, came from his speech: "A poem is lonely . . . and under way" (3:198).
10. Celan ends *gesund* Germanically with a Dalet instead of the Yiddish Tet.
1. The English version actually says "stem," not "root," but in any case the German is *Wurzel* ("root").
2. Baumann, 92.
3. Letter of 19 May 1961, partially quoted in Wiedemann-Wolf, *Antschel Paul*, 5, 71, 85, 88. Jens's article: "Leichtfertige Vorwürfe gegen einen Dichter," *Die Zeit*, 9 June 1961: 13.
4. Celan took these lines from a Columbia album of Yiddish songs sung by Belina Behrend, *Es brennt*, SMC 73715. The song he cites can be found in *Yidishe folkslider mit melodien*, ed. I. L. Kohn (New York, 1957), 411. The ghetto adaptation, by Kasriel Broydo, is in *Lider fun di getaot un lagern*, ed. S. Kaczerginski (New York, 1948), 16.
5. Information from Hans Mayer, in James K. Lyon, "'Ganz und gar nicht hermetisch': Uberlegungen zum 'richtigen' Lesen von Paul Celans Lyrik," in *Psalm und Hawdalah: Zum Werk Paul Celans* (Bern, 1987), 180. "Benedicta" is also the name taken by Edith Stein (1891–1942) when, having converted from orthodox Judaism, she became a nun. Celan had bought a biography of her in 1959.
6. Meinecke, *Wort und Name*, 277.
7. Gershom G. Scholem, *Zur Kabbalah und ihrer Symbolik* (Zurich, 1960), 186; *On the Kabbalah and Its Symbolism*, trans. Ralph Manheim (New York, 1969), 139.
8. In the actual song, we hear a turn from "It should be this way" to "It must be this way." The song, performed simply with a sparse guitar accompaniment, does not in fact stop after the phrase Celan cites but ends after one more line: "It can in this world now be no other way." It brings to mind the last movement of Beethoven's last quartet, Opus 135, which opens with musical mottoes on the words *Muss es sein? Es muss sein!* ("Must it be? It must be!").
9. Neugroschel does so in Celan, *Speech-Grille*, 197.
0. Celan told a scholar that he saw one in a church in Burgundy. There is a large twelfth-century fresco at Berzé-la-Ville near Cluny, showing Christ Almighty enthroned against a blue background within an almond-shaped border: Albrecht Schöne, *Literatur in audiovisuellen Medium: Sieben Fernsehdrehbücher* (Munich, 1974), 154.
1. Heidegger, *Was ist Metaphysik?* (1929; Bonn, 1931), 10: *Wie steht es um das Nichts?*
2. Gershom Scholem, *Von der mystischen Gestalt der Gottheit* (Frankfurt, 1962), 128.
3. At the time of "Mandorla," Celan published some Emily Dickinson translations, among them her skeptical "Four Trees—upon a solitary Acre" (5:399): *Neue Rundschau* 72/1 (1961): 36–39. His version uses "stand" and "eye" several times where she does not. Where Dickinson labels "Unknown" the "Plan / They severally—promote—or hinder," Celan asks of each tree, "whose way does it prepare and whose / does it stand opposite? [*steht er entgegen*]"—the same phrase that links "eye" to "Nothing" in "Mandorla." (Olschner calls attention to the similar wording in *Der feste Buchstab*, 293.) Her open-endedness suited him less than a question about opposition.
4. This couplet recalls the sardonic rhyme *blau / genau* from "Todesfuge": "this Death is a master from Deutschland his eye it is blue / he shoots you with shot made of lead shoots you level and true."
5. Chalfen, 7.

26. Celan owned Scholem's 1960 book, *Zur Kabbala und ihrer Symbolik*, which contains a chapter on "Die Vorstellung vom Golem in ihren tellurischen und magischen Beziehungen."
27. Scholem. *Von der mystischen*, 128.
28. In 1960 Celan was sent a book on Prague's Jewish cemetery, with pictures of Rabbi Loew's tomb and of gravestones depicting hands making the priestly blessing: Bollack, "Paul Celan sur la langue," in Colin, *Argumentum*, 120.
29. Celan was conscious of the High Holy Days in 1961. On 13 September 1961 he wrote to Nelly Sachs, "It is the Jewish New Year": Celan/Sachs, 79.
30. *Sinn und Form* 14/5–6 (1962): 703.
31. Rosenzweig, *Briefe*, 1237; *Franz Rosenzweig: His Life and Thought*, ed. Nahum N. Glatzer (New York, 1961), 174.
32. 8 Jan. 1914.
33. Jokostra, *Die Zeit*, 191. Kafka was not always divided. He reportedly liked the atmosphere of Prague's old Jewish quarter evoked in Gustav Meyrink's *Der Golem* (1915): Gustav Janouch, *Conversations with Kafka* (New York, 1953), 47.
34. For 27 May 1914 Kafka's diary says: "I find the letter K ugly, it almost sickens me yet I write it down, it must be characteristic of me." He died from tuberculosis of the larynx—*Kehlkopf* in German.
35. Kafka, "Fragmente," in *Hochzeitsvorbereitungen auf dem Lande*, ed. Max Brod (Frankfurt, 1966), 348.

Chapter 11
Speaking East (1962)

1. Letter of 23 Feb. 1962, in Federmann, 18.
2. Celan, letter to Margul-Sperber, 8 Feb. 1962, in "Briefe," 57.
3. Celan vigorously marked this passage in his copy of Kafka's story.
4. Letter to Vladimir Markov, 31 May 1961, in Birnbaum, "Parallels," 38.
5. Celan learned that Mandelshtam had been unjustly charged with plagiarism: letter to Pöggeler, 30 Aug. 1961, in Pöggeler, "Kontroverses," 238.
6. Letter of 6 Oct. 1961, in Celan/Sachs, 82.
7. Celan, letter to Petre Solomon, 18 Feb. 1962, in "Briefwechsel," 63.
8. Letter of 3 Mar. 1962, in Federmann, 19.
9. Letter of 8 Mar. 1962, in "Briefwechsel," 65.
10. Celan, letter to G. B. Fischer, 25 June 1962, in Gottfried Bermann Fischer and Brigitte Bermann Fischer, *Briefwechsel mit Autoren*, ed. Reiner Stach (Frankfurt, 1990), 629.
11. Letter of 9 Mar. 1962, in "Briefe," 58.
12. Derrida, *Schibboleth*, 49, mentions the 1962 demonstration.
13. The motto occurs in Büchner's "Der Hessische Landbote." See Michael Jakob, "In-Eins-Bildung: Zur poetischen Verfahrensweise in einem Gedicht Paul Celans," in *Die Bukowina*, 367–84.
14. Bachmann, "Unter Morden und Irren," in *Das dreissigste Jahr* (Munich, 1961); trans. Michael Bullock, *Encounter*, Dec. 1963: 3–15.
15. Bachmann, *Malina*, 68ff.
16. Enzensberger, "Die Steine der Freiheit," in *Nelly Sachs zu Ehren*, 47. Celan knew this book; his "Zurich, at the Stork" appeared in it.
17. Adorno, "Zur Dialektik des Engagements," *Neue Rundschau* 73/1 (1962): 103; repr. in *Noten zur Literatur* III (Frankfurt, 1965).
18. Michael Hamburger, Introduction to Celan, *Poems*. Celan is said to have combed newspapers from the war years, looking for names of figures who later flourished innocently: Baumann, 135.

19. Fischer, *Briefwechsel mit Autoren,* 628–30.
20. Celan, letter to Margul-Sperber, 9 Mar. 1961, in "Briefe," 58.
21. Letters to Petre Solomon, 8 Mar. 1962, in "Briefwechsel," 65, and Margul-Sperber, 9 Mar. 1962, in "Briefe," 58. I am not entirely sure that this is the poem that Celan mentions in these letters, but it is the best guess.
22. Letter of 22 Mar. 1962, in "Briefwechsel," 65.
23. Letter to Margul-Sperber, 8 Feb. 1962, in "Briefe," 57.
24. Letters to Petre Solomon, 22 Mar. 1962, in "Briefwechsel," 65, and Nina Cassian, 25 Apr. 1962, in Gutu, "Die Lyrik Paul Celans," 252.
25. Letter to Petre Solomon, 22 Mar. 1962, in "Briefwechsel," 65. On 18 March 1962 Celan wrote to Gustav Chomed, a childhood friend in Czernowitz: "my homeland remains fixed, quia absurdum," in memories that "go right through my heart, here in this often so inhuman Paris that's now no longer something dreamt of. . . . Ach, you know, I wish I still lived there": Silbermann, 38.
26. Letters to Margul-Sperber, 8 Feb. 1962, in "Briefe," 56, and Federmann, 14 Mar. 1962, in Federmann, 21.
27. The copy of *Mohn und Gedächtnis* in which Celan wrote Kahler's words is in the Leo Baeck Institute, New York. Kahler, *Die Verantwortung des Geistes* (Frankfurt, 1952), 79: "Origin and Metamorphosis of Jew-Hatred" (1939).
28. Celan, letter to Petre Solomon, 5 Sept. 1962, in "Briefwechsel," 68.
29. In "Briefe," 59.
30. Letter to Margul-Sperber, 8 Feb. 1962, in "Briefe," 56.
31. Letter of 5 Sept. 1962, in "Briefe," 68.
32. Letter to Federmann, 3 Mar. 1962, in Federmann, 19.
33. Joel Golb, "Translating Tradition: A Reading of Paul Celan's 'Huhediblu,'" *ACTS* 8–9 (1988): 168–80, and Silbermann, 71–88, have insightful commentary. Colin, *Paul Celan,* 125, includes draft versions of the poem, some pointing to Kafka's "A Country Doctor."
34. Verlaine, "Sagesse," 3.3.
35. Letter to Margul-Sperber, 12 Sept. 1962, in "Briefe," 60.
36. Letter of 12 Sept. 1962, in "Briefe," 60.
37. Letter to G. B. Fischer, 4 Dec. 1962, in *PC* 21. In 1961, fifty-seven previously unpublished Mandelshtam lyrics appeared in *Vozdushnye Puti* (New York, 1961). Celan translated two of them immediately.
38. Two poems in *Die Niemandsrose* name Mandelshtam: "Afternoon with Circus and Citadel" and "Everything is different"; five allude to him: "Mandorla," "Siberian," "In One," "Crowned out," and "A Rogues' and Swindlers' Ditty"; and one, "Blackearth," draws its title from a Mandelshtam poem that Celan translated (5:135) and from Mandelshtam's April 1935 poem "Black Earth," while also echoing the opening poem of Celan's volume, "There was earth inside them."
39. Olschner, *Der feste Buchstab,* 249.
40. Sachs, "Einer war," in *Fahrt ins Staublose,* 14. Celan owned this book and marked the poem.
41. Letter to Federmann, 3 Mar. 1962, in Federmann, 19.
42. Freud, *Beyond the Pleasure Principle* (1920), in *The Standard Edition of the Complete Psychological Works of Sigmund Freud,* ed. James Strachey (London, 1935), 18:14–17. See also "Recollection," in Freud, *Collected Papers,* 2:366–76. The mother in question was Freud's daughter Sophie. In 1967, Celan wrote a poem quoting extensively from *Beyond the Pleasure Principle* (2:201).
43. Letter of 7 Sept. 1962, in Celan/Sachs, 84.
44. Letter to Petre Solomon, 6 Aug. 1962, in "Briefwechsel," 67. This was a Second World War flying squadron. Niemen is in Lithuania.
45. *Tarusskie stranicy* (Kaluga, 1961). *Pages from Tarusa: New Voices in Russian Writing,* ed.

Andrew Field (Boston, 1964), ix, says that "only a few thousand copies" of the Russian anthology, published in late 1961, reached buyers. Celan's poem dates from 20 September 1962.

46. Celan, *La Rose de personne*, 147.

47. This poem appeared in Paris in 1934, then in *Izbrannoe* (Moscow, 1961). Tsvetaeva, *Selected Poems*, trans. David McDuff (Newcastle upon Tyne, 1987).

48. French has *youpin* or the more violent *youtre*, and in English it is "Yid." Mandelshtam, in lyrics that Celan translated, does not use this word for "Jew." Shortly before writing his Tarusa poem, Celan translated "Babi Yar." There, Yevtushenko has three different terms: in sympathetic contexts, *iudei* and *evrei*, but *zhid* only in the mouth of a pogromist, whose words Celan renders "Strike down the Jews, save Russia!" (5:280–86). (I heard Yevtushenko read "Babi Yar" in Chile in 1968, and there was no doubting his ironic emphasis on the term *zhid*.) The poet Joseph Brodsky and Professor Gregory Freidin, of Stanford University, have confirmed the derogatory nature of *zhid*.

49. At one point Celan seems to have had a second Russian citation in his poems for *Die Niemandsrose*, which did not finally appear in the book: letter to G. B. Fischer, 4 Dec. 1962, in *PC* 21.

50. Postcard to Gleb Struve, 26 Feb. 1959, in Terras and Weimar, "Mandelstamm and Celan," 363. Although Celan never translated Marina Tsvetaeva, "And with the Book from Tarusa" distantly echoes some poems of hers which appeared in that Russian anthology. Celan takes his fellow-poet's faithful scarred old writing table and makes it into a bench where a galley slave utters the one word that closes his poem: "Colchis," a legendary land far east of Alba, on the Black Sea, where the Golden Fleece was sought.

51. Letter to Brigitte Bermann Fischer, 3 Oct. 1963, in *Briefwechsel mit Autoren*, 639.

52. In Hölderlin's "Bread and Wine": "But my friend! we come too late. True the gods live, / but over our heads up there in another world."

53. Letter of 4 Dec. 1962, in *PC* 21.

54. Letter to Hans Habe, 3 Dec. 1962, in Habe, "Dasselbe Unheil nur in anderer Gestalt," *Kölnische Rundschau*, 3 June 1970: 26.

55. The word *Andenken* itself carries memories of Celan's Bremen speech (3:185), which urged that verb on his listeners, and of the elegy for his newborn son (1:121). Celan attaches the same dedicatory phrase to an early 1963 magazine selection of his poems: *Neue Rundschau* 74/1 (1963): 55. Along with them, this issue published two new Celan translations from a large group of Mandelshtam's recently published Voronezh poems. One of them concerns an idol: "His human countenance—he wants and wants to remember it." The other begins: "Where I do not exist, there / I shall fly, unseen" (5:154–57). Celan wrote to his editor about these translations: "A request: The Mandelshtam verses must stand *before* mine": letter to G. B. Fischer, 4 Dec. 1962, in *PC* 21.

56. Rilke, *Sämtliche Werke*, ed. E. Zinn (Wiesbaden, 1956), 2:185.

Chapter 12
Translation Counterpoint (1961–63)

1. Letter to Petre Solomon, 18 Dec. 1963, in "Briefwechsel," 70.

2. Letter of 24 Jan. 1964, in "Zwanzig," 23.

3. In Celan's copy of Margarete Susman, *Deutung Biblischer Gestalten* (Stuttgart, 1960), 46.

4. Bonnefoy, "Paul Celan," 93, and *ACTS* 8–9 (1988): 12.

5. Letter of 5 Mar. 1963, in Celan/Sachs, 86. In June 1963 Celan refused to read in Göttingen's Pawliner Church: Böschenstein, 12.

6. This offprint (sent to Sachs on 8 Dec. 1961) appeared in *Neue Rundschau* 72 (1961). Dickinson's poem, #657 in her collected poems, in fact begins "I dwell in Possibility." Celan must have altered it to fit his inscription.

7. Letter to Bender, 10 Feb. 1961, in *Briefe,* 54.

8. Chalfen, 52.

9. Paul Celan, "J'ai traduit . . . ," ed. George Guţu, *Neue Literatur* 41–42/7–8 (1990–91): 152–56.

10. Jean Paris, *James Joyce in Selbstzeugnissen und Bilddokumenten,* trans. Guido G. Meister [who also collaborated with Celan on "Jabberwocky"] (Hamburg, 1960), 143.

11. Celan's Shakespeare translations appeared as follows: *Neue Rundschau* 71 (1960): 98ff. (sonnets 90, 137); *Neue Rundschau* 75 (1964): 204–13 (sonnets 1–5, 43, 50, 57, 60, 65, 70–71, 79, 105–06, 115–16, 119); Shakespeare, *Einundzwanzig Sonette,* trans. Celan (Frankfurt, 1967) (sonnets published previously and 107); *GW* 5.

12. George Steiner, *After Babel: Aspects of Language and Translation* (New York, 1975), 389–91.

13. Chalfen, 52, 66; Silbermann, 44.

14. Shmueli and Seidmann, interviews by the author.

15. Baumann, 106.

16. Olschner, *Der feste Buchstab,* 298.

17. When he first published this translation, it read *Laub grünt* ("Leaf greens"). Then Celan saw the need for a past tense (and a tenth syllable), so the later version reads *grünte* ("greened").

18. About a year after this translation, Celan wrote a poem that embodies happy memories of a holiday in Romania shortly after the war, and he uses the phrase *Pontisches Einstmals* ("Pontic Once-upon-a-time")—*Pontisches* referring to the Black Sea (2:72).

19. Peter Szondi, "Poetry of Constancy—Poetik der Beständigkeit: Celans Übertragung von Shakespeares Sonett 105," in *Celan-Studien,* ed. Jean Bollack (Frankfurt, 1972), 29.

20. The more predictable Stefan George and Karl Kraus versions are discussed in Henriette Beese, *Nachdichtung als Erinnerung: Allegorische Lektüre einiger Gedichte von Paul Celan* (Darmstadt, 1976), 137.

21. Otto Pöggeler, ed., *Heidegger* (Cologne, 1969), 312–13; Joseph J. Kockelmans, *On the Truth of Being: Reflections on Heidegger's Later Philosophy* (Bloomington, Ind., 1984), 244.

22. Letter of 18 Dec. 1963, in "Briefwechsel," 70.

23. Beda Allemann and Rolf Bücher, "Paul Celan: Tălmăcirea sonetelor lui Shakespeare 2," *Manuscriptum* 13/4 (1982): 170.

24. George Steiner calls Celan's handling of Frost's ending "a miniature summa of the two languages and of the alchemy of transfer": Steiner, "Songs of a torn tongue," *Times Literary Supplement,* 28 Sept. 1984: 1094.

Chapter 13
Etching and Alchemy (1963–65)

1. Letter to Petre Solomon, 18 Dec. 1963, in "Briefwechsel," 70.

2. This cycle, the first twenty-one poems of *Atemwende* (Frankfurt, 1967), appeared in a bibliophile edition as *Atemkristall* (Paris, 1965; facs. rpt. Frankfurt, 1990), with etchings by Gisèle Celan-Lestrange.

3. Letter to Edith Silbermann, 8 Sept. 1963, in Silbermann, 67.

4. 16 Oct. 1963. *Atemwende. Historisch-Kritische Ausgabe* 7/2, ed. Rolf Bücher (Frankfurt, 1990), contains drafts of the poems with Celan's datings. Celan evidently wrote five poems in September and early October 1963 but placed them among later poems in *Atemwende* (2:60–64).

5. Celan, *Poems,* trans. Hamburger, 225; Celan, *65 Poems,* trans. Brian Lynch and Peter Jankowsky (Dublin, 1985), 57; Pierre Joris, "The Late Poetry of Paul Celan" (Ph.D. diss., SUNY Binghamton, 1990), 2:33; Luitgard Wundheiler, MS.

6. See Axel Gellhaus, "Marginalien. Paul Celan als Leser," in *"Der glühende,"* 59. For "My-poem, the Lie-noem" (*Mein-gedicht, das Genicht*) see Glenn, *Paul Celan,* 140.
7. Letter of 20 May 1965, in Schwerin, "In die Rillen der Himmelsmünze das Wort gepresst," *Die Welt,* 20 Mar. 1990: 29.
8. Hochhuth, *The Deputy,* trans. Richard and Clara Winston (New York, 1964), 223.
9. Letter to G. B. Fischer, 8 Jan. 1964, in *PC* 24.
10. Jerry Glenn and Elizabeth Petuchowski first pointed out the relation between Hebrew spelling and Celan's consonants in this poem. The day after writing it, Celan marked a paragraph on the threatened nature of Jewish existence in an essay by Emmanuel Levinas on Franz Rosenzweig, "Entre deux mondes," *La Conscience juive: Données et Débats,* ed. Éliane Amado Lévy-Valensi and Jean Halperin (Paris, 1963), 136.
11. Celan, letter to Friedrich Torberg, 14 Mar. 1964, in Torberg, *In diesem Sinne . . . : Briefe an Freunde und Zeitgenossen,* vol. 1 (Munich, 1981), 75.
12. Letter to Petre Solomon, 24 Jan. 1964, in "Zwanzig," 23. There had in fact already been one positive review in Nov. 1963: Glenn, *Bibliographie,* T300.
13. Letter to G. B. Fischer, 8 June 1964, in Fischer, *Briefwechsel mit Autoren,* 652. Celan asked Fischer if there might be an editorial position at Fischer Verlag.
14. Celan, *Atemwende,* 19.
15. "In Prague" was actually written on 12 October 1963, just before the short poems that open *Atemwende,* but Celan placed it later in the otherwise chronological volume.
16. Bachmann was in Prague in January 1964 and wrote a poem called *"Prag, Jänner."* See Bernd Witte, "Eine Poetik des Todes," in *Datum,* 238.
17. R. J. W. Evans, *Rudolf II and His World* (Oxford, 1973), 241.
18. Hans Egon Holthusen, "Das verzweifelte Gedicht," *Frankfurter Allgemeine Zeitung,* 2 May 1964 (Glenn, *Bibliographie,* T328). Peter Szondi replied effectively to Holthusen: see his and Holthusen's Letters to the Editor, *Frankfurter Allgemeine Zeitung,* 25 June 1964: 6.
19. Jean Bollack, *Pierre de coeur: Un poème inédit de Paul Celan "Le Périgord"* (Perigueux, 1991), 9–12. Bollack makes a fine presentation of this unpublished poem that Celan composed in September 1964.
20. Silbermann, 68. Celan spoke of the "Paul Celan case" in his letter of 14 December 1963 to G. B. Fischer: *PC* 22.
21. Chalfen, 144, 150–51. *Solve et coagula* is an alchemical formula. He may also have recalled Yeats's "Rosa Alchemica."
22. *The Letters of Rosa Luxemburg,* ed. Stephen Eric Bronner (Boulder, Colo., 1978), 241.
23. The line "—also my—" was cut in the final version of this poem. Pöggeler, *Spur,* 319, suggests that "horns' light" may allude to the Christian notion that Moses had horns.
24. Celan's word *Qualm* for "smoke" or "fumes" is found elsewhere only in his translation of Mandelshtam's poem on the young Levite: "Jerusalem's night, the fumes of inexistence" (5:101). Glenn, in *Paul Celan,* 135–36, discusses the 1965 poem, which recalls a painting from Celan's Edgar Jené essay, "The Blood Sea Goes over Land," with its "hovering blood tent" (3:160). For manuscripts of this poem, see Colin, *Paul Celan,* 140–53.
25. Celan, *Atemwende,* 193–95. Celan's change was from *geretteter* to *mitgewanderter.*
26. Adorno, "Engagement," in *Noten zur Literatur III,* 125–27.
27. Reinhard Baumgart, "Unmenschlichkeit beschrieben: Weltkrieg und Faschismus in der Literatur," *Merkur* 202 (Jan. 1965): 48–49. That same year, someone refuted Baumgart's critique of Celan, but, as usual, the damage was done: Walter Müller-Seidel, *Probleme der literarischen Wertung* (Stuttgart, 1965), 178–80.
28. Konrad Schacht, "Auschwitz als Kunstacker," *Die Zeit* 11 (12 Mar. 1965): 47, reacting to Edgar Lohner, "Dem Verderben abgewonnen," *Die Zeit* 9 (26 Feb. 1965): 26.
29. Celan, letter in Neumann, ed., *34 x erste Liebe,* 32.
30. Alexander Lernet-Holenia, "Celans 'Todesfuge,'" *Die Zeit* 18 (30 Apr. 1965): 48. It was Celan's publisher G. B. Fischer who arranged for this defense: Fischer, *Briefwechsel mit*

Autoren, 657, 800. See János Szász, "'Es ist nicht so einfach': Erinnerungen an Paul Celan," in *PC* 330, originally published in *Neue Literatur* 26/11 (1975). Ernst Jünger may be the author Celan disapproved of.

1. At the clinic, on the inside back cover of his Shakespeare volume, Celan began a poem that had in mind Kafka, whom he was also reading there (2:94). Kafka's last diary entry (12 June 1923), on the anxiety of writing, ends: "You too have weapons." Celan's poem, after playing on Kafka's Hebrew name, says: "I promised myself weapons." The poem is called "Vom Anblick der Amseln" (From glancing at the blackbirds); on 25 December 1911 Kafka says in his diary, "In Hebrew my name is Amschel." Celan was also playing on his own given name, Antschel.

2. Celan, *Atemwende,* 214. Celan's edition, *Shakespeares Werke,* ed. L. L. Schücking (Berlin, 1955), contains the Tieck–Schlegel translation, which, like Karl Kraus's and much like Celan's, has *Ich bin ins Hirn gehaun* for the line from *Lear.* In his last year Celan told Pöggeler that Shakespeare had always remained near him and been a "solace": Pöggeler, *Spur,* 366.

3. Letter to Petre Solomon, 2 Aug. 1965, in "Zwanzig," 23.

4. Kahler, "Jews and Germans," in *The Jews among the Nations* (New York, 1967), 95, 119. Celan must have seen this essay as "Deutsche und Juden," in *Für Margarete Susman: Auf gespaltenem Pfad,* ed. Manfred Schlösser (Darmstadt, 1964), a Festschrift to which he contributed two poems. Susman, as late as 1935, had said that "The vocation of Israel as a people is not self-realization, but self-surrender for the sake of a higher, transhistorical goal": Scholem, *On Jews and Judaism,* 89.

5. Letter to G. B. Fischer, 4 Feb. 1964, in *Briefwechsel mit Autoren,* 649. Kahler had also published an essay in 1931 advocating a dynamic process between Jewishness and Germanness, leading to a higher humanness: "Juden und Deutsche," *Freie Jüdische Monatsschau* (1931): 3–11. In 1936 he published *Israel unter den Völkern* (Zurich), upholding the Jewish element in a contemporary European brotherhood.

6. Letter of 28 July 1965, in *Der Georg-Büchner Preis,* 133–34. Landauer's sentence occurs in his essay on "heretical thoughts" in the book *Vom Judentum,* which Celan owned.

7. Celan, *Atemwende,* 253–54.

8. Celan told Michael Hamburger that *ichten* was the imperfect of "to I": Celan, *Poems,* 26.

Chapter 14
Crossing into Hebrew (1965–67)

1. Celan, *Fadensonnen, Historisch-Kritische Ausgabe* 8/2, ed. Rolf Bücher (Frankfurt, 1991), 11.

2. *Die Schriftwerke,* trans. Martin Buber (Cologne, 1962), Ps. 45:5. Buber's close version of the Hebrew actually reads: *Reite für die Sache der Treue* ("Ride on behalf of the truth"). The Biblical word for "truth" is *emet.* Franz Rosenzweig had used the same Hebrew phrase as a motto on the title page of *The Star of Redemption* (1921).

3. See Rainer Nägele, "Paul Celan: Configurations of Freud," in *Reading after Freud* (New York, 1987), 135–68.

4. Lehmann, "Berührung und Dialog," 86.

5. Rosenzweig, letter to Margarete Susman, 22 Aug. 1924, in Rosenzweig, *Briefe,* 982.

6. Kafka, *Erzählungen* (New York, 1946). Stuck into Celan's copy, I found a clipping from *Le Monde* of 8 January 1966, headed "Death of a student in a psychiatric clinic." (Celan also possessed some first editions of Kafka's works.)

7. Celan, *Eingedunkelt und Gedichte aus dem Umkreis von Eingedunkelt,* ed. Bertrand Badiou and Jean-Claude Rambach (Frankfurt, 1991). There are 200 pages of poems (and notes) from this period. Celan did not publish them.

8. Letter to Petre Solomon, 20 Aug. 1966, in "Zwanzig," 24. Around this time Nelly Sachs,

whom Celan had dropped out of touch with, published a poem referring to him: ". . . and then my Thou / whom they held prisoner / and whom I was the one chosen to save / and once more in enigmas came to lose / till hard-pressed silence onto silence sunk / and thus a love acquired its coffin then": "Einmal" (1966)—see Dinesen, Nelly Sachs, 315.

9. PC 25 and Celan, Fadensonnen, 83.
10. Letter to G. B. Fischer, 21 June 1966, in Fischer, Briefwechsel mit Autoren, 658.
11. Elie Wiesel, Les Juifs du Silence (Paris, 1966), 87, 108.
12. L'Adolescence, 204. On 8 December 1966 Celan had written to Ilse Blumenthal-Weiss in New York that he was going to read Sachs's poems for half an hour. He adds: "That I'd consider it a really fine thing to read my poems sometime at the Leo Baeck Institute, I scarcely need to say" (letter courtesy of Prof. Steven Schwarzschild).
13. Celan, Fadensonnen, 117. Later he omitted the title and epigraph.
14. "Thou-less," in Celan's German Du-los, may be punning on Greek doulos, "slave": Arnold Stadler, "Sag, dass Jerusalem ist: Paul Celans 'Wallfahrt nach Jerusalem,'" Internationale Katholische Zeitschrift 18 (1989): 186.
15. Huppert, "'Spirituell,'" 320. Though the Austrian poet Huppert says he made a memo of his conversation with Celan on 26 December 1966, the quotations may not be verbatim.
16. Adorno, Negative Dialektik. Meditationen zur Metaphysik (Frankfurt, 1966), 353; Negative Dialectics, trans. E. B. Ashton (New York, 1973), 362.
17. Letter to Petre Solomon, 15 June 1967, in "Zwanzig," 27; Celan, Fadensonnen, 135.
18. Letter to Petre Solomon, 9 Jan. 1967, in "Zwanzig," 27, and L'Adolescence, 207.
19. Edmond Jabès, Le Livre de Yukel (Paris, 1964), 126. "The same questioning joins us, the same wounded word," Jabès later wrote: La Mémoire des Mots: Comment je lis Paul Celan (Paris, 1990), 9; "The Memory of Words (How I Read Paul Celan)," trans. Richard Stamelman, Tel Aviv Review 3 (Winter 1991): 139–43.
20. Jabès, Le Livre des Questions (Paris, 1963), 132.
21. A. Faller, Der Körper des Menschen (Stuttgart, 1966).
22. (Frankfurt, 1962); trans. Joachim Neugroschel (New York, 1991).
23. In 1957, Celan bought and read Scholem's Die Geheimnisse der Schöpfung, and he owned Der jüdische Mystik in ihren Hauptströmungen (Frankfurt, 1957). See Olschner, Der feste Buchstab, 42.
24. Scholem, Von der mystischen, 143, 140 (English ed., 147, 145). Celan in 1960, reading Vom Judentum, 39, marked in Hugo Bergmann's essay a note on the Shechinah as Mother Rachel weeping for her banished children. See Glenn, Paul Celan, 152–54, and Joachim Schulze, "Mystische Motive," 490, 502ff.
25. Halpern, "Night," sec. 11, in In New York (New York, 1919). Hersh Segal (whom Celan met in 1940) published Zeks Schluflider ("Six Lullabies") in Czernowitz in 1939, rpt. ed. A. Rauchwerger (Tel Aviv, 1969), including this song. For the text, see also Undzer Gezang, ed. Schmerke Kaczerginski (Warsaw, 1947), 203. I am indebted to Robert Freedman for his help and for a recording of this song by Sarah Gorby on Phillips PCC261. Kathryn Hellerstein and Ilana Shmueli also assisted me.
26. In draft this poem has Hinübergetragen with Hin crossed out and R put in to make Rübergetragen, a contraction of herübergetragen (Celan, Fadensonnen, 202). That way Celan not only prolongs the stanza's basic rhythm, stressing the first syllable in each line, he also translates the weeping not "thither" but "hither."
27. Originally Celan had alles in this stanza's third line, so that it ran: Rübergetragen alles / Geweinte. By giving Rübergetragen a line to itself, he shaped a firm, symmetrical cadence, alternating three- and two-syllable feet: Rübergetragen / alles Geweinte.
28. Before settling on "unbinded," Celan had wandelte, saying that Ziv had "wandered" or "transformed."
29. Letters of 9 and 19 Aug. 1960, in Celan/Sachs, 55, 58, and PC 17–18.
30. Ziv occurs in a morning prayer and a Sabbath evening song, "Yedid nefesh," which Celan

may have remembered. See *Gates of Prayer: The New Union Prayerbook* (New York, 1975), 159, 316. The word, originally Aramaic, also occurs in Daniel and in Talmudic sources. I am grateful to Professor Chimen Abramsky for suggestions on this poem.

1. Letter of 8 Dec. 1967, in Celan/Sachs, 94, and *PC* 18.
2. Letter of 22 Mar. 1968, in Celan/Sachs, 95, and *PC* 19.
3. Franz Büchler, "Heute und morgen," *Neue deutsche Hefte* 97 (1964): 92.
4. Ziw in this spelling bears the mark of Scholem's idiosyncratic (and not always consistent) transliteration, so that here the Hebrew זיו (zayin-yud-vav), in English *Ziv*, should phonetically be *Siw* in German. Scholem made it *Ziw*, and Celan followed him. Whether Celan knew the proper Hebrew pronunciation is not clear. In any case, an American translator has heard Celan's *Ziw* with a German Z and in his version has transliterated it *Tsiv*, which unduly estranges the word: Neugroschel, trans., "Four Poems by Paul Celan," *Midstream* 23/8 (Oct. 1977): 46.
5. Scholem, *Major Trends in Jewish Mysticism* (1941; rpt. New York, 1961), 17.
6. I posed this question in the spring of 1987 ("'Ziv, that light': Translation and Tradition in Paul Celan," *New Literary History* 18/3 [Spring 1987]: 613–31). Since then, Shimon Sandbank has translated into Hebrew and commented on this and two other Celan poems that end with a Hebrew word: "Paul Celan: Three Poems" [in Hebrew], *Haaretz*, 2 Oct. 1987. Sandbank nicely chooses *bahir* for *hell* ("bright")—a likely equivalent that gains extra brightness from the Kabbalist book *Bahir*. The last line in Hebrew is *Ziv, oto ohr*. A collection of Sandbank's Hebrew translations of Celan was due to appear in late 1994.
7. Christoph Perels, "Erhellende Metathesen: Zu einer poetischen Verfahrungsweise Paul Celans," *Sprache in technischer Zeitalter* 62 (Apr.–June 1977): 162, raises this possibility.
8. Celan, *Fadensonnen*, 245–49. On "Just Think" see Glenn, *Paul Celan*, 150–54.
9. Stefan Bodo Würffel, "Ermunterung und Erlösung: Zu einem Motiv in den späten Gedichten Paul Celans," *Literatur und Kritik* 125 (June 1978): 259.
10. *Neue Zürcher Zeitung*, 24 June 1967; *M.B.*, 7 July 1967; *Die Stimme* 23/211 (Aug. 1967): 6.
11. *Haaretz*, 18 Aug. 1967.
12. *Akzente* 6 (1967): 486.
13. *L'Adolescence*, 207–09.

Chapter 15
Prophecy out of Exile (1967)

1. Pöggeler, *Spur*, 259.
2. See Heidegger's 1966 *Der Spiegel* interview in *Martin Heidegger and National Socialism*, ed. Günther Neske and Emil Kettering (New York, 1990), 63.
3. Baumann, 59.
4. See George Steiner, *Heidegger* (Hassocks, Sussex, 1978), 111–21, and much subsequent discussion. On the Nazi salute, see James Luther Adams's letter to the *New York Times*, 19 Feb. 1988.
5. Baumann, 58–80, has a full account of Celan's visit to Freiburg. Südwest Rundfunk recorded the reading.
6. Baumann, 60.
7. Gadamer, *Wer bin Ich und wer bist du?: Ein Kommentar zu Paul Celans Gedichtfolge 'Atemkristall'* (Frankfurt, 1973), 15.
8. Pöggeler, *Spur*, 248.
9. Schwerin, "Bitterer Brunnen," 80.
10. The version translated here appeared separately in a bibliophile edition (Paris: Brunidor, 1968). There has been an increasing amount of commentary on this poem. See Pöggeler, *Spur*, 259–71, and J. D. Golb, "Celan and Heidegger: A Reading of 'Todtnauberg,'" *Seminar* 24/3 (Sept. 1988): 255–68. See also Michael Hamburger, "Footpath with Logs at the Limit

of Language," *The Independent* (London), 22 Dec. 1990, and Pierre Joris, "Paul Celan in English, Circa 1989," in *The Poetry of Paul Celan*, ed. Haskell Block (New York, 1991), 65–67. I am grateful to Gisèle Celan-Lestrange for a conversation on this poem in November 1984.

11. Schäfer, "Die nicht . . . ," 487. Colored woodcuts of both *Arnika* and *Augentrost* ("eyebright") are found in *Das kleine Blumenbuch*, the Insel flower manual that Celan had in Czernowitz.

12. Celan added this question in a later version: Rolf Bücher, "Welt-Buch bei Celan," in *"Der glühende*," 122.

13. Letter to Kahler, 28 July 1965, in *Der Georg-Büchner-Preis*, 134.

14. Heidegger, "Hölderlin und das Wesen der Dichtung," in *Erläuterungen zu Hölderlins Dichtung* (1950; Frankfurt, 1951), 47. Celan had a copy of this book.

15. Pöggeler, "Celans Begegnung mit Heidegger," *Zeitmitschrift* 5 (1988): 123–32, maintains that "Heidegger concerned himself intensively with Celan and his motive for this was the Holocaust." He also says that the administrators of Heidegger's literary estate wrote mistakenly to Celan's widow that up to Celan's death, Heidegger hadn't known Celan was Jewish.

16. The edition was dated 12 January 1968. For Heidegger's response, I am indebted to Gisèle Celan-Lestrange. See also an account of the genesis of "Todtnauberg" by its printer, Robert Altmann, quoted in Philippe Lacoue-Labarthe, *La Poésie comme expérience* (Paris, 1986), 150–53. Altmann says that Celan read in Vaduz, Liechtenstein, on 1 August 1968 in connection with an exhibition that included "Todtnauberg," and that Heidegger's letter was exhibited in Vaduz in 1970.

17. "Words become names," Celan said in early 1968: Allemann, "Paul Celan," in *Deutsche Dichter der Gegenwart*, ed. Benno von Wiese (Berlin, 1973), 440. "At bottom my word formations are not inventions. They belong to language at its very oldest. My concern? To get free of words as mere designations. I'd like to hear again in words the *names* of things": Celan in March 1970, reported in Clemens Podewils, "Namen / Ein Vermächtnis Paul Celans," *Ensemble* 2 (1971): 69.

18. See Jerry Glenn and Elizabeth Petuchowski, "Zusammentreffenden Wellen der Interferenz in Paul Celans Gedicht 'Fahlstimmig,'" *Celan-Jahrbuch* 5 (1993): 115–38.

19. Erhard Schwandt, "Korrekturen zum Bericht von Reinhard Döhl," *Deutsche Akademie für Sprache und Dichtung, Jahrbuch 1966* (Darmstadt, 1967): 191–206.

20. Letter of 23 Nov. 1967, in "Zwanzig," 30. Lia Fingerhut had drowned in early 1962.

21. *Lesestationen im Spätwort* plays on *Spätlese*, the "late gleaning" of ripe grapes.

22. The weekend after his birthday Celan went to Cologne to record a television broadcast (Schöne, *Literatur*). In Cologne he bought Ludwig Binswanger's *Wahn* ("Madness") (Pfullingen, 1965). The early pages are marked by Celan.

23. Beda Allemann and Rolf Bücher, "Textgenese als Thematisierung und als Fixierungsprozess: Zum Entwurf von Paul Celans Gedicht 'Du sei wie du,'" in *Edition und Interpretation*, ed. Lois Hay and Winfried Woesler (Bern, 1981), 177.

24. Orgad (Celan, *Davar*, 26) has *Hayi asher tihyi* for *Du sei wie du*.

25. John E. Jackson, *Revue de Belles-Lettres* 96/2–3 (1972): 61; Jean Daive, *Études Germaniques* 25/3 (1970): 249; Celan, *Contrainte de lumière*, trans. Bertrand Badiou and Jean-Claude Rambach (Paris, 1989), 179; Celan, *Luce Coatta*, trans. Giuseppe Bevilacqua (Milan, 1987), 89; Pierre Joris, "Late Poetry," 2:563; Beatrice Cameron, "Anticomputer: An Essay on the Work of Paul Celan" (Ph.D. diss., University of California, Berkeley, 1973). Cameron later retranslated the poem, rendering Eckhart's phrases in English: *Seven Gates* 5 (1988): 41. Michael O'Connor's translation uses Wycliffe: *Literary Review* 17 (1974): 507.

26. To close *Lichtzwang*, Celan chose "Du sei wie du" and two other poems attuned to Meister Eckhart's negations from the same days of winter 1967. One of them calls divinity "Disheightened, inwarded," and ends: "Quit of death, quit / of God" (2:326). In the other Celan tells himself "in place of all rest" to merely "stand herein: / throughgrounded by Nothing-

ness, / rid of all / prayer, / fine-fugued, after / the pre-Script" (2:328). Forgoing hope, faith, and peace, this command comes "after"—later than, yet still according to—Scripture.

27. Werner Weber, "'Auf, werde Licht': Zu einem Gedicht von Paul Celan," *Neue Zürcher Zeitung,* 29 Mar. 1970: 49 (rpt. in *UPC*), informed by Celan, identified Eckhart as the source. See Meister Eckhart, *Die deutschen und lateinischen Werke: Predigten,* ed. Josef Quint (Stuttgart, 1958), 1:230.

28. George Steiner, "A Terrible Exactness," *Times Literary Supplement,* 11 June 1976: 710 (Steiner recurs interestingly to Yiddish and Middle High German in a later letter, *Times Literary Supplement,* 13 Aug. 1976: 1012) and Wilhelm Höck, "Von welchem Gott ist die Rede?," in *UPC* 274.

29. Besides Wycliffe, I consulted Dame Julian of Norwich, Richard Rolle of Hampole, and Middle English lexicons.

30. Letter of Apr. 1936, in *Ah, Sweet Dancer: W. B. Yeats, Margot Ruddock, A Correspondence,* ed. Roger McHugh (London, 1970), 81. I am indebted to Jeffrey Donaldson for this reference.

31. The hymn "Lecha dodi" is discussed in Scholem, *On the Kabbalah,* 141 (Celan owned the German edition).

32. Sandbank, "Paul Celan."

33. Celan seems to have favored the book of Isaiah. In his copy of the Luther Bible, he penciled Hebrew chapter numberings in Isaiah.

34. Scholem, *The Messianic Idea in Judaism* (New York, 1971), 318.

35. Letter to Gershom Scholem, 10 Mar. 1921, in Rosenzweig, *Briefe,* 699, and *Franz Rosenzweig,* ed. Glatzer, 100. Twice that I know of in the 1960s Celan inscribed a book of his in Hebrew for a Jewish student: in June 1964 (Alvin Rosenfeld, letter to the author, 12 Feb. 1983) and in February 1968 (Böschenstein, 14).

Chapter 16
An Embabeled Tongue (1968–69)

1. Celan, *Poems,* trans. Hamburger, 27. Celan inscribed another book for Hamburger with *offenerweise* ("openly").

2. [Siegbert Prawer], "Poems, Noems," *Times Literary Supplement,* 7 Dec. 1967: 1190, and Celan, *Poems,* trans. Hamburger, 25–26.

3. Joachim Günther, "Der lesende Paul Celan," *Der Tagesspiegel,* 20 Dec. 1967:4; rpt. in *UPC* 203.

4. Celan's younger friend, the critic Peter Szondi, left unfinished at his death an account of this poem's circumstances: "Eden," in *Celan-Studien,* 113–25; rpt. in *L'Éphémère* 19–20 (Winter–Spring 1972–73): 416–23. For a summary of further discussion, see Haskell M. Block, "Interpreting Celan: Szondi, Gadamer and Others," in *Poetry of Paul Celan,* ed. Block, 38–43, and *Boundary 2's* Spring 1984 issue on Szondi.

5. Celan, *Schneepart. Historisch-Kritische Ausgabe,* vol. 10, pt. 2, ed. Rolf Bücher, with Axel Gellhaus and Andreas Lohr-Jasperneite (Frankfurt, 1994), 90.

6. Beda Allemann and Rolf Bücher, "Bemerkungen zur historisch-kritischer Celan-Ausgabe," *Text und Kritik* 53–54 (2d ed., 1984): 94. Celan wrote this for his prospective editor Allemann.

7. Celan, *Schneepart. Faksimile der Handschrift aus dem Nachlass* (Frankfurt, 1976).

8. Quoted in Dietlind Meinecke, "Einleitung," *UPC* 30.

9. Letter to Margul-Sperber, 7 Dec. 1966, in "Briefe," 61; Petru Dumitriu, "À propos d'une traduction allemande," in *Les Cahiers de l'Herne. Henri Michaux* (Paris, 1966), 258.

10. Kurt Leonhard, "Pourquoi j'ai traduit Michaux," in *Les Cahiers,* 261.

11. Michaux, *Vers la complétude* (Paris, 1967), 23. See Böschenstein, "Paul Celan and French Poetry," trans. Joel Golb, *ACTS* 8–9 (1988): 186.

12. Michaux, "Sur le chemin de la vie," *Études Germaniques* 25 (1970): 250; cited in *ACTS* 8–9 (1988): 190.
13. Böschenstein, "Extraterritorial: Anmerkungen zu Ingeborg Bachmanns deutschen Ungaretti. Mit einem Abhang über Paul Celans Übertragung des Spätwerks," in *Zur Geschichtlichkeit der Moderne*, ed. Theo Elm and Gerd Hemmerich (Munich, 1982), 314–21, and Olschner, *Der feste Buchstab*, 308–17.
14. *L'Éphémère* 4 (Sept. 1967): 66–73.
15. In August 1967 Celan wrote one rather unforceful poem, "To a Brother in Asia" (2:259), touching the Vietnam War. Perhaps it felt remote from him in those years.
16. Wallmann, "Auch mich," 89; Szász, "'Es ist nicht so einfach,'" in *PC* 336; Celan, *Schneepart. Historisch-Kritische Ausgabe*, 128.
17. *Israel à travers les âges* (Paris, 1968).
18. Baumann, 87–90. Lutrand later urged Celan to visit Israel: Elmar Tophoven and Ilana Shmueli interviews.
19. Letter to Gideon Kraft, 23 Apr. 1968, quoted partially in Chalfen, 89. Two days later, in a poem, he spoke of being "clamped Red- / wooded between / good and harm" (2:368).
20. Textbook: *Wort und Sinn* (Paderborn, 1968). Anthology: *Welch Wort in die Kälte gerufen: Die Judenverfolgung des Dritten Reiches im deutschen Gedicht*, ed. Heinz Seydel (Berlin, 1968). Celan is said to have allowed "Todesfuge" to be printed in this anthology because the editor also included poems by his cousin Selma Meerbaum-Eisinger, who died in the same Transnistrian camp to which his parents were deported. The quotation is from Kurt Bräutigam, *Moderne deutsche Balladen* (Frankfurt, 1968), 78, cited in Glenn, *Paul Celan*, 70.
21. Review of Celan's reading in Freiburg, June 1968, quoted in Olschner, *Der feste Buchstab*, 207; review of reading in Liechtenstein, 1 August 1968, by Alois Büchel, *Liechtensteiner Volksblatt*, 8 Aug. 1968: 1; Mayer, "Erinnerungen," 1154, 1161.
22. Postcard of 14 Apr. 1968 (text only in Celan/Sachs). The painting is in the National Gallery. In April 1968, Celan also bought Georg Simmel's *Rembrandt* (Leipzig, 1916): Lydia Koelle, "Celans Jerusalem," in *"Der glühende,"* 303. See Pöggeler, *Die Frage nach der Kunst: Von Hegel zu Heidegger* (Freiburg, 1984); Roland Reuss, "Rembrandts Celan," *Celan-Jahrbuch* 3 (1989): 47–98.
23. However, sometime in 1968, according to Böschenstein, "Gespräche," 8, Celan asked him to moderate or omit mentioning any Christian associations he saw in poems such as "Psalm."
24. Wurm, "Erinnerung," 40.
25. Celan, *Schneepart. Historisch-Kritische Ausgabe*, 24. Celan must have written this epigraph onto his typescript from memory, because he quotes it slightly wrong.
26. Bialik, *Kol shirei* (Tel Aviv, 1961), 182.
27. Scholem, *Von mystischen*, 143 (the page where Celan found *Ziv*).
28. Quoted in Arno Reinfrank, "Schmerzlicher Abschied von Paul Celan," *Die Horen* 83 (1971): 73. Celan is most likely referring to *Fadensonnen*.
29. Celan's word *Gesänge* was also Buber's for the Song of Songs. I've adopted "canticles" from Michael Hamburger's version of this poem in Celan, *Poems*, 335.
30. Heidegger, *Vorlesungen zur Phänomenologie des inneren Zeitbewusstseins* (Halle, 1928), 396.
31. Rilke, *Sämtliche Werke*, 2:94.
32. *Le Monde*, 26 Apr. 1969.
33. Landauer, letter of 16 Oct. 1913, in Landauer, *Sein Lebensgang in Briefen*, ed. Martin Buber (Frankfurt, 1929), 1:448.
34. Letter to Siegfried Unseld, 8 Aug. 1969, in *Geschichte des Suhrkamp Verlages: 1 Juli 1950 bis 30 Juni 1990*, ed. Unseld (Frankfurt, 1990), 82: *Adornos Tod: ich bin betroffen, bestürzt.*
35. In "Zwanzig," 33.

Chapter 17
To Name Jerusalem (1969)

1. Facsimile in *GW* 3 and *Literatur und Kritik* 125 (June 1978): 275.
2. Manfred Winkler, "Epilog auf Paul Celan," *Die Stimme* 26/245 (July 1970): 6.
3. Pöggeler, *Die Frage*, 399; David Seidmann interview; Jean Bollack interview; Olschner, *Die feste Buchstab*, 42.
4. Ilana Shmueli, letter to the author, 21 Nov. 1993; Amichai, interview by the author, Jerusalem, June 1982.
5. Shmuel Hupert, "Encounters in Jerusalem—1969" (Hebrew), *Yediot Aharonot*, 27 May 1983. In Israel Celan met the novelist Aharon Appelfeld, who was born on the same street in Czernowitz where Celan lived from 1935 on. Appelfeld says that Celan's Hebrew was rather good and that they also joked in Yiddish: Appelfeld, interview by the author, Stanford, 9 Sept. 1989. Celan told Appelfeld he envied him writing in Hebrew.
6. Amichai, *Shirim* (Tel Aviv, 1967).
7. This and further quotes from Celan in this chapter (unless otherwise identified) are from Ilana Shmueli, "Denk dir: Paul Celan in Jerusalem," *Jüdischer Almanach*, 1995: 10–36.
8. The Jerusalem reading was held in the new Journalists House, Beit Agron, 9 October: Chalfen, "Paul Celan in Jerusalem," *Die Stimme* 238 (Nov. 1969): 5; Celan, *Davar*.
9. Chalfen, "Paul Celan."
10. Werner Kraft, "Gedicht und Wirkung: Zu zwei Gedichten von Paul Celan," *Neue deutsche Hefte* 168 (1980): 740.
11. Gershom Schocken, "Paul Celan in Tel Aviv," *Neue Rundschau* 91 (1980): 257. The Tel Aviv reading took place on 15 October.
12. Zvi Yavetz interview. Yavetz says that after this reading at Ohel Shem, Celan "cried all night": letter to the author, 26 Apr. 1985.
13. *Zeks Schluflider*, ed. Rauchwerger.
14. Tape recording, Kol Yisrael. In the interview as broadcast, Celan's voice fades into Hebrew translations of his words.
15. Shmueli, letter to the author, 21 Nov. 1993; Schwerin, "Bitterer Brunnen," 81. Celan left Israel on 17 October.
16. Letter to David Seidmann, *Die Stimme* 26/244 (June 1970): 8, and typescript copy.
17. Letter to Martha and Manuel Singer, *Die Stimme* 26/246 (Aug. 1970): 7.
18. Schwerin, "Bitterer Brunnen," 78. Later in Paris, asked about the landscape in Israel, Celan said: "No patience for landscape," and added: "A quote from Brecht": Rudolf Wittkopf, letter to the author, 30 Sept. 1984.
19. Yavetz interview. Yavetz eventually succeeded, but it was too late.
20. Shin Shalom, *Galiläisches Tagebuch* (1932; Heidelberg, 1954), 153, and letter to Shalom, 27 Oct. 1969, *Die Stimme* 26/246 (Aug. 1970): 7.
21. On these poems, the second cycle of the posthumously published *Zeitgehöft* (Frankfurt, 1976), see Böschenstein, "Erste Notizen zu Celans letzten Gedichten: Zur zweiten Abteilung von 'Zeitgehöft,'" *Text und Kritik* 53–54 (July 1984): 62–68 (another version of this essay appears in Broda, ed., *Contre-jour*); Bernd Witte, "Schattenland," *Neue Rundschau* 89/1 (1978): 97–112; Dieter Herde, "Problematik und Sprachform von Paul Celans lyrischem Spätwerk" (M.A. thesis, Aachen, 1981); Richard Reschika, *Poesie und Apokalypse: Paul Celans 'Jerusalem-Gedichte' aus dem Nachlassband 'Zeitgehöft'* (Pfaffenweiler, 1991); Arnold Stadler, *Das Buch der Psalmen und die deutschsprachige Lyrik des 20 Jahrhunderts: Zu den Psalmen im Werk Bertolt Brechts und Paul Celans* (Cologne, 1989).
22. Celan, *Davar*, trans. Orgad; Sandbank, private communication.
23. *Aber sie sind doch hebräisch geschrieben!*: Yehuda Amichai, Preface to Lasker-Schüler, *Hebrew Ballads* (Philadelphia, 1985), ix. The story, originally recounted by Rachel Katinka, can be

found in Lasker-Schüler, *Dichtungen und Dokumente,* ed. Ernst Ginsberg (Munich, 1951), 597–98.

24. Olschner, "'STEHEN' und Constantia: Eine Spur des Barock bei Paul Celan," in *Paul Celan: "Atemwende". Materialen,* ed. Gerhard Buhr and Roland Reuss (Würzburg, 1991), 201–17.

25. Celan, *Enclos du temps: Zeitgehöft,* trans. Martine Broda (Paris, 1985).

26. Böschenstein, "Erste Notizen," 63. Karl Kraus derived his journal title *Die Fackel* from this passage in Revelation: Timms, *Karl Kraus,* 57.

27. Mazar, *The Mountain of the Lord: Excavating Jerusalem* (New York, 1975), 138. This stone is now in the Israel Museum, Jerusalem. See Josephus, *The Jewish War,* 4.582, and Mishnah Sukka, 5.5.

28. Celan in Jerusalem told his friend, "Keine Ausgrabungen, bitte!" (Please, no excavations!). If he never saw or learned of the carved stone, that makes its pertinence to his poem all the more arresting—not simply a source but an ever present corroboration of his figurative insight.

29. Stéphane Mosès relates "Die Posaunenstelle" to Exodus and other Hebraic sources in "Paul Celan: Die Posaunenstelle," in *Spuren der Schrift: Von Goethe bis Celan,* ed. Mosès (Frankfurt, 1987); English version in *Languages of the Unsayable: The Play of Negativity in Literature and Literary Theory,* ed. Sanford Budick and Wolfgang Iser (New York, 1989), 209–24. For a rebuttal of Mosès' Biblical and liturgical reading, see Jean Bollack, "'Die Posaunenstelle' von Paul Celan," *Celan-Jahrbuch* 4 (1991): 39–53. Pöggeler, "Mystical Elements in Heidegger's Thought and Celan's Poetry," in *Word Traces,* ed. Fioretos, 91–93, refers the poem to the revelation at Sinai but makes no mention of the New Testament Book of Revelation. He notes that when Israeli troops reached the Western Wall in Jerusalem in June 1967, the army's chief rabbi blew the shofar there. In a one-sentence parenthesis, Pöggeler says that at excavations near the wall "a stone was found, showing that already in ancient times the shofar was blown here."

30. Letter to Scholem, 10 Mar. 1921, in Rosenzweig, *Briefe,* 100.

31. Another cryptic term hovers near the surface of this poem, a term that Celan's first and third lines together almost pronounce: *Leerstelle* ("vacant space"). This unusual word actually occurs in "Conversation in the Mountains," where two Jews talk about speech itself and a "No One" who never answers. At one point they are silent, but "it's merely a pause, it's a word-gap, it's a vacant space [*eine Leerstelle*], you can see the syllables all standing around." In "Die Posaunenstelle" the virtual presence of *Leerstelle* may also involve its grammatical sense—a place opened up in a sentence and needing to be filled—as well as its theoretical usage for the "places of indeterminacy" or "structural gaps" that make readers responsive and literature whole.

32. Heinz Michael Krämer, *Eine Sprache des Leidens: Zur Lyrik von Paul Celan* (Munich, 1979), 180.

33. Celan wrote a brief poem in 1967: "Now that the prayer stools are burning, / I eat the book / with all its / insignia" (2:258).

34. Letter to Gerhart Baumann, 20 Nov. 1969, in Baumann, 124.

35. Celan had read closely in Scholem passages such as this: "On the basis of the uniting of the poles, the distinction between male and female ceases in the Godhead": *Von der mystischen,* 181.

36. George Steiner recommends "lay" for its sexual sense, saying: "In one of the greatest love-poems of our time, Celan concludes in jubilation": "An Enclosure of Time," *Times Literary Supplement,* 4 Feb. 1977: 132.

37. Böschenstein, "Hölderlin und Celan," and Klaus Manger, "Die Königszäsur: Zu Hölderlins Gegenwart in Celans Gedicht," *Hölderlin-Jahrbuch* (1982–83): 147–55, 156–65.

38. Celan underlined and side-scored this sentence in chap. 8 of Wilhelm Michel, *Das Leben Friedrich Hölderlins* (1940; Frankfurt, 1967), 435.

39. On the page where he found the verb "plow away," Celan marked the bit about how

Hölderlin was dangerously involved in some lottery scheme by "a baptized Jew": Michel, *Das Leben*, 435.

40. The word I translate as "shardstrewn," *zerscherbten*, comes from *Scherbe*, Scholem's term for "shard" in the Kabbalah. Given this lyric's tense sequence and messianic impulse, I have used just as many syllables for each line as Celan did.

Chapter 18
A Question of Last Things (1970)

1. Letter of 5 Feb. 1970. This copy of Halevi is different from the one Celan bought in 1960.
2. Glatzer, ed., *Franz Rosenzweig*, 257.
3. Letter to Hilde de la Motte, 26 Jan. 1970, in *Autorenkalender '81*.
4. Quoted in Wittkopf, letter to the author, 30 Sept. 1984.
5. Cid Corman met Celan in 1955 and thereafter translated many of his poems. In October 1969 he published two groups of translations: *Origin* 15 (1969): 18–59, and *Caterpillar* 8/9 (1969): 4–22. He reports that Celan brought legal action against him: Review of Celan, *Poems*, trans. Hamburger, in *Sulfur* 3 (1982): 230.
6. Rokeah, "Gedenkblatt für Paul Celan," *Neue Zürcher Zeitung*, 12 July 1970: 49.
7. Mayer, "Erinnerungen," 1160.
8. Letter to Gustav Chomed, 19 Mar. 1970, in Silbermann, 38.
9. Szász, *PC* 335, and Baumann, 127. Bernhard Böschenstein invited Celan to Stuttgart, Gerhart Baumann invited him to Freiburg. Celan also intended to go to a meeting in Princeton in May 1970: Pearl Fichman, letter to the author, 26 June 1985.
10. Hanne Lenz, letter to Ilse Blumenthal-Weiss, 12 Feb. 1971.
11. Szász, "'Es ist nicht so einfach,'" *Neue Literatur* 26/11 (1975): 33.
12. Eike Wolff, "Rückwärtsgesprochene Namen. Paul Celan liest neue Gedichte," *Stuttgarter Zeitung*, 23 Mar. 1970: 24, rpt. in Glenn, *Bibliographie*, T870; Kurt Lothar Tank, "Lichtzwang der Lyrik: Zum Tode von Paul Celan," *Deutsches Allgemeines Sonntagsblatt* 20 (17 May 1970): 21.
13. Mayer, "Erinnerungen," 1162.
14. Reinfrank, "Schmerzlicher Abschied," 72; Hans-Jörg Modlmayr, "Paul Celan und die Deutschen," *Die Horen* 83 (1971): 74; Baumann, 130. Böschenstein, 16, suggests that Celan, aware that the Hölderlin Society still had members from its founding under Nazi auspices in 1943, was wary and read harder poems than usual.
15. Sachs, letter to Celan, 12 May 1960, in Celan/Sachs, 39.
16. Böschenstein interview and Böschenstein, 17.
17. Baumann, 48, 129, 79–80.
18. Weber, "'Auf, werde Licht,'" 49; Baumann, ". . . Durchgründet," 282.
19. Wurm, "Erinnerung," 40.
20. "Celan me dépasse" (Celan leaves me behind) Beckett said years later, and asked if Celan's life showed his disarray: André Bernold, *L'Amitié de Beckett, 1979–1989* (Paris, 1992), 58.
21. Daive, *Décimale Blanche*. Böschenstein, "Paul Celan and French Poetry" and "Remarks on Celan's Last Translation," *ACTS* 8–9 (1988).
22. Buber's book (1909; Leipzig, 1921) has an epigraph from Meister Eckhart: "What I have in mind most is wordless." Janouch, *Conversations with Kafka*, 47, 57.
23. For Werner Weber, in April 1970, Celan wrote out his 1968 Rembrandt poem (2:392) with its glance at Psalm 16: "Thou wilt not leave my soul in hell": Weber, *Forderungen: Bemerkungen und Aufsätze zur Literatur* (Zurich, 1970), 202.
24. Kafka's verb is *gutmachen* ("make good"), as in Germany's "reparation" payments.
25. Diary entry of 25 Sept. 1917; Celan, letter to Ilana Shmueli, 12 Apr. 1970.
26. Mandelshtam, who called his first two books "Stone," once said: "Poetry is the plow that

turns up time so that the deep layers of time . . . appear on top": Mandelstam, *Selected Essays*, 52.

27. Celan showed keen interest in the Kabbalist conception of *tsimtsum*, God's self-limitation or self-shrinking (*Selbstverschränkung*): Scholem, *Von der mystischen*, 77–81.
28. Celan's last letter to Suhrkamp insisted that his late poems were not obscure: "For him these poems are free, open and unending": publisher's note on *Schneepart* dust jacket.
29. Mary Lowenthal Felstiner years ago suggested "come the Sabbath."
30. In composing "Hochmoor" on 20 July 1968, Celan at first wrote *Sabbathkerzen*, then crossed out the *h*: Celan, *Schneepart. Historisch-Kritische Ausgabe*, 161.
31. The first appearance was in *Neue Rundschau* 69 (1958): 405.
32. Moritz Zobel, *Der Sabbat* (Berlin, 1935). Scholem added an *h* when he cited this book in his study of the Kabbalah, where Sabbath promises an end to exile: *Zur Kabbalah*, 276.
33. I have heard, once and without corroboration, that in 1953 Celan attempted suicide from the Pont Mirabeau. Celan's address appears under his poems as early as 7 Nov. 1969: Shmueli, "Denk dir," 27. It fell to Edmond Lutrand to identify Celan's body: Baumann, 90.
34. Wurm, "Erinnerung," 40. Wurm's account seems to run together events from the end of March 1970 with the end of April.
35. Michel, *Das Leben*, 464; Schwerin, "Bitterer Brunnen," 81.
36. Writing to Ilana Shmueli about his "condition" in late February 1970, Celan said: "the doctors have much to answer for, every day is a burden, what you call 'my own health' is probably never to be, the damage reaches to the core of my existence. . . . They've healed me to pieces!" (*Man hat mich zerheilt*): Shmueli, unpub. manuscript.
37. Kahler, *The Inward Turn of Narrative*, trans. Richard and Clara Winston, Foreword by Joseph Frank (Princeton, 1973), xv. Kahler wrote, among other things, *The Tower and the Abyss* and *Man the Measure*.
38. Letter to Werner Weber, 22 May 1970, *Unicorn Journal* 4 (1972): 98.
39. Bahr, "Paul Celan," 191; Baumann, 143; Dinesen, *Nelly Sachs*, 350.
40. Paul Celan's grave, along with those of François Celan and Gisèle Celan-Lestrange, lies in field 31, row 12.
41. *Les Lettres françaises* 1334 (13 May 1970): 5.
42. Lévinas, "De l'être à l'autre," *Revue de Belles-Lettres* 96/2–3 (1972): 198, and in *Chicago Review* 29/3 (1978): 16–22.
43. Szász, "Es ist nicht," *Neue Literatur*, 31; Baumann, 139, 144.
44. Letter to Gleb Struve, 29 Jan. 1959, in Terras and Weimar, "Mandelstamm and Celan," 362.
45. *Die Stimme*, June and July 1970.
46. Hans-Jürgen Heise, "Nach Paul Celans Tod," *Neue deutsche Hefte* 17/3 (1970): 101.
47. Günter Heintz, "Paul Celans Todesfuge," *Blätter für den Deutschlehrer* 14 (1970): 109.
48. Hartmut Lück, "Die Komponisten und die Todesfuge: sieben Vertonungen des Gedichtes von Paul Celan," West German Radio broadcast of 4 Feb. 1983. One setting, by an eighteen-year-old German student, appeared in a series called "New Music for Children and Youth": Jürgen Weisser, "Todesfuge: Musik für Sprecher und 6 (ad.lib. 7) Spieler (Regensburg, 1984). There were, as of 1991, about one hundred musical compositions on Celan's texts: Martin Zenck, ". . . : es sind / noch Lieder zu singen jenseits / der Menschen," in *Atemwende: Materialen*, 267. Jewish German Dance Theater, "But what about the Holocaust?"
49. Bernd Jentzsch, ed., *Der Tod ist ein Meister aus Deutschland* (Munich, 1979). During the six-hour TV series, broadcast during April and May of 1990, each episode opens with a full-screen image of Celan's face, then pans over death camps and monuments as his voice is heard reciting "Todesfuge" in its entirety. A West German Marxist also warned lest nowadays the poem be replaced in textbooks by mannered, subjective lyrics: Ursula Püschel, "Exilierte und verlorene," *Kürbiskern* 4 (1977): 117.

50. At this event, a Bach Society chorus began by singing the first Yiddish Holocaust song, "Undzer Shtetl Brennt" by Mordechai Gebirtig. Then, after Ida Ehre had recited "Todesfuge," Philipp Jenninger gave his ill-fated, would-be conciliatory speech, which led to his having to relinquish his position: stenographic report of the Bundestag for 10 Nov. 1988; *Die Zeit*, 18 Nov. 1988, Politik: 7.

51. Letter to Walter Jens, 19 May 1961.

52. Jean Améry, *At the Mind's Limits: Contemplations by a Survivor on Auschwitz and its Realities*, trans. Sidney Rosenfeld and Stella P. Rosenfeld (Bloomington, Ind., 1980), x. Améry's Preface, for a 1977 edition, was written in 1976.

53. Primo Levi, *If Not Now, When?*, trans. William Weaver (New York, 1985), 168. I wrote to Primo Levi asking him if he had indeed taken the phrase from Celan, and he replied: "I 'stole' this image from Celan's TODESFUGE, which struck me deeply (as a difference from many other of his poems, that I am sorry not to understand). But, as you know, in literature the borderline between stealth and homage is blurred" (14 June 1986, in English). In *La ricerca delle radici: Antologia personale* (Turin, 1981), 211, Levi wrote: "I've managed to penetrate the meaning of only a few among his lyrics; an exception is this 'Fugue of Death.' I read that Celan repudiated it, didn't consider it his most typical poetry; no matter, I carry it within me like an *innesto* [graft, inoculation]."

54. Szondi wrote several essays toward a book on Celan during the year after Celan died. See "Lecture de Strette: Essai sur la poésie de Paul Celan," *Critique* 258 (May 1971): 387–420; Szondi's *Celan-Studien*; and the Szondi issue of *Boundary 2* (Spring 1984).

Index

Books by Paul Celan

Index 334

Poems by Paul Celan

Prose and Speeches by Paul Celan